Riches Within
Your Reach!

Complete and Unabridged

"Would you know Life abundant,
Love doubled for all you give?
There is a means no surer
Than helping someone to live."
—Ellen H. Jones

Wilder Publications, Inc.
PO Box 243
Blacksburg, VA 24060-0243

ISBN 10: 1-60459-999-5
ISBN 13: 978-1-60459-999-2
First Edition

10 9 8 7 6 5 4 3 2 1

Riches Within Your Reach!

By Robert Collier

The four books in this volume were collected and published as *Riches Within Your Reach* by author Robert Collier in 1947. Their original dates of publication were:

The God in You (1937)
The Magic Word (1940)
The Secret of Power (1945)
The Law of the Higher Potential (1947)

Table of Contents

THE SECRET OF POWER

THE LAW OF THE HIGHER POTENTIAL

Prologue

Why is it that most of the great men of the world, most of the unusually successful men, started life under a handicap?

Demosthenes, the greatest orator the ancient world produced, stuttered! The first time he tried to make a public speech, he was laughed off the rostrum. Julius Caesar was an epileptic. Napoleon was of humble parentage, and so poor that it was with the greatest difficulty that he got his appointment to the Military Academy. Far from being a born genius, he stood forty-sixth in his class at the Military Academy. And there were only sixty-five in the class. His shortness of stature and extreme poverty discouraged him to such an extent that in his early letters to friends, he frequently referred to thoughts of suicide.

Benjamin Franklin, Abraham Lincoln, Andrew Jackson and a number of our Presidents started life in the poorest and humblest of homes, with little education and no advantages. Stewart, who started what is now the John Wanamaker Store, came to New York with $1.50 in his pocket, and no place where he could hope to get more until he himself earned it. Thomas Edison was a newsboy on trains. Andrew Carnegie started work at $4 a month. John D. Rockefeller at about $6 a week.

Reza Khan, who became Shah of Persia, started as an ordinary trooper in the Persian army. Mustapha Kemal, Ruler of Turkey, was an unknown officer in the Turkish army. Ebert, first President of Germany after World War I, was a saddle maker. A number of our own Presidents were born in log cabins, without money, without education.

Sandow, the strongest man of his time, started life as a weakling. Annette Kellerman was lame and sickly, yet she became diving champion and one of the world's most perfectly formed women. George Jowett was lame and a weakling until he was eleven years old. An older boy bullied him and beat him until he aroused such a feeling of resentment in young Jowett that he determined to work and exercise until he could pay back that bully in kind. In two years, he was able to beat the bully. In ten years, he was the world's strongest man!

Why is it that men with such handicaps can outstrip all of those naturally favored by Nature? Why is it that the well-educated, well-trained men, with wealthy and influential friends to help them, are so often pushed aside, to make way for some "nobody" whose family no one ever heard of, but whose sheer ability and force make him a power to be reckoned with?

Why? Because men with early advantages are taught *to look to material things for success* ... to riches or friends or influence or their own training or abilities. And when these fail them, they are at a loss where to turn next.

But when a man has no special skill or ability or riches or influence, he has to look to something outside these for success, something beyond material means. So he turns to the God in him, to his cell of the God-Mind, and of that cell he demands that it bring him fame or fortune or power or position. What is more, if he continues to demand it with persistent faith, HE GETS IT!

You see, in every adversity there lies the seed of an equivalent advantage. In every defeat there is a lesson showing you how to win the victory next time. The turning point in the lives of most successful men has come at some moment of crisis, when everything looked dark, when there seemed no way out. That was when they turned to their inner selves, when they gave up hope in material means and looked to the God in them for help. That was when they were able to turn each stumbling block into a stepping-stone to success.

> Isn't it strange that princes and kings,
> And clowns that caper in sawdust rings,
> And common folks like you and me,
> Are builders for eternity?
>
> Each is given a bag of tools,
> A shapeless mass, a book of rules;
> And each must make, ere life is flown,
> A stumbling block or a stepping stone.

You are one with the great "I AM" of the universe. You are part of God. Until you realize that—and the power it gives you—you will never know God. "We are parts of one stupendous whole, whose body Nature is, and God the soul." God has incarnated Himself in man. He seeks expression. Give Him work to do through you, give Him a chance to express Himself in some useful way, and there is nothing beyond your powers to do or to attain.

It matters not what your age, what your present circumstances or position. If you will seek your help outside your merely physical self, if you will put the God in you into some worthwhile endeavor, and then BELIEVE in Him, you can overcome any poverty, any handicap, any untoward circumstance. Relying upon your personal abilities or riches or friends is being like the heathen of old, whom the Prophet of the Lord taunted. "You have a God whom you must carry," he derided them. "We have a God *who carries us!*"

The God of personal ability or material riches or friends is one that you must continually carry. Drop him, and immediately you lose everything. But there is a God in you who will carry you—and in the doing of it, provide you with every good thing this world can supply. The purpose of this book is to acquaint you with this God *in you, The God That Only The Fortunate Few Know.*

As the poet so well expressed it—

> *In your own self lies Destiny. Let this*
> *Vast truth cast out all fear, and prejudice,*
> *All hesitation. Know that you are great,*
> *Great with Divinity. So dominate*
> *Environment and enter into bliss.*
> *Love largely and hate nothing. Hold no aim*
> *That does not chord with Universal Good.*
> *Hear what the voices of the Silence say—*
> *All joys are yours if you put forth your claim.*
> *Once let the spiritual laws be understood,*
> *Material things must answer and obey.*

Some might think that merely a poet's dream, but along comes Dr. J. B. Rhine of Duke University to prove it scientific fact as well.

In his new book "The Reach of the Mind," Dr. Rhine points out that in the past, Science seemed to feel that man was entirely material. It had discovered how glands regulate personality through their chemical secretions; it had shown that the child mind matures only as the brain develops; that certain mental functions are linked with specific areas of the brain, and that if one of these is injured, the corresponding mental function is lost.

So Science believed that it had accounted for all the processes of thought and action, that it could show a material basis for each.

But now Dr. Rhine and other experimenters have proved that knowledge can be acquired *without the use of the senses!*

Not only that, but they have also proved that the powers of the mind are not bound by space or limited by time! Perhaps their greatest discovery is that the mind can influence matter *without physical means.*

This has been done through prayer, of course, since time began, but such results have always been looked upon as supernatural. Dr. Rhine and other experimenters show that any normal person has the power to influence objects and events.

To quote "The Reach of the Mind"— "As a result of thousands of experimental trials, we found it to be a fact that the mind has a force that can act on matter. . . . There must, therefore, be an energy convertible to physical action, *a mental energy.*"

The one great essential to the successful use of this mental energy seems to be intense interest or desire. The more keyed up a person is, the more eager for results, the more he can influence those results.

Dr. Rhine showed through many experiments that when the subject's interest is distracted, when he lacks ability to concentrate his attention, his mental energy has little or no power over outside objects. It is only as he gives his entire attention to the object in mind, as he concentrates his every energy upon it, that he gets successful results.

Dr. Rhine's experiments prove scientifically what we have always believed—that there is a Power over and above the merely physical power of the mind or body, that through intense concentration or desire we can link up with that Power, and that once we do, nothing is impossible to us.

It means, in short, that man is not at the mercy of blind chance or Fate, that he can control his own destiny. Science is at last proving what Religion has taught from the beginning—that God gave man *dominion* and that he has only to understand and use this dominion to become the Master of his Fate, the Captain of his Soul.

> *Body and mind and Spirit, all combine*
> *To make the creature, human and Divine.*
> *Of this great Trinity, no part deny.*
> *Affirm, affirm, the great eternal I.*
> *Affirm the body, beautiful and whole,*
> *The earth-expression of immortal soul.*
> *Affirm the mind, the messenger of the hour,*
> *To speed between thee and the Source of Power.*
> *Affirm the Spirit, the eternal I—*
> *Of this great Trinity, no part deny.*
>   —ELLA WHEELER WILCOX

The God in You

THE GOD IN YOU

The declaration of Independence starts with the preamble that all men are born free and equal. But how many believe that? When one child is born in a Park Avenue home, with doctors and nurses and servants to attend to his slightest want, with tutors and colleges to educate him, with riches and influence to start him in his career, how can he be said to be born equal to the child of the Ghetto, who has difficulty getting enough air to breathe, to say nothing of food to eat, and whose waking hours are so taken up with the struggle for existence that he has no time to acquire much in the way of education!

Yet in that which counts most, these two are born equal, for they have equal access to the God in themselves, equal chance to give Him means of expression. More than that, the God in one is just as powerful as the God in the other, for both are part of that all-powerful God of the Universe who rules the world.

In effect, we are each of us individual cells in the great Mind of the universe—the God Mind. We can draw upon the Mind of the Universe in exactly the same way that any cell in our own body draws upon our brain for whatever it needs outside its immediate surroundings.

All men are born free and equal, just as all the cells in your body are equal. Some of these cells may seem to be more fortunately situated than others, being placed in fatty portions of the body where they are so surrounded with nourishment that they seem assured of everything they can need for their natural lives.

Others may be in hard-worked parts where they are continually having to draw upon the lymph around them, and through it upon the blood stream and the heart, and where it seems as though they cannot be sure of sustenance from one day to the next. Still others may be in little-used and apparently forgotten parts where they seem to have been left to dry up and starve, as in the scalp of the head when the hair falls out and the fatty tissue of the scalp dries, leaving the cells there to shrivel and die.

Yet despite their apparent differences in surroundings and opportunity, all these cells are equal, all can draw upon every element in the body for sustenance at need.

To see how it is done, let us take a single nerve cell in our own brain, and see how it works.

Look up the diagram of a typical nerve cell in any medical work, and what do you find? From one side of the cell, a long fibre extends which makes connection with some part of the skin, or some group of cells such as a muscle. This fibre is part of the nerve cell. It is the telephone line, carrying orders or stimuli from the cell to the muscle it controls, or from the sensory nerve in the skin to the cell in the brain. Thoughts, emotions, desires, all send impulses to the nerves controlling the muscles concerned, and provide the stimuli which set these muscles in action, thus transforming nervous energy into muscular energy.

So if you have a desire which requires the action of only a single muscle, what happens? Your desire takes the form of an impulse to the nerve cell controlling that muscle, the order travels along the cell-fibre to the muscle, which promptly acts in accord with the stimulus given it. And your desire is satisfied.

But suppose your desire requires the action of more than one muscle? Suppose it needs the united power of every muscle in the body? So far we have used only the long nerve fibre or telephone line connecting the nerve cell with the muscle it controls. But on the other side of each nerve cell are short fibres, apparently ending in space. And as long as the nerves are at rest, these fibres do lie in space.

But when you stir up the nerve cells, when you give them a job that is greater than the muscles at their command can manage, then these short fibres go into action. Then they bestir themselves to some purpose. They dig into the nerve cells near them. They wake these and stimulate them in turn to stir up those on the other sides of them until, if necessary, every cell in the brain is twitching, and every muscle in the body working to accomplish the job you command.

That is what happens in *your* body if even a single cell in your brain desires something strongly enough, persistently enough, to hold to its purpose until it gets what it wants. And that is what happens in the God-body when you put the same persistence into your desires.

You see, you are a cell in the God-body of the Universe, just as every cell in you is a part of your body. When you work with your hands, your feet, your muscles, you are using only the muscles immediately connected with your brain cells. When you work with the money you have, the riches or friends or influence you control, you are using only the means immediately connected to your brain cell in the mind of God. And that is so infinitesimally small a part of the means and resources at the command of that Great God-mind.

It is just as though you tried to do all the work required of your body today by using only the tiniest muscle in your little finger, when by stirring up the surrounding nerve cells, you could just as well draw upon the power of the whole mind, or of the entire body if that were needed. It is as though one of your nerve cells undertook to do the work of the whole body, and tried, with the single muscle at its command, to do it!

You'd think that foolish, if one tiny nerve cell out of the billions in your brain, undertook any such gigantic job. You'd know it was hopeless ... that no one cell, and no one muscle, could ever accomplish all that work. Yet you, as a single cell in the God-mind, have often attempted just as impossible jobs. When all you had to do to accomplish everything you desired was to stir into action the cells around you!

How can you do this? In the same way that any cell in your own brain does it. *Pray!* In other words, get an urgent, insistent desire. The first principle of success is DESIRE— knowing what you want. Desire is the planting of your seed. It needs cultivation, of course, but the first important step is the PLANTING. Desire stirs the nerve cells in your brain to use the muscles under their control to do the work required of them. Desire will set your nerve cell in the God-mind vibrating, using the muscle under its command and stirring into action all the nerve cells around it until they, too, are working with you to bring about the thing you wish.

That is the reason it was said in the Vedas thousands of years ago that if any two people would unite their psychic forces, they could conquer the world! That is the reason Jesus told us—"If two of you shall agree as touching anything they shall ask, it shall be done unto them. For when two or three are gathered together in My name, there am I in the midst of them, and I shall grant their request."

When two or more nerve cells unite for a certain action, they get that action, even if to bring it about they have to draw upon every cell in the whole body for help!

This does not mean that anything is impossible to a single cell or a single person—merely that 'when two or more are united for a common purpose, the results are easier. But there is no good thing any man can ask, believing, that he cannot get.

In the first chapter of Genesis, it is written that God gave man dominion over the earth. And it is true. It is just as true as that any nerve cell in your whole body has dominion over your body. If you doubt it, let one nerve be sufficiently irritated, and see how quickly it puts every nerve in your body to work to remove that irritation.

One nerve cell in your body, with a strongly held purpose, can bring into action every cell in your body to accomplish that purpose. One nerve cell in the God-body (in other words, one man or woman) with a strongly held purpose, can bring into action every cell in the Universe, if these be necessary to the accomplishment of that purpose!

Does that mean anything to you? Does it mean anything to know that the words of prophets and seers are true, that the promises of the Scriptures can be depended upon, that there really is a Power in the Universe that responds to the urge of the lowliest man or woman just as readily as to the command of the highest?

The world is yours! It matters not whether you be prince or pauper, blue-blooded or red, white-skinned, black, yellow or brown. The God-body of the Universe makes no more distinction between cells than do you in responding to the impulses of the nerve cells in your own body.

Rich or poor—it's all one to you. Highly placed or low—one can cause you as much trouble, or give you as great satisfaction, as another. And the same is true of the God-body of the Universe. All men are created free and equal. All remain free and equal nerve cells in the God-mind of the Universe.

The only difference lies in our understanding of the power that is ours. How much understanding have you? And what are you doing to increase it? "Seek first understanding, and all things else shall be added unto you." Easier to believe that now, isn't it? With the right understanding, you could run the world. Can you think of anything more important than acquiring understanding?

What turned the complaining, discouraged, poverty-stricken and quite ordinary young Bonaparte into the greatest military genius of his age, "Man of Destiny" and master of most of Europe?

The Talisman of Napoleon, the Talisman of every great and successful man, the only Talisman that will stir the whole body of the Universe into action, is the same Talisman as that needed to put the entire physical body at the service of any one nerve cell—*a purpose so strongly held that life or death or anything else seems of small consequence beside it!* A purpose— and the persistent determination to hold to it until it is accomplished.

Love sometimes makes such a Talisman—the love that goes out to dare all and do all for the loved one. Greed oftentimes brings it into being—hence many of the great fortunes of today. The lust for power is a potent Talisman, that has animated men since time began. Greater still is the zeal of one who would convert the world. That Talisman has carried men through fire and flood, into every danger and over every obstacle. Look how Mohammed, a lowly camel driver, became the ruler of and prophet to millions.

Faith in charms, belief in luck, utter confidence in another's leadership, all are Talismans of greater or lesser power.

But the greatest of all is belief in the God inside YOU! Belief in its power to draw to itself every element it needs for expression. Belief in a definite PURPOSE it came here to fulfill, and which can be fulfilled only through YOU!

Have you such a faith? If not, get it! For without such a faith, life is purposeless, meaningless. What is more, until you lay hold of that Talisman, life will never bring anything worth while to you!

What was it won for Grant over his more brilliant opponents? The grim, dogged, persistent purpose to fight it out along those lines if it took all summer! What is it that has made England victor in so many of her wars, in spite of inept leadership and costly blunders? That same bull-dog determination, which holds on in spite of all reverses and discouragements, until its fight is won. What was it that wore out the unjust judge, in the parable that Jesus told?

And he spake a parable unto them to this end, that man ought always to pray, and not to faint; saying, "There was in a city a judge, which feared not God, neither regarded man;

"And there was a widow in that city; and she came unto him, saying, 'Avenge me on mine adversary'

"And he would not for a while; but afterward he said within himself, 'Though I fear not God, nor regard man; yet because this widow troubleth me, I will avenge her, lest by her continual coming she weary me.'"

And the Lord said, "Hear what the unjust judge saith. And shall not God avenge his own elect, which cry day and night unto him, though he bear long with them?"

If the nerve in a tooth keeps crying out that a cavity in that tooth needs attention, won't you finally drop everything and seek out a dentist who can satisfy that nerve's needs? And if any other nerve prays continuously for attention, won't you do likewise with it?

Well, you are a nerve in the God-body. If you have an urgent need, and keep praying and insisting and demanding the remedy, don't you suppose you will get it just as surely?

A definite purpose, held to in the face of every discouragement and failure, in spite of all obstacles and opposition, will win no matter what the odds. It is the one nerve cell working against the indifference, the inertia or even the active opposition of the entire group. If the cell is easily discouraged, it will fail. If it is willing to wait indefinitely it will have to wait. But if it keeps stirring up the cells next to it, and stimulating them to stir those beyond, eventually the entire nerve system will go into action and bring about the result that single cell desires—even if it be only to rid itself of the constant irritation.

You have seen young fellows determined to go to college. You have thought them foolish, in the face of the obstacles facing them. Yet when they persisted, you know how often those obstacles have one by one magically disappeared, until presently they found themselves with the fruition of their desires. A strongly held purpose, persisted in, believed in, is as sure to win in the end as the morrow's sun is to rise. And earnest prayer is to the God-body what a throbbing nerve is to yours. Hold to it, insist upon it, and it is just as sure of a hearing. But remember:

He that wavereth is like the wave of the sea, driven by the wind and tossed; yet not that man think that he shall receive anything of the Lord.

All are born free and equal. All may not start with the same amount of wealth or opportunity immediately available to them, but all can go to the Source of these and get just as much of them as is necessary to satisfy their desires.

We are surrounded by riches. We have available unlimited wealth. But we have to learn how to draw it to us.

Years ago, at Kimberley in South Africa, a poor Boer farmer tried to glean a living out of the rocky soil. His boys oftentimes picked up pieces of dirty-looking crystal and used them as pebbles to throw at some wandering sheep. After years of fruitless effort, the farmer abandoned his attempts to make a living out of this rocky soil, and moved to a more fertile spot. Today, the farm he tried so hard to cultivate is the site of the Kimberley Diamond Mines, one of the richest spots on the face of the globe. And the bits of dirty crystal that his boys threw at the sheep turned out to be diamonds in the rough!

Most of us are like that poor Boer farmer. We strive and struggle, and frequently give up, because of ignorance of our powers, ignorance of the good things around us. We remain in poverty until along comes someone and shows that we were standing on a diamond mine all the time.

Russell Conwell tells the story of a Pennsylvania farmer whose brother went to Canada and became an oil driller. Fired with the brother's tales of sudden wealth, the farmer sold his land and went to Canada to make his fortune. The new owner, in looking over the farm, found that where the cattle came to drink from a little creek, a board had been put across the water to hold back a heavy scum which was washed down by the rains from the ground above.

He examined this scum, and thought it smelled like oil. So he had some experts come out and look the ground over. It proved to be one of the richest oil fields in the state of Pennsylvania.

What riches are you overlooking? What opportunities? Opportunity," says a famous writer, "is like oxygen. It is so plentiful that we fairly breathe it." All that is necessary is a receptive mind, a willingness to try, and the persistence to see things through.

There is some one thing that YOU can do better than anyone else. There is some line of work in which you can excel—if you will just find that one thing and spend all your time and effort in learning to do it supremely well.

Don't worry if it seems to be some humble thing that anyone ought to be able to do. In a magazine some time ago, there was the story of a Polish immigrant who could speak scarcely a word of English, who had no trade or training and had to take any sort of job that offered. He happened to get one in a nursery, digging up dirt for the flowers. He dug so well that soon he was attending to the planting of many of the commoner varieties of flowers.

Among these were the peonies. He loved those big peonies, gave them such careful attention that they thrived and grew more beautiful than ever. Soon his peonies began to attract attention, the demand for them grew, until he had to double and then quadruple the space devoted to them. Today he is half owner of that nursery.

Two artists opened an office together, doing any kind of work they could get. One noticed that wherever he happened to do cartoons for people, the results were so effective that they came back for more. So he made an especial study of cartoon drawing. Today his earnings are in the $25,000 class, while his fellow artist is still barely making ends meet as a jack of all trades.

A retail clerk found that she had a special gift for satisfying complaining customers. She liked to straighten out the snarls that others had caused, and she did it so well that she soon attracted the attention of her employers. Today she is head of the complaint department.

There is the switchboard operator with the pleasing voice, the reception clerk with the cheery smile, the salesman with the convincing manner, the secretary with the knack of saving the boss' time, the drummer with the jolly manner. Every one of us has something. Find out what one thing you can do best, cultivate it and you can be the biggest man in that line in the world.

Success is where you are and within yourself. Don't try to imitate what someone else is doing. Develop what YOU have. There is something in you that will enable you to reach the top in some one line. Put the spot light on your own characteristics, your own abilities. Find what you can do best, what people like you best for. Then cultivate that.

When the great Comstock Lode was first discovered, a fortune was taken out of it. Then the ore petered out. The owners presently gave up and sold out to a new group. These men spent several hundred thousand dollars in a fruitless attempt to locate the rich lode, and they too were ready to give up. But someone thought to try a bore hole to the side of one of the entries, and struck an almost solid mass of ore so rich that nearly $300,000,000 was taken from it.

In the early days of the prairie farms, newcomers were frequently able to buy for a song the homesteads of the original settlers, because the latter had been able to find no water. They had dug wells, but had been unable to reach the streams beneath. Oftentimes, however, by digging only a few feet further, the newcomers found water in abundance. The first settlers had quit when success was almost within their grasp. The greatest success usually comes from one step beyond the point where defeat overtook you. "He who loses wealth, loses much," says an old proverb. "He who loses a friend, loses more. But he who loses his courage, loses everything."

Three things educators try to instil into children:

1st—Knowledge
2nd—Judgment
3rd—Persistence.

And the greatest of these is Persistence. Many a man has succeeded without education. Many even without good judgment. But none has ever got anywhere worth while without persistence. Without a strong desire, without that inner urge which pushes him on, over obstacles, through discouragements, to the goal of his heart's desire.

"Nothing in the world can take the place of persistence," said Calvin Coolidge. "Talent will not. Nothing is more common than unsuccessful men with talent. Genius will not; unrewarded genius is almost a proverb. Education will not; the world is full of educated derelicts. Persistence and determination alone are omnipotent. The slogan 'Press on' has solved and always will solve the problems of the human race."

Russell Conwell, the famous educator and lecturer who founded Temple University, gathered statistics some years ago on those who succeed, and his figures showed that of 4043 multimillionaires in this country at that time, only 69 had even a High School education. They lacked money, they lacked training, but they had the URGE to get somewhere, the *persistence* to keep trying ... and they succeeded!

Compare that with the figures Conwell gathered on the sons of rich men. Only one in seventeen died wealthy! Lacking incentive, having no urge within them to get ahead, they not only failed to make their mark, but they lost what they had.

The first essential of success is a feeling of lack, a need, a *desire* for something you have not got. It is the powerlessness of the cripple or invalid that makes him long for strength, gives him the necessary persistence to work for it until he gets it. It is the poverty and misery of their existence that makes the children of the Ghetto long for wealth, and gives them the persistence and determination to work at anything until they get it.

You need that same urgent desire, that same determination and persistence if you are to get what you want from life. You need to realize that whatever it is you want of life, it is there for the taking. You need to know that you are a cell in the God-mind, and that through this God-mind you can put the whole Universe to work, if necessary, to bring about the accomplishment of your desire.

But don't waste that vast power on trifles. Don't be like the fable of the woodsman who, having worked long and hard for the wishing Fairy and accomplished the task she set him, was told that he might have in reward any three things he asked for. Being very hungry, he promptly asked for a good meal. That eaten, he noticed that the wind was blowing up cold, so he asked for a warm cloak. With his stomach full and a warm cloak about him, he felt sleepy, so he asked for a comfortable bed to lie upon.

And so, with every good thing of the world his for the asking, the next day found him with only a warm cloak to show for his labors. Most of us are like that. We put the mountain in labor, just to bring forth a mouse. We strive and strain, and draw upon all the powers that have been given us, to accomplish some trifling thing that leaves us just where we were before.

Demand much! Set a worth-while goal. Remember the old poem by Jessie B. Rittenhouse from "The Door of Dreams" published by Houghton Mifflin Co., Boston.

I bargained with Life for a penny
And Life would pay no more,
However I begged at evening
When I counted my scanty store.

For Life is a just employer;
He gives you what you ask,
But once you have set the wages,
Why, you must bear the task.

I worked for a menial's hire,
Only to learn, dismayed,
That any wage I had asked of Life,
Life would have paid.

Don't you be foolish like that. Don't bargain with Life for a penny. Ask for something worth putting the Universe to work for. Ask for it, demand it—then stick to that demand with persistence and determination until the whole God-mind HAS to bestir itself to give you what you want.

The purpose of Life from the very beginning has been dominion—dominion over every adverse circumstance. And through his part of dominion, his nerve cell in the Mind of God and his ability through it to get whatever action he may persistently demand—man HAS dominion over everything.

There is a Spark of Divinity in YOU. What are you doing to fan it into flame? Are you giving it a chance to grow, to express itself, to become an all-consuming fire? Are you giving it work to do? Are you making it seek out ever greater worlds to conquer? Or are you letting it slumber neglected, or perhaps even smothering it with doubt and fear?

And God said, Let us make man in our image, after our likeness; and let him have DOMINION over the fish of the sea, and over the fowl of the air, and over the cattle, and over all the earth, and over every creeping thing that creepeth upon the earth.

Do you know what is the Unpardonable Sin in all of Nature? Read the following chapters, and you will see!

Affirmation:

And every morning I will say, There's something happy on the way. And God sends love to me. God is the light of my life, the Source of my knowledge and inspiration. God in the midst of me knows. He provides me with food for my thoughts, ideas for excellent service, clear perception, Divine intelligence.

THE GOAL OF LIFE

Mind is the Master-power that moulds and makes,
And Man is Mind, and evermore he takes
The tool of Thought, and, shaping what he wills,
Brings forth a thousand joys, a thousand ills:—
He thinks in secret, and it comes to pass:
Environment is but his looking glass.

—JAMES ALLEN

"In the beginning God created the heaven and earth. And the earth was without form and void; and dark ness was upon the face of the deep. And the Spirit of God moved upon the face of the waters. And God said ..."

In the beginning was Mind, Energy, without form, without direction . . . like so much static electricity. Then came the Word, the mental image, to make all that power dynamic, to give it form and direction. What matters it the form it took first, so long as it had definite direction? It required an Intelligence to give it shape. That is the first great fact of the Scriptures. NOT that the heavens and earth were created, or light brought forth, but that *any form presupposes a Directing Intelligence!*

You cannot have dynamic electricity without a generator—an intelligence to conceive and direct it. No more can you have an earth or a flower, without an Intelligence to give them form from the static energy all about.

In the beginning, not merely was the earth without form and void, but the whole universe was the same way. Just as the interspaces of the universe are today. Everything was static—energy in flux. But "the Spirit of God moved upon the face of the waters. And God said, Let there be light."

St. John puts it—"In the beginning was the Word. And the Word was with God. And the Word was God." And what is the "Word"? As often mentioned before, a word is not a mere sound issuing from the lips, or so many letters written by hand. A word is a mental concept, an idea, an image.

In the beginning was the mental image! Read over that first chapter of Genesis, and you will see that in everything God created, the "Word" came first—then the material form. The "Word" had to come first—you cannot build a house without first having a clear image of the house you are going to build. You cannot make anything, without first conceiving a mental image of the thing to be created. Not even God could do that!

So when God said—"Let the earth bring forth grass," He had in mind a clear mental picture of what grass was like. As the Scriptures put it—"The Lord God made the earth and the heavens, and every plant of the field *before it was in the earth*, and every herd of the field *before it grew*." First the "Word," the mental image—then the creation.

It requires intelligence to form a mental concept. The animals cannot do it. They can recall images of things they have seen. They cannot conceive concepts from pure ideas. So, as stated above, creation pre-supposes a mental image, and a mental image means a directing Intelligence behind it.

That is the first conclusion that a reading of the Scriptures forces upon us. And the second is that like reproduces like.

Go over that first chapter again, and you will find that no less than six different times is the assertion repeated that "everything reproduces after its kind ..." "Let the earth bring forth grass, the herb yielding seed, and the fruit tree yielding fruit *after his kind*, whose seed is in itself.... Let the earth bring forth the living creature after his kind, cattle, and creeping thing, and beast of the earth after his kind."

Then God made man in His own image, after His likeness. Notice that! After telling us repeatedly that everything reproduced after its own kind, the Scriptures go on to say that God made man *in His own image*. That can mean only one thing—that man, too, is a God! For throughout all nature, hybrids are sterile. Nothing can breed out of its own kind. Different races, different strains of the same species, can interbreed, but all must be of the same kind.

So when God made man in His own image, and bade him be fruitful and multiply, He thereby showed that man was no hybrid, but of the true breed of God. And to prove it, he gave man dominion over the "fish of the sea, and over the fowl of the air, and over every living thing that moveth upon the earth." And He bade man replenish the earth, *and subdue it,* and have dominion.

Simple instructions, and easily carried out—in part— but as for subduing the earth, and having dominion over it, mankind is still in the primer class. Yet if man is a God— *and he is*—then he *can* do it. And anything so worthwhile as that is worth all our effort to learn how to do.

For if we are gods and true sons of God—as the Scriptures frequently assure us—then we must possess all the properties of God. We must be creators. Then why don't we create happier conditions? Why don't we do away with poverty and disease and all unhappiness?

Why? Because it takes understanding and faith to use our powers, and so few have the patience to work for them. Men will study for years to become doctors, or lawyers, or engineers. And they will start the practice of their professions in fear and trembling, realizing that it will be years before they will have gained enough practical knowledge from experience to be really competent in their work.

Yet they will read a book or two on psychology or some of the mental sciences, and if they cannot put the principles into practice next day, they give up in disgust and condemn the principles as tommyrot!

Of all fields of study, none offers such possibilities as the study of the inner powers of man. None offers such sure rewards to the persevering, sincere student. Yet there is no field so neglected by the average man. Nine men out often—yes, ninety-nine out of a hundred—merely drift through life. With generators inside them capable of producing power enough to accomplish any purpose, they get nowhere.

They use their generators, of course, but to what purpose? To sigh over some movie idol—or thrill over the exploits of some notorious racketeer—or wax indignant at the thieving of a fat city grafter. Vicarious emotions, all of them—yet because it is so much easier to enjoy one's thrills vicariously, most people go through life experiencing few others.

They speed up their generators, but with no resultant good to themselves. Their experiences are all dream pictures. When they leave the movies, or put down their paper or book, they wake up! They never make the effort necessary to bring those thrills into their own lives.

Suppose the envelope of air that surrounds the globe were a great storage battery of electrical energy. Every thought, every fervent desire, every emotion, adds to the energy there. Every time you run your generator—with feelings of love or hate or fear or envy or hope or faith— you put additional energy into that storage battery.

But to draw energy out of this storage battery, you must have good conductors, good wires, the wires of a definite purpose, strongly held. And to keep the energy from dissipating requires the insulation of faith.

You cannot get much current from a storage battery by merely touching your wires to its posts, letting them slip on and off continuously. You have to twist them securely around the posts, fasten them there firmly with the screw cap, to get a constant current.

And you cannot use plain wires, or the current will run off into the first conductor that comes in contact with it. Your wires must be insulated, so the current will go directly from the battery to the appliance you wish it to run.

It is the same with the storage battery of power all around you. You can draw upon it at will, you can get flashes of power from it at the touch of fervent prayer or under the stress of any other high emotion, but if you want a continuous flow of power, you must have first a firmly held purpose, then the insulation of serene faith. Given these, there is no limit to the power you can draw, or the purposes to which it can be put.

Now how would this help if you were out of a job, had a wife and children waiting for something to eat, a home that was about to be taken away from you—and you had been praying and trying in every way you knew to raise the necessary money? How could you use the idea? What would you need to do?

Remember, in the Bible, how it is told that the apostles labored all night long, and caught nothing, yet when Jesus bade them cast their nets on the right side, and they did so, their nets were filled to overflowing?

You have been praying and trying, and you have caught nothing. Now it is your turn to cast your nets on the right side. And casting them there means to disregard the material world around you for a moment, and do your fishing in the world of energy!

All around you is energy—unappropriated energy that you can turn into any form you wish. The same flux out of which God created the world! And you are a god, a creator, a true son of the Father. You have the same power to make of your world what you like that He has. It requires only the same method He used.

First, the "Word," the mental image. What is it you want? Position, power, love, riches, success? Make your mold. The best flux in the world will not make a usable shape unless you have a mold to pour it in. So make your mold, your mental image. See it clearly in your mind's eye. Don't make it the home or position or riches that belong to someone else. Use them as a model, if you like, but make your own out of virgin material.

Second, the flux. "The Spirit of God moved on the face of the waters." Throw your net, your spirit, around as much of the unappropriated energy about as you need to fill your mold. Then hold to it with the dogged grip of the bulldog. It is yours. You have filed your claim upon it, and no one can take it away from you unless you weaken and let go. Hold to that knowledge with grim, unshakable purpose, and there is nothing you cannot get.

"Whatsoever you ask for when you pray, believe that you receive it, and you shall have it." Whatever you want, make your mental hold, then throw your net around the flux necessary to fill it, and hold on to it until that flux has hardened. It is yours. You *have* it. You have only to believe, to *know that you have it,* in order to give that flux time to harden so that all can see it.

But to lose faith is to pull away the mold while your flux is still liquid. It will run like quicksilver in all directions, and you have to start all over again, making a new mold, casting your net around new energy, starting again to give it time to harden and become manifest.

In every man there is a Seed of Life, with infinite power to draw to itself whatever it conceives to be necessary to its expression. It doesn't matter who you are, what your environment or education or advantages, the Seed of Life in you has the same power for good.

What is it makes a poor immigrant-boy like Edward Bok, overcome every handicap of language and education, to become one of the greatest editors the country has known?

What is it accounts for the fact that, as before-mentioned, of 4043 multimillionaires in this country a few years before the first World War, all but 69 started so poor that they had not even a high school education?

Isn't it that the more circumstances conspire to repress it, the stronger becomes the urge of the Life in you for expression? The more it lacks channels through which to expand, the more inclined it is to burst its shell and flow forth in all directions?

It is the old case of the river that is dammed, generating the most power. Most of us are so placed that some opportunity for expression is made easy for us. And that little opportunity serves like a safety valve to a boiler—it leaves us steam enough to do something worth while, yet keeps us from getting up enough power to burst the shell about us, and sweep away every barrier that holds us down.

Yet it is only such an irresistible head of steam as that which makes great successes. That is why the blow which knocks all the props from under us is often the turning point in our whole career. Take the case of a man I know who, five years after losing his job, reached his goal as head of a rival company and the greatest authority on his product in the country. Do you suppose he would ever have won these rewards had he continued as salesman for his original company?

No, indeed! He was getting along too well. He had a comfortable home, a fine family, a good income and congenial working conditions. Why should he disturb them? The old fable of the dog with the bone looking at his reflection in the water, keeps many a man from taking a chance at a better opportunity when he has a reasonably good one within his grasp. He's afraid he may be giving up the real for the chimera.

Yet playing safe is probably the most unsafe thing in the world. You cannot stand still. You must go forward—or see the world slide past you. This was well illustrated by figures worked out by one of the big Economic Services. Of all those who have money at 35, 87% lose it by the time they are 60.

Why?—Because the fortunes they have take away the need for initiative on their part. Their money gives to them easy means of expressing the urge in them, without effort on their part. It gives them dozens of safety valves, through which their steam continually escapes.

The result is that they not only accomplish nothing worth while, but they soon dissipate the fortunes that were left them. They are like kettles, the urge of life keeping the water at boiling point, but the open spout of ease letting the steam escape as fast as it forms, until presently there is not even any water left.

Why do the sons of rich men so seldom accomplish anything worth while? Because they don't have to. Every opportunity is given them to express the urge in them through pleasant channels, and they dissipate through these the energies that might carry them to any height. The result? They never have a strong enough "head of steam" left to carry through any real job.

With us ordinary mortals, however, sooner or later comes a crisis in our affairs, and how we meet it determines our future happiness and success. Since the beginning of time, every form of life has been called upon to meet such crises. So the goal of life has always been DOMINION—a means of overcoming all obstacles, of winning dominion over circumstances.

In "Weekly Unity" Magazine, some years ago, there was the story of a couple who wanted to dispose of their house and move to another town. But the so-called "Depression" was on at that time, and houses were a drug on the market. Real Estate Agents held out no hope, so "Why not try prayer?"—a friend asked. "What can we lose?" they asked each other. So they sat down together and tried to realize—

1. That there is only one Mind, that they were parts of that Mind, and that those to whom they must sell were also parts of it.

2. That this God-Mind is working for the good of all—for their good and for that of those who were seeking just such a home as theirs.

3. That this God-Mind was glad to help them, glad to help those seeking such a home, so all they had to do was to put their home in His hands, and leave the working out of the problem confidently and serenely to Him.

Within a short time, they sold the house for a good price for CASH. In another issue, "Unity" told about a dealer who had bought a number of pianos on credit, and borrowed some of the money from the bank to pay for them. The pinch came, and the bank notified him that his note must be paid by a certain date. He went home worried and miserable. With the help of his wife, however, he was able to throw off the worry and put it up to the God Inside Him to find the necessary funds.

That afternoon, one of the clerks came to him and said there was a man cursing and swearing about something he had bought from him the day before. He went over to the man and found him ranting and raging about an inexpensive article he had purchased for his son, on which some of the strings had broken. The shopkeeper promptly gave him a better article to replace it. That took all the wind out of the complaining customer's sails, and he became so apologetic that he felt he had to buy something else to make up for his boorish behavior. It developed that he was planning to get a fine piano for his daughter's birthday, and the money he promptly paid for this proved to be more than enough to take care of the dealer's note at the bank.

The goal of life since the beginning of time has been DOMINION over just such circumstances as these, and only through the God in you can you win it. "My soul, wait thou only upon God," bade the prophet of old, "for my expectation is from Him."

But don't limit the channels through which His help can come to you. Don't insist that it should be through a legacy from some rich uncle, or a raise in your pay or the winning of some prize or order. Develop any channel that looks promising, but leave ALL the channels open. And then act as though *you already possessed the thing you want.*

Don't say—"When this bill is paid—or this crisis past—I shall feel so relieved." Instead, say—"I AM relieved, I feel so content and peaceful now that this load is off my shoulders."

How will you act when you get the thing you want? Well, a think that way—and before you know it, you will BE that way. lines by Ella Wheeler Wilcox—

> *Thought is a magnet; and the longed-for pleasure*
> *Or boon or aim or object is the steel;*
> *And its attainment hangs but on the measure*
> *Of what thy soul can feel.*

How would you conduct yourself if you full realized your one-ness with God, if you could truly believe that He is constantly offering you life, love and every good thing your heart can desire? Well, that is exactly what He is doing!

So act as if you already had the thing you want. Visualize it as yours. See the picture clearly in every detail in your mind's eye. Then LET GOD make it manifest. Do what you can, of course, with what you have, where you are, but put your dependence upon God, and LET His good gifts come to you.

Look at the first chapter of the Scriptures. When God wanted light, did He strive and struggle, trying to make light? No, He said—*"Let there be light."*

When you want something very much, instead of trying to MAKE it come your way, suppose you try asking for it and then LETTING it come. Suppose you just relax, and *let* God work through you instead of trying to *make* Him do something for you. Suppose you say to yourself—"I will do whatever is given me to do. I will follow every lead to the best of my ability, but for the rest, it is all up to the God in me. God in me knows what my right work is, where it is, and just what I should do to get it. I put myself and my affairs lovingly in His hands, secure that whatever is for my highest good, He will bring to me."

Emerson used to say that when we discern Truth, we do nothing of ourselves but allow a passage for its beams. They express the same thought in electricity through the equation $-C = E/R$: The current delivered at any given point is equal to the voltage divided by the resistance. With too much resistance, no current is delivered, no matter how much may be available.

When we worry and are tense and fearful, we set up so great resistance that God finds it difficult to get through to us. We have to LET GO before we can become good conductors. Like John Burroughs, we must be able to say— "Serene I fold my hands and wait, nor care for wind or tide or sea. No more I strive against time or fate, for lo! Mine own shall come to me."

Unity has a favorite Prayer of Faith, written by Hannah More Kohaus, which all of us might well use when we are worried or sick or in need. If you will relax and repeat it slowly aloud, it is calculated to help you in any crisis:

Robert Collier

God IS MY help in every need;
God does my every hunger feed;
God walks beside me, guides my way
Through every moment of the day.

I now am wise, I now am true,
Patient, kind, and loving, too.
All things I am, can do, and be,
Through Christ the Truth that is in me.

God is my health, I can't be sick;
God is my strength, unfailing, quick;
God is my all; I know no fear,
Since God and love and Truth are here.

A GOLDEN RULE MOTTO

I shall pass through this world but once.
Any good, therefore, that I can do
Or any kindness that I can show
To any human being Let me do it now. Let me
Not defer it or neglect it for
I shall not pass this way again.

—ANONYMOUS

ONLY A COG IN A WHEEL

A man there was of unusual gifts
Bearing an honored name,
Life came to him with outstretched hands
Proffering wealth and fame;
But he carelessly turned his head away,
The prize made little appeal,
Contenting himself with a minor part,
He was only a cog in a wheel.

When opportunity knocked at his door,
It found him asleep and deaf;
Long and patiently it waited there,
But he did not come to himself.
His golden chances were wasted like chaff,

He took no account of the real;
Each day a monotonous grind to him,
He was only a cog in a wheel.

In the image of God this man was made,
With power to do and to serve;
Strong of mind and body was he,
But he lacked essential nerve.
So he drifted along from day to day,
Without ambition or zeal,
Playing a dull and nondescript part,
He was only a cog in a wheel.

What place do you fill in life's great machine—
Are you using your gifts aright?
Today have you wrought some truly fine thing—
Can you claim to have fought a good fight?
Will it surely be said that you "played the game"—
That your life was productive and real?
Or will the world say, as it goes on its way,
He was only a cog in a wheel?

—ANONYMOUS

Many versions as to the true description of Christ have been given to the world. Among the most authentic is this one, written by Publius Lentulus, President of Judea, to Tiberius Caesar, and first appeared in the writings of Saint Anselm of Canterbury in the Eleventh Century.

"There lived at this time in Judea a man of singular virtue—whose name is Jesus Christ whom the barbarians esteem as a prophet, but his followers love and adore him as the offspring of the immortal God. He calls back the dead from the graves and heals all sorts of diseases with a word or touch. He is a tall man, well shaped, and of an amiable and reverend aspect—his hair of a color that can hardly be matched, falling into graceful curls, waving about and very agreeably couched about his shoulders, parted on the crown of his head, running as a stream to the front after the fashion of the Nazarites; his forehead high, large and imposing; his cheeks without spot or wrinkle, beautiful with a lovely red; his nose and mouth formed with exquisite symmetry; his beard of a color suitable to his hair, reaching below his chin and parted in the middle like a fork; his eyes bright and blue, clear and serene, look innocent, dignified, manly and mature. Often times however, just before he reveals his divine powers, his eyelids are gently closed in reverential silence. In proportion of body most perfect and captivating; his arms and hands are delectable to behold. He rebukes with majesty, counsels with mildness, his whole address, whether in word or deed, being eloquent and grave. No man has seen him laugh, yet his manners are exceedingly pleasant, but he has wept frequently in the presence of men. He is temperate, modest and wise. A man for his extraordinary beauty and divine perfection, surpassing the children of men in every sense."

YOUR MENTAL BROWNIES

Mankind, like Ancient Gaul, can be divided into three parts.

1st—Those who are still in a state of simple consciousness, living, acting and thinking as the animals do. Men and women in this class can be said to exist—nothing more.

2nd—Those in a state of self-consciousness. This comprises the great bulk of the higher races of mankind. They reason, they study, they work, they sorrow and enjoy. But they are forced to depend for all good things upon their own efforts and they are subject to all manner of circumstances and conditions beyond their control. Theirs is a state of struggle.

3rd—Those entering into or who have reached the intuitional or higher consciousness, that state which Jesus termed the Kingdom of Heaven within us.

Just as, in the childhood of the race, there was brought forth an Adam and Eve with such advanced receptual intellects that they presently developed conceptual ideas (i.e. named impressions and the ability to classify them, compare them and draw conclusions from them), so today are to be found here and there the advance guard of the Mental Age—men and women as far ahead of the ordinary conceptual intellect of their fellows as this is in advance of the simple consciousness of the animal.

You see, the animal recognizes only images. Each house is to him a new house, with its own associations of food or famine, of kindness or blows. He never generalizes, or draws conclusions by comparing one house with another. His is the simple or receptual consciousness.

Man, on the other hand, takes his recept or image of a house and tabs it. He names it a house and then classifies it according to its kind. In that way, he turns it from a mere image into an idea or concept. It is as though he were traveling on a railroad train and keeping a tally of every house he passed. To the animal, it would mean filling his mind with the pictures of a hundred or more houses. To a man, it would be merely a matter of jotting down in the tablets of his memory—"100 houses, 25 of the Colonial type, 15 Tudor style, etc."

If his mind were too full of images, there would be no room in it to work out conclusions from those images, so man classifies those images into concepts or ideas, and thus increases his mental capacity a millionfold.

But now the time has come in his mental development when his mind is so full of concepts that a new short cut must be found. Here and there a few have already found this short cut and penetrated to the highest plane of consciousness—the intuitional or "Heaven" consciousness.

What is this higher consciousness? Bucke calls it the Cosmic Consciousness, and defines it as a consciousness of the world about us, a consciousness that does not have to stop and add concept to concept like a column of figures, but which can work out the answer immediately, intuitively, as a "lightning calculator" can work out a problem in mathematics, apparently without going through any of the intermediate stages of addition and subtraction, of labored reasoning from premise to conclusion.

You see, the conscious you is merely that aggregation of images and sensations and concepts known as the brain. But beyond and above this reasoning mind is your intuitive mind—the Soul of you—which is one cell in the great Oversoul of the Universe, God. It is the connecting link between God and you. It is part of Him. It shares in all His attributes, all His power and wisdom and riches. And at need it can draw upon the whole of these. How? In the same way that any cell of your body can draw upon the vitality of the whole body—by creating the need, *by using what it has.*

There is nothing mysterious about the way life works. It is all a logical growth. In the intellect, the young child first registers impressions, then it recognizes and tabs them, finally classifying them and using them as the basis for reasoning out ideas. By the use of impressions and images, the child can know the world it sees and feels. By concepts, it can construct in imagination the world it has not seen. Is this all? Is it the end?

"No!" answers Bucke in "Cosmic Consciousness." "As life arose in a world without life; as simple consciousness came into existence where before was mere vitality without perception; as self-consciousness soared forth over land and sea; so shall the race of man which has been thus established make other steps and attain to a yet higher life than any heretofore experienced or even conceived.

And let it be clearly understood that the new step is not merely an expansion of self-consciousness, but as distinct from it as that it's from simple consciousness, or as is this last from mere vitality without any consciousness at all.

But how shall we know this new sense? How recognize its coming? The signs are evident in every man and woman of high mentality. You have seen accountants who could write down a column of figures and give you the total without consciously adding one to another. You can recall instances when you have anticipated word for word what someone was about to say to you, when you have answered the telephone and known before he spoke who was at the other end of the wire, when you have met a stranger and formed a "snap judgment" of him which afterwards turned out to be marvelously correct. We call this intuition. It is the first stage of the Cosmic Consciousness. It is a perfectly logical step in the growth of the intellect.

In the jump from Simple Consciousness to Self-Consciousness, man combined groups of recepts or images into one concept or idea, just as we combine the three Roman numerals III into the one symbol 3. No longer did he have to hold in his mind each individual tree in a forest. He grouped them all together under one heading of trees, and called the group a forest.

Now he is advancing a step farther. Instead of having to first study each tree individually to learn the properties of that forest, he is getting that knowledge from the soul within him, which is part of the great Oversoul of the forest and of the Universe, and therefore knows all things. In other words, he is getting it intuitively.

That is the first step in reaching the Heaven consciousness—to cultivate your intuitions, to encourage them in every possible way. Your soul is a cell in the great God-body just as every cell in your body is part of you. And as part of the Oversoul of the Universe, it has access to all the knowledge of the Universe. But it needs exercise, it requires development.

When you want to develop any cell or set of cells in your body, what do you do? You exercise them, do you not? You use them to the limit of their abilities. Then what happens? They feel weak, exhausted. They become thin and emaciated. Why? Because you have broken up those cells, used the energy in them, and they have not yet had time to draw upon the blood stream for more. For the first few days or weeks that you continue that hard usage, they remain weak and nerveless. Again why? Because the amount of energy your "governor" is accustomed to apportioning those cells is not sufficient for such heavy work. But keep persevering, and what happens? Those cells not only harden until they are equal to any call you can make upon them, but they grow in size and power. They have put in a permanent order upon the "governor" for more life-giving energy, and as long as they can find use for it, that energy will keep coming to them.

That is the first thing you must do to grow in intuitive consciousness—cultivate what you have, use it on every possible occasion even though you seem to strain it beyond its powers at first. Listen for that still, small voice. And listen to it. "And thine ears shall hear a word behind thee," promised the Prophet of old, "saying—This is the way, walk ye in it, when ye turn to the right hand, and when ye turn to the left."

What is the vision of the artist, the inspiration of the writer, the discovery of the chemist or inventor, but his intuitive consciousness at work? Ask almost any great author, and he will tell you that he does not work out his plots. They "come to him"—that's all. "The key to successful methods," says Thomas A. Edison, "comes right out of the air. A real new thing like a general idea, a beautiful melody, is pulled out of space—a fact which is inexplicable."

Inexplicable—yes, from the viewpoint of the conceptual intellect—but quite understandable from the intuitive point of view.

So much for the first step. It is one possible to any man or woman of high intellect. When it involves a problem or a work of art or a story or a new discovery, it requires only filling the mind with all available concepts related to the desired result, then putting it up to the God in you to work out the answer.

The second step is the earnest desire for a higher consciousness. That sounds simple enough. Everybody would like to be able to learn without going through all the labor of adding percept to recept, making concepts of these and then figuring out the answers. So if the earnest desire is all that is needed, it ought to be easy.

Yet it is not. It is the hardest step of all. Why? Because the desire must be your *dominant* desire. It must not be merely a means to the end of obtaining riches or winning to high position.

All agree on this: This Heaven consciousness comes only as the result of a tremendous desire for spiritual truth, and a hunger and thirst after things of the spirit.

Perhaps that can be better understood when you remember how many ordinary people have had partial glimpses of it when almost at the point of death, or when coming out from under the influence of anaesthetics.

What, then, are the necessary conditions?

First, an understanding of the power latent in you, an understanding that, regardless of how much or how little education you have received, there is in you a power (call it the subconscious, or your soul, or your good genii or what you will) capable of contacting the Intelligence which directs and animates all of the universe.

Second, the earnest desire for spiritual growth. To possess this, a man need not be an ascetic, or give up his family or his business. In fact, he should be the better husband and father and business man for it. For the man of business today is no longer engaged in cheating his neighbor before the neighbor can cheat him. He is trying to *serve,* and to the extent that he succeeds in giving more and better service than others, he succeeds. Can you conceive of any finer preparation for the Heaven consciousness?

Third, the ability to thoroughly relax. As Boehme put it—"To cease from all thinking and willing and imaging. Your own 'self-conscious' hearing and willing and seeing hinder you from seeing and hearing God."

"When a new faculty appears in a race," says Bucke, "it will be found in the very beginning in one individual of that race; later it will be found in a few individuals; after a further time, in a larger percentage of the members of the race; still later, in half the members; and so on until, after thousands of generations, an individual who misses having the faculty is regarded as a monstrosity."

The Heaven consciousness, or Cosmic Consciousness as Bucke calls it, has reached the point of being found in many individuals. When a faculty reaches that point, it is susceptible of being acquired by all of the higher type of members of that race *who have reached full maturity.*

And it is never too late to develop this Intuitive Consciousness, for your mind never grows old. In his book, "The Age of Mental Virility," Dr. Dorland points out that more than half of mankind's greatest achievements were accomplished by men over 50 years old, and that more of these were done by men over 70 than by those under 30.

In tests made by Dr. Irving Lorge of Teachers College, Columbia University, it was found that while SPEED of learning might decline with years, the mental powers do not decline. When the speed penalty was eliminated, people of 50 and 60 made higher scores than those around 25. Dr. Lorge sums up his tests in these words:

As far as mental ability is concerned, there need be no "retiring age." The probabilities are that the older a person becomes, the more valuable he becomes. He possesses the same mental power he had in his young manhood, plus his wealth of experience and knowledge of his particular job. These are things that no youngster, however brilliant, can pick up.

You have an Intuitive Consciousness, which has evidenced itself many a time in "Hunches," and the like. Remains, then, only to develop it. Robert Louis Stevenson pointed the way when he told how he worked out the plot for Dr. Jekyll and Mr. Hyde.

"My Brownies! God bless them!" said Stevenson, "Who do one-half of my work for me when I am fast asleep, and in all human likelihood do the rest for me as well when I am wide awake and foolishly suppose that I do it myself. I had long been wanting to write a book on man's double being. For two days I went about racking my brains for a plot of any sort, and on the second night I dreamt the scene in Dr. Jekyll and Mr. Hyde at the window; and a scene, afterward split in two, in which Hyde, pursued, took the powder and underwent the change in the presence of his pursuer."

You have had similar experiences. You know how, after you have studied a problem from all angles, it sometimes seems worse jumbled than when you started on it. Leave it then for a while—forget it—and when you go back to it, you find your thoughts clarified, the line of reasoning worked out, your problem solved for you. It is your little "Mental Brownies" who have done the work for you!

The flash of genius does not originate in your own brain. Through intense concentration you have established a circuit through your subconscious mind with the Universal, and it is from IT that the inspiration comes. All genius, all progress, is from the same source. It lies with you merely to learn how to establish this circuit at will so that you can call upon IT at need. It can be done.

"There are many ways of setting the Brownies to work," says Dumont in "The Master Mind." "Nearly everyone has had some experience, more or less, in the matter, although often it is produced almost unconsciously, and without purpose and intent. Perhaps the best way for the average person—or rather the majority of persons—to get the desired results is for one to get as clear an idea of what one really wants to know—as clear an idea or mental image of the question you wish answered. Then after rolling it around in your mind—mentally chewing it, as it were—giving it a high degree of voluntary attention, you can pass it on to your Subconscious Mentality with the mental command: 'Attend to this for me—work out the answer!' or some similar order. This command may be given silently, or else spoken aloud—either will do. Speak to the Subconscious Mentality—or its little workers—just as you would speak to persons in your employ, kindly but firmly. Talk to the little workers, and firmly command them to do your work. And then forget all about the matter—throw it off your conscious mind, and attend to your other tasks. Then in due time will come your answer—flashed into your consciousness—perhaps not until the very minute that you must decide upon the matter, or need the information. You may give your Brownies orders to report at such and such a time—just as you do when you tell them to awaken you at a certain time in the morning so as to catch the early train, or just as they remind you of the hour of your appointment, if you have them all well trained."

Have you ever read the story by Richard Harding Davis of "The Man Who Could Not Lose?" In it the hero is intensely interested in racing. He has studied records and "dope" sheets until he knows the history of every horse backward and forward.

The day before the big race he is reclining in an easy chair, thinking of the morrow's race, and he drops off to sleep with that thought on his mind. Naturally, his subconscious mind takes it up, with the result that he dreams the exact outcome of the race.

That was mere fiction, of course, but if races were run solely on the speed and stamina of the horses, it would be entirely possible to work out the results in just that way. Unfortunately, other factors frequently enter into every betting game.

But the idea behind Davis' story is entirely right. The way to contact your subconscious mind, the way to get the help of the "Man Inside You" in working out any problem is:

First, fill your mind with every bit of information regarding that problem that you can lay your hands on.

Second, pick out a chair or lounge or bed where you can recline in perfect comfort, where you can forget your body entirely.

Third, let your mind dwell upon the problem for a moment, not worrying, not fretting, but placidly, and then turn it over to the "Man Inside You." Say to him—"This is your problem. You Can do anything. You know the answer to everything. Work this out for me!"And utterly relax. Drop off to sleep, if you can. At least, drop into one of those half-sleepy, half-wakeful reveries that keep other thoughts from obtruding upon your consciousness. Do as Aladdin did— summon your Genie, give him your orders, then forget the matter, secure in the knowledge that he will attend to it for you. When you waken, *you will have the answer!*

"The smartest man in the world is the Man Inside," said Dr. Frank Crane. "By the Man Inside I mean that Other Man within each one of us that does most of the things we give ourselves credit for doing.

"I say he is the smartest man in the world. I know he is infinitely more clever and resourceful than I am or than any other man is that I ever heard of.

When I cut my finger it is he that calls up the little phagocytes to come and kill the septic germs that might get into the wound and cause blood poisoning. It is he that coagulates the blood, stops the gash, and weaves the new skin.

"I could not do that. I do not even know how he does it. He even does it for babies that know nothing at all; in fact, does it better for them than for me.

"When I practice on the piano I am simply getting the business of piano playing over from my conscious mind to my subconscious mind: in other words, I am handing the business over to the Man Inside.

"Most of our happiness, as well as our struggles and misery, comes from this Man Inside. If we train him in ways of contentment, adjustment and decision, he will go ahead of us like a well-trained servant and do for us easily most of the difficult tasks we have to perform."

Read that last paragraph again. "Most of our happiness, *as well as our struggles and misery*, comes from this Man Inside."

How, then, can we use him to bring us only the good things of life?

By BLESSING instead of ranting and cursing, by TRUSTING instead of fearing. Every man is what he is because of the dominating thoughts that he permits to occupy his mind and thus suggests to the Man Inside.

Those thoughts that are mixed with some feeling of emotion, such as anger or fear or worry or love, magnetize that Man Inside and tend to drive him to such action as will attract to you similar or related thoughts and their logical reactions. All impulses of thought have a tendency to bring about their physical equivalent, simply because they set the Man Inside You to work trying to bring about the physical manifestations of your thought images. Jesus understood this when He said—"By their fruits shall ye know them."

What, then is the answer?

1. Realize that your thoughts are the molds in which the Man Inside You forms your circumstances, that "As a man thinketh, so is he."

2. Remember that there is nothing in all of God's Universe which you need to fear. For God is Love, and you are one with God. So make friends with your problems. Don't try to run away from

them. Walk up to them, bring them into the open, and you will find that they are not obstacles, but stepping-stones to something better.

3. If you are worrying or fearful, stop it. Put your affairs into the hands of the God in You—and forget them! Remember that all things are possible with God, and all things are possible with you when you realize that you are one with Him. So look to God instead of to your difficulties. Look to the things you WANT—not to those you fear.

4. Forget the past. Remember—"Now is the accepted time. Now is the day of salvation." Look ahead to the great things that are before you—not backward at the regrets of the past. Look to what you want to see manifested. Think of each day as in itself a life, and say each morning—"I wake to do the work of a man."

5. Bless all things, for under even the most unprepossessing exterior lies a kernel of good. Remember that "When Fortune means to man most good, she looks upon him with a threatening eye."

In "Unity Weekly," the story is told of a farmer who, when he plows a field, blesses every seed he puts into it, and visualizes the abundant harvest it will bring. His neighbors marvel at the size of his crops.

In another issue, they tell of a guest in a western hotel who was impressed by the atmosphere of joy and peace in the room she occupied. Living in it seemed to be an inspiration. She was so filled with the presence of good in it that she asked the maid who had occupied it before, to give it such a restful atmosphere. The maid told her it was not the occupant, but herself; that whenever she worked in a room she blessed it, and as she left it, she stood in the door for a moment affirming peace and restfulness for it and blessing for the one who would occupy it.

Arthur Guiterman has written a blessing for every home that each of us might well use:

> Bless the four corners of this house,
> And be the Lintel blest;
> And bless the hearth, and bless the board,
> And bless each place of rest;
> And bless the door that opens wide
> To stranger, as to kin;
> And bless each crystal windowpane
> That lets the starlight in;
> And bless the rooftree overhead,
> And every sturdy wall;
> The peace of God, the peace of man,
> The peace of love, on all.

CONSECRATION

> Laid on Thy altar, my Lord divine
> Accept my gift this day for Jesus' sake;
> I have no jewels to adorn Thy shrine,

Nor any world-famed sacrifice to make.
But here I bring within my trembling hands
This will of mine—a thing that seemeth small
And only Thou, dear Lord, canst understand
How, when I yield Thee this, I yield mine all.
Hidden therein Thy searching eyes can see
Struggles of passion, visions of delight,
All that I love or am, or fain would be—
Deep loves, fond hope, and longing infinite.
It hath been wet with tears and dimmed with sighs:
Clinched in my grasp till beauty it hath none.
Now, from Thy footstool, where it vanquished lies,
The prayer ascendeth, O, may Thy will be done.
Take it, Oh, Father, ere my courage fail:
And merge it so in Thine own will that e'en
If in some desperate hour my cries prevail
And thou give back my gift, it may have been
So changed, so purified, so fair have grown,
So one with Thee, so filled with peace divine,
I may not know, or feel it as my own,
But gaining back my will, may find it Thine.

—AUTHOR UNKNOWN

THE SEED OF LIFE

The fundamental law of the Universe is that every form of life holds *within itself* vitality enough to draw to it every element it needs for growth and fruition. But it is only as it casts off all outside support, and puts its dependence solely upon the life force that created it and left its spark within it, that it is able to draw to itself the elements it needs for complete growth and fruition.

Take the giant redwoods of California. By no law known to man can they draw water to their foliage hundreds of feet in the air! Yet they do draw it—hundreds of gallons every day.

It is not done through pressure from below—from the roots. It is done by pull from above! In other words, the need is first established, then the need itself provides the means or the "pull" to draw to it the elements it must have for expression!

All through Nature, you will find that same law. First the need, then the means. Use what you have to provide the vacuum, then draw upon the necessary elements to fill it. Reach up with your stalk, spread out your branches, provide the "pull" and you can leave to your roots the search for the necessary nourishment. If you have reached high enough, if you have made your magnet strong enough, you can draw to yourself whatever elements you need, no matter if they be at the ends of the earth!

God formed a Seed of Himself in you. He gave it power to attract to itself everything it needs for its growth, just as He did with the seed of the tree. He gave it power to draw to itself everything it needs for fruition, just as He did with the tree. But He did even more for you. He gave your Seed of Life power to attract to itself everything it needs for its *infinite expression!*

You see, Life is intelligent. Life is all-powerful. And Life is always and everywhere seeking expression. What is more, it is never satisfied. It is constantly seeking greater and fuller expression. The moment a tree stops growing, that moment the life in it starts seeking elsewhere for means to better express itself. The moment you stop expressing more and more of Life, that moment Life starts looking around for other and better outlets.

The only thing that can restrict Life is the channel through which it works. The only limitation upon it is the limitation you put upon it.

The secret of success lies in this: There is inside you a Seed of God capable of drawing to you any element you need, to bring to fruition whatever of good you desire. But like all other seeds, its shell must be broken before the kernel inside can use its attractive power. And that shell is thicker, harder, than the shell of any seed on earth. Only one thing will break it—*heat from within*—a desire so strong, a determination so intense, that you cheerfully throw everything you have into the scale to win what you want. Not merely your work and your money and your thought but the willingness to stand or fall by the result—to do or to die. Like the Master when He cursed the fig tree for its barrenness, you are willing to demand of the Seed of Life in you that it *bear fruit or perish.*

That is the secret of every great success. That is the means by which all of life, from the beginning of time, has won what it needed.

What was it gave to certain animals protective shells, to others great speed, to still others a sting, to those who needed them claws or horns? What gave to the bold and strong the means to destroy, to the weak and cowardly facilities for hiding or escape? What but the Seed of Life in each, giving to every form of life the means that form craved to preserve its skin.

Since the very creation of the earth, Life has been threatened by every kind of danger. Had it not been stronger than any other power in the Universe—were it not indeed a part of God Himself—it would have perished ages ago. But God who gave it to us endowed it with unlimited resource, unlimited energy. No other force can defeat it. No obstacle can hold it back.

What is it that saves men in dire extremity, who have exhausted every human resource and finally turned to God in their need? What but the unquenchable flame of God in them—the Seed of Life He has given to each of us—with power to draw to us whatever element we feel that we need to save us from extinction.

The story is told of a little girl four years old, who had been taught to believe in a protecting Deity. She got lost one day, and was gone for hours. Her mother was on the verge of desperation when at last she saw her child coming home. She was all alone, yet seemed to be holding somebody's hand and her lips were moving as if she were carrying on a sprightly conversation. Her mother opened the front door just in time to see her drop the invisible hand and to hear her say:

"You may go now, God. This is where I live. And thank you very much!"

It was all quite simple as she explained it to her mother. She had wandered about until she got tired and hungry. Then she realized that she didn't know the way home.

"I knew I was losted, Mother," she said, "so I asked God to take me home. I knew that He knew the way. Then I started for home and God showed me where to go. And here I am."

"Why, then," some will ask, "does not the God in you exert itself to bring you food when you are hungry, drink when you are thirsty, clothing when you are cold, money when you are in debt?" Why? Because you don't put your dependence upon it for these. You look for these things to your hands or your friends or some means within the power of those around you. It is only when you despair of all ordinary means, it is only *when you convince it* that it must help you or you perish, that the Seed of Life in you bestirs itself to provide a new resource.

That is why psychological or metaphysical means so seldom cure a patient who continues to put some of his dependence upon drugs or treatments. It is not that the spirit in you is a "jealous God." It is that it takes a real need to stir Him into action. As long as you show that you feel there is a chance of your being saved through some other means, the Seed of Life in you is not going to bestir itself to help you. And as long as it sees that you are depending upon your friends or the stock market or some other method to supply your urgent need of money, it is not going to worry itself about it.

"Unity Weekly" tells of a woman alone in a big city, jobless, anxious and discouraged, and worried about her husband who was seeking work in another town.

Because there was no one else to whom she could look for help, she prayed until she was able to put utter faith in God, to believe that He would look after her and to put all her dependence upon Him. Then she was able to go out into the street with springy step, with a heart full of confidence and a face that radiated belief in herself and in her ability to do things. She threw away her sheet of Want Ads, and on impulse, turned into a cheerful looking building and found a desirable job! Within a day or two after, an unexpected check came to her in the mail, and a letter of good news from her husband.

Another case was that of a subnormal boy, about to be rejected by a school. His mother had taught him to believe in God, so he kept repeating to himself—"God will tell me what to do." God did—to such good purpose that a few years later he graduated at the head of his class!

Then there was a woman who was expected to die from a seemingly incurable and painful disease. She asked that her bed be moved to a window, and as she looked out at the starry spaces in the long hours of the night, she thought of God—of His power, of His goodness, of His love for every creature, of Jesus saying that not even a sparrow fell without His marking it. And as she pondered all this, belief in His ability and His willingness to cure her came to her, until presently there began to flow into her consciousness the belief that she WAS cured, and she amazed her attendants by sitting up and asking for something to eat. Today she is alive and well.

How can YOU stir the boundless force of the God in you into action? How can YOU draw upon its infinite resource for your urgent needs?

Utter faith, utter dependence—that is the only answer. No half-way measures will do. If you want help and have exhausted all the methods that physicians and surgeons and practitioners can offer you, and want now to go direct to the Source for new Life, new health and strength, you cannot keep on dabbling with drugs and treatments and hope to stir the Seed of Life in you into action. You must drop everything else. You must put your whole dependence upon the infinite power of that Seed of God in you. You must get the attitude of our revolutionary patriots—"Sink or swim, live or die, survive or perish, I give my hand and my heart to this cause. Either I live by it or I die with it!"

Get that attitude of mind, and the stirring of your Seed of Life into action is simple.

Say to yourself—"I am one with the Life Force that runs the Universe, the great I AM of which Jesus said—'Before Abraham, was I AM.' I AM energy. I AM power. I AM filled with omnipotent life. The vitality of God permeates every fiber of my being. I AM well and whole in every part of my body. I AM made up of billions of cells of Intelligent Life, and that Intelligence is guiding me to Health and Happiness and Prosperity."

E. Stanley Jones, author of CHRIST OF THE INDIAN ROAD, tells how he broke down completely with nervous exhaustion and brain fatigue at the end of eight years of missionary work in India, just when he had learned the ways of the people, and conditions seemed ripe for him to do the most good.

He was terribly depressed and disappointed, until one night in the midst of his prayers, he seemed to hear a voice saying—"Are you yourself ready for this work to which I have called you?" "No, Lord," he answered, "I am done for. I have reached the end of my resources." "If you will turn that over to me," the voice told him, "*and not worry about it,* I will take care of it." "Lord," he responded gladly, "I close the bargain right here!"

That was many years ago. The Doctors had just told him he would have to leave India and go back home for a couple of years to rest. Instead, he threw himself with renewed energy into his work, and he never before knew such health as he has had since. He seems to have tapped a new source of life for body, mind and spirit. *Yet all he had to do was to take it!*

Does this mean that you are to make no effort to help yourself? By no means! This was never meant for a lazy man's world. The whole purpose of existence is growth, and all nature is continually growing. Whenever anything stops growing, it starts to die.

We were given hands to work with, brains to think with. We were expected to use these.

For while it is not the roots that send the moisture to the tops of the tall trees, it is the roots that dig down to the moisture and nutriment to start it flowing. It requires an urgent need to draw to you resources beyond the power of your hands, just as it requires the exaporation of the moisture in the leaves to pull the water to the tops of the tallest trees, but unless the hands or the roots do their part first, that need will never be satisfied. The trouble with most people is that they go as far as their hands or their immediate abilities will take them, and stop there. It is as though a tree sent up its stem only as high as the root pressure carried the water from the earth. That would give us a forest of stunted trees, just as dependence upon their hands gives us the masses who live in poverty and misery.

It is only when you multiply your hands by thousands, it is only when you conceive and start great projects impossible of attainment by you alone, that you call forth the power of the Seed of Life in you, to draw to you every element you need for complete growth and fruition.

When George Mueller of England started his first orphanage, he had no money, no backers, no material resources to depend upon. He saw the need, that is all, so he went as far as he could in supplying that need. And each time, when he had reached the end of his resources, yet kept confidently trying, the need was met! In fifteen years, he built five orphanages and spent more than $5,000,000—all without a single visible means of support!

When St. Theresa proposed to build an orphanage, she was asked how much she had on which to start. When it developed that her total wealth was only three ducats, her superiors laughed at the idea. "It is true," she answered them, "that with only three ducats I can do nothing, but with God and three ducats I can do anything!" And she proceeded to prove it by building the orphanage whose good work made her famous.

In the fields of philanthropy and religion, you can find hundreds of similar stories. And in the fields of business, you find many thousands more. How many times have you read of some great institution that was founded on nothing but hard work and the faith of its founder. Henry Ford began on little else. Stewart started what is now the John Wanamaker store with a total cash capital of $1.50.

Sometimes, in fact, it seems to be an advantage not to have enough money when you start a new project. Then you don't put your faith in the money—you put it in IDEAS. In other words, you look to MIND to supply the means.

Someone expressed it well when he said we must work as if everything depended upon us, and at the same time, pray as if everything depended upon God.

What does an oculist do when you go to him for glasses? Fit your eyes with glasses that take away ALL the strain and enable you to see perfectly? No, indeed! The best oculists give you glasses a little short of the strength necessary to take all the strain off your eyes. They relieve you of the heavy burden, but they leave your sight just enough short of perfection to keep your eyes working towards that end.

The result? When you go back six months or a year later, your eyes are stronger—you can take glasses which do less of your work—until in time you do without them altogether.

What do business leaders advise young people today? Live within your income? No, indeed! *Go into debt!* Reach out! Spread yourself! Then dig the harder to catch up!

You are entitled to just as much of the good things of life as Ford or Rockefeller or Morgan, or any of the rich men around you. But it is not THEY who owe it to you. And it is not the world that owes you a living. The world and they owe you nothing but honest pay for the exact service you render them.

The one who owes you everything of good—riches and honor and happiness—is the God inside you. Go to him! Stir him up! Don't rail against the world. You get from it what you put into it—nothing more. Wake up the God inside you! Demand of him that he bring you the elements you need for riches or success. Demand—and make your need seem as urgent as must have been the need of the crustacean to develop a shell, of the bird to grow wings, of the bear to get fur.

Demand—and KNOW THAT YOU RECEIVE! The God in you is just as strong as ever He was in those primitive animals in pre-historic days. If He could draw from the elements whatever was necessary to give the elephant its trunk, the camel its hump, the bird its wings, and to each creature the means it required to enable it to survive, don't you suppose He can do the same today to provide YOU with the factors you consider essential to your well-being?

The answer is that you have already brought into being your "hump" or your "trunk" or whatever it was that you felt you must have. You are, in short, what your thoughts and fears and beliefs have made you. *Your present condition reflects the successful result of your past thought!*

Astonishing as it may sound to many people, you are now living in a world of your own making. But you don't have to keep on living there if you don't like it. You can build a new world in exactly the same way you built that one—only it would be well to build it on a different model.

It is the Einstein doctrine of the extended line, which must return to its source. An evil thought or act goes out upon its course, but the Eternal Lawmaker has decreed that it must return to its creator. A good act or thought is governed in the same way. "By their fruits, ye shall know them."

So don't complain of your lot. Don't rail at the difficulties and obstacles that confront you. Smile on them! Treat them as friends. *Bless them*—for they can be made to bless you!

You see, they have not been sent from Heaven to punish you. You asked for them yourself. They are of your own making, and they are your friends, because they call forcibly to your attention some wrong method you have been using. All you have to do is to change your methods, and the results will automatically change with them. It is just as though you were doing some problem in multiplication, and you kept saying—"One times one is two." That would throw your whole result out of balance, and it would stay out until you learned your mistake and made one times one equal one.

> You are not higher than your lowest thought,
> Or lower than the peak of your desire.
> And all existence has no wonder wrought
> To which ambition may not yet aspire.
> O Man! There is no planet, sun or star
> Could hold you, if you but knew what you are.

What, then, is the method to be used to get what you want from life?

1st—DESIRE. Decide what it is you want. Make it something so worthwhile that all other things will seem small and unimportant beside it, something so urgent that you can say to the God Inside You—"Give me this or I perish!"

2nd—See yourself having it. Visualize the thing you want. See yourself with it. Try to get the FEEL of having it, the joy and thankfulness you would get out of it. In Burton Rascoe's Memoirs, he tells how he worked out his life on a predetermined schedule, in which everything came true because he thought it, he desired it and he BELIEVED it. Here are a few typical lines from it:

When I was fifteen years old, I wanted to live in Chicago some time and I knew I would; the university I wished to go to was the University of Chicago and I knew I would; there was only one newspaper in the world I ardently wished to work on—the "Chicago Tribune"—and I knew five years in advance that I would some day work there; when I was a reporter I knew I would be some day literary editor.

When I was literary editor of the "Chicago Tribune" I knew I would some day live in New York and be literary editor of the "New York Tribune".

In 1927 I wanted $50,000 and knew I would get it; within less than a year I had over $100,000, almost without any effort on my part.

3rd—Be thankful for having received it. Remember the admonition of the Master—"Whatsoever things ye ask for when ye pray, believe that ye RECEIVE them, and ye shall have them." You cannot believe that you actually receive the things you ask for without being thankful for them. So give thanks, sincere thanks, for having received the things you prayed for, and try to FEEL grateful. Remember to SMILE! Repeat aloud daily Adelaide Proctor's poem—

My God, I thank Thee, who has made the earth so bright;
So full of splendor and of joy, beauty and light;
So many glorious things are here, noble and right.

I thank Thee too that Thou hast made joy to abound;
So many gentle thoughts and deeds circling us round,
That in the darkest spot of earth Thy love is found.

4th—*Act as though you HAD already received* the thing you asked for. Faith without works is dead. Do some physical thing each day such as you would do if you had the object you prayed for. If you are asking for money, for instance, GIVE a little, even though it be only a dime, just to show the freedom from money worry that is now yours. If you are asking for love, say a kindly word to each of those with whom you come in contact. If you are asking for health, dance about your room, sing, laugh, do some of those things you will do when you have fully manifested the good health you crave.

5th—*Show your affection* for the thing you asked for. Give your love to it, pour it out just as you would if you had the object in your hands. Only by making it REAL to you in your thoughts can you materialize it in your life.

We go, you know, in the direction of our thoughts. What we long for—*and expect*—that we are headed towards. So look for the kind of things you want to see. Look for them in your own life—and in the lives of those around you. Look for them—AND BEGIN DOING THEM! Remember those lines of Goethe's:

Are you in earnest? Seize this very minute;
What you can do, or dream you can, begin it;
Boldness has genius, power, and magic in it.
Only engage, and then the mind grows heated;
Begin, and then the work will be completed.

AFTER ITS KIND

Do you know what is the most important lesson in the whole Bible? Do you know what principle was considered so vital that God is said to have used it on three of the six days of creation, and it is repeated no less than six times in the first chapter of Genesis alone? Just this:

"Everything Reproduces After Its Kind!"

Go back over the miracles of increase in the Bible. What do you find? When the widow of Zarephath gave Elijah her oil and meal, what did she get? MORE OIL AND MEAL, did she not? Not gold, or riches, but INCREASE AFTER ITS KIND.

When another widow begged Elisha to save her sons from bondage, he asked—"What hast thou in the house?" And when told—"Naught save a pot of oil," it was the *oil* he increased, was it not?

When the multitude lacked for bread and the Apostles asked Jesus what they should do, He did not turn the stones into bread, or bring forth gold with which to buy. No, He asked—"How many loaves have you?" And when told five, and two fishes, He based His increase upon *them*.

You see, it all comes back to terms of electrical energy, for what is energy but power, and what are personality, skill, ability, riches, but different forms of power? If you want to increase your stock of these, what must you do? Put them to work, must you not? Put them out at interest, as in the parable of the talents. No energy ever expanded until it was released. No seed ever multiplied until it was sown. No talent ever increased until it was used.

You want more power, more riches, greater ability, a wider field of usefulness. How are you going to get them? *Only by putting out at interest that which you have!*

And the way to do this lies—NOT in working for riches as such—BUT FOR INCREASE IN THE FORM OF ENERGY YOU HAVE!

Now, what have YOU in the house? What seed can you plant, what service can you give?

In "Weekly Unity" some years ago, there was the story of a mother who had been well-to-do, but had lost everything and was now hard put to it to provide food and clothing for her small boys. It was near Christmas, and she was bewailing to a friend the fact that she could buy no gifts for her children, much less remember old friends and relatives.

The friend smiled. "Money is not what you need," she told her. "Can money buy the gifts that live in your heart? If I were in your place, I should stop repining and, instead, seek the guidance of your Inner Self."

The mother took the advice, and one night, as she dropped off to sleep after having prayed for guidance, she saw a beautiful tree, lighted with tapers, and beneath each light hung a small envelope. As she looked more closely, she saw that the names written on the envelopes were those of friends and relatives to whom she longed to give.

Opening one of the envelopes, she found a piece of blank paper and she seemed to hear a voice saying: "Write, and let that which you write bear witness of Me. As you write, give from your heart the treasures that are stored there in My name. I will fulfill every blessing according to your word."

The mother woke, and going immediately to her desk, began to write her blessings. She wrote words of life and wholeness for an aunt who had been bound with rheumatism for months; words of courage for an uncle who was having a difficult time with his farm; words of guidance for a young cousin who had seemed to lose her way a bit. Inspired by that Inner Self, she wrote ten blessings that night.

She had never thought that she could write, but her own heart thrilled at the beauty of the words that came to her, and she was lifted up by their power and simplicity. "Don't ever again say you have nothing to give," one of her friends told her later. "I never received so richly in all my life." And throughout the years, the blessings that this mother gave out have continued to bear fruit.

"Give me gold," prayed Levesco, "that I may be helpful, not helpless. Give me gold that I may taste the pure joy of making others happy. Give me gold that I may see the beauties of this world in moments of leisure. Give me gold that I and mine may be secure in our declining years."

A worthy prayer, indeed. But prayer alone is not enough. You must plant the seed before you can hope to reap the harvest. You must give before you can get.

"DO THE THING," said Emerson, "and you shall have the power. But they who do *not* the thing, have not the power. Everything has its price, and if the price is not paid— not that thing but something else is obtained. And it is impossible to get anything without its price.

"For any benefit received a tax is levied. In nature nothing can be given—all things are sold.

"Power to him who power exerts."

Russell Conwell, the famous lecturer, who built the Baptist Temple in Philadelphia and founded Temple University, was in the beginning merely the pastor of a very poor flock. His congregation consisted of working people, and many of them were in need. So he was continually offering prayers for money.

One Sunday, it occurred to him that the old Jewish custom had been to make a gift or offering first, and then pray for what you wanted. So he announced that the following Sunday, he would reverse his usual method of procedure. Instead of offering his prayer first, he would first take up the collection, and he wanted all who had special favors to ask of God to give freely as an "Offering." We quote the result from "Effective Prayer":

The question was asked afterward if anyone who made a special offering on that particular day had not been answered, and there was no exception in the mass of testimony to the efficiency of each prayer that day. The recitals of the marvels which followed that prayerful offering were too startling for general belief. The people had complied with the conditions, and God had answered clearly according to His promise. They had brought the tithes into the storehouse, and the Lord had poured out the blessings as an infallible result.

Cases of sudden and instaneous recovery of the sick were related by hundreds. One poor man whose child was insane prayed for her recovery. That afternoon when he went to the sanitarium, she met him in her right mind.

A lady sold her jewelry and brought the proceeds as an offering as she prayed for healing from sciatic rheumatism. She fell going from the Church, and arose to find the rheumatism gone.

One old gentleman involved in a ruinous lawsuit brought all the profits of the previous week and deposited them as he prayed for a just outcome. Within the week, the suit was withdrawn.

A woman with an overdue mortgage on her home determined to risk all on one prayer, and gave all she had as she prayed. When plumbers came to repair a leak the following week, they discovered a loose board in the floor under which her father had hidden all his money. The sum was more than enough to pay off the mortgage in its entirety.

There were probably fifty such cases.

You have to sow before you can reap. You have to give before you can get. And when you sow, when you give, you must give freely with no strings to it. As Jesus put it— "Except a kernel of wheat fall into the ground and die, it abideth alone. But if it die, it beareth much fruit."

You remember the old-fashioned hand-pumps that are still to be found on many farms. To start them, you had to pour in a bucket of water, in order to create a vacuum and thus be able to draw water from the well. The same principle applies in using a siphon. You pour in water to drive out the air and create a vacuum. Once the vacuum is formed, your water flows, and you can get unlimited quantities of it without having to give more. But you get none from pump or siphon until you first give some.

You must give to get. You must sow the seed you have before you can reap the harvest. You cannot merely lend it. You must GIVE it, freely and fully. "Except a kernel of wheat fall into the ground and DIE," said the Master. Except your seed of riches be given freely and fully, you get nothing from it.

"But if it die, it beareth much fruit." If it be dead to you—if it is gone beyond hope of return, then you can look for a harvest.

"He that findeth his life shall lose it," said the Master on another occasion, "but he that loseth his life for My sake shall find it." He that gives all he has in the service of his fellows shall find that in so doing, he has planted seeds which will bring him a harvest of happiness and plenty.

You have probably read the story of Charles Page, as given in the "American Magazine" a few years ago. Page was then a millionaire oil operator in Oklahoma, but a few years before he had little or nothing, and his wife was so sick he feared he was going to lose her as well. The surgeons at the hospital had given up hope for her, so as all other avenues seemed closed, Page turned to God.

"Oh, Lord," he prayed, "don't take her away from me. I just couldn't bear it."

The words rang in his ears—and they had an empty ring. As a prayer, it seemed to fall flat. Why should the Lord interfere for him, if the only reason he could offer was that he couldn't bear it? Plenty of husbands just as devoted as he had lost their wives. Why should the Lord specially favor him?

The thought came home to him with the power of a blow. What had he ever done that the Lord should go out of His way to help him? What reason had he to look for special consideration from above? None! He'd been a decent enough citizen, but no more so than the average, and kneeling there he couldn't recall a single thing he had done which would entitle him to ask favors from the Lord.

The thought appalled him. What chance had he? Must he then lose the one dearest to him in all the world, just because he had never done enough to be worthy of keeping her? No! No! That was unthinkable. It wasn't too late. He would start that very minute. What was it the Master had said? "Whatsoever ye do unto the least of these My brethren, ye do it unto Me."

The next morning a poor widow was in transports of joy to find under her doorsill money enough to carry her safely through the winter.

But that evening inquiry at the hospital elicited the information that Page's wife was no better. For a little his faith faltered. Then, as he thought back over the reason for his act, it flamed up anew. Why had he helped the widow? Not because he was interested in her welfare, not even because it was the right thing to do, but because he was trying to buy off the Lord. Thinking of it in that light, it sounded ridiculous. He got down on his knees again.

"I ain't makin' a bargain with You, God," he promised. "I'm doin' this because it's the *right thing* for me to do."

This time it seemed to him his message carried. He felt strangely cheered and relieved. His prayer had gone through.

Now comes the remarkable part of this incident. His wife, much to the astonishment of the surgeons, took a turn for the better, and within a comparatively short time was well!

From that day to this Charles Page has never failed in his Covenant with God. Times there were when everything looked black. Times when it meant a real struggle to find the Lord's share. But his faith never faltered. He knew if he did his part, he could depend upon God for His.

For a long time, he gave a tenth of all his earnings. Then he increased it to a fourth. Later to a half, and finally to all except what he needed for personal and family expenses. He has given away literally millions.

"But don't get the idea," he warns, "that I'm telling you how to get rich. It's the *giving*, not the *getting*, that is important. Personally, I believe that it's only playing fair to tithe, or give a part of your income to God. But it must be a gift, not an investment. Do you get the difference? If you tithe in the right spirit, you will get your reward just as sure as a gun's iron; but the reward may not come in the form of money. Often it's something far better than money . . ."

"What you keep to yourself you lose," wrote Munthe. "What you give away, you keep forever." And Irene Stanley expressed much the same thought in her little poem—

> *You have to let go of the rung below*
> *When you reach for the round above.*
> *There is no other way to climb, you know,*
> *You have to let go of the rung below.*
> *Each upward step brings more of the glow*
> *And warmth of the Sun of hove,*
> *You have to let go of the rung below,*
> *When you reach for the round above.*

You see, God incarnates Himself through you. But He cannot be shut up. He must be given out, expressed. You put Him into everything you do, whether towards failure or success. You are inseparable from the creative force. You are part of the fountain head of supply.

What then must you do to win riches and success? GIVE! Give freely of what you have.

Give, and it shall be given unto you; good measure, pressed down, and shaken together, and running over, shall men give unto your bosom. For with the same measure that ye mete withal it shall be measured to you again.

—LUKE 6:38.

Does that require too great faith? You do not marvel at the farmer who freely throws all his seed into the ground, knowing he will never see it again, but must depend upon its fruit for his increase. He shows perfect faith. Should you show less?

Remember the first Law of Life, the law that was considered so important that it was repeated six times in the first Chapter of Genesis:

"Everything increases after its kind."

Do you expect that law to be changed for you? Do you expect to reap without sowing? "There is that scattereth and increaseth yet more," said that wisest of ancient sages, King Solomon. "And there is that withholdeth more than is meet, *but it tendeth to poverty.*

"The liberal soul shall be made fat, and he that watereth, shall be watered himself."

You see, Life is logical. Life follows definite, fundamental laws. One of these laws is that you reap as you sow, that "He that hath a bountiful eye shall be blessed."

For all motion is cyclic. It circulates to the limit of its possibilities and then returns to its starting point. Thus any unselfish expenditure of energy returns to you laden with gifts. Any unselfish act done for another's benefit is giving part of yourself. It is an outward flow of power that completes its cycle and returns laden with energy.

Everything we get, we pay for—good or bad. Personal gain comes through impersonal service. Personal loss comes through selfishness.

As Emerson puts it—"A perfect equity adjusts its balance in all parts of life. *Every act rewards itself.*" Any act of ours that injures another, separates us from God. Any act of ours that helps others, brings us closer to God and Good. One may think that his cheating of another is a secret between them, but by his cheating, he has shaken the trust of another in human brotherhood and damaged his idealism. Isn't that a definite affront that is going to stand between him and God when the one who cheated tries to enlist God's help in enlarging the activities of his own life?

Wouldn't it have been better to say to himself: "God gives me all my money. Surely He has given me enough for all the needs of my business, or if He hasn't already given it, it is on the way. If I need more, He will give me more. So I am not even going to think about trying to make 'easy money' by taking advantage of others. God provides me with plenty, and I am going to run this business as if He were always here beside me."

One on God's side is a majority. You are always together with God. So make Him an active partner in your business. Look to Him for its needs, give the same loving service you feel that He would give. Then cast off all worries fears, and *put your business lovingly in His hands.* When the future looks dark, when problems confront you, just say to yourself:

> *God lights the way; no more I grope,*
> *Nor stumble on in troubled hope.*
> *I sow no seeds of care and strife;*
> *But those of love, and joy, and life.*
> *No more I strive to plan my lot;*
> *The Father fills my cup unsought.*

What is the Unpardonable Sin? What but damming the sources of God's supply. What but trying to shut up the God in you, trying to keep Him from expressing Himself.

When the giant monsters of antiquity ceased developing, and depended upon their size and strength and fierceness, they perished. When the vast Empires of China and Greece and Persia and Rome stopped reaching out and tried merely to hold what they had, they died. When the rich man or big business of today stops giving service and merely hangs on to his fortune, he loses it.

You cannot stand still. You must go forward—or die.

There is a God in you seeking expression. You cannot keep Him shut up. You must give Him channels through which to express Himself, or He will rend you and come out of you.

What would you think of a man who spent years in developing great muscles, then tried to keep them great by not using them, by not wearing them out? You'd call him a fool, wouldn't you, because everyone knows that the only way to develop muscles is to use them, the only way to keep them strong is to continually exercise them.

What everyone does not seem to know is that all of life works in the same way. You cannot hold on to anything good. You must be continually giving—and getting. You cannot hold on to your seed. You must sow it—and reap anew. You cannot hold on to riches. You must use them and get other riches in return.

The Unpardonable Sin is to stand in the way of progress, try to stop the cycle of life.

You must give to get. You must sow to reap. The unprofitable servant in Jesus' parable was not the first or the only one to be cast into outer darkness where is weeping and gnashing of teeth, from burying his talent. The ones who became rulers over many things were those who freely used what they had—who started riches *flowing!*

So when a "talent" is given you, don't try to hide it away or bury it. Don't dam up the channels of supply with the few dollars you have, and thus prevent the unlimited riches of God from flowing to you.

Set up your generator, which is the service you have to offer your fellowman. Turn on the steam by giving to it all the power, all the skill, all the intelligence you have. Then start the flow of riches with your faith by cheerfully pouring into the channel of service all that you have. That means buy the things that are necessary to your development and that of your family. Pay your just debts, though it leaves you without a cent in your purse. Put your dependence—NOT on the few dollars you have in hand, but on the great ocean of supply above and about you. Use the few dollars you have to create the vacuum which shall poke a hole in the bottom of that ocean, and start the unending flow of riches pouring into you.

You remember that Jesus once likened the power of God to the leaven in bread. You put a tiny yeast cake into a great pan of dough and it affects the whole mixture. It makes it GROW. Apparently it INCREASES the quantity of flour, milk, eggs and other ingredients—certainly it makes them bulk to several times their original size.

That yeast is the "God in you" that you put into your circumstances, your affairs. Put it into fears and worries, and it will increase them until they can hardly be borne. Put it into your expenses, and it will make them ever greater. Put it into love and life and good work, and it will bring these back to you increased a hundredfold.

"Let's have a league of optimists," writes Elizabeth Swaller in LET'S HAVE IT,

> *To boost the world along.*
> *We are so weary of the thought*
> *That everything is wrong!*

> We're surfeited with talk of lack,
>   Depression, gloom and fear.
> If we but think of brighter things,
> Good times will soon be here.
>
> 'Tis time to turn and face about
> And court conditions fine.
> By boosting, I shall prosper yours,
> And you will prosper mine.

Put your yeast into optimistic thoughts, into kindly words, into loving acts of service. Remember, the hardest part of anything is the start. If you want something, pray for it—*then* START doing, being, giving—whatever is needful to set the yeast acting. You don't have to make the dough expand when you put the yeast into it. The yeast attends to that. All you have to do is to give the yeast a chance to get in its work!

So if you want to receive something of good, show your faith by GIVING of what you have. Put a little yeast into your affairs. It doesn't matter how poor you are, how much in debt, how weak or sickly. You can always give something. But remember that everything increases after its kind, so give of what you want to receive. Sow the seeds of the harvest you want to reap, whether it be love, energy, service or money.

And PRAY! Nearly 2,000 years before Christ, it was said in the Vedas that if two people would unite their psychic forces, they could conquer the world. Then came Jesus, to put it even more definitely: "Again I say unto you, that if two of you shall agree on earth as touching anything that they shall ask, it shall be done for them of my Father which is in Heaven. For when two or three are gathered together in my name, there am I in the midst of them."

In one of his books, Russell Conwell tells of a little group in his church who were in such straitened circumstances that they decided to get together and see if, by uniting their prayers, they could not improve their finances.

So they met at the house of one of their number who happened to be a bookbinder by trade, and decided that each week the whole group would unite their prayers to solve the difficulties of some one member.

The bookbinder was the first one chosen. He owed a great deal of money, and had no means of paying his debts. So that evening, the group prayed that he might receive help in meeting his obligations. It was then agreed that at noontime every day until the next meeting, each member would stop whatever he was doing, and spend a minute or two in silent prayer that the bookbinder's needs might be met.

The meeting was on Tuesday evening. The next day after lunch, as was his custom, the bookbinder dropped into a publishing house nearby for a chat with some friends. He met there a man from Washington who told him that "for the first time in his life, he had forgotten his train," and must now get back home on some urgent business, without placing a contract which he had intended to give to a New York bookbinder.

The bookbinder suggested that he also was in that business, and possibly could help him, but the other objected that the particular class of work he wanted could be done only in New York. Upon the binder persisting, however, he explained his needs, and being convinced that they could be filled right there in as satisfactory a way and on more reasonable terms than in New York, he not only gave the binder the contract, *but advanced enough money to more than take care of his difficulties!*

The binder hurried to the other members of his group and told them of his good fortune. His problem was so completely solved that he felt they ought to start work at once for some other member, because all were so badly in need. All felt so elated over their success in helping the binder solve his problem, that they chose the most difficult case of all as the next.

This was a jeweler who had grown so old and forgetful that his business was in a deplorable condition. Bankruptcy seemed so sure that his son had moved out of town to avoid sharing the disgrace.

Two or three days after the group started working on the jeweler's problem, the son came to town for a day to attend a funeral. On the return trip from the cemetery, he fell into conversation with one of the other mourners, in the course of which the latter mentioned that he was looking for an expert in clock making to superintend a new factory he was erecting in another city.

The son told him his father was a master of that art, but no good at managing finances. The upshot of it was that the jeweler applied for the position, at the same time explaining his present financial difficulties. The manufacturer liked his letter, went over the whole situation with him, and ended by taking over the store as a retail outlet, paying off the old debts, and forming a business connection with the jeweler which prospered both amazingly.

An old lady who owned a small notion store was next. Soon after the group united in prayer for her, a fire destroyed the store next door to her. The owner decided to build bigger than before, and offered her not only an attractive price for her store, but an interest in his business, which paid her enough to live in comfort the rest of her days.

Every Member of that Group Became Prosperous!

Do you, too, want something very much? Then give— *and pray!* Get yourself a small toy bank—a paper one will do. Each day put something into it, even though it be only a penny. Give that money to God. Give it to Him at the time you put it into the bank, but leave it there until it amounts to a dollar or more. Then use it for any good charitable purpose that presents itself.

Don't give it to some panhandler. Try to use it where it will do the recipient some good. Use it to help him to help himself, as in buying some book for him that will show him the way out of his difficulties.

And as you give, *pray!* Pray not only for yourself, but for others.

Every morning at seven, we shall pray for protection for our own family, and for all students of this Course who will join with us in "uniting their psychic forces" by "agreeing as to the thing they should ask." For this prayer, you cannot do better than repeat the ninety-first Psalm.

Every day at noon, we shall pray for abundant supply for all of those among our readers who will join with us in praying for the whole group. For this prayer, hold in your hand any money you intend to give that day for any good purpose, and any checks or money you intend to use to pay bills, and say with us:

I bless you . . . and be thou a blessing. May you enrich all who touch you. I thank God for you, but even more I thank Him that there are billions like you where you came from. I bless that Infinite Supply. I thank God for it and I expand my consciousness to take it in. (Here try to see in your mind's eye a Niagara of money flowing to you and to all who are praying with you. See yourself and all of us bringing in a great net full of money like the nets the Apostles pulled in bursting with fish.) I release that Infinite Supply through all my channels and the channels of all the students of this Course just as I freely release the money I hold in my hand, giving it where it will do the most good. The Spirit that multiplied the loaves and fishes for Jesus enters into this money, making it grow and increase and bring forth fruit an hundredfold. All of God's channels are now open and flowing for us. The best in ourselves for the world—the best in the world for us.

Then PREPARE for prosperity. When the Israelites of old were suffering from drought, and begged the Prophet Elisha to help them, what was the first thing he told them to do? Fill the valley with ditches—prepare to RECEIVE the water that they asked for!

You see prayers and affirmations are not for the purpose of influencing God. He has already done His part. All of good is always available to each of us. Our prayers and affirmations are for the purpose of bringing our own minds to the point where we can ACCEPT God's gifts! We don't need to work on conditions—we need only to work on ourselves. The only place we can cure our lacks and our troubles *is in our own minds!* When we have done it there, we shall find that they are cured everywhere.

"Whatsoever things ye ask for when ye pray," the Master assured us, "believe that ye HAVE RECEIVED them, and ye shall HAVE them."

That is the basis of all successful prayer, whether for the healing of our bodies, or for material benefits. Once you convince your Higher Self, which is the God in you, that you HAVE the thing you want, *it will proceed immediately to bring it into being!*

But how, you may ask, can I convince my Higher Self that I have riches or any other good thing, when my common sense tells me that I am in debt up to my ears and creditors are hounding me day and night?

You can't—if you keep thinking and acting DEBTS. But here is a psychological fact: The Higher Self accepts as fact anything that is repeated to it in convincing tones often enough. And once it has accepted any statement as fact, it proceeds to do everything possible to MAKE IT TRUE!

That is the whole purpose of affirmations—to bring the God in You to accept as true the conditions that you desire, to the end that He will then proceed to bring them into being. It is a sort of auto-suggestion. You keep saying to yourself that you ARE rich, that you HAVE the things you desire, until the constant repetition is accepted by the Higher Self and translated into its physical equivalent.

Debts? Don't worry about them. Remember that the shadow of growing grain kills the weeds. Keep your mind on the good you want and it will kill off the evil you fear, just as the turning on of light dispels darkness. A farmer does not have to hoe the weeds out of growing wheat, any more than you have to sweep the darkness out of a room. Neither do you have to worry about debts or lack. Put all your thoughts and all your faith in the riches you are praying for, and let them dispel the debts.

But don't worry if you can't summon such faith right out of the blue. Most of us have to lead up to it gradually. Start with Coué's well-known affirmation—"Every day in every way we are getting richer and richer." Use that to prepare your Higher Self for the stronger affirmations. Then, when your faith has grown stronger, *claim the thing you want!* Affirm that you HAVE it—and insofar as possible, ACT AS THOUGH YOU HAD IT!

Write it in your heart that each day is the best day of the year, that NOW is the accepted time, NOW is the day of salvation. Then thank God for the good you have been praying for, believe that you HAVE received and give thanks.

Remember this: God's will always works when you offer no resistance to it. So pray—and then LET His good come to you. Don't fight the conditions about you. Don't try to overcome the obstacles in your path. BLESS them—know that God is in them—that if you will LET them, they will work WITH you for good. Have faith not only in God, but in people and things. Don't look for a miracle to happen. Don't expect an angel from Heaven to come and open the way. Know that God works through ordinary people and things, and it is through them that your good will come.

So bless THEM. Serve them as you would the Lord, doing each thing that is given you to do as though you were the greatest genius. And all day long, as the thought occurs to you, keep repeating to yourself—"Every day in every way I am getting richer and richer," or whatever it is that you desire.

There is something about praying for *others* that oftentimes does one more good than praying for oneself. You see, you cannot give anything to others without first possessing it yourself. When you wish another evil, you draw that evil to yourself first and you usually get a part of it. When you bring good to another, you bring it through yourself, and you share in it.

Remember the experience of Job in the olden days. Despite his lamentations and prayers, he lost all his riches, and his afflictions remained with him. But then misfortune fell upon his friends as well, and in his sympathy for them, Job forgot his own ailments and prayed for his friends. And it is written that—"The Lord turned the captivity of Job, *when he prayed for his friends.* And the Lord gave him twice as much as he had before."

> For who upon the hearth can start a fire,
> And never warm the stone?
> Or who can cheer another's heart,
> And not his own?
> I stilled a hungry infant's cry,
> With kindness filled a stranger's cup,
> And lifting others,
> Found that I was lifted up!

HOW TO DEVELOP FAITH POWER FOR SUCCESSFUL LIVING

To you, faith has doubtless been a term properly applied in sermons and theological books, but which has but little or no practical place or meaning in the world of action and deeds—in the world in which most of us live most of our time, and perform most of our actions.

We assure you that Faith Power is something having a most intimate and important relation to Personal Power along practical lines, and is something which, in the current phrase, "you need in your business."

Mr. Leon Jolson, president of the huge Necchi Sewing Machine Company, is today worth many millions of dollars. A few years ago he was a poor Polish immigrant who couldn't even speak English. The newspaper account of his spectacular rise to success quoted him as saying, "I had unfaltering faith. I prayed for guidance every step of the way. I used head and foot work."

The general conception of Faith—the idea of Faith held by most persons—is that it is an emotional state independent of, if not indeed actually contrary to Reason. However, we believe that the most important reasoning of practical everyday life is based on Faith. We do not know positively that the sun will rise tomorrow morning—all that we know is that in the history of the race the sun always has risen in the morning, and we "believe" that it will continue the practice on the morrow; but we do not "know" absolutely that such will be the case, we cannot prove it absolutely by argument—even by mathematics—unless we admit the existence of Universal Law, or the law of Causation, whereby "the same causes, under the same conditions will produce the same effects."

You may object to all this as silly—but, instead, it is the strictest application of the rules and laws of practical thought. Of course, you say that we "know" that the sun will rise tomorrow morning, and may even tell to a second the time of its rising. Certainly we "know" this—but we know it only by an act of Faith. That Faith, moreover, is the belief that there exists Universal Law—that "natural things act and move under Law"—that "the same causes, under the same conditions, produce the same results."

In the ordinary affairs of life and action you act according to Faith. You do this so naturally and instinctively, so constantly and habitually, that you are not aware of it. You start on an airline flight. You buy your ticket, having faith that the plane will start from the airport named on the ticket, and approximately on the time noted in it. You have faith that it will proceed to the destination promised. You do not "know" these things from actual experience—for you cannot so know what lies in the future: you take them for granted, you assume them to be true, you act upon Faith.

You take your seat. You do not know the pilot or the co-pilot—you have never seen them, nor do you even know their names. You do not know whether or not they are competent, reliable, or experienced. All that you know is that it is reasonable to suppose that the plane company will select the right kind of men for the task—you act upon Faith, upon Faith rationally interpreted. You have Faith in the company, in the management, in the system of flights, in the equipment, etc. and you stake your life and wholeness of body upon that Faith. You may say that you only "take a chance" in the matter; but, even so, you manifest Faith in that "chance," or else you wouldn't take it. You wouldn't "take a chance" of standing in the path of a rushing express train, or of leaping from the Empire State Building, would you? You manifest Faith in something—even if that something be no more than the Law of Averages.

You place your money in a bank; here again you manifest Faith—Faith rationally interpreted. You sell goods on credit to your customers—Faith again. You have Faith in your grocer, your butcher, your lawyer, your physician, your clerks, your insurance company. That is to say Faith of some kind, or of some degree—else you would not trust anything whatsoever to them. If you "believe" that a man is dishonest, incompetent, or insane, you do not place confidence in him, nor trust your affairs or interests to him; your Faith is in his "wrongness," and not in his "rightness"—but it is Faith, nevertheless. Every "belief" short of actual, positive knowledge, is a form or phase of Faith.

You have the Faith that if you step off a high building into space, you will fall and be injured, perhaps killed: this is your Faith in the Law of Gravitation. You have a similar Faith in certain other physical laws—you have the Confident Expectation that evil results to you will follow certain courses of action concerning these physical laws. You have Faith that poisons will injure or destroy your physical body, and you avoid such. You may object that you "know" these things, not merely "believe" them; but you don't "know" anything directly and immediately until you experience it—and you cannot experience it—and you cannot experience a future happening before its time. All that you can do concerning each and every future experience is to "believe" certain things concerning it—and that "belief" is nothing else but Faith, interpreted more or less rationally and correctly.

You do not "know" certainly and positively, by direct experience, or by pure reason, a single thing about the happenings of tomorrow, or of some day next week, or of the corresponding day of next year. Yet you act as if you did possess such knowledge—but why? Simply because of your Faith in the Law and Order of the Universe; of the operation of the Law of Causation; whereby effects follow causes; of the law of Probabilities, or of the Law of Average; or of some other Natural Law. But your knowledge of and belief in such Laws are but forms of your Faith, i.e., Confident Expectation that "things will work out according to the rule observed in past actions." You cannot get away from Faith in your thoughts and beliefs concerning the present and the future, any more than you can run away from your shadow in the bright daylight.

From the foregoing, and the reflections aroused in your mind by the consideration of it, you will perceive that Faith has as true and as sound position and place in the psychology of the human being as have Reason and Intellect.

Without the Confident Expectation of Faith, there will be no kindling of the flame of Insistent Desire—no application of the steel of Persistent Determination. Unless Faith expresses itself in the Confident Expectation of the obtaining or attainment of the thing desired and willed, then will Desire find it difficult to "want it hard enough," and Will will find it impossible to "persistently determine to obtain it." Desire and Will depend upon Faith for their Inspirational Forces—by means of the latter, the Energizing Forces of Desire and the Dynamic Forces of Will are inspired and vitalized, and have the Breath of Life breathed into them.

HOW SICKNESS IS CURED BY FAITH

Among the many phases and forms of the application and manifestation of the mental principle of Faith Power is that important phase or form known generally as "Faith-Cure."

Faith-Cure is a term applied to the practice of curing disease by an appeal to the hope, belief, or expectation of the patient, and without the use of drugs or other material means. Formerly, Faith-Cure was confined to methods re-quiring the exercise of religious faith, such as the "prayer cure" and "divine healing," but has now come to be used in the broader sense, and includes the cures of Mental Science.

It is now generally agreed that the cures made by the various practitioners of the numerous schools and forms of Faith-Cure have as their underlying effective principle the mental condition or state of Faith; this principle operating so as to call forth the innate power of the mental-physical organism to resist and to overcome the abnormal conditions which manifest as disease. Thus, all cures wrought by the mental forces of the individual, under whatever name or method, are, at the last, Faith-Cures.

This innate power of the organism so lodged in the subconscious mentality, is found to respond readily to the ideas accepted as true by the individual—to his "beliefs," in short. These beliefs are forms of Faith, at the last.

From the psychological point of view, all these different kinds of faith-healing, as indeed all kinds of faith-healing, as indeed all kinds of mind-cure, depend upon suggestion. In faith-healing proper not only are powerful direct suggestions used, but the religious atmosphere and the autosuggestions of the patient co-operate, especially when the cures take place during a period of religious revival or at other times when large assemblies and strong emotions are found. The suggestibility of large crowds is markedly greater than that of individuals, and to this greater faith must be attributed the greater success of the fashionable places of pilgrimage.

Analyzing the phenomena attributed to Suggestion, and reducing the idea of Suggestion to its essential elements, we find that Suggestions consists of: (1) placing a strong idea in the mind—grafting it on the mind, as it were; (2) arousing the Expectant Attention of the results implied or indicated in the suggested idea; and (3) setting into operation the activities of the subconscious mentality in the direction of bringing about the result pictured by the Expectant Attention, which in turn has been aroused by the suggested idea. There you have the whole idea of Suggestion in a nutshell!

Now then, all phenomena of Faith-Cure, and of Suggestion as well, are seen to depend upon the presence and action of the element or principle of Faith Power in the mentality of the individual.

By an application of the first of the above stated elements of this greater principle of your being, and of Nature as a whole, you may keep yourself in health, strength and general desirable physical well-being; or you may bring about by it a gradual return to health and physical well-being if you have lost these; again, if you allow this principle to be directed wrongly and abnormally, you may lose your physical well-being and health, and may start on the downward path of disease, the end of which is an untimely death. Your physical condition is very largely dependent upon the character and kind of the Ideas and Ideals which you permit to be planted in your mind and by the degree of Expectant Attention, or Faith, which you permit to vitalize these Ideas and Ideals.

Briefly stated, the course to be followed by you in this matter is as follows: (1) Encourage Ideas and Ideals of Health, Strength, and Vitality—the ideas of Physical Well-Being—to take lodgment in your mind, there to send forth their roots sprouts, blossoms and fruit; cultivate these Ideas and Ideals and vitalize them with a goodly amount of Expectant Attention, Confident Expectation and Faith along the lines of these conditions which you desire to be present in yourself; see yourself "in your mind's eye" as you wish to be, and "confidently expect" to have these conditions manifested in you by your subconscious mentality; (2) never allow yourself to hold the ideas of diseased abnormal conditions, and, above all, never allow yourself to cultivate the mental habit of "expecting" such conditions to manifest in your body—cultivate the attitude of Faith and Hope, and discard that of Fear; (3) if your mind has been filled with these negative, harmful and destructive mental Ideas and Expectancy, and if your body has manifested Disease in response to them, you should proceed to "kill out" these noxious mental weeds by a deliberate, determined and confident cultivation of the right kind of Ideas and Ideals and states of "Expectancy"; it is an axiom of advanced psychology that "the positives tend to inhibit and to destroy the negatives"—the weeds in the mental garden may be "killed out" by the careful and determined cultivation of the positive plants of Hope, Faith and Confident Expectation of the Good and Desirable.

Faith Power is present and active—it is potent and powerful—and it is friendly to you if you recognize and realize its existence; it is ready to serve you, and to serve you well, provided that you call upon it properly and furnish it with the proper channels through which to flow in its efforts to manifest itself. This is the great truth back of the special lesson of Faith-Cure!

THE MIGHTY SUBCONSCIOUS MIND

The Subconscious—that great field or plane of mental activity—is the seat of far greater power, and the source of far deeper and broader streams of mental force, than the average person even begins to realize. In that field, or on that plane, are performed over seventy-five percent of man's mental activities.

Our mental world is far more extensive than we usually conceive it to be; it has great comparatively unsounded depths, and equally grand comparatively unsealed heights. The explored and charted areas of our conscious mentality are incidental and subordinate to those broad areas of which even the brightest minds of our race have merely explored the borderland; the expanded uncharted interior of the strange country still awaiting the exploring expeditions of the future. Our position in relation to this great *Terra Incognita* of the mind is similar to that of the ancient civilized world toward the earth as a whole; we are as yet awaiting the Columbus who will explore the Western Continent of the mind, and the Livingstones and Stanleys who will furnish us with maps of the mental Darkest Africa.

Yet, even the comparatively small explored areas of the Subconscious have revealed to us a wonderful land—a land filled with the richest raw materials, precious metals, wonderful species of animal and plant life. And our daring investigators have discovered means of applying and using some of the wonderful things which have been discovered in even that borderland of the new mental world.

The Subconscious entertains deep-rooted convictions and beliefs concerning the general success or non-success of the individual. The person who has constantly impressed upon his subconscious mentality that he is "unlucky" and that "Fate is against me," has created a tremendous power within himself which acts as a brake or obstacle to his successful achievement. He has created an enemy within himself which serves to hold him back, and which fights against every inner effort in the direction of success. This hidden enemy hampers his full efforts and cripples his activities.

On the contrary, the person who believes that "luck is running my way," and that "things are working in my favor," not only releases all of his latent energies but also actually stimulates his full powers—along subconscious lines as well as conscious.

Many men have become so convinced of their propitious Destiny that they have overcome obstacles which would have blocked the progress of one holding the opposite conviction. In fact, most of the men who have used their failures as stepping-stones to subsequent success have felt within themselves the conviction that they would triumph in the end, and that the disappointments and temporary failures were but incidents of the game.

Men have believed in their "stars" or in the presence and power of something outside of themselves which was operating in the direction of their ultimate triumph. This has given to them an indomitable will and an unconquerable spirit. Had these same men allowed the conviction of the operation of adverse and antagonistic influences to take possession of their souls, they would have gone down in the struggle—and would have stayed down. In either case, however, the real "something" which they have believed to be an outside thing or entity, has been nothing more nor less than the influence and power of their own Subconscious— in one case pulling with them, and in the other pulling against them.

The man with his Subconscious filled with belief and Faith in his non-success, and in the inevitable failure of his efforts—the man whose Confident Expectation is that of non-success, failure and inability, and whose Expectant Attention is directed toward such an outcome and the incidents and circumstances leading up to it,—is like a man in the water who is swimming against the stream. He is opposing the strong current, and his every effort is counteracted and overcome by the adverse forces of the stream. Likewise, the man whose Subconscious is saturated with the conviction of ultimate victory and final success—whose Confident Expectation is directed toward that end, and whose Expectant Attention is ever on the look-out for things tending to realize his inner beliefs—is like the swimmer who is moving in the direction of the current. Such a man not only is not really opposed by the forces of the stream, but, instead, has these forces at work aiding him.

The importance of having the Faith, Confident Expectation and Expectant Attention of the Subconscious directed toward your success, achievement and successful ultimate accomplishment—and the importance of not having these mighty forces operate against yourself—may be realized when you stop to consider that in the one case you have three-quarters of your mental equipment and power operating in your favor, and in the other case you have that three-quarters operating against you. And that three-quarters, in either case, not only is working actively during your waking hours, but also "works while you sleep." To lose the assistance of that three-quarters would be a serious matter would it not? But far more serious is it to have that three-quarters actually working against you—having it on the side of the enemy! This is just what happens when the Subconscious gets into action under the influence of wrongly directed Faith, Expectant Attention and Confident Expectation.

Get busy with your Subconscious. Train it, educate it, reeducate it, direct it, incline it, teach it, suggest to it, along the lines of the Faith in Success and Power and not those of the Faith in failure and weakness. Set it to work swimming with that current. The Subconscious is much given to Faith—it lives on Faith, it acts upon Faith. Then see that you supply it with the right kind of Faith, and avoid as a pestilence that Faith which is based on fear and is grounded in failure and despair. Think carefully—and act!

HOW TO DEVELOP ENTHUSIASM FOR YOUR WORK

Faith is the underlying principle of that remarkable quality of the human mind which is known as Enthusiasm. It is its essence, it is its substance, it is its actuating principle. Without Faith there can be no manifestation of Enthusiasm. Without Faith there can be no expression of the activities of Enthusiasm. Without Faith there can be no exhibition of the energies of Enthusiasm. Without Faith the quality of Enthusiasm remains dormant, latent and static—Faith is needed to arouse it, to render it active, to cause it to become dynamic.

Moreover, the Faith required for the manifestation and expression of Enthusiasm must be positive Faith—Faith in the successful outcome of the undertaking—Faith exhibiting its positive phases—Faith in the attainment of that which is desirable and which is regarded as good. You can never manifest Enthusiasm toward that which you confidently expect to be a failure, nor toward that which you feel will bring undesirable results and effects. Negative Faith has no power to arouse Enthusiasm; the presence of Positive Faith is necessary to awaken this wonderful latent mental or spiritual force.

Enthusiasm is a mental or spiritual force which has always been regarded by mankind with respect—often with a respect mingled with awe. To the ancients it seemed to be a special gift of the gods, and by them it was regarded as animating the individual with almost divine attributes of power, and as causing him to absorb a portion of the essence of the divine nature. Recognizing the fact that men under the influence of Enthusiasm often accomplish almost superhuman tasks, the ancients came to believe that this added power and capacity arose from the superimposition of power from planes of being above that of humanity. Hence, they employed terms to define it which clearly indicated their belief in its transcendent nature.

The term "Enthusiasm," is directly derived from the ancient Greek term meaning, "to be inspired by the gods." The two compositive elements of the original term are, respectively, a term denoting "inspiration," and one denoting "the gods" or "divinity," the two terms in combination meaning literally "inspired by the gods."

You have found that when you become quite intensely interested in a subject, object, study, pursuit or cause, so that your Enthusiasm is thoroughly aroused then there comes to you a highly increased and greatly intensified degree and amount of mental energy and power. At such times your mind seems to work with lightning-like rapidity, and with a wonderful sense of ease and efficiency. Your mental powers seem to be quadrupled—your mental machinery seems to have some miraculous oil poured into the proper place, thus removing all friction and allowing every part of the mechanism to move smoothly and easily and with wonderful speed. At such times you feel, indeed, actually "inspired." You feel that a new world of attainment would be opened to you if you could make this mental condition a permanent one.

Looking around you in your world of practical everyday work and effort, you will see why business men and other men of affairs regard as an important factor of successful work that mental quality known as "enthusiastic interest" on the part of the persons performing that work. This "enthusiastic interest" in the work or task is found to call forth all the mental and physical powers of the worker. He not only puts into his task every ounce of his ordinary capacity, but he also draws upon that hidden reserve force of his Subconscious mentality and adds that to his ordinary full energy. When he approaches the fatigue limit his "enthusiastic interest" carries him on, and before long he has "caught his second wind" and obtained his fresh start.

Ask any successful sales-manager for a list of the essential characteristics of the successful salesman, and on that list you will find this capacity for or habit of "enthusiastic interest" occupying a prominent place. This, not only because of its highly important effect upon the work of the salesman himself, but also because "Enthusiasm is contagious," and the lively, quickened interest of the salesman tends to communicate itself to the subconscious mentality of his customer.

In the same way the Enthusiasm of the public speaker, orator, advocate or statesman energizes and quickens his entire intellectual and emotional nature, thus causing him to do his best, likewise communicating itself to his audience by means of "mental contagion." The man with "his soul afire" tends to fire the souls and hearts of those around him. The spirit of the enthusiastic leader, foreman, or "boss" is "caught" by those under him.

Enthusiasm is clearly a manifestation of the emotional phase of man's mentality, and it appeals directly and immediately to the emotional nature of others. Likewise, it is clearly a product of the subconscious mentality, and accordingly it appeals directly and immediately to the subconscious mentality of others. Its effect is characteristically animating, energizing, inspiring, "quickening." It not only stirs the feelings and sets fire to the spiritual nature but it also stimulates and vivifies the intellectual faculties. The "live wires" in the world of men are those individuals who possess the quality of "enthusiastic interest" highly developed and habitually manifested when the occasion calls for it. Overdone, it defeats its object—the Golden Mean must be observed; but lacking it the man is what is known in the idiom of practical men as a "dead one."

The man of true Enthusiasm is characterized by his abiding Faith in his proposition or subject; by his lively interest in it; by his earnestness in presenting it and working toward its accomplishment; by his untiring, indefatigable efforts on its behalf. Faith, however, is the foundation upon which all the rest is built; lacking Faith, the structure of Enthusiasm falls like a house of cards.

The more Faith a man has in that which he is doing, toward which he is working, or that which he is presenting to others, the greater will be the manifestation of his own powers and capacity, the more efficient will be his performance of the work, and the greater will be his ability to influence others and to cause them to see things in the light of his own belief and interest. Faith arouses and sustains Enthusiasm; lack of Faith deadens and inhibits it; Unfaith and positive disbelief kill it. It is clear that the first step toward the cultivation and development of Enthusiasm is that of the creation of Faith in the subject or object toward which you wish to manifest and express Enthusiasm.

If you have no Faith in the subject or object of your activities, then you will never be able to manifest Enthusiasm concerning that subject or object.

Life without Faith and Enthusiasm is a living death— persons living that life are mere walking corpses. If you would be a "live wire" instead of a "dead one," you must begin to arouse and develop Enthusiasm in your heart and soul. You must cultivate that keen and quickened Interest, and that lively and earnest Faith in what you are doing, and in the things to which you are giving your time and work. You must mentally "breathe in," and inspire that Spirit of Life which men for many centuries have called "Enthusiasm," and which is the twin-sister of Inspiration. Then will you know the exhilaration of that "enkindled and kindling fervor of soul"—that "ardent and lively zeal"— the mark of true Enthusiasm.

THE FLAME OF DESIRE ESSENTIAL TO FAITH

Desire is the second factor of Mental Power. You must not only "know definitely exactly what you want," and manifest it by means of Idealization; you must also "want it hard enough," and manifest it in Insistent Desire. Desire is the flame and fire which create the steam of Will. The Will never goes out into effective action except when drawn forth by active and sufficiently strong Desire. Desire furnishes the "motive" for Will; Will never becomes active in absence of a "motive." When we speak of a man having a "strong will," we often mean really that he has strong desire—Desire strong enough to cause him to exert every ounce of power and energy in him toward the attainment or accomplishment of the object of Desire.

Desire exerts a tremendous influence upon all of the mental faculties, causing them to put forth their full energies and powers and to perform their work efficiently. It stimulates the intellect, inspires the emotions and quickens the imagination. Without the urge of Desire there would be but little mental work performed. The keynote of Desire is "I Want"; and to gratify and satisfy that "want" the mind puts forth its best energies. Without Desire you would do but little thinking, for there would be no motive for such. Without Desire you would perform no actions, for there would be no moving-reason for such. Desire is ever the "mover to action"—to action mental as well as physical.

Moreover, the degree and the intensity of your work, mental or physical, is determined by the degree of Desire manifested in you concerning the object or end of such work. The more you want a thing, the harder will you work for it, and the easier will such work seem to you to be. The task performed under the influence and incentive of strong Desire will seem much easier than would be the same task performed without such influence and incentive—and infinitely easier than would the same task appear if its end and object were contrary to your Desire. No argument is needed to establish these facts—they are matters of common knowledge and are proved by the experience of everyday life.

The degree of force, energy, will, determination, persistence and continuous application manifested by an individual in his aspirations, ambitions, aims, performances, actions and work, is determined primarily by the degree of his Desire for the attainment of these objects—his degree of "want" and "want to" concerning that object. So true is this principle that some who have studied its effects have announced the aphorism: "You can have or be anything you want—if you only want it hard enough."

Without Faith it is practically impossible for you to manifest strong, ardent, insistent Desire. If you are filled with doubt, distrust, unfaith or disbelief in a thing, or concerning the successful accomplishment or attainment of anything, you will not be able to arouse the proper degree of desire for that thing or for its accomplishment and attainment. Lack of Faith, or, still more, positive disbelief, tends to paralyze the Desire Power; it acts as a brake or as a damper upon its power. Faith, on the contrary, frees the brakes of Desire, or turns on the full draft of its fire.

Here is the principle in concise form: Faith encourages and sustains, promotes and maintains Desire in its highest degree of efficiency; doubt, disbelief, distrust, and unfaith retard and restrict, inhibit and paralyze this efficient manifestation of Desire.

THE MIGHTY POWER OF A STRONG WILL

Will-Action is the third factor of Mental Power. You must not only "know clearly just what you 'want," and see it in your "mind's eye" in ideal form—you must not only "want it hard enough," and arouse its power to a degree of insistence and demand which will not brook denial or defeat—you must also call into service the persistent, determined, indomitable application of the Will, which will hold your energies and powers steadfastly and relentlessly to the task of accomplishment and attainment. You must "will to will" and must make your Will will itself in the act of Willing.

Will is perhaps the most mysterious of all of the mental powers. It seems to dwell on a mental plane alone by itself. It lies nearer and closer to the "I AM I" or Ego, than does any other phase of mentality. It is the principal instrument of the "I AM I"—the instrument which the latter employs directly and immediately. Its spirit is Persistent Determination—its essence is Action. Whenever you act, then do you employ your Will. Will Power is the dynamic phase or aspect of Mental Power. All other mental force is more or less static—it is only when the Will becomes involved in the process that Mental Power manifests its dynamic phase or aspect. Wise men have held that "All Power is Will Power at the last"; and that, "All activities are forms or phases of Will-Action, at the last." In the Cosmos, as well as in the individual, Will Power is the essential and basic phase of Power.

HOW TO ATTRACT THE PERSON YOU WANT

The Law of Mental Attraction, or Mental Gravitation, acts along lines very similar to those of the action of physical Gravitation. There is present and active the mutual and reciprocal "pull" between Thoughts and Things, and between Thoughts and Thoughts—Thoughts, however, are Things at the last analysis. This principle extends even to so-called inanimate objects: this mystery is explainable under the now well-established law that there is Mind in everything, even in the apparently inanimate objects of the universe, even in the atoms and particles of which material substances are composed.

Not only do you attract thought-vibrations, thought-waves, thought-currents, thought-atmospheres, etc. of a harmonious character, and to which your thoughts have a natural affinity; you also attract to yourselves (by the power of thought attraction) other persons whose thoughts have an affinity and harmony with your own. In the same way you attract to yourself (and are attracted toward) other persons whose interests run along the same general lines as your own.

You draw to yourself the persons who may be necessary for the successful carrying out of the plans and purposes, the desires and ambitions, which fill your thoughts most of the time; and, in the same way, you are drawn toward those into whose plans and purposes you are fitted to play an important part. In short, each person tends to attract toward himself those other persons whom he needs in order to materialize his ideals and to express his desires—providing that he "wants hard enough" and providing that the other persons are in harmonious affinity with his plans and purposes.

Persons who have had their attention directed toward the operations of the Law of Mental Attraction, and who have learned to apply the principles of its manifestation in their own affairs in life, observe many wonderful instances of its power in the happenings of their everyday life. Books, newspaper items, magazine articles bearing on some subject which is prominent in their thoughts, all these come to hand in an almost uncanny way. Persons who fit into the general scheme of the thought-plan come into one's life. Peculiar "happenings" come to pass in the same way. Things arise which "fit in" with the general idea. Unexpected circumstances arise which, although often at first sight seemingly obstructive and undesirable, in the end are found to dovetail perfectly into the whole scheme of things. No wonder that many persons having these experiences are at first inclined to attribute them to supernatural or superhuman influence—but they are in full accordance with Natural Law, and are a part of the powers of man, when rightly understood.

Your conditions and environment, the circumstances and happenings which come to you, are very largely the result of the operation of the Law of Mental Attraction—and they are accordingly, to a great extent, manifestations in objective, material form of your mental ideas, ideals and pictures, the force and nature of such manifestation depending largely upon the degree of Faith and Confident Expectation possessed and expressed by you in your thoughts upon these subjects and events—or upon the degree of doubt, disbelief, distrust and unfaith, those negative phases of Faith which serve to slow down the action of Faith Power or perhaps even to reverse its machinery.

You create environment, conditions, circumstances, events, assistance, means to ends, by Mental Power operating along the lines of the Law of Mental Attraction. Mental Attraction, like all forms or phases of Mental Power, is the transformation of the subjective Ideal into objective Reality—the thought tends to take form in action, the mental form tends to take on objective materiality and substance. The ideal is represented by the clear, strong, definite, mental picture or ideal form manifested in Idealization. Desire furnishes the flame and heat which generate the steam of Will needed in the creative process; but the Idealization is impaired and weakened, the Desire dies away, the Will loses its determination, unless Faith be there to create the Confident Expectation. The less the Faith and Confident Expectation, or the greater the doubt, disbelief, distrust, unfaith and lack of confidence, the weaker is the Idealization, the weaker the Desire, and the weaker the Will Power manifested.

Without Faith there can be no Confident Expectation; without Faith, the Fires of Desire die away; without Faith, the Steam of Will ceases to be generated; and thus Attainment becomes impossible. Whenever you think of the Law of Mental Attraction, think of Faith—for Faith is its very soul—its inspiration.

BELIEVE IN YOURSELF

Among the many characteristics and qualities which make for success of the individual there is none more fundamental, essential and basic than that of Self Confidence and Self Reliance—both of these terms being but expressions of the idea of Faith in Oneself. The man who has Faith in himself not only brings under his control and direction those wonderful powers of his subconscious mentality, and the full power of his conscious mental faculties and instruments, but also tends to inspire a similar feeling in the minds and hearts of those other individuals with whom he comes in contact in the course of his pursuit of the objects of his endeavors. An intuitive perception and realization of one's own powers and energies, capacity, and efficiency, possibilities and capabilities, is an essential attribute of the individual who is destined to success.

A study of the world of men will disclose the fact that those men who eventually succeed, who "arrive" ultimately, who "do things," are marked by this deep intuitive Faith in themselves, and by their Confident Expectation of Ultimate success. These men rise superior to the incidents of temporary defeat; they use these failures as stepping-stones to ultimate victory. They are living expressions of Henley's *Invictus*—they, indeed, are the Masters of their Fate, the Captains of their Souls! Such men are never Really defeated; like rubber balls, they have that "bounce" which causes them to rise Triumphantly after each fall—the harder they are "thrown down," the higher do they rise on the rebound. Such men are always possible—nay, probable and certain—victors, so long as they maintain this intuitive Faith in Self, of Self Confidence; it is only when this is lost that they are really defeated or destroyed.

The failures in life are discovered usually to be either (1) those who have never manifested this Faith in Self, or Self Confidence; or else (2) those who have permitted themselves to lose the same under the "Bludgeonings of Chance."

Those who have never felt the thrill of Faith in Self, or of Self Confidence, are soon labeled by their fellows as lacking the elements of successful achievement—the world soon "gets their number" and places them where they belong. Their lack of Self Faith and Self Confidence is felt by those with whom they come in contact; the world lacks Faith in them and has no Confident Expectation of their success.

The study of the life-story of the successful men in all walks of life will illustrate this principle to you so forcibly that, having perceived it, you will never again doubt its absolute truth. In practically every case you will find that these successful men have been knocked down, and bowled out, many times in the early days of their careers—often even later on in life. But the knock-out, though perhaps dazing them for a short time, never robbed them of their gameness, their will-to-succeed. They always arose to their feet before they were counted out; and they always firmly, but resolutely, faced Fate. Though their "heads were bloody, they were unbowed," as Henley triumphantly chants. Fate cannot defeat such a spirit; in time, Destiny recognizes the fact that "here is a man"—and being feminine, she falls in love with him and bestows her favors upon him.

When you have found your Real Self—"That Something Within"—this "I AM I"—then have you found that Inner and Real Self which has constituted the subject and object of that Faith and Confident Expectation which have inspired, animated, enthused and sustained the thousands of men who have reached the Heights of Attainment by the Path of Definite Ideals, Insistent Desire, Confident Expectation, Persistent Determination, and Balanced Compensation. It is this Intuitive perception and consciousness of the Real Self which has caused men to live out the ideal of *Invictus* in the spirit of that glorious poem of Henley. Nothing but this inner realization would have been sufficient to fill the soul of man with this indomitable spirit and unconquerable will.

INVICTUS
BY W. E. HENLEY

Out of the night that covers me,
Black as the pit from pole to pole,
I thank whatever gods there be
For my unconquerable soul.

In the fell clutch of circumstance
I have not winced or cried aloud;
Under the bludgeonings of chance
My head is bloody but unbowed.

Beyond this vale of doubt and fear
Looms but the terror of the Shade

And, yet, the passing of the years
Finds, and shall find me, unafraid.

It matters not how straight the gate,
How charged with punishments the scroll
I am the Master of my Fate,
I am the Captain of my Soul.

The wise teachers of the race have for centuries taught that this Faith in the Real Self, in the "I AM I," will enable the individual to convert into the instruments of his success even those circumstances which apparently are destined to defeat his purposes; and to transmute into beneficent agencies even those inimical forces which beset him on all sides. They have discovered, and passed on to their followers, the knowledge, that such a Faith is a spiritual Power, a living force, which when trusted and rightly employed will annihilate the opposition of outward circumstances, or else convert them into workers for good.

Your Real Self is a ray from the great Sun of Spirit—a spark from the great Flame of Spirit—a focal point of expression of that infinite SELF OF SPIRIT.

The earnest Faith in your Real Self, and your Confident Expectation concerning its manifestation and expression in your work, your endeavors, your plans, your purposes, serve to bring into action your full mental and spiritual power, energy, and force. It quickens your intellectual powers; it employs your emotional powers efficiently and under full control; it sets into effective action your creative imagination; it places the powers of your will under your mastery and direction. It draws upon your subconscious faculties for inspiration and for intuitive reports; it opens up your mind to the inflow of the illumination of your superconscious spiritual faculties and powers. It sets into operation the Law of Mental Attraction under your direct control and direction, whereby you attract to yourself, or you to them, the circumstances, events, conditions, things and persons needed for the manifestation of your ideals in objective reality. More than this, it brushes away the obstacles which have clogged the channels of your contact with and communication with SPIRIT itself—that great source of Infinite Power which in this instruction is called POWER.

Discover your Real Self, your "I AM I"—then manifest your full Faith in and toward it; and cultivate your full Confident Expectation concerning the beneficent results of that Faith.

THE INFINITE LOVES YOU
BECOME AN INVINCIBLE SOUL

The Message of Truth: You, yourself, in your essential and real being, nature, and entity, are Spirit, and naught but Spirit—in and of SPIRIT; spiritual and not material. Materiality is your instrument of expression, the stuff created for your use and service in your expression of Life, Consciousness and Will: it is your servant, not your master; you condition, limit and form it, not it you, when you recognize and realize your real nature, and awaken to a perception of its real relation to you and you to it. The report of SPIRIT received by its accredited individual centers of expression, and by them transmitted to you is this:

In the degree that you perceive, recognize, and realize your essential identity with ME, the Supreme Presence-Power, the Ultimate Reality, in that degree will you be able to manifest My Spiritual Power. I AM over and above you, under and beneath you, I surround you on all sides. I AM also within you, and you are in ME; from Me you proceed and in Me you live and move and have your being. Seek Me by looking within your own being, and likewise by looking for Me in Infinity, for I abide both within and without your being. If, and when, you will adopt and live according to this Truth, then will you be able to manifest that Truth—in and by it alone are Freedom and Invincibility, and true and real Presence and Power, to be found, perceived, realized and manifested.

Francis Thompson, in his mystic poem entitled *The Hound of Heaven* describes with a tremendous power, and often with an almost terrible intensity, the hunt of Reality for the unwilling individual Self. He pictures Divinity as engaged in a remorseless, tireless quest—a seeking, following, tracking-down of the unwilling individual soul. He pictures the separated spirit as a "strange, piteous, futile thing" that flees from the pursuing Divinity "down the nights and down the days." The individual spirit, not knowing its relation to and identity with the pursuing Absolute, rushes in a panic of terror away from its own good. But, as Emerson says, "You cannot escape your own Good"; and, so the fleeing soul is captured at last. By Faith in the Infinite, however, the individual soul overcomes its terror of the Infinite and, recognizing it as its Supreme Good, it turns and moves toward it. Such is the mystic conception of the effect and action of Faith in the Infinite.

The complete poem, *The Hound of Heaven*, covers five pages; but we here present a condensed version of these beautiful and gripping lines by Francis Thompson. If you are not reciprocating the Great Love of God, you may have a feeling of remorse and resolve to do better. If this feel: does not come to you; you must have a heart of stone.

THE HOUND OF HEAVEN
BY FRANCIS THOMPSON

I fled Him, down the nights and down the days;
  I fled Him, down the arches of the years;
I fled Him, down the labyrinthine ways
  Of my own mind; and in the mist of tears
I hid from Him, and under running laughter.
    Up vistaed hopes I sped;
    And shot, precipitated,
Adown Titanic glooms of chasmed fears,
From those strong Feet that followed, followed after.
    But with unhurrying chase,
    And unperturbed pace,
Deliberate speed, majestic instancy,
    They beat—and a Voice beat
    More instant that the Feet—
"All things betray thee, who betrayest Me."

I said to Dawn: Be sudden—to Eve: Be soon;
    With thy young skiey blossoms heap me over
        From this tremendous Lover—

Still with unhurrying chase,
And unperturbed pace,
Deliberate speed, majestic instancy,
    Came on the following Feet,
    And a voice above their beat—
"Naught shelters thee, who wilt not shelter Me."

In the rash lustihead of my young powers,
    I shook the pillaring hours
And pulled my life upon me; grimed with smears,
I stand amid the dust of the mounded years—
My mangled youth lies dead beneath the heap.
  My days have crackled and gone up in smoke.
    Designer Infinite!—

Ah! must Thou char the wood ere Thou canst limn with it?
My freshness spent its wavering shower in the dust;
And now my heart is as a broken fount.

Now of that long pursuit
Comes on at hand the bruit;
That Voice is round me like a bursting sea:
"How little worthy of any love thou art!
Whom wilt thou find to love ignoble thee
Save Me, save only Me?
All which I took from thee I did but take,
Not for thy harms,
But just that thou mightest seek it in My arms.
All which thy child's mistake
Fancies as lost, I have stored for thee at home:
Rise, clasp My hand, and come!"

Halts by me that footfall:
Is my gloom, after all,
Shade of His hand, outstretched caressingly?
"Ah, fondest, blindest, weakest,
I am He Whom thou seekest!
Thou dravest love from thee, who dravest Me."

Prentice Mulford said: "A Supreme Power and Wisdom governs the Universe. The Supreme Mind is measureless and pervades all space. The Supreme Wisdom, Power, and Intelligence are in everything that exists, from the atom to the planet. The Supreme Power has us in its charge, as it has the suns and endless system of worlds in space. As we grow more to recognize this sublime and exhaustless Wisdom, we shall learn more and more to demand that Wisdom, draw it to ourselves, and thereby be ever making ourselves newer and newer. This means ever perfecting health, greater power to enjoy all that exists, gradual transition into a higher state of being, and the development of powers which we do not now realize as belonging to us. Let us then daily demand Faith, for Faith is power to believe and power to see that all things are parts of the Infinite Spirit of God, that all things have Good or God in them, and that all things, when recognized by us as parts of God, must work for our good."

To sum up:

1. There exists a greater underlying Something that is beneficent and well-disposed toward you, and which tries to help, aid and assist you whenever and wherever It can do so.

2. Faith and Confident Expectation regarding the beneficent power of that Something tends to open the channels of Its influence in your life; while doubt, unbelief, distrust, and fear, tend to dam up the channel of its influence in your life, and to rob it of the power to help you.

3. To a great extent, at least, you determine your own life by the character of your thought; by the nature and character of your thoughts you furnish the pattern or mold which determines or modifies the efforts of the Something to aid you, either in the direction of producing desirable results or else in bringing about undesirable results by reason of your damming up the sources of your Good.

In the *Book of Psalms* in our own Scriptures, are to be found several of the great masterpieces of the esoteric teachings concerning Faith Power—in them is given the essence of the Secret Doctrine concerning Faith in the Infinite. Chief among these are the Twenty-Third Psalm, and the Ninety-first Psalm, respectively. So important are these two great esoteric poems—so filled with practical helpful information are they—that we deem it advisable to reproduce them here that you may avail yourself of their virtue and power at this particular stage of this instruction. Accordingly, they are given on these pages.

THE PSALM OF FAITH
Psalm 23

The Lord is my shepherd; I shall not want. He maketh me to lie down in the green pastures; he leadeth me beside the still waters. He restoreth my soul; he leadeth me in the paths of righteousnes for His name's sake. Yea, though I walk through the valley of the shadow of death, I will fear no evil; for thou art with me; Thy rod and Thy staff they comfort me. Thou preparest a table before me in the presence of mine enemies; Thou anointest my head with oil; my cup runneth over. Surely goodness and mercy will follow me all the days of my life, and I will dwell in the house of the Lord forever.

THE PSALM OF SECURITY
Psalm 91

He that dwelleth in the secret place of the most High shall abide under the shadow of the Almighty. I will say of the Lord, He is my refuge and my fortress: my God in Him will I trust. Surely He shall deliver thee from the snare of the fowler, and from the noisome pestilence. He shall cover thee with His feathers, and under His wings shalt thou trust: His truth shall be thy shield and buckler. Thou shalt not be afraid for the terror by night; nor for the arrow that flieth by day; nor for the pestilence that walketh in darkness; nor for the destruction that wasteth at noonday. A thousand shall fall at thy side, and ten thousand at thy right hand; but it shall not come nigh thee. Only with thine eyes shalt thou behold and see the reward of the wicked. Because thou hast made the Lord, which is my refuge, even the most high, thy habitation. There shall no evil befall thee, neither shall any plague come nigh thy dwelling. For He shall give His angels charge over thee, to keep thee in all thy ways. They shall bear thee up in their hands, lest thou dash thy foot against a stone. Thou shalt tread upon the lion and the adder: the young lion and the dragon shalt thou trample under feet. Because he hath set his love upon Me, and therefore will I deliver him; I will set him on high, because he hath known My name. He shall call upon Me, and I will answer him and honor him. With long life will I satisfy him, and show him my salvation.

LEAD KINDLY LIGHT

The teachers and students of the Inner teachings, the Ancient Wisdom, the Secret Doctrine, are also aware of the esoteric

spiritual significance of the lines of the well-known hymn "Lead Kindly Light," written by Newman in a period of spiritual stress. Few who read or sing this hymn realize its esoteric spirit and meaning—none but "those who know" perceive and recognize that which dwells under the surface of those wonderful words and lines.

THE CHANT OF FAITH POWER
(Lead Kindly Light)
Lead kindly Light, amid the encircling gloom; Lead Thou
me on. The night is dark, and I am far from home; Lead Thou
me on. Keep Thou my feet; I do not ask to see the distant scene;
one step enough for me, Lead Thou me on.

Carry with you ever the spirit of the ancient aphorism of the wise sage, which is; "Faith is the White Magic of Power."

The Magic Word

THE LAW OF INCREASE

I am Success, though hungry, cold, ill-clad,
I wander for a while, I smile and say,
"It is but a time, I shall be glad
Tomorrow, for good fortune comes my way.
God is my Father, He has wealth untold,
His wealth is mine—health, happiness and gold."
—ELLA WHEELER WILCOX

In a pamphlet written by Don Blanding, he tells of a time during the trying years of the Great Depression, , when he found himself financially, mentally and physically "broke." He was suffering from insomnia and from a physical lethargy amounting almost to paralysis. Worst of all, he had a bad case of "self-pity," and he felt that the self-pity was fully justified.

He was staying at a small Art Colony (on credit), trying to rebuild his wrecked life and wretched body. Among those at the Colony was Mike, an Hawaiian boy. Mike seemed to be always cheerful. Mike seemed to be always prosperous. And, naturally, Blanding wondered why. For Mike, when he had known him before, had been blessed with few of this world's goods.

So one day he asked Mike what good fairy had waved her wand over him and turned all that he touched into gold.

For answer, Mike pointed to a string of letters he had pasted over his bed—"L-I-D-G-T-T-F-T-A-T-I-M."

Blanding read them, but could make no sense out of them. "What are they, the 'Open, Sesame' to the Treasure Cave?"

"They have been the 'Open, Sesame' for me," Mike told him, and went on to explain how they had helped him. It seems that Mike, too, had experienced his ups and downs, but in the course of one of his "downs," he had happened upon a teacher who showed him the power of PRAISE and THANKFULNESS.

"There is an inherent law of mind," says Charles Fillmore, "that we INCREASE whatever we PRAISE. The whole of creation responds to praise, and is glad. Animal trainers pet and reward their charges with delicacies for acts of obedience; children glow with joy and gladness when they are praised. Even vegetation grows better for those who love it. We can praise our own ability, and the very brain cells will expand and increase in capacity and intelligence, when we speak words of encouragement and appreciation to them."

God gave you dominion over the earth. Everything is your servant, but remember it is said in the Scriptures that God brought every beast and fowl to Adam, *to see what he would call them.* You are like Adam in this, that you can give to everything and everybody with whom you come in contact the name you like. You can call them good or bad. And whatever you call them, that is what they will be—good servants or evil. You can praise or curse them, and as you do, so will they be to you.

There is one unfailing Law of Increase—*"Whatever is praised and blessed, MULTIPLIES!"* Count your blessings and they increase. If you are in need of supply, start in now to praise every small piece of money that comes to you, blessing it as a symbol of God's abundance and love. Salute the Divinity represented by it. Bless Him and name Him Infinite and Abundant Supply. You will be surprised how soon that small piece of money will increase to many pieces. Take God into your business. Bless your store, bless every one that works for you, each customer that comes in. Know that they represent the Divinity called Abundance, so bless them as such.

If you are working for someone else and want a better job or more pay, start by BLESSING and being THANKFUL *for what you have.* Bless the work you are doing, be thankful for every opportunity it gives you to acquire greater skill or ability or to serve others. Bless the money you earn, no matter how little it may be. Be so thankful to God for it that you can give a small "Thank Offering" from it to someone in greater need than yourself.

Suppose the Boss does seem unappreciative and hard. Bless him just the same. Be thankful for the opportunity to SERVE faithfully, no matter how small the immediate reward may seem to be. Give your best, give it cheerfully, gladly, thankfully, and you will be amazed how quickly the INCREASE will come to you—not necessarily from your immediate boss, but from the Big Boss over all.

I remember reading a letter from a woman in the drought belt in which she said that they, unlike most of their neighbors, had an abundant supply of water, and excellent crops. "When my husband plows a field," she writes, "I ask God to bless each furrow. Each seed that goes into the seeder is blessed, and the realization held that it will produce abundantly according to His righteous law. Our neighbors marveled at the abundance of hay that we cut this year. The hay was sold before the third cutting was put up.

"Each day, in the silence, I put the ranch 'Lovingly in the hands of the Father.' I ask God to bless everybody that comes in contact with the ranch."

Few realize the power of praise and blessing. Praise may be called the great liberator. You remember the story of Paul and Silas. They lay in jail bound with chains, but they did not despair. They rejoiced and sang hymns of praise, and lo, the very walls were shaken down and they were set free.

Praise always magnifies. When we praise God and then look about us and praise His invisible presence in all that we see, we find that the good is so magnified that much becomes evident that we ordinarily fail to see. Running through all of Jesus Christ's acts as well as His teachings we find the glowing element of praise. When He looked at five loaves and two small fishes and realized that He had a multitude to feed, His first thought was a thought of praise. "And looking up to heaven, he blessed."

Go back over the Old Testament and see how often you are adjured to "Praise the Lord and be thankful, that THEN shall the earth yield her increase." Probably no life chronicled in the Scriptures was more beset with trials and dangers than that of King David. And what was his remedy? What brought him through all tribulations to power and riches? Just read the Psalms of David and you will see.

> Jehovah reigneth; let the earth rejoice;
> Let the multitude of isles be glad.
> Bless Jehovah, O my soul;
> And all that is within me, bless his holy name . . .
> Who forgiveth all thine iniquities;
> Who healeth all they diseases.

"If anyone could tell you the shortest, surest way to all happiness and all perfection," wrote William Law, "he must tell you to make it a rule to yourself to thank and praise God for everything that happens to you. For it is certain that whatever seeming calamity happens to you, if you thank and praise God for it, you turn it into a blessing. Could you therefore work miracles, you could not do more for yourself than by this thankful spirit; for it turns all that it touches into happiness."

How then can YOU increase your supply? How can you get more of riches and happiness and every good thing of life? In the same way as the Wise Men and the Prophets of old. In the same way that Jesus twice fed the multitudes. In the same way that He filled the disciples' nets to overflowing with fish, after they had labored all night and caught nothing.

By EXPANDING what you have! And the way to expand is through love, through praise and thanksgiving— through saluting the Divinity in it, and naming it Infinite and Abundant Supply.

Throughout the Bible we are told—"In everything by prayer and supplication WITH THANKSGIVING let your requests be made unto God." Again and again the root of inspiration and attainment is stressed. *Rejoice, be glad, praise, give thanks!*

And that was what our Hawaiian boy had done. That was the secret of his prosperity and success. The Talisman he had pasted over his bed meant—"Lord, I do give Thee thanks for the abundance that is mine." Every time he looked upon it, he repeated those words of thankfulness. The happy ending lies in the fact that these words of praise and thanksgiving proved to be as potent a talisman for Don Blanding as they had for Mike, the Hawaiian.

"Whose offereth praise, glorifieth Me," sang the Psalmist of old. And it is as true today as it was thousands of years ago. Praise, thankfulness, understanding—these three supply the golden key to anything of good you may desire of life.

In "Think What You Want" magazine, some time ago, H. W. Alexander told how praise helps. "Sincere praise is money in your pocket," he said.

It is a spiritual and moral uplift. It is a tonic to the giver and the receiver. It rebounds to both a thousand times. I know a company whose sales during the depression went from $2,600,000 a year to $8,000,000. Praise was the inspiration.

In a divorce court not so long ago was recorded the story of a man who from a laborer's job climbed to the Presidency of his business. A friend asked him why he quit his almost lifetime companion, though she was well provided for. Said he, "Well my wife of today appreciates my ability, tells me right along, wheras my childhood sweetheart knows my weaknesses and tells me about them. I like appreciation." His income tax is on a $100,000 salary.

Little things count. Your secretary has a new dress, a new hat, a fashionably fluffy ruffle—tell her so. The file clerk finds your letters quickly—tell her so. The cop on the beat is sure to see the school boys are safely over with a wave of his hand. Tell him he is tops.

One of the finest persons who worked for me was an elderly servant woman. She had a tough time in life, poorly educated, used split infinitives, came early in the morning to clean the house. She often said to me as I left in the morning, "Sure, you look good today. You've got a big job, you work hard, you'll win." She *thought* I was good, and when I went out I *was* good. Top executives who read this know very well the truth of what the chauffeur, maid, gardener—who gives them a cheery word of praise, means to them at market time, conference time, or directors' time—it rings in their mind— oh, yes, they remember. You can't fly too high.

And the mother who *thinks* her boy or girl is about right, aids them on as no one else can.

I have this belief—that big or little, praise does win friends, wins respect for yourself, wins you a monetary return, and it helps a Pullman porter, a housewife, an industrialist to bigger, better things. It costs you nothing but a smile—but do be sincere.

To the wives who may read this: You know your man. He can't fool you. But be just as honest as you can, praise him, send him out to work with a smile, with praise, and you'll wear sables—try it.

Like attracts like. Praise and appreciation bring back greater praise and appreciation to you. If you want health, happiness, in your life, if you are seeking riches and success, attune your thoughts to these. BLESS the circumstances that surround you. Bless and praise those who come in contact with you. Bless even the difficulties you meet, for by blessing them, you can change them from discordant conditions to favorable ones, you can speed up their rate of activity to where they will bring you good, instead of evil. It is only lack of RESPONSIVENESS to good that produces the lacks in your life. Good works on the plane of EXPANSION. Good revolves at a high rate of activity. You can key your activity to that same rate by an expectant, confident state of mind. You can bring all your surroundings and circumstances up to that same level by BLESSING them, PRAISING the good in them, saluting the DIVINITY in them.

In the pages that follow, we shall show you how the practice of blessing and praising all things has brought good to all who have tried it, how you can use these same methods to attract every good thing *you* may desire.

Into whatsoever house ye enter, first say—"Peace be to this house!"

IN THE BEGINNING

For life is the mirror of king and slave,
'Tis just what we are and do;
Then give to the world the best you have,
And the best will come back to you.

We often speak of psychology and metaphysics as new sciences, and think that the study of these began within the last half-century. Yet if you refer to the very first book of the Bible, you find more profound examples of applied psychology than in any textbook of today.

Take the story of Jacob as an instance. You remember how Jacob agreed to serve Laban seven years for the hand of Rachel in marriage. And how, through the guile of his father-in-law, Jacob had to serve a second seven years. Even then, when he would have gone back to his own country, Laban begged him to tarry yet a while longer, and agreed to pay Jacob as wages "all the speckled and spotted cattle and all the brown cattle among the sheep, and the speckled and spotted among the goats."

Since Laban first removed from the herds all cattle of this kind, the chances of Jacob's getting rich on the speckled offspring of solid-colored cattle seemed poor indeed.

But Jacob evidently knew his Scriptures, and the idea we think so new, that first comes the "word" (or mental image), then the physical manifestation, was in his mind even when he made the bargain.

For what did he do?

And Jacob took him rods of green poplar, and of the hazel and chestnut tree; and pilled white strakes in them, and made the white appear which was in the rods.

And he set the rods which he had pilled before the flocks in the gutters in the watering troughs when the flocks came to drink, that they should conceive when they came to drink.

And the flocks conceived before the rods, and brought forth cattle ringstraked, speckled, and spotted.

And Jacob did separate the lambs, and set the faces of the flocks toward the ringstraked, and all the brown in the flock of Laban; and he put his own flocks by themselves, and put them unto Laban's cattle.

As it came to pass, whensoever the stronger cattle did conceive, that Jacob laid the rods before the eyes of the cattle in the gutters that they might conceive among the rods.

But when the cattle were feeble, he put them not in; so the feebler were Laban's, and the stronger Jacob's.

And the man increased exceedingly, and had much cattle, and maidservants, and menservants, and camels, and asses.

You have heard of the English cuckoo. Too lazy to rear and care for its own young, it goes to the nests of other birds when they are off seeking food, notes the markings on their eggs, then comes back later *and lays in their nest eggs of those same exact markings!*

Various saints of the middle ages are said to have had markings on their hands, feet and sides similar to those on the crucified Saviour, acquired from constant contemplation of His image. And only recently I read of an adopted child, which was reported to have developed markings similar in all respects to those of the real son of its foster-parents, although the son had died some months before the adopted child was born. The parents were satisfied it was a case of reincarnation, but it seemed to me merely a materialization in the foster-child of the images in the mother's mind. She had grieved inexpressibly over her loss. She had adopted the waif to try to fill the void left by her own little boy. And striving to see in his every action some reminder of her lost one, those images so strongly held in her mind actually expressed themselves in the body of her foster-child.

It all comes back to that first line of the first chapter of the Gospel of St. John—"In the beginning was the Word." For what is a "Word"? A mental image, is it not? Before an architect can build a house, he must have a mental image of what he is to build. Before you can accomplish anything, you must have a clear mental image of what it is you want to do. Turn to the Scriptural account of the creation of the world. What is the outstanding fact you find there?

IN EVERY THING GOD CREATED, THE "WORD CAME FIRST— THEN THE MATERIAL FORM!

Just listen: "And God said, Let there be light... And God said, Let there be a firmament . . . And God said, Let us make man ..."

First the "word," then the material form. Scientists tell us that words denote ideas, mental concepts—that you can always judge how far a race has advanced in the mental scale by the number of words it uses. Its vocabulary is the measure of its ideas. Few words—few ideas, few mental images.

Therefore, when God said—"Let the earth bring forth grass," He had in mind a clear mental image of what grass was like. In other words, He had already formed the mold. As the Scriptures put it—"The Lord God made the earth and the heavens, and every plant of the field *before it was in the earth,* and every herb of the field *before it* grew." He made the mental image, the mold. It needed then only to draw upon the energy about Him to fill that mold and give it material form.

And that is all you, too, need to do to give your word of power material form—first make the mental image, the mold, then pour into it the elements necessary to make that image manifest for all to see.

What do you want first?—Health—Happiness? Riches?

For perfect health, begin by taking the life out of every distorted image of sickness or imperfection. Charge those nerve centers of yours to withdraw their supporting hands, and let your image of disease collapse like the pricked bubble it is.

THEN IMAGE THE PERFECT MOLD OF WHATEVER ORGAN HAS BEEN DISEASED.

Image the perfect mold of it so vividly that you can clearly see it in your mind's eye, then charge The God in You to reach out with its millions of hands for all the elements it needs to make that perfect image manifest.

First the word (the mental image), then the creation. But the creation will never become manifest without faith. So when you have made your image, when you have set The God in You to work pouring into it the elements it needs for life, *"believe that you receive!"* See with the eyes of your mind that perfect organ functioning as it was meant to, *and thank God for it!*

For riches, the same principle holds true. Take your life out of every image of debt, of lack, of unfulfilled obligation. The God in you is a God of plenty. He cannot owe money. He cannot be limited. There are no circumstances powerful enough to force Him to live in poverty or want.

Yet He, remember, is devoted entirely to your advancement. So how can you be tied down by debt or limitation of any kind?

How? Because YOU have insisted upon it. Instead of a God of plenty, you have worshiped one of want. Instead of reaching out for what you needed, you have tied the hands of The God in You and tried to do their work with the paltry powers of your material hands.

Unloose The God in You! Give Him a job and set Him to work. Make your mental image of the great business or other service you long for, then set The God in You to work bringing to you every element you need to make that image real. And don't wait until you receive the whole of it, but as fast as any element becomes manifest, USE it!

If you have only 10-cents, USE it to start your great idea. If you have only the idea, START it, even though you can take only the first step. First the word, remember, then the creation. And there can be no creation without faith.

Show your faith by using each element as fast as it makes itself manifest, even though there be no sign that any other element is following, and before you know it, your whole structure will be complete.

Have you ever read Genevieve Behrend's account of how she got $20,000, when, from all material points of view, her chances of ever seeing that amount of money were just about nil?

"Every night before going to sleep," she writes, in YOUR INVISIBLE POWER:

I made a mental picture of the desired $20,000 which seemed necessary to go and study with Troward. Twenty imaginary $1,000 bills were counted over each night in my bedroom, and then, with the idea of more emphatically impressing my mind with the fact that this twenty thousand dollars was for the purpose of going to England, and studying with Troward, I wrote out my picture, saw myself buying my steamer ticket, walking up and down the ship's deck from New York to London, and finally saw myself accepted as Troward's pupil. This process was repeated every morning and every evening, always impressing more and more fully upon my mind Troward's memorized statement: "My mind is a center of Divine operations." I endeavored to keep this statement in the back part of my consciousness all the time, with no thought in mind of how the money might be obtained. Probably the reason why there was no thought of the avenues through which the money might reach me was because I could not possibly imagine where the $20,000 would come from. So I simply held my thought steady and let the power of attraction find its own way and means.

One day while walking on the street, taking deep breathing exercises, the thought came: "My mind is surely a center of Divine operation. If God fills all space, then God must be in my mind also; if I want this money to study with Troward that I may know the truth of Life, then both the money and the truth must be mine, though I am unable to feel or see the physical manifestations of either. Still," I declared, "it must be mine."

While these reflections were going on in my mind, there seemed to come up from within me the thought: "I AM all the substance there is." Then, from another channel in my brain the answer seemed to come, "Of course, that's it; everything must have its beginning in mind. The Idea must contain within itself the only one and primary substance there is, and this means money as well as everything else." My mind accepted this idea, and immediately all the tension of mind and body was relaxed. There was a feeling of absolute certainty of being in touch with all the power Life has to give. All thought of money, teacher, or even my own personality, vanished in the great wave of joy which swept over my entire being. I walked on and on, with this feeling of joy steadily increasing and expanding until everything about me seemed aglow with resplendent light. Every person I passed appeared illuminated as I was. All consciousness of personality had disappeared, and in its place there came that great and almost overwhelming sense of joy and contentment.

That night when I made my picture of the twenty thousand dollars it was with an entirely changed aspect. On previous occasions, when making my mental picture, I had felt that I was waking up something within myself. This time there was no sensation of effort. I simply counted over the twenty thousand dollars. Then, in a most unexpected manner, from a source of which I had no consciousness at the time, there seemed to open a possible avenue through which the money might reach me. Just as soon as there appeared a circumstance which indicated the direction through which the twenty thousand dollars might come, I not only made a supreme effort to regard the indicated direction calmly as the first sprout of the seed I had sown in the absolute, but left no stone unturned to follow up that direction, thereby fulfilling my part. By so doing, one circumstance seemed naturally to lead to another, until, step by step, my desired twenty thousand dollars was secured.

For happiness, the method is no different. Your God is a God of love, and real love can know no unhappiness, for love gets its happiness from giving.

There are laws to interfere with almost every other activity of humanity, but none to keep you from giving as much as you like. An unselfish giving results in getting, just as surely as planting results in harvesting. Give with no thought of reward but the good of the one you are helping, and good is bound to flow back to you.

Love begets love, you know, so take your life out of every thought of enmity, of repining, of unhappiness. In place of these, see yourself in your mind's eye giving every manner of happiness to all whom you would have love you. Image that in your mind's eye, then set The God in You to work bringing you opportunities to make all these loved ones happier. And as fast as each opportunity presents itself, USE it! No matter how tiny an opportunity it may be, *use it!* No matter if it be merely the chance to say a pleasant word, to give a kindly smile, to bring a happy thought, *use it!*

And in the using, you will find that doubly great happiness has come to you.

Each of us is a miniature sun, his circumstances and surroundings his solar system. If debts and disease and troubles form part of your system, what is the remedy? *Let go of them, of course!* If you want new planets of riches and youth and happiness, how can you get them? In the same way the sun does, and only in that way—by throwing off from yourself.

this: Nothing can come into your solar system except from you
ou. If it comes from outside, it is not yours and has no power over
take hold of it mentally and accept it as yours. If you don't want
it, you can refuse to accept it, refuse to take hold of it, refuse to believe in its
reality—then put in the place it seems to occupy, the perfect condition of your
own imaging.

If there is something lacking in your solar system, you have only to "speak
the word"—create the mental image, then hold to that image in serene faith
until The God in You has filled it with those elements that make it visible to
all.

It is your own fault when you allow yourself to become the victim of
personal impotence or of undesirable external situations. As Emerson put
it—"Nothing external to you has any power over you." You fear these negative
seemings simply because you BELIEVE in them, when all the time it is only
that BELIEF that gives them power and authority.

Remember, YOU are the central sun of your own solar system. YOU have
dominion over everything within that system. YOU can say what shall enter,
what shall stay there. And you have infinite attractive power to draw to you
anything of good you may desire. Nothing stands between you and your
fondest desires but lack of understanding of or faith in this power of
attraction.

But once you send out the desire, you must have perfect faith in the result.
You cannot accomplish anything by expressing a desire and then spending
your time fearing and worrying lest you will not find the work you seek, or not
have the money in time to pay your bills, or that some other evil thing will
happen to prevent good from coming to you. The law of attraction cannot
bring both good and evil at the same time. It must be one or the other. And
it is up to YOU to decide which it shall be.

"After any object or purpose is clearly held in thought," says Lilian Whiting,
"its precipitation in tangible and visible form is merely a question of time.
Columbus saw in vision a path through trackless waters around the world. The
vision always precedes and itself determines the realization."

Dare you to say—"Every day in every way I am getting richer and richer"? If
you dare—and will follow up the word with the mental image of yourself
HAVING all the riches you desire—Spirit substance will make your word
manifest and show you the way to riches.

You were designed by the Father to be master of your fate and captain of
your soul. If you are not exercising that mastery, it is because you are lying

down on the job. Instead of mastering your thoughts and mental images, you are letting them bow down before mere things.

No thing can make you unhappy if you "will exercise your divine power of love and blessings towards it. Everything is good in its essence, and that good essence will respond to your call of blessing, and its good will come forth to meet you.

> The world stands out on either side
> No wider than the heart is wide;
> Above the world is stretched the sky—
> No higher than the soul is high;
> The heart can push the sea and land
> Farther away on either hand;
> The soul can split the sky in two,
> And let the Face of God shine through.

TREASURE MAPPING FOR SUPPLY

So many people have won to success and happiness by making "Treasure Maps" to more easily visualize the things they wanted, that "Nautilus" magazine recently ran a prize competition for the best article showing how a "Treasure Map" had helped to bring about one's heart's desire. Caroline J. Drake won the contest.

"I had been bookkeeper," she wrote, "in a large department store for seven years when the manager's niece, whose husband had just died, was put in my place.

I felt stunned. My husband had died ten years previously, leaving a little home and some insurance. But sickness and hospital bills had long since taken both home and money. I had supported the family for eight years and kept the three children in school, but had not been able to save any money. The eldest child, a boy, had just finished high school but as yet had found nothing to do to help along.

Day after day I looked for work of any kind to do which might pay rent and give us a living. I was thirty-five years old, strong, capable and willing; but there was absolutely no place for me. For the first time in my life I was afraid of the future. The thought that we might have to go on relief appalled me.

Thus three months passed. I was behind two months with the rent when the landlord told me I would have to move. I asked him to give me a few days longer in which to try and find work. This he agreed to do.

The next morning I started out again on my rounds. In passing a magazine stand I stopped and glanced over the papers and magazines. It must have been the answer to my many prayers that led me to pick up the copy of a magazine which stared me in the face. Idly I opened it and glanced at the table of contents. My mind was in such a turmoil that I was barely conscious of the words which my eyes saw.

Suddenly my eye was caught by a title about 'treasure-mapping' for success and supply. Something impelled me to buy a copy of the magazine, which proved to be the turning point in our lives.

Instead of looking for work, I went home. Still under the influence of that "Something" (which I did not then understand) I began to read the magazine. Strange and unreal as it then seemed, still I did not doubt. I read each article eagerly and in its order. When I came to the article about treasure-mapping to bring success and supply, something about the idea seemed to hold me in its grip. As a child I had always loved games, and this idea of making a treasure-map reawakened that old desire.

I read the article several times. Then, with a bunch of papers which I hunted up, I set to work to make my treasure-map of success and supply. So many things came into my mind to put on that treasure-map! First, there was the little cottage at the edge of town. Then there was a little dress and millinery shop which I had always longed for. Then, of course, a car. And in that cottage would be a piano for the girls; a yard in the back where we could work among the flowers of an evening or a morning. My enthusiasm grew by leaps and bounds. From magazines and papers I cut pictures and words and sentences—all connected with the idea of success and abundance.

HOW I MADE THE "TREASURE-MAP"

Next I found a large sheet of heavy white paper and began building that map. In the center I pasted a picture of a lovely little cottage with wide porches and trees and shrubbery around it. In one corner of the map I put a picture of a little storeroom and underneath I pasted the words, "Betty's Style Shop." Close to this I pasted pictures of a few very stylish dresses and hats.

At different places on the map I placed sentiments and mottoes—all carrying out the idea of success, abundance, happiness and harmony.

I do not know how long I worked on that treasure-map which was to be the means of attracting into our lives the things which we had need of and desired. I could already feel myself living in that cottage and working in the little dress shop. Never had I felt so completely fascinated and thrilled with an idea as with that treasure-map and what I was sure it would bring us. I tacked the map on the wall of my bedroom, right in front of my bed, so that the first thing I saw in the morning and the last thing at night would be that treasure-map of my desires.

Every night and morning I would go over every detail of that map until it fairly seemed to become a part of my very being. It became so clear that I could call it instantly to mind at any moment in the day. Then in my Silence period I would see myself and the children going through the rooms of the cottage, laughing and talking, arranging the furniture and curtains. I would picture my daughters at the piano singing and playing; I would see my son sitting in the library with books and papers all around him. Then I would picture myself walking about my shop, proud and happy; people coming in and going out. I would see them buying the lovely hats and dresses, paying me for them and going out smiling.

During all this time, I was learning more and more of the power of the mind to draw to us the things and conditions like unto our thoughts. I understood that this treasure-map was but the means of impressing upon my subconscious mind the pattern from which to build the conditions of success and harmony into our lives. Always, after each of my Silence periods, I would lovingly thank God that the abundance and harmony and love were already ours. I believed that I *had* received; for mentally living in the cottage and working in the shop was to me the certain fact that I would take possession of them in the material world just as in the mental.

When the children found out what I was doing, they entered heartily into the spirit of the game and each of them soon had a treasure-map of his own.

It was not many weeks before things began to happen. One day I met an old friend of my husband's and he told me that he and his wife were going west for several months and asked if we would come out and take care of their house for the rent. A week later we were settled in that cottage, which was almost the very picture of the one I had on my treasure-map. A little later my son was offered work evenings and Saturdays in an engineering office, which proved the means of his entering college that fall.

We had been in the cottage nearly two months when I saw an advertisement in the local paper for a woman to take charge of a lady's dress shop. I answered the ad and found that the owner was having to give up the shop for several months, perhaps permanently, on account of her health. Arrangements were quickly made so that I was to run the business and share half the expenses and the profits.

Within six months after we started treasure-mapping for supply, we had accomplished practically everything that map called for. When the owner of the cottage came back several months later, he made it possible for us to buy the place and we are still here.

The business, too, is mine now. The lady decided not to come back, so I bought the business, paying her so much a month. It is a much larger and more thriving business now—thanks to the understanding of the power of thought which I gained through my study and practice.

In another article in "Nautilus," Helen M. Kitchel told how she used a "Treasure Map" to sell her property. She pasted an attractive picture of her house on a large sheet of paper, put a description of it underneath and then surrounded picture and description with such mottoes as— "Love, the Divine Magnet, attracts all that is good"—and others of a similar nature. She hung her map where she could see and study it several times a day, and repeated some of the affirmations or mottoes whenever the thought of making a sale occurred to her.

She also started a little private letter box which she called "God's Box" and in it, whenever the thought occurred to her, she placed a letter written to God telling of her needs and desires. Then each month she went over the letters, taking out and giving thanks for those that had been answered.

Within a year her house was sold, on the very plan she herself had outlined in one of her "Letters to God," on the exact basis and for the exact price she had asked in that letter.

Another method is to "Talk with God." Go somewhere where you can be alone and undisturbed for a little while, and talk aloud to God exactly as you would to a loving and understanding Father. Tell Him your needs. Tell Him your ambitions and desires. Describe in detail just what you want. Then thank Him just as you would an earthly father with whom you had had a similar talk and "who had promised you the things you asked for. You will be amazed at the result of such sincere talks.

"My word shall not come back to me void, but shall accomplish that whereunto it was sent." Whatever you can visualize—and BELIEVE in—you can accomplish. Whatever you can see as yours in your mind's eye, you can get. "In the beginning was the Word." In the beginning is the mental image.

Corinne Updegraff Wells had an article in her little magazine "Through Rose Colored Glasses" that illustrates the power of visualizing your ambitions and desires. "Many years ago," she says, "a young girl who lived in a New York tenement was employed by a fashionable Fifth Avenue modiste to run errands, match samples and pull basting threads.

Annie loved her job. From an environment of poverty she had become suddenly and miraculously an inhabitant of an amazing new world of beauty, wealth and fashion. It was thrilling to see lovely ladies arrive in fine carriages, to watch the social elite preen before Madam's big gold framed mirrors.

The little errand girl, in her starched gingham, soon became filled with desire and fired with ambition. She began imagining herself as head of the establishment instead of its most lowly employee. Whenever she passed before mirrors she smiled at a secret reflection she saw of herself, older and more beautiful, a person of charm and importance.

Of course, nobody even suspected the secret existence of this make-believe person. Hugging her precious secret, Annie smiled confidently at that dazzling reflection in the mirror and began playing an exciting game, "I'll pretend I'm already Madam. I'll be polite and look my best and have grand manners and learn something new each day. I'll work as hard and take as much interest as though the shop were really and truly mine."

Soon fashionable ladies began whispering to Madam: "Annie's the smartest girl you've ever had!" Madam herself began to smile and say: "Annie, you may fold Mrs. Vandergilt's gown if you'll be very careful," or, "I'm going to let you deliver this wedding dress," or, "My dear, you're developing a real gift for color and line," and, finally, "I'm promoting you to the work-room."

The years passed quickly. Each day Annie came more and more to resemble the image she alone had seen of herself. Gradually the little errand girl became Annette, an individual; then Annette, stylist; and finally, Madam Annette, renowned costume designer for a rich and famous clientele.

The images we hold steadfastly in our minds over the years are not illusions; they are the patterns by which we are able to mould our own destinies.

> *You never can tell when you do an act*
> *Just what the result will be,*
> *But with every deed you are sowing a seed,*
> *Though the harvest you man not see.*
> *Each kindly act is an acorn dropped*
> *In God's productive soil;*
> *You may not know, but the tree shall grow*
> *With shelter for those who toil.*
>
> *You never can tell what your thought will do*
> *In bringing you hate or love,*
> *For thoughts are things and their airy wings*

Are swifter than carrier doves.
They follow the law of the universe—
Each thing must create its kind,
And the speed o'er the track to bring you back
Whatever went out from your mind.

—ELLA WHEELER WILCOX

"WANTED: RAIN!"

From one to two inches, and free from hail if possible. Is badly needed to save remaining crops and fill the reservoirs. Must be delivered soon to do any good. Will pay highest market price.

Can be delivered any place; prefer general rain. Showers gratefully accepted, but prefer real, honest-to-goodness downpour.

This offer made by the following firms for the general good of the community, and in the general belief that anything worth having, is worth asking for.

BELLE FOURCHE, South Dakota needed one thing— RAIN—to save remaining crops and fill the reservoirs. Why not advertise for it, thought L. A. Gleyre, publisher of THE NORTHWEST POST. A novel idea—advertising to the Lord—never been tried in just that way before, but at least there was no harm in trying. The prayerful advertisement reprinted above was the result.

"We proposed to each merchant in town," says Mr. Gleyre, "that he pay $2.50 for his name at the bottom of the page ad, with the provision that if no material rain fell between the date of the advertisement and the following Tuesday midnight, the ad was entirely at our expense.

The idea took immediately . . . we could probably have filled a double truck. While the week was rolling by, our people had a new one to think about—their minds were actually taken off the scarcity of rain and made to function along the line of whether THE NORTHWEST POST was going to make good with their ad. The majority of our merchants were pleased with the idea. Some actually believed we had some inside information from the weather bureau which prompted our offer. A few, including one or two preachers, while not saying so to us, took occasion to say it was sacrilegious, etc.

During the specified week, light rains fell in some parts of our territory. Belle Fourche had three very light sprinkles—not enough to count, for we agreed that the rain should be a downpour. Toward the end of the week excitement ran rife and interest continued to grow. Some of our warm friends made bets we would win. Others openly hoped we would, while everyone agreed that it would be tremendously helpful if we did win.

We won—but lost. Just six hours after midnight, Wednesday morning, it rained pitch-forks-and-saw-logs-for-handles. It was exactly what we advertised for—a swash-buckling, rip-snortin' downpour of rain. It measured from one-half to two inches, and one remote point reported seven inches of rainfall!

But we didn't charge any merchant a cent. We lost by six hours.

I think it attracted more attention than anything we have done in years. To this day we are asked to advertise for something needed.

Where did that rain come from? Did the advertisement bring it? Does the Rain Dance of the Hopi Indians bring it? Did the prayer of Elijah bring it, as told in the Bible?

Yes! At least, so we believe, and we think we can show you good reason for that belief. Not only that, but we believe that back of these answers to prayer is the fundamental law of life and supply!

For of all the promises of Jesus, there is but one that promises us WHATEVER WE ASK shall be done for us! That one positive assurance is *based on this condition*—"If two of you agree on earth as touching anything they shall ask, it shall be done for them of my Father which is in Heaven."

And again He said—"Where two or three are gathered together in My name, there am I in the midst of them." Why is this? Why the necessity for several to unite in asking for a thing in order to be sure of getting it?

A good many years ago, Professor Henry of Princeton made an experiment with a charged magnet. First he took an ordinary magnet of large size, suspended it from a rafter and with it lifted a few pounds of iron.

Then he wrapped the magnet with wire and charged it with the current from a small battery. Instead of only a few pounds, the now highly charged magnet lifted 3,000 pounds!

That is what happens when one person prays, believing, and another adds his prayers and his faith. In effect, the second person is charging the magnet of the first one with his current, MULTIPLYING the power of the other's prayer a dozen times over.

In "Nautilus" magazine some months ago, Elizabeth Gregg told how five people prayed—agreeing—and the most pressing personal problem of each was soon solved. It seems that the husband of a Mrs. A. had been sick with ulcerated stomach for months. She had prayed repeatedly, without result, so one day she picked four of her friends whom she knew to be badly in need of help in different ways, and got them to agree to meet together on a certain day each week and see if, by uniting their prayers in perfect agreement, they might not improve their condition.

At the first meeting, it was decided to pray for the recovery of Mrs. A.'s husband, so these five women, sitting in silence, mentally pictured the husband strong and well, going about his work in a happy way. Then they gave thanks that their prayer had been answered.

"It was agreed," the article goes on to say, "that promptly at twelve o'clock noon each day until the next meeting, each of the five women would stop whatever she was doing and spend five minutes in silent prayer, agreeing with each other, that the husband be freed from sickness.

Three days after that first meeting, the husband was entirely free from pain. By the end of the week, he was on his way to complete recovery.

Next came the problem of Mrs. B., a widow whose home was to be sold in six weeks for failure to meet her payments. With earnestness and faith the women concentrated at the stated time each day upon the desire that the way would open for her supply. And true to the law, the way did open. Just a day before the week was up a well-to-do lady in the town called and asked Mrs. B. if she would take care of her children, eight and ten, for a few weeks while she, the mother, was away. The sum she offered would take care of the back payments on the home and provide living expenses. Shortly after the lady returned she made arrangements for Mrs. B. to take care of an invalid aunt, which gave the widow a steady and lucrative income.

Next was the problem of Mrs. C, whose husband had been out of work for several months. A few days after the week of agreement was up the husband received a letter from a cousin living at a short distance offering him work in his lumber mill. So, again the law was fulfilled.

Then the case of little Miss D., who for years had been estranged from her family, came under the law for solution. But in this case it was several weeks before any outward sign of fulfillment appeared. However, love had entered the heart of Miss D. during this time and for the first time since the estrangement she gave way to her new feeling and wrote to each of the family asking forgiveness for what she now acknowledged had been intolerance on her part. By return mail came letters from her family, letters also filled with the spirit of love. Thus, for the fourth time in the work of these women did the law work unfailingly.

The last problem was that of Mrs. E., who owned a little dress shop but whose business had been almost ruined since the larger and newer shop just across the street had opened. Envy and hate had filled the heart of Mrs. E. so that she resisted all overtures at friendship which the owner of the new shop had made. Then, from her study of Truth she learned that no one need compete with anyone; that there is full abundance for all when we learn how to claim it. So, instead of envying, she now joined with the others in sending out love and good will to her competitor, as she had called her.

A few weeks later the owner of the new store called and asked if Mrs. E. would take over the management of her store for six months while she was in the East on business. She explained that when she returned it might be advantageous to both of them to form a partnership. This was later done and today Mrs. E. is half owner of a thriving dress and millinery shop and there is perfect harmony between her and the woman she once hated.

Russell Conwell, author of "Acres of Diamonds," tells of dozens of such cases. He tells of a kidnaped child returned unharmed through the power of united prayer; of a lost child found in the same way; of men and women cured of apparently incurable diseases; of businesses saved, of positions won, of love renewed and families reunited. There is no good thing you can ask, believing, that shall not be given you.

"What will you have?" quoth God. "Pay for it and take it." And the paying consists of complying with the law of agreement, by praying–if you pray alone–that the good you are asking for yourself shall be given to all others as well, by "agreeing as to what ye shall ask" if you are praying in a group.

Did you ever read the diary of George Mueller covering the early days of his great work? George Mueller, you know, was the man who started an orphanage with no money in hand, no rich patrons, no prospects–just absolute trust in God. Read the following extracts from his diary and see how that trust was justified:

Nov. 18, 1830. Our money was reduced to about eight shillings. When I was praying with my wife in the morning, the Lord brought to my mind the state of our purse, and I was led to ask Him for some money. About four hours after, a sister said to me, "Do you want any money?" "I told the brethren," said I, "dear sister, when I gave up my salary, that I would for the future tell the Lord only about my wants." She replied, "But He has told me to give you some money." My heart rejoiced, seeing the Lord's faithfulness, but I thought it better not to tell her about our circumstances, lest she should be influenced to give accordingly; and I also was assured that, if it were of the Lord, she could not but give, I therefore turned the conversation to other subjects, but when I left she gave me two guineas.

On March 7. I was again tempted to disbelieve the faithfulness of the Lord, and though I was not miserable, still, I was not so fully resting upon the Lord that I could triumph with joy. It was but one hour after, when the Lord gave me another proof of His faithful love. A Christian lady brought five sovereigns for us.

April 16. This morning I found that our money was reduced to three shillings; and I said to myself, I must now go and ask the Lord earnestly for fresh supplies. But before I had prayed, there was sent from Exeter two pounds, as a proof that the Lord hears before we call.

October 2. Tuesday evening. The Lord's holy name be praised! He hath dealt most bountifully with us during the last three days! The day before yesterday five pounds came in for the orphans. O how kind is the Lord! Always before there has been actual want he has sent help. Yesterday came in one pound ten shillings more. Thus the expenses of yesterday for housekeeping were defrayed. The Lord helped me also to pay yesterday the nineteen pounds ten shillings for the rent.

I saw more clearly than ever that the first great and primary business to which I ought to attend every day was to have my soul happy in the Lord. The first thing to be concerned about was not how much I might serve the Lord, how I might glorify the Lord; but how I might get my soul into a happy state, and how my inner man might be nourished.

REVIEW OF THE YEAR 1838

As to my temporal supplies. The Lord has been pleased to give me during the past year 350 pounds, 4 shillings, 8 pence. During no period of my life has the Lord so richly supplied me. Truly, it must be manifest that, even for this life, it is by far the best thing to seek to act according to the mind of the Lord as to temporal things. We have to make known our need to God in prayer, ask His help, and then we have to believe He will give us what we need. Prayer alone is not enough. We may pray never so much, yet, if we do not *believe* that God will give us what we need, we have no reason to expect that we shall receive what we have asked for.

"In the heart of man a cry, in the heart of God supply." But as Mueller said, prayer alone is not enough. If we do not BELIEVE that God will give us what we ask for, we have no reason to expect that we shall receive it.

How can we cultivate such belief? Jesus gave us the cue. "Unless ye be converted (turned about) and become as a little child, ye shall in no wise enter the Kingdom of Heaven." And again—"Unless a man be born again, he shall not enter the Kingdom."

How can we become as a little child? How can we be born again? The first essential would seem to be to determine what there is about a child that we must imitate. What one thing is universal with all little children? DE-

PENDENCE, is it not? Utter dependence upon those around them, utter faith in them to provide their needs. And the greater the Dependence, the better those needs seem to be supplied.

Take the embryonic child in its mother's womb, for instance. At inception, it measures only .004 centimeters. In nine months, it multiplies in size a billion times. That is what happens to it during its state of most utter dependence. In the next eighteen to twenty-one years, when it comes to depend more and more upon itself, it increases only sixteen times.

Does that mean we should make no effort ourselves? By no means! The admonition given us was—"Work and pray!" And the "work" is emphasized first. But it does mean that when we have done all that is in our power, we can confidently and serenely leave to the Lord whatever else is necessary to the accomplishment of our desire.

Three thousand years ago, there was a poor woman whose husband had just died and left her with two small sons and a heavy burden of debt.

The amount was not much, as debts go today, but when you have not a cent, even a small debt looks big as a mountain. And the widow had nothing at all.

So in the fashion of those days, her creditor purposed to sell her sons into bondage. For even in those semi-barbaric times, property was more valuable than life. The right of human beings to life, liberty and the pursuit of happiness had never even been heard of. So she, having nowhere else to turn, went to the Prophet Elisha, and begged him to help her in her need.

And what do you suppose Elisha did? Took up a collection? Or appealed to the fund for widows and orphans? Not he! "What have you in the house?" he asked.

He believed in using the means at hand, believing that God always provides unlimited supply if we but have the courage and faith to use what we have.

So he merely asked what the widow had to start with, and when told—"Naught save a pot of oil," he bade her borrow vessels from the neighbors *and pour out into them the oil that she had.* In other words, she was to *start the flow.* And it is written that so long as she had vessels to receive it, *the oil kept flowing.*

When the vessels were all filled, Elisha bade her sell the oil and pay her debt, and then start afresh with her sons beside her.

What have YOU *in your house?* When troubles assail you, do you sit back and bemoan your fate, waiting for some friend to help, or do you take stock of what you have, and set to work using it?

You remember the story of the man who came from the hospital after an accident, completely paralyzed. Of all his body, he could move only one finger. In those circumstances, wouldn't you have given up? But he didn't. "If I can move but one finger," he decided, "I'll use it to do more than one finger ever accomplished before!" He did—and lo and behold! In a little while, the fingers next that one began to show life, too. Before many months had passed, he was using every muscle in his body.

I know of a man who lost everything he had in the clothing business. From an expensive apartment, he had to move his family into the poorest rooms in town, where they and their neighbors did not know from one day to another, where the next meal was coming from. They were downcast—yes. But discouraged? No!

He went around to some of his old creditors—got them to trust him for a few knit neckties that they could not sell anywhere else—found a printer who would give him credit for a few hundred envelopes, letterheads and postage—and sent those ties to lists of men culled from the occupational directory of the telephone book. As fast as the money for them came back, he bought more ties and mailed them out, he and his family doing the work of enclosing, addressing and stamping in their cramped little apartment. Before that type of selling became passe, *he had made two hundred thousand dollars out of it.* Yet most men in the same circumstances give up and quit. Life's biggest mistakes, according to Harrington Emerson, is to under-estimate your power to develop and to accomplish. Ella Wheeler Wilcox says:

> *Ships sail east, and ships sail west,*
> *By the very same breezes that blow;*
> *It's the set of the sails, and not the gales,*
> *That determine where they go.*

Success is not a thing—not a guerdon that awaits you at some far-off shrine. Success lies in doing well whatever thing you are doing *now*. It is more a matter of mental attitude than of mental or physical capacity. You have all the fundamentals of it right now. But it is only the USE of them that can make you successful.

"All very well," perhaps you say, "but look at the handicaps I am under. There is Jim Jones, whose father left him a million—and all mine left was some debts to add to my own."

Have you ever read Emerson's comparison of Alaska and Switzerland? Alaska, according to him, is in six respects much better off than Switzerland.

It has tremendous resources of virgin forests; Switzerland has practically none. It has great stores of gold and silver and copper and lead and tin and coal; Switzerland has practically none. It has fisheries—the greatest in the world; Switzerland has none.

It has in proportion to its area, greater agricultural possibilities than Switzerland—over a hundred thousand square miles suitable for agriculture. It has a tremendous seacoast; Switzerland none. And yet if Alaska were supporting the same number of people to the square mile as Switzerland, it would have 120,000,000 inhabitants.

Now the Swiss have marketed what? Natural resources? No! The Swiss are a people who take a block of wood that was worth ten cents and convert it into a carving worth a hundred dollars.

They will take a ton of metal, steel, brass and so on, and put it together in such form as to make it worth several million dollars.

They take cotton thread that they buy from this country at twenty cents a pound, and they convert it into lace worth a couple of thousand dollars a pound.

And because as a nation they have learned the art of utilizing their latent capacities, they have prospered abundantly.

What is the moral? Simply this: It is not money that counts. It is not natural resources. It is the way *you use what you have!* You can succeed with what you have at this moment, if only you learn to use it rightly.

"Ask not for some power that has been denied you. Ask what ability you have which can be made to develop into something worth while. *What is in your hand?*"

"We are too apt to think," says Bruce Barton, "that if we had some other man's equipment or opportunity, we could do great things. Most successful men have not achieved their distinction by having some new talent or opportunity presented to them. They have developed the opportunity that was at hand."

Great successes are simply a group of little successes built one upon another, in much the same way that John MacDonald's first great subway was merely a long line of little cellars—*strung together!* As Professor James put it—

As we become permanent drunkards by so many separate drinks, so we become saints in the moral, and authorities and experts in the practical and scientific spheres, by so many separate acts and hours of working. Let no one have any anxiety about the upshot of his work or education, whatever the line of it may be. If he keeps faithfully busy each hour of the working day, he may safely leave the final result to itself. He can with perfect certainty count on waking some fine morning, to find himself one of the competent ones of his generation, in whatever pursuit he may have singled out.

What makes a great musician? Practice—keeping everlastingly at it until playing becomes second nature. What makes a great artist, a great lawyer, a great engineer, a great mechanic or carpenter? Persevering study and practice. You may have a natural liking for a subject, so the study of it is easier to you than to others, but the big successes in life have seldom been the brilliant men, the natural wonders, the "born orators" or the talented artists. The great successes have been the "grinds."

"A few years ago," said Dr. John M. Thomas, president of Rutgers University, "Rutgers had a student called a 'greasy grind' by some of his classmates. This was S. Parker Gilbert, Agent-General for Reparations under the Dawes plan. He may have been a 'greasy grind,' but at thirty-two he was earning $45,000 a year. And, according to Owen D. Young, Chairman of the Board of Directors of the General Electric Company, Gilbert held for several years the most important political position in the world."

A good many men in and out of college have an idea that to study is foolish. "No one ever gets anywhere from studying," they say. S. Parker Gilbert is only one of thousands of cases that prove to the contrary.

The most important job in the world for you is the one above yours. And the way to get it is to study—to "grind"— until you can put more of knowledge, more of skill, more of initiative into it than any man around you. Only thus can you win success.

Why do so many fail? Because they do not try hard enough, work persistently enough. The doors of opportunity are always closed. They have been since the world began. History tells us of no time when you could walk down a street and find any doors of opportunity standing open and inviting you to come in. Doors that are worth entering are usually closed, but the resolute and courageous knock at those doors, and keep knocking persistently until they are opened.

You remember the parable of the importunate friend:

And He said unto them, Which of you shall have a friend, and shall go unto him at midnight and say unto him, Friend, lend me three loaves; for a friend of mine in his journey is come to me, and I have nothing to set before him?

And he from within shall answer and say, Trouble me not; the door is now shut, and my children are with me in bed; I cannot rise and give thee.

I say unto you, though he will not rise and give him because he is his friend, yet because of his importunity he will rise and give him as many as he needeth.

And I say unto you, Ask, and it shall be given you; seek, and ye shall find; knock and it shall be opened to you.

Why do so many fail to receive that for which they ask? Because they are not importunate enough. They do not convince the God in them that their prayer is something they MUST have. They ask and knock once or twice, and because the door is not immediately opened, they give up in despair. Remember—"He that wavereth is like a wave of the sea, driven with the wind and tossed. Let not that man think that he shall receive anything of the Lord."

If you have faith in God or man or self,
Say so; if not, push back upon the shelf
Of silence all your thoughts till faith shall come.
No one will grieve because your lips are dumb.
                                        —ELLA WHEELER WILCOX

CATALYSTS OF POWER

Doubt not, fear not, work on, and wait;
As sure as dawn shall conquer dark,
So love will triumph over hate,
And Spring will bring again the lark.
                                        —DOUGLAS MALLOCH

Nearly two thousand years before Christ, it was said in the Vedas (the sacred writings of the Hindoos) that if any two people would unite their psychic forces, they could conquer the world, even though singly they could do nothing.

Then came Jesus to tell us even more positively that if two of us agree as touching anything we may ask, it shall be done for us.

Jesus never made any such positive promise of certain results when we pray alone. Why should it be necessary for two to unite their desires or prayers in order to be sure of results? If you add 2 to 2, you get only 4. If you add your muscular power to mine, you can lift only twice as much as either of us could lift alone. Yet if you add your prayers to mine, you get—not merely twice the power, but a hundred or a thousand times as much.

Why should this be? We have the word of many great psychologists that it is so. Judge Troward of England, who was to the British Empire what Professor Wm. James was to America, is authority for the statement, as is

Brown Landone and a score of psychologists of lesser note. What is the reason?

Perhaps the answer lies in what the chemists call CATALYSTS. In chemistry there are certain substances which, when added to others, release many thousands of times as much power as they themselves contain. These catalysts, without losing any of their own energy, multiply the energy in other substances by thousands and sometimes even by millions! Perhaps that is what happens when two or more unite as touching the thing they shall pray for. Perhaps one is a CATALYST, multiplying the power of the other by thousands upon thousands of times. Certain it is that even Jesus, when those about Him were not in sympathy with Him and did not believe in Him, as on the occasion of His visit to Nazareth, worked no mighty works. Perhaps that is why, when He sent out His disciples to heal the sick, He sent them out "two by two."

Be that as it may, one thing is sure: If two or more of you will get together for a minute or two each day, and really agree as touching the thing you shall ask and the way you shall ask for it, you will get amazing results. Mind you, it is not enough to merely pray together for the same thing. You must unite your thought. You may ask me to pray with you that you may be healed of an ulcerated stomach, and when we pray, you may be picturing those sores and thinking of the pain and trouble they have been causing, while I am picturing the perfect organ that God gave you. That is not uniting our forces. That is setting them in opposition. We must both think health. We must both see in our mind's eye the thing we WANT—not the one we fear or wish to be rid of.

The same is true of debts. You may be thinking of all the money you owe, of the mortgage that is falling due, of the cut in pay you had to take, while I am trying to help you by thinking of the Infinite Supply that God is sending you. We'll never accomplish much that way. We've BOTH got to think of and visualize RICHES—not debts or lack. We've got to remember that the debts or other wrong conditions are merely the LACK of riches or health or other good thing, and that when we provide the good, the evil disappears as naturally as darkness disappears when you turn on the light. So what we must think of and see in our mind's eye is the light—i.e. the riches or the perfect health or the love or other good thing we desire.

If two can unite in doing that, there is no good thing they can ask, believing, that they cannot get. In the preceding chapter, we quoted the article by Elizabeth Gregg in "Nautilus," telling how five women prayed together, and every prayer was answered. And in Chapter Five, we told of a similar group in Russell Conwell's church who accomplished even more marvelous results through united prayer. You have problems too great to be solved by you alone. And you have friends with problems that they are unable to handle. Why not get together and unite your forces? Why not meet for fifteen minutes once a week, talk over your difficulties, decide upon the case that seems most pressing, and then at a certain time each day, all of you drop whatever you are doing and give a minute or two to uniting your thought and your prayers? You CAN do it, and you will be amazed at the power of your united prayers. There is nothing of good you can ask, believing, that cannot and will not be done for you.

> No star is ever lost we once have seen.
> We always may be what we might have been.

THE FIRST COMMANDMENT

If with pleasure you are viewing
   Anything a man is doing,
If you prize him, if you love him,
   Tell him now.
Don't withhold your approbation
   Until the Parson makes oration
And he lies with many lilies on his brow.

For no matter how you shout it
   He won't really know about it,
He won't count the many teardrops
   That you shed.
If you think some praise is due him,
   Now's the time to pass it to him.
For he cannot read his tombstone when he's dead.

What shall I do to be saved?" asked the rich young man of Jesus 1900 years ago. And today most of us are asking essentially the same question—"What shall I do to be saved from poverty and sickness and unhappiness, here and now as well as in the hereafter?"

"Keep the commandments!" was the Master's answer to the rich man. And later, when asked—"What is the greatest commandment," He told His hearers: "Thou shalt love the Lord thy God with all thy heart, and with all they soul, and with all thy mind: *This is the first and great commandment. And the second* is like unto it. Thou shalt love thy neighbor as thyself. On these two commandments hang all the Law and the Prophets."

Sounds simple enough, but just what is "loving God"? Is it going to Church and being a professed Christian? Or is it simply BEING THANKFUL AND HAPPY!

Going to Church and being an example to your neighbors is excellent, but is there any way in which you can show your love for God better than by being happy? Happiness implies praise, satisfaction with what God has done, thankfulness for His good gifts. Happiness means that you are enjoying life, appreciating it to the full, radiating joy to all about.

And loving your neighbor is just making him happy, too—praising him and blessing him and doing what you can to help him.

Can you think of any commandment, any law, that would do as much towards universal peace, towards settling the strife between labor and capital, towards bringing the millennium, as these two?

1. Be thankful and happy yourself.
2. Try to make your neighbor happy.

"On these two commandments hang all the Law and the Prophets."

Someone has wisely said that the first step towards universal peace is to have peace in our own hearts—to wish our neighbors well, to bless and praise even those who have used us despitefully. Evelyn Gage Browne expressed the thought when she wrote—

> This old world needs the tender touch,
> The kindly word, the lifting hand,
> The love that blesses us so much,
> And friendly hearts that understand.

It is said that a woman once went to Krishna and asked him how to find the love of God. "Who do you love most?" he inquired. "My brother's child," she answered. "Go back and love him more," advised Krishna. She did so, and lo! Behind the boy, she saw the form of the Christ child.

The same thought is expressed in the old legend of the group that went out to find the Christ child. There were knights and great ladies and monks and clergymen and all manner of people, and among the latter was a kindly old shoemaker. Everyone laughed at the idea of his going out when so many of the great ones of the earth were ahead of him. But after they had all come back disappointed, the bent little shoemaker walked joyfully in, accompanied by the Christ child himself.

"Where did you find Him?" they asked. And the Christ Child answered for him—"I hid myself in common things. You failed to find me because you did not look with the eyes of love."

Millions of books have been written about love, but most of them know not even the meaning of the word. To them, love is passion, self-gratification. Real love is not that. Real love is GIVING. It seeks only the good of the loved one. Yet in giving love freely, you get it, for it is like energy in that it expands only as it is released. It is like a seed in that it multiplies only when you sow it. As Ella Wheeler Wilcox put it—

> Give love, and love to your heart will flow,
> A strength in your utmost need;
> Have faith and a score of hearts will show
> Their faith in your word and deed.

Carlyle defined wealth as the number of things a man loves and blesses, which he is loved and blessed by.

Who are the unhappiest creatures on earth? Not the poor or the sick—but those who keep all their love for themselves. They may be worth millions, they may have dozens of servants to attend to their every want, but they are bored to extinction. They are miserable. Why? Because they have stopped giving, and as the words of a beautiful hymn express it—

> For we must share, if we would keep
> That blessing from above.
> Ceasing to give, we cease to have—
> Such is the Law of Love.

Life is expansion, mentally and physically. When you stop growing, you die. That is literally true in the case of your body cells, and figuratively true mentally, for when you cease to progress mentally, you are as good as dead. The undertaker may not call for a year or two, but so far as useful purposes are concerned, you might as well be buried.

And just as life is action, so is happiness service. For in helping and praising others and making them happy, you win happiness for yourself. Charles Kingsley once said that we knew our relations to God only through our relations with each other. No man can love God while he hates his neighbor. No man can love God while he is himself unhappy or deliberately makes another unhappy.

To be unhappy implies a criticism of God. An unhappy man cannot be grateful, he cannot be trustful, he cannot be at peace—and without these, how can he love God?

Yet if he lives only for himself, he is bound to be unhappy. "For whosoever shall save his life shall lose it," said the Master. "But whosoever shall lose his life for My sake, the same shall save it." He who loses himself in the service of others shall find therein life and love and happiness.

Longfellow tells of sending first an arrow into the air, and then a song, and seeming to lose them. But presently he found the arrow in an oak tree, and the song, from beginning to end, he found in the heart of a friend.

"He prayeth well," wrote Coleridge, "who loveth well both man and bird and beast.

> He prayeth best, who loveth best
> All things both great and small;
> For the dear God who loveth us,
> He made and loveth all.

When Jane Addams graduated from college, the doctors told her she had only six months to live. If a doctor told you that, what would you do? Most of us would simply sit down and die, and feel very sorry for ourselves in the doing of it.

Not so Jane Addams. "If I have only six months to live," she said, "I'll use those six months to do just as much as I can of the things I want most to do for humanity."

And she so lost herself in the work that she forgot to die. Eight years after the time predicted for her demise, she started Hull House, the Chicago settlement that is known the world over. Not only that, but her health was as good or better than that of the doctors who had prophesied her end.

Everyone has heard of Luther Burbank and of the marvelous success he had in growing things. He could take even a prickly cactus plant and from its shoots grow a plant without thorns or prickers, from which cattle could get sustenance on even the dryest soil.

How did he work such wonders with all manner of growing things? Through the magic of love! He blessed each little plant, he praised and nursed and loved it. And the life in it responded by giving him such results as no man before him had ever dreamed of. Here is the message that Luther Burbank sent to his friends on his last birthday:

As you hold loving thoughts toward every person and animal and even toward plants, stars, oceans, rivers and hills, and as you are helpful and of service to the world, so you will find yourself growing more happy each day, and with the happiness comes health and everything you want.

"Love and you shall be loved," said Emerson. "All love is mathematically just, as much as the two sides of an algebraic equation." The old philosopher who said—"Take out of life anything you want, *and pay for it,*" stated an eternal truth. You get as you give. It is well to remind one's self of this frequently by repeating now and then, when inclined to be disturbed by seeming difficulties—"I so love that I see all good and give all good, *and all good comes back to me.*"

The most universal desire in all the world is man's natural desire for happiness. It is the purpose of existence. It is God's plan—to make man WIN happiness through struggle and service, through adding to the happiness of others.

Why is it that a moving-picture actor makes a thousand times as much as a teacher, or as an average business man or even a clergyman? Because he makes many thousand times as many people happy. He enables them to forget their troubles, to live their ideals, their dreams, through his picturing of them. When the rest of us find some way to make as many people happy, we shall share in like rewards.

A long time ago, Emerson wrote—"He who addresses himself to modes and wants that can be dispensed with, builds his house off the road. But he who addresses himself to problems every man must come to solve, builds $$$ house on the road, and every man must come to it."

Just ask yourself—What have I to GIVE that will add to the happiness of those around me? You will be surprised how many simple little ways of brightening the lives of others will present themselves, and how great the reward these ways can bring, when multiplied by hundreds or thousands.

A man down in Washington was too poor to buy his child toys, yet he wanted above everything to make that child happy. So with his pocket-knife, he carved out of discarded pieces of lumber a rough sort of Kiddie-car. It made such a hit, not only with his own youngster but with every child around, that he took it to a manufacturer and made a fortune out of it.

Years ago, a young veterinary over in England had a mother who was confined to a wheel chair. To soften the jolts for her, he fastened a strip of rubber around the iron tires. Those strips of rubber, through constant improvement, developed into the famous Dunlop tire, which have sold by the million.

There are similar stories to be found by the hundred. The only limit to your opportunities is the limit of human happiness. And that has not yet been reached.

"My husband died a short time ago," writes a poor, harassed widow, "leaving his estate so involved that it looks as though we shall lose everything. What can I do? I have two young children to clothe and feed and educate, and I've never made a penny in my life. Tell me, is it wrong to pray for death, for I don't know what else we can do?"

Is it wrong to pray for death? What do *you* think? Is praying for death showing love for God, confidence in Him? What did the Prophet of old, in similar case? "My husband is dead," wailed the widow to Elisha, "and the creditor is come to take unto him my two sons to be bondmen." Did Elisha demand that God rain down gold upon her? On the contrary—he asked what she had in the house, and with it he helped her to win her own salvation.

Read the story of Mary Elizabeth, and you will find an almost exact parallel. A widow with three children, no money, and the creditor "Poverty" demanding those children for bondservants. But the oldest of them asked herself—"What have we in the house?"—and found an ability to make others happy through delicious candy. Today the whole family is independently wealthy.

> You have no talent? Say not so.
> A weaker brother you can lift
> And by your strength help him to go
> Renewed and blessed—this is your gift.

> No talent? Some one needs a word
> Of courage, kindness, love, and cheer—
> Which only you can speak—to gird
> His spirit against grief and fear.

> Yours is a special gift that none
> But you can use. Oh, lift your heart!
> So much of good will be undone
> Unless you do your own great part.

> You are God's helper day by day;

He comforts, guides, and speaks through you;
He needs just you in this blest way.
No talent? Oh, that is not true!
                    —EVELYN GAGE BROWNE

The ancient Greeks had a legend that all things were created by love. Everyone was happy, because love was everywhere, and each vied with the other to make those around him happy.

Then one night while love slept, fear crept in, and with it came disease and lack and all unhappiness. For where love attracts, fear repels. Where love gives freely, fear is afraid there will not be enough for all, so holds on to everything it has.

What was the knowledge of good and evil against which God warned Adam in the Garden? Wasn't it a knowledge of things *to fear?*

In the second chapter of Genesis, we are told that Adam and Eve were naked and were not ashamed. Why? Because they knew no evil—therefore they feared no evil.

But they ate of the Tree of Knowledge of good and evil. They learned about evil. They hid themselves in the Garden in fear of evil. And immediately evil things began to happen to them, and have continued happening to their descendants ever since.

In the Garden of Eden, everything was abundance. The earth gave of its fruit bountifully. Then man learned fear. And having been given dominion over the earth, his fear reacted upon it. He feared it would hold back its fruits. He feared there would not be enough for all. He feared the snake and the wild animal, which before had been docile to his love.

What was the result? Instead of giving of its abundance gladly, he had to wrest its fruits from the earth. Instead of the luscious fruits and herbs of the Garden, the earth gave him the product of his fears—thorns and thistles. Instead of friendship between him and the beasts of the forest, there was the natural fruit of fear—suspicion and enmity.

From the time he ate of the Tree of Knowledge of Good and Evil, man has reaped the fruits of fear. And as long as his belief in evil holds, he will continue to reap the fruits of fear.

God is love. And what is the first characteristic of love? *To give.* God is constantly giving to us *all that we will accept.*

But that is, alas, woefully little. For the first characteristic of fear is to shut up every opening, whether of income or outgo. Fear repels. Fear holds on to what it has, lest it should be unable to get more. Fear takes only what it can grab. It will not open its doors and let good come in. It is too much afraid of evil.

The result is that good comes to us through fear only after great struggle and suffering, even though the good be all the time trying to manifest itself. It is like a fortress built upon the highest peak of a great mountain. It is so fearful of evil coming to it that it has put itself as far as possible away from good as well.

Love opens the petals of the flowers and the leaves of all growing things to the sun, giving freely of its fragrance, and thereby draws to itself every element it needs for growth and fruition.

Love asks—What have we in the house that will make others happy?—and thereby attracts to itself everything necessary for its own happiness.

What is the first and greatest commandment? To give out love, to make the world a happier place than you found it. Do that, and you cannot keep happiness from coming to you, too.

"I often wonder," says Andrew Chapman, "why people do not make more of the marvelous power there is in Kindness. It is the greatest lever to move the hearts of men that the world has ever known—greater by far than anything that mere ingenuity can devise, or subtlety suggest. Kindness is the kingpin of Success in life; it is the prime factor in overcoming friction and making the human machinery run smoothly. If a man is your enemy, you can not disarm him in any other way so surely as by doing him a kind act."

THE LADY OR THE TIGER

In ancient times, it is said that there lived a king whose methods of administering justice were original in the extreme.

He built a huge arena to seat himself and all his people. Under it, he put two doors. When a culprit was brought before him, accused of any crime, the king gave him his choice of which door he would open. If the accused man chose the right door, there came forth from it a beautiful lady, who was forthwith wed to him. But if he chose the wrong door, there came out of it a fierce and hungry tiger, which immediately tore him to pieces.

The king had a beautiful daughter, and upon a time it came to pass that a handsome young courtier fell in love with her and she with him. That was a grievous crime, for it did not at all suit the king's plans that his daughter should marry a commoner, no matter how well favored he might be. So the poor suitor was promptly clapped into a cell, and informed that on the morrow he must stand trial in the arena like any common culprit.

The princess was heartbroken. She tried prayers, she tried tears, but her father was adamant. Any common man who dared lift his eyes to her deserved death, and death he should have—death, or marriage to someone in his own station.

Failing to move her father, the princess tried the guards. But no amount of gold would persuade them to free her lover. This much she did accomplish, though—she learned from which door the tiger would come, from which the lady. More, she learned who the lady was, and horror of horrors, it was one she had seen more than once casting amorous glances at her lover!

The morning found her torn between love and jealousy. She could not see her lover killed before her eyes—and yet, would it not be better to suffer that moment of agony, and be able to remember him as loving only her, than to see him day after day in the arms of another, see the triumph in that other's eyes, see his own eyes turn away from her to the beauty in his arms?

As in a dream, she took her place on the dais at her father's right hand. As in a dream, she saw her lover step forth, saw him look to her for a sign, saw herself signal to him to choose the right hand door—then hid her face that she might see no more.

Which had she chosen—the Lady or the Tiger? Which would you choose in like circumstances? Judging from the newspapers of the day, all too many, even in our so-called civilization, would choose the tiger. Why? Because they would rather see their lover dead than in the arms of another. Their idea of love is passion, self-gratification, and if they can't have their loved one for themselves, they don't want anyone else to have him, regardless of how he or the other may suffer.

At some time and in one modified form or another, that choice of the Lady or the Tiger comes to most people, and your answer depends solely upon what kind of love yours is. If it is real love, you will not hesitate for a moment, for real love is selfless and free from all fear. (And that is all jealousy is—*fear!*) Real love gets its happiness from giving. It lavishes itself upon the object of its affections without thought of return. And by its very prodigality, it brings back real love to itself.

For love is a magnet. Like the magnet of iron which gives off electricity, by its very giving it draws to itself its own. And again like the iron magnet, when its strength is done, when all power has gone out of it, it has only to rub against a stronger magnet to be renewed!

What is it that makes men and women fall in love? Not beauty; that attracts attention. But love requires more than beauty. Love requires personality, *charm*, MAGNETISM!

And what is magnetism? What but the power you GIVE OUT! It is vitality, it is abounding interest in people and things, it is LOVE!

You cannot be self-centered and still give out magnetism. You cannot think only of the gratification of your own desires and still expect to win or hold another's love.

Love gives out a current of love, and all who come within its aura are attracted to it. Selfishness, jealousy, hate, are like layers of insulation around a magnet. They not only shut off all love from going out, but they keep any from getting in. A selfish man, a jealous man, an angry man, has no magnetism. He repels everyone he comes in contact with. He has shut off his own current, and insulated himself against any from the outside.

I remember reading a story of a man who had become involved in a serious law-suit. He was bitter and resentful, for he felt that his opponents had been most unfair and unjust. But the suit was apparently going against him.

He went to a teacher of the mental sciences and laid his case before him. The teacher told him he would never get anywhere with his case until he rid himself of his resentment and hatred. "Bless your opponents," he advised. "Know that in some way not yet apparent they are doing you a favor. Say to yourself, whenever thoughts of resentment creep in—'I live by the law of love.' And then try to do just that."

The man tried it, and found that he could not keep saying and using this affirmation without its affecting everything he did. There came a most unexpected opportunity to do a great favor for his opponents. Reluctantly he did it, and lo and behold, it opened the way to a fair settlement of the whole case—a settlement that proved eventually far more profitable to him than winning the case would have done.

"Doubt not, fear not, work on and wait; as sure as dawn shall conquer dark, so love will triumph over hate." So writes Douglas Malloch, and in a recent issue of "Nautilus" magazine, Sonia Shand tells of a "Love Game" which bears out the same idea.

It is based, she says, on Shakespeare's "Taming of the Shrew." You remember, in the play, no matter what Katharine said or did, Petruchio acted as though she were falling in with his wishes, and the more contrary she became, the more he would praise her for her sweet submission to his every wish. Well, this game is as simple as that. No matter what happens during the time you are playing your game of Love, you smile and say it is good and wonderful.

Whether a feared bill collector comes blustering to your door, or the neighbors' children pull up your favorite flowers, or any one of the hundred annoying things that are part of your daily existence happen, just smile and give thanks for them as though they were great blessings instead of annoying trials.

Release the feeling of love toward each and every annoying thing as though it were the best that ever happened to you. You will be amazed at the results that come from this little game, because in love, no matter how tiny the grain of it, there is unlimited power for good, and it is never wasted.

You have heard the old adage that a soft answer turneth away wrath. This game has the same principle incorporated in it, with a lot more added to it. Nonresistance is one thing, but by itself it is negative. Add your praise and blessings to it, and you turn it into a positive force for good.

To love all things is our natural heritage. It was what made Adam and Eve so happy in the Garden of Eden. The snake of Fear crept into their hearts and turned them out of Eden, but we can each of us get back in if we will use the game of Love.

Try it. And while you are playing it, be sure to glorify *yourself*. See yourself as the perfect individual you always had hoped some day to become. Be the charming, gracious, noble self, who is raised by the powers of Love to a level above all sordid, petty, annoying and ugly things of life. Be that for one hour each day, and you will be amazed how quickly you will be that all the day.

You can use this Love Game in the home, in business, in whatever you are doing and wherever you are working.

If you are a business man, perhaps worried by a heavy load of debts and obligations, bless your creditors with the thought of abundance as you begin to accumulate the wherewithal to pay off your obligations. Keep the faith they had in you by including them in your prayer for increase. Begin to free yourself at once by doing all that is possible with the means you have, and as you proceed in this spirit the way will open for you to do more. For through the avenues of Spirit, more means will come to you and every obligation will be met.

If you are a creditor, be careful of the kind of thoughts you hold over your debtor. Avoid the thought that he is unwilling to pay you or that he is unable to pay you. One thought holds him to be dishonest and the other holds him to be subject to lack, and either of them tends to close the door to the possibility of his paying you soon.

Declare abundant supply for both creditors and debtors, and thus help them to prosper. Pray and work for their good as well as for your own, for yours is inseparable from theirs. You owe your debtor quite as much as he owes you and yours is a debt of love. Pay your debt to him and he will pay his to you.

Take anything in your life that seems not to be going well, and give a few minutes each day to "treating" it. Remind yourself first that harmony and true success are the Divine purpose of your life, that there are no exceptions to this law, therefore this particular difficulty must come under it. That being so, this thing that troubles you cannot be inharmonious or negative, once you know the truth about it. Know, therefore, the truth must be that in some way this difficulty is working out for your good, that beneath its hard and ugly outer shell, there is a kernel of perfect good for you. So bless the good within.

How does the kernel of the black walnut break its tough shell and send up a green shoot that presently grows into a great tree? By heating within! And that is the way you have to break the shell of every difficulty and trial that confronts you—by BLESSING the kernel of good you know to be within it, by praising and loving it until it expands and bursts its shell and springs forth as the fragrant plant of good for you.

Praise, blessing, thanksgiving, LOVE—these will solve any difficulty, tame any shrew of sickness or trouble. Start each day by saying—"This is the day which Jehovah hath made; I will rejoice and be glad in it. I thank God for abundant life, I thank God for enduring love. I thank God for joy, I thank God for glorious health, I thank God for infinite supply. I have awakened to a new day. I join the birds and all created things in glorious praise and thanksgiving. Lord, I do give Thee thanks for the abundance that is mine."

> If I have faltered more or less
> In my great task of happiness;
> If I have moved among my race
> And shown no glorious morning face;
> If beams from happy human eyes
> Have moved me not; if morning skies,
> Books and my food, and summer rain
> Knocked on my sullen heart in vain;
> Lord, Thy most pointed pleasure take
> And stab my spirit broad awake.
>
> —ROBERT LOUIS STEVENSON

EXERCISE FOR CHAPTER THIRTEEN

Remember, in "Vanity Fair," the owner of a fine estate who always carried acorns in his pocket, and when strolling about his grounds, if he came to a vacant spot, he would dig a little hole with his foot and drop an acorn into it. "An acorn costs nothing," he was fond of saying, "but it may spread into a prodigious bit of timber."

The same is true of words of praise, of blessing. They cost nothing, but when planted in the waste places of human consciousness, they become tremendously productive of happiness. As Willa Hoey expressed it—

> *It's the little things we do and say*
> *That mean so much as we go our way.*
> *A kindly deed can lift a load*
> *From weary shoulders on the road,*
> *Or a gentle word, like summer rain,*
> *May soothe some heart and banish pain.*
> *What joy or sadness often springs*
> *rom just the simple, little things!*

Write it on your heart that each day is the best day of the year. There is no tomorrow, you know; there is no yesterday. There is only the eternal NOW. So make the most of your happiness *now*, while you can.

You create your own environment, so only YOU are to blame if some existing situation seems unhappy. That being so, only YOU can rectify it. You must cure it in your own thought before it can be remedied anywhere else. "Nothing is evil, but thinking makes it so."

Instead of thinking unhappy thoughts, sickly thoughts, thoughts of poverty and lack, talk to the God in You about the good things you want. Start with what you have, and suggest to him each day that you are getting stronger, healthier, richer, happier. Talk to Him as to a rich and loving Father, describing the improvements you see in your affairs, the finer body you have in your mind's eye, the more important work you should be doing, the lovelier home, the richer rewards. Talk them over for ten minutes each day when you are alone with Him. You will be amazed at how readily He will help you to carry out your suggestions.

Don't worry about how He is to bring about the conditions you desire. Just talk to Him confidently, serenely, happily—and then leave the rest to Him. And for your prayers, here is an affirmation used by Unity which has been found unusually effective:

"My Father-God, I place all my dependence in Thee, Thou giver of every good and perfect gift. Thou who art the source of my being art also the source of my supply. All that I shall ever need is in Thy mind for me, prepared for me from the beginning. Omnipresent substance, the garment with which Thou clothest Thy universe, with which Thou nourishest all Thy creation, is also mine to have and to use for my every desire and for the blessing of others of Thy children. I open myself fully through my faith in Thee, through my vision of Thy abundance, through my expectancy of its manifestation for me. I open my hands, my pocketbook, my wardrobe, my business, my bank account, and from Thy rich storehouse Thou dost fill every vessel that I hold out to Thee full to overflowing with Thine own omnipresent good and in Thine own good measure, pressed down, shaken together, running over. I thank

Thee, my Father-God, that through the Christ in me I can touch Thine omnipresent substance and all my world be clothed with Thy opulence. I praise and give thanks that now and throughout eternity I am one with Thee and that in this union all Thine is mine and mine is Thine forever and ever."

Throughout this book, we shall give you numbers of affirmations to use for different conditions. Don't try to use them all at once. Use one until it becomes so familiar that you find yourself repeating it too parrotlike. Then change to another. All are helpful. The mere statement—"I am good," "I am strong," "I am capable," is an upbuilding affirmation that tends to start your subconscious trying to bring about that condition in you, just as negative statements such as "I am poor or sick" tend to make those conditions true. So try to remember always to PRAISE God in every thing and every condition that confronts you. Praise Him and look for the Divinity in each.

Praise God that Good is everywhere;
Praise to the Love we all may share—
The Life that thrills in you and me;
Praise to the Truth that sets us free.

THE THREE LAWS OF LIFE

For thousands of years, philosophers have wrangled over the problem of why men without scruple or conscience should so often succeed, while good men of equal ability fail. Some tell us it is because the wicked have their innings in this world and will suffer for it through eternity, while we shall have our turn at happiness and plenty then. That is a bit unsatisfying, especially when those near and dear to us are suffering for lack of things we should be able to give them. But for many, it has to suffice.

But not for all! A few have learned that there are definite laws governing success—just as definite and just as certain of results as the laws of Physics.

These basic laws govern everything you do. They rule all of mankind, whether mankind likes it or not. They are unlike man-made laws in that they govern high and low alike. They defer neither to rich nor to poor, to weak nor to powerful—only to those with an understanding heart. It was with them in mind that the wisest of ancient kings bade us seek first understanding, and all things else would be added to us. Summed up, those laws are:

1. *The Law of Averages*, under which man in the mass is no better off than the animals, his chances of happiness and success in life but little better than one in a hundred.

2. *The Law of Tendency*, which is towards Life-GIVING. To the extent that a man allies himself with this great fundamental force of nature, to that extent he improves his chances for success.

3. *The Law of Capillary Attraction*, which gives to every nucleus the power to draw to itself those things necessary for its growth and fulfillment. It is through this third law that man is able to rise above the Law of Averages. It is by using it with the Law of Tendency that he is able to reach any height, attain any goal.

Under the Law of Averages, man in the mass is subject to alternate feast or famine, happiness or misery—just as the animals are. Nature seems carelessly profligate. She brings forth enough fish to choke the sea—then lets the many die that the few may live. She gives life with a prodigal hand— then seems entirely careless of it, letting the mass suffer or perish so long as the few survive.

To man she has given inexhaustible riches—but the few have most of it while the many toil to serve them.

That is Nature's Law of Averages in the animal kingdom. That is Nature's Law of Averages for man in the mass. But for man the individual she reserves a different fate.

As long as he chooses to be governed by the Law of Averages, man must be content with his one chance in a hundred of prosperity and happiness. But let him separate himself from the mass, and he can choose his own fate.

And the way to separate himself from the mass is—not to journey to some desert or forgotten isle, not to mew himself up in a solitary cell—but to hitch his wagon to the star of some strong purpose, and thereby pull himself out of the mass of self-centered, self-seeking, merely animal humanity, and ally himself with the great fundamental Law of the Universe, which carries all mankind upon its crest.

The word "Man," you know, means steward or distributor. The purpose of man here on earth is to utilize and distribute God's good gifts. To the extent that he cooperates in this purpose, he is allying himself with the forces behind all of nature. To the extent that he looks out only for his own selfish ends, he is opposing it. "I came," said Jesus, "that they might have life, and have it more abundantly." And He demonstrated His mission by giving more of life to all who sought it.

And what is "Life"? Life is energy. Life is power. Life is supply. Life is the creative force out of which the world and everything in it was made in the beginning, and is made now.

As I see Him, God is the Life-Principle which permeates and directs the universe. His "sons" are the individual subconscious minds or Spiritual Selves back of each of us, pouring Life into us, guiding and governing (to the extent we permit them) all the complicated functions of our bodies, all our outward circumstances and conditions.

These "sons" are like vast Genii, possessing all riches, all happiness, all wisdom on their own plane, but forced to reflect those God-like gifts upon the material plane only as we (their mirrors) can understand and express them.

They pour their Life-Energy through us in a continuous stream, like the strips of steel that are fed into stamping machines in a steel mill. Going in, it is potential life, potential power, potential riches. But like the strips of steel, coming out it is only what we have expressed through it— what our stamping machine (our innermost beliefs) has impressed upon it.

Whatever we truly believe, whatever we love and bless and hold constantly in thought as our own, it brings into being in our lives, in our bodies, in our circumstances. Like light shining through a prism it is broken up into its component colors in passing through our conscious minds. But like the prism, our minds can be darkened by fear and worry to shut off all the happier colors. It is a perfect stream of Life-Energy that starts through us, but just as a poorly made die in a stamping machine can cut crude and ugly patterns on the best of steel, just as a faulty prism can turn beams of sunshine into shadows, so can your beliefs turn perfect Life-Energy into manifestations of sickness and poverty and misery. God does not inflict them upon you—you do.

The first essential, then, is to change the pattern—to watch your beliefs as the Director of the U. S. Mint watches the molds which cast the coins he turns out. Instead of picturing the things you FEAR, and thus stamping their mold upon the Life-Energy passing through you, picture the conditions you WANT. "What things soever ye ask for when ye pray," said Jesus, "believe that ye RECEIVE them, and ye shall HAVE them!"

What do YOU want? Know that your spiritual self HAS it. Like the perfect flower in the tiny unopened bud, it is all there, needing only the sunshine of your faith to bring it forth.

You have seen trees in the winter, all the twigs bare, with no sign of the brilliant foliage soon to spring from them. Yet the leaves are already there, perfectly formed, waiting only for the warm sunshine to bring them out. In the same way, the things YOU want are already around you, no matter how bare everything may look. They need only the sunshine of your faith to bring them forth.

That is the first step, *to have faith!* That is the pattern which molds all your circumstances—*your beliefs.* Get that pattern right. It is there that unscrupulous men get ahead of their less understanding brethren. Knowingly or unknowingly, they have hit upon the fact that the first essential of material success is to believe in themselves, believe that the world belongs to them, believe that it *owes* them a living. They may not knowingly BLESS the things they want, but they LOVE them, long for them, put them above everything else in life, and since God is love, it sometimes seems that we have only to love a thing greatly to get it.

To that extent, they are right. Their trouble is that they do not bother to look around for right sources from which to draw their supply. They take whatever is not nailed down, and sooner or later they run afoul of the Law of Tendency and end in ruin.

This Law of Tendency is our next step, for it *requires co-operation* with the Life-Giving forces of the universe— *swimming with the tide.*

The Law of Tendency is based upon the fact that the whole purpose of Life is growth. The forces of nature are Life-GIVING forces. Its fundamental trends are towards the advancement of life, the good of the world. Those businesses and those individuals whose work is in line with that tendency are swept forward by the great tide of good. Those whose work tends to hinder the forward movement of life are sooner or later brushed aside and cast upon the rocks.

Ella Wheeler Wilcox expressed the thought beautifully when she wrote—The world has a thousand creeds, and never a one have I, Nor church of my own, though a million spires are pointing the way on high.

But I float on the bosom of faith, that bears me along like a river:

And the lamp of my soul is alight with love, for life, and the world and the Giver.

"But," I can hear you say, "I know many worthy men whose efforts were always for good, yet who are hopeless failures." True—but so do I know many swimmers who cannot keep afloat a hundred yards, even with the strongest tide behind them. The tide is the second step. The first step is to get your pattern right—in other words, learn how to swim. And having the tide with you makes that first step none the less necessary.

Believe in yourself. Look upon yourself as one of the Lords of the Universe. Know that it belongs to you. BELIEVE THAT YOU *HAVE* the things you want. Love them. Bless them. Thank God for them, even before they seem manifest. "Lord, I do give Thee thanks for the abundance that is mine."

That is the first essential. The second is to USE your powers for good—*get on the side of the* Life-GIVING *forces.*

"Sounds well," perhaps you will say, "but I'd like you to tell me how I am going to use riches for good, when my principal reason for taking this course is to learn how to GET riches to keep the wolf from my own door!"

The first essential in the creation of anything—be it a house or an automobile or a fortune—is the mental picture or image. Before God made man, He "imaged" him—He formed a mental picture of him. Then He poured His Life-Energy into that image, and it became man. Before an architect builds a house, he draws a mental picture of it, he "images" it upon paper. Then he pours materials and energy into that image and it becomes a house. Before you can build a fortune, you must form it in your mind's eye. You must "image" it on the mental plane, and in that mental image you must think of it as already yours. In other words, "believe that you HAVE it!" An easy way to do this is the "Treasure Mapping" outlined in Chapter 10.

One of the startling facts of modern science is that this universe is not a finished product. Creation is going on all around us—new worlds being formed, cosmic energy taking shape in a million different molds.

But a far more startling fact to most of us is that WE ARE CREATORS, and that we can form today the world we personally shall be living in tomorrow.

People blame their environment, their education, their opportunities, their luck, for their condition. They are wrong. There is one person to blame—and only one— THEMSELVES. They are today the result of their thoughts of yesterday and the many yesterdays that preceded it. They are forming today the mold for what they will be in the years to come.

For there is no such thing as failure. Whether you are poor and sickly, or rich and strong, you have succeeded in one thing. You have compressed the cosmic energy about you into the mold that you held before the mind's eye of your inner self. You have named the forces that worked with you "good" or "bad," and as you named them, so have they been to you as servants—Good, or Evil.

But there is a happy ending. You don't need to leave things as they are. If you don't like the present results you can rename those servants. You can bless and praise the good, no matter how tiny it may seem, and by your praise and blessing, you can expand it a thousand-fold.

Which brings us to the third step—"The Law of Capillary Attraction."

Plant a seed of corn in the ground, and it will attract to itself from the earth and the water and the air everything it needs for its growth. Plant the seed of a desire in your mind and it forms a nucleus with power to attract to itself everything needed for its fulfillment. But just as the seed of corn needs sunshine and air and water from which to draw the energies necessary to bring forth the perfect ear, so does your seed of desire need the sunshine of a perfect faith, the fruitful soil of a will-power held steadfast to the one purpose.

This is the Alpha and Omega of all accomplishment— that every seed has in it the perfect plant, that every right desire has in it the perfect fulfillment, for Desire is God's opportunity knocking at your door. The seed must be planted, it must have nourishment and sunshine. The desire must be definitely planted by the work of starting the initial step in its accomplishment, it must be nourished by a will-power which holds it to its purpose, and it must have the warm sunshine of perfect faith. Given these, it will attract to itself whatever else is necessary to its fulfillment.

You see, the Law of Capillary Attraction is based upon the principle of growth from the vitality inherent in the seed or idea itself. It is like a snowball which starts with only a handful of snow, yet by gathering to itself all it comes in contact with, ends as an avalanche!

First the seed, the desire. Next, the planting—the initial step necessary to start its accomplishment. Third, the cultivation—the continual working towards the one end. You can't just WILL a thing into existence, you know. But you can use the will as the machinist uses a vise—to hold the tool of your purpose until it accomplishes its end. Fourth, the sunshine—FAITH—without which all the others are as nothing. Without sunshine, the seed will rot in the ground, the plant will wither on the stalk. Without faith, your desire will die still-born. Believe that you RECEIVE. See the perfect plant in the seed. See the perfect accomplishment in the desire.

Prof. Wm. James of Harvard, the greatest psychologist this country has known, wrote—"If you only care enough for a result, you will almost certainly attain it. If you wish to be rich, you will be rich; if you wish to be learned, you will be learned; if you wish to be good, you will be good. Only you must, then, really wish these things, and wish them exclusively, and not wish at the same time a hundred other incompatible things just as strongly."

But be careful that your desire tends towards Life-GIVING, towards the furtherance of Good. You can't make much of a snowball pushing up hill. If you do, it will presently grow bigger than you, get beyond your control, and engulf you in the resultant catastrophe. The fruit you bring forth is going to partake of the same nature as the seed you plant. If there is no kindliness in the seed, no love of your fellow-man, nothing but self-gratification, the fruit of your tree will be the same kind. It will be bitter to others—it will turn bitter in your own mouth.

Now how does this apply to you? There are certain things you want from life—Success, Riches, Fame, Honor, Love, Happiness, Health, Strength. All of these are worthy desires. All of them are entirely possible of fulfillment for you. How are you to go about getting them?

Your job here on earth is to distribute certain God-given gifts—certain goods, certain services, certain abilities—to the end that the world may be more livable for your having been in it.

In ancient Egypt, it was believed that each person was given at birth a "Ka" or "Double," which was his REAL SELF. It had infinite power for good. The body was merely its reflection, seen through the glass of the conscious mind.

So it is with you. Your REAL Self is God's image of you—the God in You. He gave it dominion over all the earth. Can you imagine it, then, as powerless under any circumstances, as poverty-stricken, as in doubt where its supply is coming from?

If you believe in God at all, you must believe in His intelligence. And if He is intelligent, He made nothing without a purpose. Everything fits into His plan. YOU, for instance—He created you for the purpose of performing certain work. That being so, it would seem pretty certain that He gave you every ability, every means necessary for the perfect performance of that work, would it not?

But how are you to know what that work is? Easily enough, if you stop to analyze your ambitions and desires. They are your subconscious promptings. Not, of course, the merely selfish desires for the gratification of some personal vanity or passion. But the big, deep down ambitions that come to you in exalted moments. They are the promptings of The God in You, urging you to EXPRESS on the material plane the work he is already doing in the mental realm.

You have an idea, let us say, which will short-cut the work of the world, make life easier and happier for any number of its inhabitants. You take whatever steps seem good to you to accomplish that idea. But you presently reach a point where lack of money or lack of knowledge or other circumstances leave you high and dry—seemingly at your rope's end. What are you to do then?

PRAY! And how are you to pray? Jesus gave us the formula—"Whatsoever things ye ask for when ye pray, believe that ye RECEIVE them, and ye shall HAVE them."

But how can you believe that you HAVE when you are at the end of your resources and there is no possible way out in sight? How? By knowing that The God in You, your REAL SELF, already HAS the answer in the realm of the REAL. By seeing the finished result there, imaging it in your mind's eye, and then putting it up to that God in You to show you the next step necessary to reflect that result on the material plane, in the serene confidence that, since he has worked out the answer, the EXPRESSION of it step by step through you is simple.

Tell yourself—and KNOW—you ARE rich, you ARE successful, you ARE well and happy and possessed of every good thing you desire. Use your "Treasure Map" to picture these things—then believe that you HAVE them.

No matter how limited your education, no matter how straitened your circumstances, the God in You HAS the knowledge and the means and the power to accomplish any right thing you may desire. Give him a job—and it is DONE! You HAVE it! And you have only to see that finished result in your mind's eye—"BELIEVE THAT YOU RECEIVE"—in order to begin to reflect it on the material plane.

Therein lies the nucleus of every success—the nucleus which has such life that it draws to itself everything it needs for its full expression—*the belief that you* HAVE. It is the secret of power, the Talisman of Napoleon. To acquire it takes just three things.

1. Know that this is a world of Intelligence. Nothing merely happens. You were put here for a purpose, and you were given every qualification and every means necessary to the accomplishment of that purpose. So you need never fear whether you are big enough, or smart enough, or rich enough to do the things required of you. "The Father knoweth that ye have need of these things," so do the things that are given you to do in the serene knowledge that your needs will be met.

2. Know that The God in You which is your REAL Self is already DOING this work you were given to do, so all that is required of you is to SEE that

accomplished result, and REFLECT it step by step on the material plane, as the way is opened to you. "And thine ears shall hear a word behind thee, saying—This is the way. Walk ye in it."

3. Have serene faith in your God's ability to express the finished results through you. When you can SEE that result in your mind's eye as already accomplished, you will realize that you don't need to fear or worry or rush in and do things foolishly. You can go serenely ahead and do the things that are indicated for you to do. When you seem to reach a cul-de-sac, you can wait patiently, leaving the problem to The God in You in the confident knowledge that at the right time and in the right way he will give you a "lead" showing what you are to do.

The fundamental Law of the Universe, you remember, is the Law of Attraction. You attract to you whatever you truly love and bless and believe is YOURS.

Knowing that The God in You Has the fruition of your desire—knowing that the perfect leaf is in the bare twig of your present circumstances—it is easy to pour such life, love and blessings into that leaf that it bursts its bonds and blossoms forth for all to see.

So, like the Egyptians of old, let us commune with The God in Us night and morn, much as our reflection in the mirror might commune with us:

Reality of me, I greet you and salute you the perfect "me" God created. You have a perfect body, made in the image and likeness of God. Make that perfect body manifest in me. You have infinite riches—dominion over all things. Use that dominion, I pray you, to uncover and bring out in my life, my work and my surroundings the perfect reflection of (whatever your particular desire may be).

Then SEE, in your mind's eye, The God in You doing those things you wish to do, emphasizing the traits you wish to cultivate, displaying the riches or possessions you want. Know that he HAS these. And that as soon as you can SEE them through the prism of your conscious mind, as fast as you can *realize* their possession, *you, too, will reflect them for all the world to see!*

OUR PRAYERS ARE ANSWERED
BY BONNIE DAY

Our prayers are answered: each unspoken thought
And each desire implanted in the mind
Bears its own harvest, after its own kind;
Who dreams of beauty has already caught

The flash of angel wings. Who seeks to find
True wisdom shall assuredly be taught.
But thorns of fate have thorny thoughts behind;
For out of our own hearts our lives are wrought.

Be on thy guard, my soul, lest wind-blown seed
Into the fertile soil of thought should fall
And lodging place within the garden wall
Be given to bitter rue or noxious weed.
Unspoken prayers bear fruitage.
Love thoughts call Forth into being every loving deed.
Idle or earnest, still our prayers are all
Answered according to our inward creed.

A PRAYER FOR WORK

Lord give me work. All work is Thine.
Help me to make Thy business mine.
Give me my part, and let me share
Thy joy in making life more fair;
My part, and with the part the will
To make my life Thy plan fulfill.
Thus every day, Lord, help me see
My simplest task as done for Thee.
                    —ESTHER ANN CLARK

All day long and every day, the God in You keeps repeating—"I AM." But He lets YOU end the sentence. You can add "poor" or "rich," "sad" or "happy," "sick" or "well," as YOU choose. God can do for you only what you ALLOW Him to do THROUGH you. You praise and bless Him, only when you see the good and true and beautiful. You dishonor Him when you call yourself weak or sick or poor.

So claim the good! Praise God for it, thank Him and bless Him for all His good gifts.

If you are out of work at the moment, know that the Spirit of the Lord is upon you, directing you to your right work. The Spirit of God goes before you to make plain your way. It works through you to make you efficient, successful, prosperous and of real worth to your employer and associates.

Know this—and then open your channels! Give of what you have of service to others. Start where you are. Distant fields always look greener, but opportunity lies right where you are. Take advantage of every opportunity of service, even if it be only to wash dishes or do chores around your own home. Show God that you are a channel for good NOW The more you can prove that, the greater will be your opportunities, and soon those opportunities will take the form of just the right job for you.

Each night and morning, and whenever the need for a job occurs to you, repeat this affirmation:

"God in me knows what my right work is, where it is and what I ought to do to be actually engaged in it. Let this knowledge be quickened in me as a revelation to my conscious mind so I shall know what is my right work, where it is and what there is for me to do to be established in it."

Remember it is from within, and not from without, that you get in touch with all of Good. Every ill, every lack, every discordant condition, must be cured in your own thought first. It is like a radio. The programs of all the world are in the air about you, but you have to tune in on the one you want. When you turn on the radio, the program that comes to you may be some sordid tale of crime or unhappiness, or it may be merely static noises. If so, that is all you will get—until you turn the dial. But you CAN get the program you want, if you keep turning away from the others and persistently try until you find the one you want.

But you must both affirm and ACT the part. To affirm prosperity and then act like a pauper with what substance you have is to show that you do not believe your own affirmation and do not expect anything from it. It doesn't matter if you have to force yourself to take some appropriate action. Take it—and thereby increase your faith.

Every affirmation should be matched by some action expressing the faith that you HAVE received or ARE receiving, action of the sort you would engage in if the affirmed good were visibly and tangibly present.

That doesn't mean you must spend a lot of money recklessly, buy a lot of things such as you will when you have the riches you crave. It does mean you must take the mental attitude of BEING rich, HAVING the right sort of job, sprucing up, being confident and serene and unworried.

You can help others get the sort of place they want in the same way you can yourself. Here is an affirmation to use for others:

Infinite Spirit, open the way for So-and-so's right position (or home or abundance or what-not), the position he is best fitted to fill, the position that needs him and which no one else can fill so well as he. Let him be led to the right people, the right place where he can give good service for good pay. Lead him to make the right contacts. I leave it with you, and I know all is well.

In a recent issue of "Nautilus" magazine, Dortch Campbell tells how he prayed for a home—and found the one he had always dreamed of.

"The whole secret," he says, "lies in that beautiful thing called love. I prayed for a home. Every element in the answer that came was in accord with justice. The quality of love was not strained.

A house that you can call your own home is not so easy to obtain these days. For me it was most difficult. Conditions have been serious in the Mississippi Valley for nearly a decade; the cotton problem has become acute. But the house where I had lived for a long time was taken away from me. I was homeless; there was no other available, for people have not been building houses in my country.

I had to build my own home to find a roof for myself and my loved ones. But there was no mortal way to build that home. I had not sufficient money to buy even a lot. Yet the home of my own became a reality in answer to my prayers as simply and as unostentatiously as a rose unfolds.

I felt that we are far too selfish in our prayers, so I prayed for others when I prayed for myself. I asked that the contractor who should build my home should be blessed through me. I prayed for the owner of the land. I prayed for an harmonious association with the contractor. I asked that there be love and friendship between us and between all who might be associated in the undertaking. I prayed that he might find a way to finance my home and that I in turn should help him to succeed. I prayed for others as earnestly as I prayed for myself. I prayed for the landowners that they, through me, might sell other lots.

I prayed in this fashion, loving them that they in turn might love me. Deep within me, I desired that all of us might equally profit in the building of my home. This was all. There was no domination on my part, no attempt to influence or control them, no direct thought to them.

Step by step, that home came about. I obtained the lot for a very small outlay—a lot worth three times what I paid. The contractor himself actually gave me the money I required. The home became mine in such a gentle fashion that I, accustomed to prayer, stand amazed. Things— for example—like a driveway, were contributed free.

But it was not only I who was helped, and this to me is the most beautiful part of the answer to that prayer. It has been my privilege since the house was constructed to help those who helped me in getting my home. More lots have been sold, more will be sold. The contractor has closed several contracts as a result of building my home.

What we need is to be not only hearers but DO-ERS of the Word. We find Truth by trying to live it. Since God is love, it may be that we have only to love a thing greatly to get it. Can it be that the long-lost key to attainment through prayer is in feeling the loving power of God within to give us that which the heart desires?

If I can do some good today,
If I can serve along life's way,
If I can something helpful say,
    Lord, show me how.

If I can right a human wrong,
If I can help to make one strong,
If I can cheer with smile or song,
    Lord, show me how.

If I can make a burden less,
If I can aid one in distress,
If I can spread more happiness,
    Lord, show me how.

If I can do a kindly deed,
If I can sow a fruitful seed,
If I can help someone in need,
    Lord, show me how.

If I can feed a hungry heart,
If I can give a better start,
If I can fill a nobler part,
    Lord, show me how.

–GRENVILLE KLEISER

FIRST CAUSES

How can I tell if I am working a-right?"—many students ask us. And "How can I be sure I am following correct lines?"—is the question in the mind of many a man and woman when confronted by some unusual problem.

In his Edinburgh Lectures, Judge Troward gave so clear an answer to this question that I quote it here:

If we regard the fulfillment of our purpose as contingent upon any *circumstances*, past, present, or future, we are not making use of First Cause. We have descended to the level of *Secondary Causation*, which is the region of doubts, fears and limitations.

What is First Cause? Judge Troward defined it, too.

If a lighted candle is brought into a room, the room becomes illuminated; if the candle is taken away, it becomes dark again. Now the illumination and the darkness are both conditions, the one positive resulting from the presence of the light, the other negative resulting from its absence. From this simple example we therefore see that every positive condition has an exactly opposite negative condition corresponding to it, and that this correspondence results from their being related to the same cause, the one positively and the other negatively; and hence we may lay down the rule that all positive conditions result from the active presence of a certain cause, and all negative conditions from the absence of such a cause. A condition, whether positive or negative, is never primary cause, and the primary cause of any series can never be negative, for negation is the condition which arises from the absence of active causation.

How can you be sure that you are working a-right? By asking yourself one question: "On what am I putting my dependence for the riches, or the health, or the success I am seeking?" If the answer is—"Upon my ability, or my doctor, or his drugs, or the help of my friends," then you can rate your chances of success as not more than one in ten, for you are working with secondary causes, and secondary causes are always undependable.

But if your answer is—"I am throwing everything I have into my work, but I am putting my dependence for success—NOT on these *means*—but on the unquenchable, irresistible power of the Seed of Life working through me," why then you can count your chances of success as nine out of ten.

You see, it all conies back to the Fundamental Law of the Universe—that each nucleus, each seed, contains within itself vitality enough to draw to it every element it needs for its complete growth and fruition.

But the seed must germinate, the nucleus must start whirling, before either has the slightest attractive power. Until they do that, they are so much congealed life, with no more "pull" to them than any other bit of inanimate matter around them.

Suppose you want something badly—more than anything else life can offer you at the moment. The desire for that something forms a nucleus, a seed, and like every other seed, it has latent in it the power to draw to itself the elements necessary for its complete growth and fruition. But until you *do* something about it, it is an inanimate nucleus, a seed that has not been planted, a nucleus with no power of attraction because no one has taken the trouble to start it whirling.

How can you put it to work? By PLANTING your seed—in other words, by making your start. What is the first thing you would do if you KNEW you would get your desire? What is the first step you would take in its accomplishment? TAKE IT! Do something to start, no matter on how small a scale. To begin, you know, is to be half done. Make the accomplishment of that desire the *sine qua non* of your existence, give to it all the thought and energy and riches you have to bring it into being, leave all other considerations in second place until you have won what you want.

That is the way great fortunes are made. That is the way miracles are performed. That is the only way you can put life into the nucleus of your desires and start them whirling and drawing to you whatever things you need for their manifestation.

Conditions, obstacles—they don't matter. Disclaim them, disregard them, and lay claim to the thing you want regardless of conditions. Like the seed in rocky soil, they may force your nucleus to work harder, to whirl faster, but give it vitality enough, and it will draw what it needs from the ends of the earth!

So don't work on poverty. Don't work on debts. That will merely bring more of these undesirables to you. Work on your idea, work on your nucleus—*believe that you receive*— and you will speedily draw to you all the riches you need to fill out the vacuums now caused by poverty and debts.

You have seen shoots of trees spring up on rocky ledges where there was scarcely enough nourishment to keep a bit of moss alive. And you have known such shoots to grow into mighty trees. How do they do it?

The seed of a tree is a nucleus. Plant it, and the first thing it does after it heats and germinates is to burst its shell and send forth a shoot—*upward*—using for that purpose the energy latent in the seed itself. In other words, it reaches out first to express life. It uses all the power it has to bring forth fruit. When it finds it has not enough energy in itself to accomplish this, it puts forth roots to draw the necessary elements from the soil about.

But if it happens to have fallen on a rocky ledge, it soon finds there is not enough soil to give it moisture or nourishment. Does it then despair? Not a bit of it! It sends its roots into every tiny crevice until they reach moisture and nourishment. It actually splits giant rocks asunder in its search for nutriment. It burrows through or around any obstacle until it exhausts the last flicker of life in itself or gets what it wants. Wherever they are, whatsoever may stand between, the shoot of the tree sends its roots seeking every element it needs for its growth and fruition.

First the stalk—then the roots. First the need—then the means to satisfy that need. First the nucleus—then the elements needed for its growth. The seed is a primary cause. The need, the nucleus, both are primary causes. Conditions—they are secondary. Given enough life in the nucleus, it will draw to itself the necessary means for growth regardless of conditions. The life in the seed is what counts—not the place where it falls.

All through Nature, you will find that same law. First the need, then the means. Use what you have to provide the vacuum, then draw upon the necessary elements to fill it. Reach up with your stalk, spread out your branches, provide the "pull" and you can leave to your roots the search for the necessary nourishment. If you have reached high enough, if you have made your magnet strong enough, you can draw to yourself whatever elements you need, no matter if they be at the ends of the earth!

God formed a Seed of Life which is you. He gave it power to attract to itself everything it needs for its growth, just as He did with the seed of the tree. He gave it power to draw to itself everything it needs for the fruition of its DESIRES, just as He did with the tree. But He did even more for you. He gave your Seed of Life power to attract to itself everything it needs for its *infinite expression!* He asks of you only that you make your desires strong enough, your faith in their drawing power great enough, to attract to you anything necessary to their fruition.

You see, Life is intelligent. Life is all-powerful. And Life is always and everywhere seeking expression. What is more, it is never satisfied. It is constantly seeking greater and fuller expression. The moment a tree stops growing, that moment the life in it starts seeking elsewhere for means to better express itself. The moment you stop expressing more and more of Life, that moment Life starts looking around for other and better outlets.

The only thing that can restrict Life is the channel through which it works. The only limitation upon it is the limitation you put upon it.

Over in Japan, they have taken the shoots of oak trees, and by binding a wire tightly around the main root at the point where the trunk begins, they have stunted the growth to such an extent that instead of great oaks eighty or a hundred feet high, these shoots reproduce all their qualities in dwarfed trees twelve or fourteen inches in height! These stunted trees live as long as regular trees, but they express only the millionth part of the life an oak should manifest.

We look upon that as abnormal, and so it is, yet it is being done all around us every day. Men bind their subconscious minds with wires of fear and worry. They put clamps of limitation upon their channels of supply. Then they wonder why they don't express more life in their bodies, why more of happiness and comfort is not evidenced in their surroundings.

God put a seed of Himself into you. That seed He called DESIRE. He gave it infinite power to draw to itself whatever it needs for expression. But He gave you free will—in other words, He left it with you to direct that expression— to draw upon it to the full or to put clamps upon it, as you like.

There lies in you the aegis of a Napoleon, a Lincoln, an Edison—anything you wish. All that is necessary is to stir up the Seed of God in you, and give it channels for expression. You can be what you want to be, if you want it strongly enough, if you believe in it firmly enough to make it your dominant desire.

How did Annette Kellerman, from a hopelessly crippled child, become one of the world's most perfectly formed women? By stirring up the Seed of Life in her limbs, through her earnest DESIRE for strength and beauty, by giving them work to do, ways in which to express life! How did George Jowett, from a cripple at eleven, become the world's strong man at twenty-one? By stirring up the Seed of Life in him through his overmastering DESIRE to be strong—by giving his muscles first a little, then more and more of work to do.

How did Reza Khan, from an ordinary trooper in the Persian army, rise to the rulership of Persia? How did a water boy win the throne of Afghanistan?

One and all, they stirred up the Seed of Life in them through DESIRE and Faith. One and all, they reached up and out, using freely all the power they had in the serene confidence that there was plenty more behind. Obstacles? They knew that obstacles were merely negative conditions that would disappear as darkness disappears when you turn on the light. It was the *prize* they kept their eyes upon. And it was the *prize* that they reached out for and plucked!

A few years ago, if anyone had told the neighbors of these men that today they would be rulers, he would have been laughed at as crazy. "Why, just look at their position," he would have been told. "Look at their circumstances, their surroundings. Look at the condition of the country. Consider their lack of training, of experience."

Conditions—all of them. Secondary causes. And these men had the vision to see beyond them—to go back to the *primary cause*—the Seed of God in themselves. They opened new channels for it to express itself. They reached up their stalks and spread out their branches and the Seed of Life in them drew to itself every element needed to bring forth their fruit.

At the heart of you is a seed—the Seed of God, the Seed of Life. In it is a perfect body, just as in every acorn there is a perfect oak. Not only that, but there is the power in it to draw to you every element you need to manifest a perfect body.

What do you care if circumstances have conspired to make you sick, or crippled or weak or infirm or ugly or old? If you are, it is because you or those around you have put the clamps of your fears or wrong beliefs upon the Seed of Life in you, and certain of your organs are stunted or dying.

The remedy? It is simple. Remove the clamps! Disregard your infirmity? It is only a condition—a LACK of Life. Then stir up the Seed of Life in you. Stir it up and charge it to draw to itself every element necessary to fill out the perfect image of your body that is in the seed.

Impossible? Have you ever heard of anything that is impossible to God? It is a Seed of God that is in you, and there is NOTHING of good it cannot draw to you!

The Law is—Use what you have, and more will be given you.

> *Let me not ask how difficult may be*
> *The work assigned to me.*
> *This only do I ask:*
> *Is this my task?*
>
> *Let me not ask if I be strong enough,*
> *Or if the road be rough.*
> *I only ask today,*
> *Is this the way?*
>
> —CLAUDE WEIMER

"Every good tree bringeth forth good fruit," said Jesus. "But a corrupt tree bringeth forth evil fruit. Every tree that bringeth not forth good fruit is hewn down and cast into the fire. Wherefore by their fruits ye shall know them."

What did Jesus mean by "Bearing fruit"? Didn't He have in mind methods of expressing the Seed of Life in you, making opportunities for it to expand and reach out to all those you come in contact with, doing something that makes this world a better place to live in?

And how does a tree go about the bearing of fruit? It brings forth a fragrant blossom first, does it not? When the blossom goes, it leaves the pistil, which gradually ripens into the luscious fruit.

The blossom is any idea of service, any means for making life more comfortable or enjoyable for those you live or deal with. The pistil is the action of turning that blossom into the beginning of the fruit by taking the first step to start the service, no matter how small that step may be. The luscious fruit is the finished service.

"That's fine!" I can hear many say, "I have the blossom— oh, a most fragrant blossom—but no means for turning it into the pistil or the fruit."

What does the branch have with which to start fruit? Enough nourishment for a start, but nothing over. Do you see the branch worrying on that account? Not a bit of it! It uses cheerfully everything it has, serene in the knowledge that providing more is the vine's problem. The branch has only to supply the *need*. The more it finds use for, the more it gets. Another branch may be just as big, but if the first one bears twice as much fruit, it will get twice as much nourishment, for the vine apportions its life-giving forces—not by size, but by needs. Wasn't it Jesus who said—"I am the vine, ye are the branches." Can you draw on Him for more than He can provide?

"Straight from a mighty bow this truth is driven: They fail, and they alone, who have not striven." They have a proverb in the East that a road of a thousand miles begins with a single step. Goethe expressed the thought when he wrote—

> Are you in earnest? Seize this very minute;
> What you can do, or dream you can, BEGIN it!
> Boldness has genius, power and magic in it.
> Only engage, and then the mind grows heated;
> BEGIN, and then the work will be completed.

"If ye abide in me," promised the Master, "and my words abide in you, ye shall *ask what ye will*, and it shall be done unto you. For herein is my Father glorified, that ye bear much fruit."

If you stir up the Seed of Life in you by strong DESIRES, if you provide it channels through which to express itself by taking the first step towards the accomplishment of those desires, you can ask for any element you need, and it will be given you.

But if you lose this day loitering, it will be the same story tomorrow and the day after. That which you are today is the fulfillment of yesterday's aspirations;

that which you are tomorrow will be the achievement of today's vision. You can't stand still. You must go forward—or backward. Eternal progress is the Law of Being. If you meet its call, you will never fail to go on and on to greater and greater heights. As Florence Taylor so aptly put it—

> *Success is the sum of small efforts,*
> *Repeated day in and day out,*
> *With never a thought of frustration,*
> *With never a moment of doubt.*
> *Whatever your cherished ambition,*
> *Begin now to make it come true,*
> *Through efforts, repeated, untiring,*
> *Plus faith in the thing that you do.*

Health, riches, love—they are all *means* to an end, they are all conditions. The Seed of Life in you is the only thing that counts—that, and the channels you give it for expression. There is your PRIMARY CAUSE—all else is secondary. So disregard all else, and keep going back to it.

Do you want love? The mere desire is a proof of the availability of the love you want, for someone has rightly defined desire as God tapping at your door with His infinite supply. So plant the seeds of love by giving it to all you come in contact with. Plant the seeds freely, serenely, believingly, and the harvest is as sure as when you plant seeds of wheat in fertile ground.

Make it a practice to appreciate things and people. Use it all through the day whenever anything occurs that pleases you. Say silently, if you cannot do so audibly, "I appreciate you." And never miss an opportunity to say a kindly word of praise or thanks to those around you. As Amy Bower puts it—

> *We never know*
> *How jar kind words may go.*
> *There is no way to measure*
> *Friendly smiles. They carry treasures*
> *Of courage, faith and love of man.*
> *And we may watch them grow*
> *Until their warmth*
> *Infolds a multitude; returns to bless*
> *The giver too with bread of happiness.*

A good affirmation to use is—"I so love that I see all good and give all good, and all good comes back to me."

Do you want riches? Wealth is largely a matter of consciousness. Many persons who want money, and who are striving for money, actually tend toward driving it away from them by reason of their tenseness of thought and their failure to realize the "money consciousness." In order to handle millions, one must learn to think in the terms and ideas of millions. Harriman once expressed this pregnant truth when he said: "It is just as easy to think and to talk in millions as in single dollars." This wizard of finance, whose feats were regarded by the public as closely approaching those of legerdemain, made this adage one of his cardinal principles of thought and action. He "thought and talked in millions," and his thought took form in action—his mental states took on material form—his ideals became realities.

There are many men in this country—in every city in this country—who have within them the germ-powers which, if allowed to develop and grow, would cause these men to become second Harrimans, or second Morgans, or even second Rockefellers. But practically none of these persons ever will really develop into this stage; in fact, the probability is that they will evolve merely into successful small shopkeepers, small news-stand keepers, or even small peanut-stand men—successful, in each case, but always on a small scale. They are content to think in single dollars—even in dimes— instead of thinking in millions. They manifest realities in the direct ratio of their ideals. Their thought takes form in actions of like calibre. Their mental states are reproduced in material form, but they are the same size in both subjective pattern and objective form.

> Just where thou art, shine forth and glow;
> Just where thou art, 'tis better so;
> Serve thou the Lord with perfect heart,
> Not somewhere else, but where thou art.

Emerson had a saying that you could travel the world over in search of beauty, but unless you had it within yourself, you would never find it, and the same is true of every good thing of life. The first step to success lies right where you are and in what you are doing. Until you have learned the lesson your present work holds for you, until you have learned to do it joyfully, lovingly, as to the Lord, you have not taken that first step towards the goal of your ambitions. You have not really begun.

Supply is an active force. It goes only to those who are alive, who are providing so many and such powerful magnets for it that they can "pull" it to themselves regardless of what obstacles may come between.

But suppose it is health you want? Suppose you are crippled or blind or bed-ridden. What then?

Why, then your remedy lies in breaking up the congealed life in your afflicted organ, and pouring it anew into the perfect mold.

And the way to break it up is by giving all you have of life to that one desire, by working up so intense a FEELING that it shall presently burst its shell and draw to it every element it needs for its perfect expression.

You can't do that by dabbling in mental work, the while you are depending partly upon drugs, partly upon other means. You must FEEL so strongly that your salvation lies in the Seed of God within you, you must BELIEVE so utterly in its power, that you are willing to sink or swim by it alone. Like Grant, you must have the grim determination to "fight it out along those lines, if it takes all summer!"

But it will not take "all summer." Once you get the spirit of it, you will find it by far the speediest and surest method there is. Often your relief will be immediate.

A writer in "Unity" tells of a friend who was suffering from a physical inharmony that threatened to become malignant, when all at once the thought came to her—"If God can't heal me, what can *this* do?" "This" referred to the drugs she was taking. Immediately she applied a cleansing substance to the troublous part, threw away the drugs and from that day had no further trouble.

In THE FORUM, recently, Winifred Rhoades told of an amusing happening in India, It seems that a pack animal slipped at a ferry in India some years ago, and a case of medicines was spilled. The colored pills were picked up and returned to their appropriate bottles, but with the 'white pills it was impossible to tell one kind from another. However, a young native gathered them up, and in spite of the missionary doctor's warning of the danger of using them ignorantly, he promptly made them the foundation of a widespread reputation.

When the missionary next appeared in that region, the young native greeted him with joy. "I owe all my prosperity to you!" he exclaimed. It seems that the bottle containing the assorted white pills he had picked up was the favorite in his shop. Patients came from far and near to get them. And in answer to the horrified doctor's question as to how he could administer them if he didn't know what they were meant for, he announced that he gave them to patients only when he didn't know what was the matter with them.

Dr. Richard C. Cabot of Harvard told a gathering of his fellow-medicos—"The body has a super wisdom and force which are biased in favor of life rather than death. What is this force? It is God, the healing power which supplies 90 percent of recovery." And on another occasion, he said—"If nature, assisted by the proper mental and emotional moods, is capable of curing an ulcer in three or four weeks, why isn't it possible for the same force to heal the same ulcer in three or four minutes, when the curative processes have been speeded up abnormally by the subject's passing through an intense religious (*emotional*) experience?" In "Man, the Unknown," Dr. Alexis Carrel told of having actually seen a cancerous growth on a man's hand cured in a few minutes.

You see, underneath all its seeming hardness, life is really a kindly force. Life is love. It is supply. It is health. It has in it every element we need to satisfy any right desire. So there is no need to look to this man, or that drug, or some outside agency, for the things you need. Go to the Primary Cause. Go to Life. Go to God!

"There is a time in every man's education," said Emerson, "when he arrives at the conviction that he must take *himself* for better or for worse *as his portion;* that though the wide universe is full of good, no kernel of nourishing corn can come to him but through his toil on that plot of ground given to him to till.

"The power which resides in him is new in nature, and none but he knows what he can do. *Nor does he know until he has tried.*"

> "You are sick," they said, "But that isn't the truth"—
> And the woman shook her head.
> "The Bible declares, he that dwelleth in God
> Shall not say, I am sick," she said.
> And she held to the truth through a starless night,
> Till morning proved that her words were right.
>
> "You are tired," they said. But she smiled at that.
> "How can I be tired," said she,
> "When the only work is work for God,
> And He is my life, you see?"
> And she quietly went her busy way,
> With a happy song in her heart all day.

"You are poor," they said. But she only thought,
"How little they know! God speed
The day when the world awakes to find
That love is its only need."
And she still maintained, as her fortune grew,
Not money but love—if they only knew!

For the world knows not of the peace that comes
To a soul at one with God.
It is only those who are toiling on
In the path the Master trod
Who can feel, through the dark, that loving hand,
And holding it fast, can understand.

What was it that made Napoleon Master of most of Europe? Not native genius. Not brilliant intellect. In his class at the Military Academy, he stood forty-sixth—and there were only sixty-five in the class!

The genius that made Napoleon was first his intense DESIRE for power, and then *his colossal belief in his own destiny!* He had no fear in battle, because he believed the bullet was not made that could kill him. He had no hesitation in attempting the seemingly impossible, because he believed the very stars in their courses would stoop to sweep the obstacles from his path.

You see, the secret of success lies in this: There is inside you a Seed of Life capable of drawing to you any element you need, to bring to fruition whatever of good you desire. But like all other seeds, its shell must be broken before the kernel inside can use its attractive power. And that shell is thicker, harder, than the shell of any seed on earth. Only one thing will break it—heat from WITHIN—a *desire* so strong, a determination so intense, that you cheerfully throw everything you have into the scale to win what you want. Not merely your work and your money and your thought, but the willingness to stand or fall by the result—to do or to die. Like the Master when He cursed the fig tree for its barrenness, you are willing to demand of the Seed of Life in you that it *bear fruit or perish.*

That is the secret of every great success. That is the means by which all of life, from the beginning of time, has won what it needed.

What was it gave to certain animals protective shells, to others speed, to still others a sting, to those who needed them claws or horns? What gave to the bold and strong the means to destroy, to the weak and cowardly facilities for hiding or escape? What but the Seed of Life in each, giving to every form of life the means that form craved to preserve its skin.

Always the seed in each form of life responded to the call of that life—"*Give me so-and-so or I perish.*"

Since the very creation of the earth, Life has been threatened by every kind of danger. Had it not been stronger than any other power in the Universe—were it not indeed a part of God Himself—it would have perished ages ago. But God who gave it to us endowed it with unlimited resource, unlimited energy. No other force can defeat it. No obstacle can hold it back.

What is it that saves men in dire extremity, who have exhausted every human resource and finally turned to God in their need? What but the unquenchable flame of God in them—the Seed of Life He has given to each of us—with power to draw to us whatever element we feel that we need to save us from extinction.

What do business leaders advise young people today? Live within your income? No, indeed! Go *into debt!* Reach out! Spread yourself! Then dig the harder to catch up!

You are entitled to just as much of the good things of life as Ford or Rockefeller or Morgan, or any of the rich men around you. But it is not THEY who owe it to you. And it is not the world that owes you a living. The world and they owe you nothing but honest pay for the exact service you render them.

The one who owes you everything of good—riches and honor and happiness—is the Seed of Life inside you. Go to it! Stir it up! Don't rail against the world. You get from it what you put into it—nothing more. Wake up the Seed of God inside you! Demand of it that it bring you the elements you need for riches or success. Demand—and make your need seem as urgent as must have been the need of the crustacean to develop a shell, of the bird to grow wings, of the bear to give it fur.

Demand—and KNOW THAT YOU RECEIVE! The Seed of Life in you is just as strong as ever it was in those primitive animals of pre-historic days. If it could draw from the elements whatever means it required to enable them to survive, don't you suppose it can do the same today to provide you with the factors you consider essential to your well-being?

True, these factors are different from those called for in primitive times, but do you suppose that matters to the Seed of Life? Everything in this world is made up of energy. Don't you suppose it is as easy to pour that energy into one mold as into another?

Many seem to think that riches and success are a matter of luck. They are not luck. They are a matter of DEMANDING MUCH from the Seed of God inside you, and then insisting upon those demands being met.

The trouble with most people is that they are looking to some force outside themselves to bring them riches or happiness. The superstitious carry a rabbit's foot or an amulet, believing it will bring them luck. The religious carry medals or images or the relic of some Saint. It never occurs to them that they have the means of going direct to God. God seems too impalpable, too shadowy and far away. His apparent isolation, His seeming detachment from their work-a-day world, makes Him appear too unsubstantial to depend upon in real need. They want something they can see and feel and talk to. Something with a substance like their own. Hence the demand for statues and pictures and shrines and relics Hence, too, the need for Saints and Priests—intercessors, nearer to the Great One than ordinary mortals can hope to reach.

But direct contact is always better than even the most potent intermediary. And you HAVE the direct contact, any time you want to use it.

You are a Tree of Life. The seed of you is a Seed of God—part of Him as much as the acorn is part of the oak. And that Seed has all the properties of God, just as the acorn has all the potential properties of the oak. It can draw to you every element you need to make yours the most perfect tree in the garden, the most fruitful.

So, instead of depending upon the stars, or a rabbit's foot, or an amulet, or even the Saints, put your faith in the Seed of God, which is the animating part of you. No matter what your circumstances may be, no matter what obstacles may conspire to hold you down, look—NOT merely to the means at hand, NOT to circumstances or conditions— but to that never-failing power of the Seed inside you to draw to you any element you believe you MUST have to survive.

That is the way to make your "Star," your "Destiny," work for you. Only the "Star," the "Destiny," is right inside YOU. It is the Seed of God, the Seed of Life in YOU which your desire, your faith and your need have started into action. It is stronger than any circumstances. It can overcome any condition. So bless it and baptize it, *and stir it up!*

Bless it morning and evening, but when the urgent need arises—DEMAND! Demand that it bestir itself. Demand that it draw to you whatever elements you need. Demand— and *give all* as you demand all—make it a matter of life or death, survive or perish.

There is a point in the tree, you know, below which the "pull" of the leaves has little power. That is the point to which the roots must deliver the water, or the tree will never flower or bear fruit.

There is a point in your circumstances or your business at which the pull of your Seed of Life does not make itself felt. That is the point to which your efforts must deliver the fruit of your work, or your desire will die still-born.

So when you demand, first GIVE—throw every bit of effort you have into reaching the point at which the Seed of Life will take over the work. Give all that you can to the work in hand, and don't forget to give to the Lord as well. It is this which makes so successful the prayers of those who, demanding riches, throw all their scanty store into the plate, and depend solely upon that Seed of God in them to supply their needs. When you can do this, believing, the world is yours.

> When things go wrong, as they sometimes will,
> When the road you're trudging seems all up hill,
> When the funds are low and the debts are high,
> And you want to smile, but you have to sigh,
> When care is pressing you down a bit,
> REST—if you must—but don't you quit.
>
> Success is failure turned inside out—
> The silver tint of the cloud of doubt,
> And you never can tell how close you are,
> It may be near when it seems afar.
> So stick to the fight when you're hardest hit—
> It's when things seem worse that you mustn't quit.

EXERCISE FOR CHAPTER SIXTEEN

All things therefore whatsoever ye would that men should do unto you, even so do ye also unto them; for this is the law and the prophets.

Someone in Omaha studied that Golden Rule, and out of it found the solution to much of Nebraska's jobless problem in the last big depression. He brought together a number of jobless men and women, and started them doing things to help others!

Forgetting their own troubles, they looked about them for ways to help others more unhappy and unfortunate than themselves and organized the All Omaha Self Help Society. They do farming, craft work and canning. They build houses, repair them, tend yards, do housework, care for children, and perform any service that offers which is of value to the community. Where money is available, they accept pay for their services and turn it into wheat and flour and fuel and shelter. They have improved their condition and that of all around them, without waiting for business to pick up or for some government agency to give them a lift. And in scores of parts of the country, similar groups have done the same.

In times of quandary, when you seem at the end of your rope, if you will only stop and think awhile, you will nearly always find that you have the BEGINNINGS of the solution of your problem in your mind, or somewhere ready to your hand. Use that beginning to start—no matter on how small a scale.

Alice Foote MacDougall built a business that, before the depression of the '30's, was worth $5,000,000. Yet she started with a little booth in Grand Central Station where she sold coffee. One blustery winter's day, everyone that came in seemed so cold and hungry that she sent home for her waffle iron and the necessary ingredients, and served waffles free to all who came for coffee. Those free waffles made her famous. They were the start that built for her a string of restaurants and a good-sized fortune.

The stories of that kind we might tell are legion. There was the poor farmer's wife who gave some of the strawberry preserves she was making to a youngster from High School who had stopped by for a drink. He thought them so good that he asked if he couldn't sell some of them to neighbors. From that start she built a profitable business.

The famous Jones Farm Sausage got its start from the talk of neighbors and friends who had tasted this delicious sausage at the Jones' table. And many another successful business has started on as small a scale.

The great thing is the start—to see an opportunity for service, and to start doing it, even though in the beginning you serve but a single customer—and him for nothing.

> In life's small things be resolute and great
> To keep thy muscles trained.
> Knowst thou when Fate thy measure takes?
> Or when she'll say to thee
> "I find thee worthy, do this thing for me!"

STRONG DESIRE ESSENTIAL TO SUCCESS

I

Desire Power is one of the many phases of Personal Power—of that Personal Power which flows into and through the individual from that great source of the All-Power of All-Things which in this instruction is know as POWER.

You do not create your own Personal Power of any kind, though you may modify it, adapt it, develop it, and direct it. POWER, the source of All-Power, has always existed and will always exist. You generate Personal Power by drawing upon the great Source and Fount of All-Power; by opening your natural channels to its inflow; and by supplying it with the proper physical and mental mechanism by means of which it is enabled to express and manifest itself efficiently.

An old writer once said: "Few speakers succeed who attempt merely to make people think—they want to be made to feel. People will pay liberally to be made to feel or to laugh, while they will begrudge a sixpence for instruction or talk that will make them think. The reasons are palpable and plain: it is heart against head; soul against logic; and soul is bound to win every time." Cardinal Newman once said: "The heart is commonly reached, not through reason, but through the imagination, by means of direct impressions, by descriptions. Persons influence us, voices melt us, deeds inflame us."

One has but to recall instances of the great influence exerted over the public mind by the emotional appeals to affection or dislike, to prejudices for or against, to desires, ambitions, aspirations, cravings, longings and things eagerly "wanted," made by orators, politicians, statesmen, actors and preachers, in order to realize the potent effect of Emotion, Affection and Desire upon men's thoughts, opinions, beliefs and convictions.

A modern writer says: "A large part of the business of life consists in moving the emotions and desires of men so as to get them to act." Another says: "The successful man is he who is able to persuade the crowd that he has something that they want, or that they want something that he has." The successful salesman, advertising man or any other man who has things to sell other men, all bring into play the force of Desire in those whom they are seeking to interest in their projects. They appeal to the "want" or "want to" side of the mind of men. They play upon men's sympathies, their prejudices, their hopes, their fears, their desires, their aversions.

Men "do things" and "act" because of the motive power of their emotional nature, particularly in the form of Affection and Desire. This is the only reason impelling or influencing men to "do things." Were this motive power absent, there would be no action or doing of things; there would be no reason or cause for such action or doing, in that event. We act and do solely because we "like" and "want." Were the emotional element absent, there would be no element of volition. Without Desire we would make no choices, would exercise no decision, would perform no actions. Without the "want" and "want to," there would be no "will to do," and no "doing." Desire is the motive power of Action; take away the motive power and there cannot be and will not be any movement, activity or volition. Without the motive power of Desire, the machinery of voluntary action ceases to operate, and comes to a complete standstill.

An old writer, whose words have been preserved for us though his name is unknown to the present writers, enunciates a profound truth in the following rather startling statement:

"Every deed that we do, good or bad, is prompted by Desire. We are charitable because we wish to relieve our inner distress at the sight of suffering; or from the urge of sympathy, with its desire to express its nature; or from the desire to be respected in this world, or to secure a comfortable place in the next one. One man is kind because he desires to be kind—because it gives him satisfaction and content to be kind. Another man is unkind because he desires to be so—because it gives him satisfaction and content to be so. One man does his duty because he desires to do it—he obtains a higher emotional satisfaction and content from duty well done than he would from neglecting it in accordance with some opposing desires. Another man yields to the desire to shirk his duty—he obtains greater satisfaction and content from refraining from performing his duty, in favor of doing other and contrary things which possess a greater emotional value to himself.

The religious man is religious in his actions, because his religious desires are stronger than are his irreligious ones—he finds a greater satisfaction and content in religious actions than in the pursuits of the worldly-minded. The moral man is moral because his moral desires are stronger than his immoral ones—he obtains a greater degree of emotional satisfaction and content in being moral than in being immoral. Everything we do is prompted by Desire in some shape or form, high or low. Man cannot be Desireless, and still act in one way or another—or in any way whatsoever. Desire is the motive-power behind all action—it is a natural law of Life. Everything from the atom to the monad; from the monad to the insect; from the insect to man; from Man to Nature; and possibly from Nature to God; everything from lowest to highest and from highest to lowest— everything that is—is found to act and to do things, to manifest action and to perform work, by reason of the power and force of Desire. Desire is the animating power, the energizing force, and the motive-power in, under, and behind all natural processes, activities and events.

There is a general rule concerning Desire which it is important that you should note and remember. The rule is as follows: *"The degree of force, energy, will, determination, persistence and continuous application manifested by an individual in his aspirations, ambitions, aims, performances, actions and work is determined primarily by the degree of 'want' and 'want to' concerning that object."*

So true is this principle that some who have studied its effects have announced the aphorism: *"You can have or be anything that you want—if you only want it hard enough."* To "want a thing hard enough" is equivalent to "paying the price" for it—the price of the sacrifice of lesser desires and "wants"; the casting off of the non-essentials, and the concentration of Desire upon the one essential idea or thing, and the application of the will to its attainment or accomplishment.

Much that we have been in the habit of ascribing to the possession and the manifestation of a "strong will" has really been due to the element of Will which is called Conation, i.e., Desire tending toward expression in Will-action. The man filled with an ardent, fierce, burning, craving and urge for and toward a certain object, will call to his aid the latent powers of his Will, and of his Intellect—these under the motive power and stimulus of Desire will manifest unusual activity and energy toward the accomplishment of the desired end. Desire has well been called the Flame which produces the heat which generates the Steam of Will.

Very few persons, comparatively, know how to Desire with sufficient intensity and insistence. They content themselves with mere "wishing" and mild "wanting." They fail to experience that Insistent Desire, which is one of the important elements of the Master Formula of Attainment. They do not know what it is to feel and manifest that intense, eager, longing, craving, insistent demanding, ravenous Desire which is akin to the persistent, insistent, ardent, overwhelming desire of the drowning man for a breath of air; of the shipwrecked or desert-lost man for a drink of water; of the famished man for bread and meat; of the fierce, wild creature for its mate; of the mother for the welfare of her children. Yet, if the truth were known, the desire for success of the men who have accomplished great things has often been as great as these.

We are not necessarily slaves to our Desires; we may master the lower or disadvantageous desires by Will, under the Power of the "I AM I," or Master Self. We may transmute lower desires into higher, negatives into positives, hurtful into helpful, in this way. We may become Masters of Desire, instead of being mastered by it. But before we may do so, we must first desire to do so, to accomplish and to attain this end. We may even rise to the heights of Will—the place where the "I AM I" may say, truthfully, "I Will to Will" and "I

Will to Desire"; but even there we must first desire to so "Will to Will" and "Will to Desire."

Even at these sublime heights of Egohood, we find Desire to be the fundamental and elemental Motive Power: this because it abides at the very heart of things—the heart of ourself—the Heart of Life. Even there, we essay and accomplish the highest deeds and acts of Will solely and simply because they serve to "content our spirit," to give us the highest degree of "self satisfaction"—to gratify, satisfy and give expression and manifestation to our greatest, most insistent, most persistent and strongest "want" and "want to."

MAGNETIC POWER OF DESIRE

The strongest and most persistent desires of the individual tend to attract to him (or him to) that which is closely related to or correlated with those desires," That is to say: the strong insistent desires of a person tend to attract to him those things which are closely related to such desires; and, at the same time, tend to attract him toward those related things. The Attractive Desire of Desire operates in two general ways, viz., (1) to attract to the individual the things closely related to his desires; and (2) to attract the individual to such related things.

In your own experience, in all probability, you have experienced many cases of the operation of this subtle law of Nature. You have become intensely interested in some particular subject, and your desire for further progress and attainment along the lines of that subject has been actively aroused. Then you have noticed the strange and peculiar way in which persons and things related to that subject have come under your observation and attention—sometimes even being apparently forced upon you apart from any act on your part. In the same way, you have found yourself attracted in certain directions in which, unknown to you, were to be found persons or things related to the subject of your desire, information concerning that subject, conditions in which the subject was involved or being manifested. In short, you have found that things happened "as if" you were either attracting persons, things and circumstances to you, or else that you were being attracted, drawn or "led" to such persons, things or circumstances.

Under such conditions, you will find arising on all sides certain events connected with and related to the subject of your desire; books containing information concerning it; persons having some connection with it; conditions in which that subject plays an important part. You will find, on the one hand, that you seem to have become a center of attraction for things, persons and circumstances related to that subject; or, on the other hand, that you are being attracted to certain centers of attraction related to that subject. In short, you will discover that you have set into operation certain subtle forces and principles which have "correlated" you with all related to that subject.

More than this, you will find that if you will maintain for a considerable time a continuous and persistent interest and desire in that particular subject, you will have established a vortex-center of attraction for that which is related to the subject. You will have set into operation a mental whirlpool, steadily spreading its circumference of influence, which draws into itself and to your central point the related and correlated things, persons and circumstances. This is one of the reasons why after you "get things going" in any particular line of interest and desire, things tend to "come easier" to and for you as time passes. In such cases, that which required enormous effort in the earlier stages seems to move almost automatically in the later ones. These are matters of common and almost universal experience with those who have been actively engaged in any particular line of work in which strong interest and insistent desire have been aroused and maintained.

So, you see, Desire Power tends not only to develop and evolve within you the qualities and powers necessary to enable you to manifest and express yourself along the lines of the desires persistently held by you; it also tends to attract to you, and you to them, the things, persons, circumstances and conditions related to or correlated with the subject of such desires. In other words, Desire Power employs every means at its disposal in order to express and manifest itself more fully, and (through you) to attain its object and end—its greatest possible degree of satisfaction and realization. When you have thoroughly aroused Desire Power within you, and have created for it a strong, positive focal center of influence, you have set into operation powerful forces of Nature, operating along subconscious and invisible lines of activity. In this connection, remember the adage: *"You may have anything you want—if you only want it hard enough."*

The attractive force of Desire Power operates in many different ways. In addition to the "drawing power" operating along the lines of "something like telepathy" of which we have spoken, it also operates in other ways on the sub-conscious planes of the mind in order to influence, guide and direct the person to the other persons, things, conditions and circumstances related or correlated to or with the particular desire which is being persistently and insistently held by that person. Under its influence, the subconscious mentality raises to the levels of consciousness new ideas, thoughts, plans, which if applied will tend to "lead" the person in the direction of the things which will serve to aid him in the realization of those desires which he is insistently harboring.

In this way, the person is led to the related things, just as in the other ways the things are led to him. Desire Power pushes, as truly as it pulls—it urges you forward as truly as it attracts things to you. In some cases the process is entirely subconscious, and the person is amazed when he finds "by chance" (!) that he has "stumbled upon" helpful things in places in which he had least expected to find them, and in places to which he had apparently been led by Chance. But there is no Chance about it; persons are undoubtedly "led to" helpful things and conditions, but by Desire Power operating along the lines of the subconscious mentality, and not by Chance.

Many successful men could tell how often in their respective careers, at critical times, the most peculiar happenings have been experienced by them, seemingly "by chance" or "by accident,' which served as the means of transforming defeat into victory. In this way they acquired "by chance" some important bit of information serving to supply the missing link in their mental chain, or else giving them a clue to that which had previously escaped their thought. Or, perhaps, they unexpectedly "ran into" the person who afterward turned out to be the one particular person who alone could have helped them in certain ways. Or, again, they have picked up at random the particular newspaper, magazine or book which either gave them the required information, or else mentioned some other book or thing which filled the need.

These things happen so often, and in such a striking way, that many men of active experience have learned to expect them, to rely upon them, and to act upon them. Not knowing the true underlying causes of the happenings, they usually refrain from mentioning their experiences to their friends for fear of being regarded as superstitious or credulous; but if the subject happens to be introduced in confidential conversation between men of this kind, it will be found that the instances cited are numerous, and are so strikingly similar in general nature that the careful thinker is forced to the conclusion that there is some fundamental principle involved in the events, and that there is a logical sequence of cause and effect indicated.

Not knowing the true cause of these happenings, men are prone to ascribe them to "luck," fate, destiny, chance or else to think of them simply as "one of those things beyond explanation." Some men who have become familiar with them have learned to recognize them readily when they experience them, by reason of a "feeling" that "here is another of those things." They learn to distinguish between a mere general and vague notion, and a "sure enough hunch." Sometimes, men think that these things are the result of the aid of a kindly Providence operating in their behalf; others feel that they have helpers "on the other side"; still others feel that there is "something almost uncanny" about the whole thing; but so long as it is perceived to operate in their behalf all are willing to take advantage of the aid of the Unknown Power.

Of course, the subconscious mentality of the individual is the "helper," or "directing genius" in such cases, and the happenings are merely phases of the general phenomena of the Subconscious. But, nevertheless, Desire Power is the animating principle involved. The subconscious mentality, like the conscious mentality, is energized and aroused into activity by the urge of Desire Power. Desire Power employs every possible form of energy, activity and motive-power at its command; and also presses into service all kinds of machinery and instruments, mental and physical. The Fire of Desire kindles every faculty of the mind, on conscious and subconscious planes, and sets them all into active work on its behalf. Without Desire Power in some form or phase, none of these faculties would manifest activity; where activity is manifested by them, there is always implied the presence and urge of Desire Power.

Sometimes Desire Power will operate in strangely indirect ways in order to accomplish its results. By means of the "under the surface" perception of the subconscious faculties, Desire Power seemingly perceives that "the longest way 'round is the quickest way home," and it proceeds to cause the individual to pursue that "longest way 'round" in order to attain his desire in the shortest possible time. In such cases it often acts so as to upset and overturn the plans which one has carefully mapped out; the result makes it seem to one that failure and defeat, instead of victory and success, have come to him. It will sometimes tear the person away from his present comparatively satisfactory environment and conditions, and then lead him over rock roads and hard trails; and finally, when he has almost despaired of attaining success, he finds it literally thrust upon him.

Such instances are not invariable, of course, but they occur sufficiently often and with such characteristically marked features that they must be recognized. It often happens that, as one who has experienced it has said, "It seems as if one were grabbed by the back of his neck, lifted out of his set environment and occupation, dragged roughly over a painful road, and then thrust forcibly but kindly upon the throne of success or at least into the throne room with the throne in plain sight before him."

But, at the last, those who have experienced these strenuous activities of Desire Power operating through the subconscious nature and in many other ways are found to agree universally in the statement, "The end justified the means; the thing is worth the price paid for it." It requires philosophy and

faith to sustain one when he is undergoing experiences of th
knowledge of the law and principle in operation will of course
The right spirit to maintain in such cases is that expressed in ___ .
a great life, if you don't weaken."

Desire Power employs freely the subconscious faculties in its work of
Realization through Attraction. It employs these in man just as it employs
them in the case of the homing pigeon, the migrating birds, the bee far from
its hive—it supplies the "homing instinct" to the man seeking success, as well
as to the animal seeking refuge. It is said that animals separated from their
mates, seemingly are attracted to them over long distances. Lost animals find
their way home, though many miles over strange country have to be traveled.
Let a person establish a "refuge" for birds, and the birds will soon begin to
travel toward it—even strange species from long distances putting in an
appearance. Water fowls travel unerringly toward water; the roots of trees manifest the same sense of direction toward water and rich soil.

In high and low, the Law of Desire Attraction manifests its power. Man is
under the law, and may even cause the law to work for him when he
understands its nature. Man may harness Desire Power just as he has
harnessed other great forces of Nature—may harness it and set it to work for
him. Once set to work for him, this power will work "without haste, and
without rest" toward the end impressed upon it— it will work for him while he
is awake and working otherwise, and when he is asleep and resting from his
conscious work. Desire is the "force of forces," because it is the inmost kernel
of all the other forms of natural force, physical or mental. All force depends
upon inner Attraction or Repulsion—and these are but the manifestation of
Desire Power, positive or negative.

THE MASTER FORMULA FOR GETTING WHAT YOU WANT

The Master Formula of Attainment, stated in popular form, is as follows:

*"You may have anything you want, provided that you (1) know exactly what you
want, (2) want it hard enough, (3) confidently expect to attain it, (4) persistently
determine to obtain it, and (5) are willing to pay the price of its attainment."*

We shall now ask you to consider three of the above five elements of the
Master Formula of Attainment, viz., the element of Definite Ideals, or
"knowing exactly what you want"; the element of Insistent Desire, or "wanting
it hard enough"; the element of Balanced Compensation, or "being willing to
pay the price of its attainment." Each of these three elements is highly

important, and should be carefully examined and considered. Let us begin with the first requisite, i.e. "Knowing exactly what you want."

When you consider the question, "Exactly what do I want?" you will be apt to regard it as one quite easy to answer. But after you begin to consider the question in detail, and in real earnest, you will discover two very troublesome obstacles in your way on the road to the correct answer. The two obstacles are as follows: (1) the difficulty in ascertaining a clear and full idea of your desires, aspirations, ambitions, and hopes; and (2) the difficulty in ascertaining which ones of a number of conflicting desires, aspirations, ambitions, and hopes you "want" more than you do those opposing them.

You will find yourself with "the divine discontent" of a general dissatisfaction with your present condition, circumstances, possessions and limitations. You will feel, perhaps strongly, the "raw desire" of the elemental Desire Power within you, but you will not have clearly outlined in your mind the particular directions in which you wish that elemental force to proceed into manifestation and expression.

You will often feel that you wish that you were somewhere other than where you now are; that you were doing something different from what you are now doing; that you possessed things other and better than you now possess; or that your present limitations were removed, thus giving you a wider and fuller expression and manifestation of the power which you feel to be within you: all these general feelings will be experienced by you, but you will not be able to picture clearly to yourself just what "other things" you really want to take the place of those which are now your own.

Then, when you attempt to form the clear picture, and definite idea, of what you want, you will find you want *many* things, some of them opposing each other, each offering attractive features, each bidding actively for your favor and acceptance—thus rendering a choice and definite decision very difficult. You find yourself suffering from an embarrassment of riches. Like the perplexed lover in the song, you say, "How happy would I be with either, were t'other fair charmer away." Or, like the psychological donkey who was placed at an equidistant point between two equally tempting haystacks, and who died of hunger because he couldn't make up his mind which one he wanted most, you may remain inactive because of strong conflicting desire-motives.

It is because of one or both of the above-mentioned conditions that the great masses of persons do not avail themselves of the great elemental urge of Desire Power. It is there, ready to exert its power, but they lack definite direction and power of decision, and so remain, like the vegetables or the lower animals, content to allow Nature to work along the instinctive lines of self-protection, propagation, etc., without employing initiative or self-direction.

The few of the race who break these barriers, and who strike out for themselves, are found to have known very clearly "just what they wanted," and to have "wanted it hard," and to have been willing to pay the price of attainment. In order to set to work the forces of Desire Power in a special direction, the individual must make clear an ideal path over which they may travel, as well as to arouse the forces so as to cause them to travel over that path.

Self-Analysis. You will find that a scientific application of the principle of Self-Analysis, or mental stock-taking, will aid you materially in overcoming the two great obstacles in the Path of Attainment, which we have just mentioned. Self-Analysis in this case consists of a careful analysis of your elements of Desire, to the end that you may discover which of these elements are the strongest, and that you may clearly understand just what these strongest elements are really like in character. You are advised to "think with pencil and paper" in this work of self-analysis—it will greatly aid you in crystallizing your thought and, besides, will give a definite and logical form to the results of your work. The following suggestions and advice will aid you materially in this task.

Begin by asking yourself the question: *"What are my strongest desires? What do I 'want' and 'want to' over and above anything and everything else? What are my highest Desire-Values?"* Then proceed to "think with pencil and paper," and thus to answer your important question above stated.

Take your pencil and begin to write down your strongest desires—your leading "wants" and "want tos"—as they come into your consciousness in response to your inquiry. Write down carefully the things and objects, the aims and ideals, the aspirations and ambitions, the hopes and confident expectations, which present themselves for notation in the course of your mental stock-taking. Note all of them, without regard to the question of whether or not you ever expect to be able to secure or attain them.

Put them all down on the list, no matter how ridiculous and unattainable they may seem to you at the time. Do not allow yourself to be overcome by the magnificent aims and ideals, aspirations and ambitions, which thus present themselves. Their very existence in your Desire-nature is, in a measure, the prophecy of their own fulfillment. As Napoleon once said: "Nothing is too magnificent for a soldier of France!" You are that soldier of France! Do not impose limitations on your Desire-nature in this way. If a magnificent desire is within you, it should be respected—so put it down on the list.

By this process of Self-Analysis you bring to the surface of your consciousness all the various feelings, desires, longings and cravings which have been dwelling in your subconscious mind. Many of these deep desires are like sleeping giants—your exploration of your subconscious mental regions will arouse these—will cause them "to sit up and take notice," as it were. Do not be frightened by these awakening sleepers. Nothing that you find there is alien to you. Even though you may find it necessary to transmute them, or to inhibit them in favor of more advantageous desires, at a later stage of your work, do not now deny them a place on your list—put them down on paper. The list must be an honest one, therefore be honest with yourself in the analysis.

At first, you will find that your list is a more or less higgledy-piggledy conglomeration of "wants" and "want tos," apparently having but little or no logical order or systematic relation. Do not let this disturb you, however—all this will be taken care of as you proceed; order and arrangement will establish themselves almost automatically when the proper time arrives. The main thing at this stage is to get all of your stronger desires into the list. Be sure to exhaust your subconscious mind of strong desires—dig out of that mine anything and everything that has strength in it.

The next step is that of the cold-blooded, ruthless, elimination of the weakest desires, with the idea and purpose that in the end there will be a "survival of the fittest" on your list. Begin by running over your list, striking off the weaker and less insistent—the mere temporary and passing—desires, and those which you clearly recognize as likely to bring you but little if any permanent satisfaction, continued happiness and lasting content.

In this way you will create a new list of the stronger desires, and those having a greater permanent and satisfying value. Then, examining this list, you will find that some of the items will still stand out from the others by reason of their greater comparative strength and greater degree of permanent value. Make a new list of these successful candidates, including only those possessing the greatest strength and value to you, and dropping the others from the list. Then continue this process of elimination of the weakest and the least satisfying until you reach that point where you feel that any further elimination would result in cutting away live wood.

By this time you will have become aware of a most significant and important fact, namely, that as your list has grown smaller, the strength and value of the surviving desires have grown greater. As the old gold-miners expressed it, you are now "getting down to pay dirt"—getting down to the region in which the nuggets and rich ore abide. When you have reached this stage, you will do well to stop work for the time being; this will give you a needed mental rest, and will also furnish your subconscious mentality with the opportunity to do some work for you along its own particular lines.

When you again take up your list for consideration, you will find a new general order and arrangement of its items pictured in your mind. You will find that these remaining desires have grouped themselves into several general classes. Your subconscious mental faculties will have performed an important task for you. Then you will be ready to compare these general classes, one with the other, until you are able to select certain classes, which seem stronger than the others. Then you will be ready to proceed to the task of eliminating the weaker general classes, making a new list of the stronger ones.

After working along these general lines for a time, with intervals of rest and recuperation, and for subconscious digestion and elimination, you will find that you have before you a list composed of but a comparatively few general classes of "wants" and "want tos"—each of which possesses a far greater degree of strength and value than you had previously suspected. Your subconscious mind has been working its power upon these classes of desires, and they have evolved to a higher stage of strength, definiteness, clearness and power. You are beginning at last to find out "just what you want," and are also well started on your way to "wanting it hard enough."

General Rules of Selection. In your task of selection, elimination, "boiling down" and chopping away the dead wood, etc., you will do well to observe the three following general Rules of Selection:

I. *The Imperative Requisite.* In selecting your strongest desires for your list, you are not required to pay attention to any fears lurking in your mind that any of the particular desires are apparently unattainable—that they are beyond your power of achievement, and are rendered impossible by apparently unsurmountable obstacles. You are not concerned with such questions at this time and place—ignore them for the present. You are here concerned merely with the question of whether or not your "want" or "want to" concerning a certain thing is felt "hard enough" for you to sacrifice other desirable things—whether you feel that the particular desire is of sufficient value for you to "pay the price" of its attainment, even though that price be very high. Remember the old adage: "Said the gods to man, 'Take what thou wilt—but pay for it!' " If you are not willing to "pay the price," and to pay it in full, then you do not "want it hard enough" to render it one of your Prime Desires.

II. *The Test of Full Desire.* We have told you that, *"Desire has for its object something that will bring pleasure or get rid of pain, immediately or remote, for the individual or for some one in whom he is interested."* Therefore, in passing upon the comparative strength and value of your respective desires, or general classes of desires, you must take into consideration all of the elements of Desire noted in the above definite statement—the indirect as well as the direct elements of personal satisfaction and content.

You must weigh and decide the value of any particular desire, or class of desires, not only in the light of your own *immediate* satisfaction and content, but also in the light of your *own future* satisfaction and content; not only in the light of your own *direct* satisfaction and content, but also in the light of your *indirect* satisfaction and content derived from the satisfaction and content of others in whom you are interested. Your future satisfaction and content often depend upon the sacrifice of your present desire in favor of one bearing fruit in the future. You may be so interested in other persons that their satisfaction and content has a greater emotional value to you than the gratification of some desire concerned only with your own direct satisfaction and content. These Desires-values must be carefully weighed by you. If you leave out any of these elements of Desire, you run the risk of attaching a false value to certain sets of desires. You must weigh and measure the value of your desires by the use of the standard of the full content of Desire.

III. *Seek Depth of Desire.* You will find it advisable to omit from your list all purely superficial and transient feelings, emotions and desires. They have but a slight value in the case. Instead, plunge into the deep places of your mental being or soul; there you will find abiding certain deep, essential, basic, permanent feelings, emotions and desires. In those regions dwell the "wants" and the "want tos" which when aroused are as insistent and as imperative as are the want of the suffocating man for air; the want of the famished man for food; the want of the thirsting man for water; the want of the wild creature for its mate; the want of the mother for the welfare of her child.

These deep desires are your real emotional elements— the ones most firmly and permanently imbedded in the soil of your emotional being. These are the desires which will abide when the transient, ephemeral ones have passed and are forgotten. These are the desires for which you will be willing to "pay the price," be that price ever so high in the form of the sacrifice and relinquishment of every other desire, feeling or emotion. Measure your desires by their essential depth, as well as by their temporary weight. Select those which are embedded so deeply in the soil of your emotional being that they cannot be uprooted by the passing storms of conditions and circumstances.

The Struggle for Existence. You are now approaching the final stages of your discovery of "just what you want." You now have a list of Insistent Desires—the survivors in the Struggle for Existence on the part of your many desires and classes of desires. If you have proceeded earnestly and honestly in your work of Self-Analysis and Selection, you will have a group of sturdy Desire-giants before you for final judgment. By a strange psychological law these surviving candidates have taken on much of the strength and energy of those which they have defeated in the struggle; the victors will have absorbed the vitality of those whom they have defeated, just as the savage hopes to draw to himself the strength of the enemies killed by him in battle. Your Desire Power has now been concentrated upon a comparatively small group of desires, with a consequent focusing of power.

You will now find that your "wants" and "want tos" have arranged themselves into two great classes, viz., (1) the great class of those desires which while *different* from other desires, or classes of desires, are not necessarily *contradictory* to them nor *directly opposed* to them; and (2) the great class of those desires which are not only *different*, but are also actually *contradictory* and *opposed* to other desires or classes of desires.

The merely *"different"* classes may abide in mutual harmonious existence and relation with or to each other, just as do light and heat, or the color and odor of a flower. But two *contradictory* and *opposing* classes of desires cannot co-exist and coordinate their energies in the same individual; both remaining in the fore, there will be friction, inharmony, strife, and mutual interference.

One might as well try to ride two horses moving in different directions, as to try to maintain in equal force two opposing or contradictory sets of desires. The two sets, each one pulling in an opposite direction and with equal strength, will bring the Will to a standstill. The individual, in such a case, will either oscillate between the two attracting poles, or else he will come to a "dead center" between them. Something must be done when you find an opposing set of desires of this kind well to the fore in your category of strong desires. You must set in operation a process of competition, from which one set must emerge a victor and the other set be defeated.

In this process of competition, you will need to employ your best and keenest powers of analysis and judgment. In some cases the matter may be settled quickly, and the decision easily arrived at, because when your full attention is turned upon the two competitors, one will be seen to stand out so much more clearly than the other that the latter will be almost automatically retired. The full power of Reason and Feeling focused in such a case will usually result in a quick and sure decision.

But there are instances in which both of the opposing sets of desires seem to possess an equal power and value in your emotional and intellectual scale.

Here you are apparently in the condition of the poor donkey, previously mentioned, who starved to death because he was unable to decide which of the two haystacks was to be eaten. The matter must be decided by the introduction of an additional element which will add weight to one set or the other, and thus bring down the balance on that particular side. This added element is usually found in one or the other of the following two classes of mental processes, viz., (1) Imagination, and (2) Association. Let us consider each of these.

The Element of Imagination. The imagination, employed in the case of the desire-conflict now before us, usually is very effective in bringing about a decision. In employing it, you have but to imagine yourself, first, in the actual possession of the object of the one set of desires; and then, instead, in possession of the object of the second set. In this process you draw upon your own recollections and experiences, and upon your recollection of the experiences of others. You imagine "how it would feel" to have attained the object of, first, *this* "want" or "want to," and then *that* one. You place yourself in imagination in the position that you would occupy in case you should attain the object of *this* desire, or of *that* one. Then you pass judgment as to which seems to be the better, i.e., to afford the greater degree of satisfaction and content, present and future, direct and indirect.

This process has the advantage of overcoming the handicap placed upon a future satisfaction in favor of a present one. The future experience is brought into the field of the present, and thus may be compared with a present experience relieved of the handicap of time. This is a matter of great importance, for ordinarily the present-time value of an emotional feeling or desire is far greater than that of a past-time or future-time value of a similar experience. The test of imagination usually results in (1) strengthening the present value of a really advantageous emotional feeling and desire, and (2) in weakening the present value of an apparently advantageous, but really disadvantageous, one. The use of the memory and the imagination is to be highly recommended in the task of deciding the real and actual value of an emotional state or desire.

The Element of Association. The element of association introduced into a desire-conflict will often result speedily in a determination and decision in favor of one side as against the other. Association will add strength to one set of desires, and will weaken the opposing set, in most cases. The Association of Ideas is that psychological law which binds one set of ideas, or mental states, to others; so that by bringing one set into consciousness we tend to bring there also the associated sets. In the present case we bring into consciousness the associated consequences of each set of desires.

You may proceed to apply the test of Association as follows: Seek to uncover and discover as many as possible of the associated results of the attainment of the set of desires in question—strive to think of "what else will happen" in case you attain that set of desires. This is something like inquiring into the family and social connections of two rival suitors or sweethearts—weighing their respective relations and associations and the probable future consequences of marriage with either of them.

It is always well, in cases of doubt concerning the comparative value of conflicting sets of desires, to consider carefully just what other things are associated with each of the two respective sets of desires—just what other results are likely to accompany the attainment of the object or end of each set of desires under consideration. In other words, you should ascertain the kind of relations and friends possessed by each of the rival suitors or sweethearts. In this way you will often find that one of the two apparently equal sets of desires has some very agreeable and advantageous relations and associates, while the other has some very disagreeable and disadvantageous ones.

You thus discover, figuratively speaking "just what kind of family you are marrying into"; and you thus take stock of the respective associated and related "in laws," friends, associates and entanglements of each of the suitors. This is of great value, since in spite of the oft asserted statement that "I am not marrying the whole family," one usually really does do just that very thing.

The idea of the application of the test of Association in such cases may be expressed in a few words, as follows: The real test of any particular desire depends not alone upon the immediate results likely to accompany its attainment, but also upon the associated and related results which follow in its train of association and correlation—the results which necessarily "go with it," and which are so closely bound up with it that they cannot easily be detached from it. In some cases, the test of Association will reveal the fact that the price of the attainment of a certain set of desires is excessive—often actually prohibitive. In other cases, on the contrary, you will find by this test that you are getting a great bargain by reason of the "extras" which go with the thing itself. The objects of some desires are thus found to be "damaged goods"; while those of others are found to have an associative value not apparent to the casual observer.

An Appeal to the Touchstone. In cases in which careful analysis, deliberation, the tests of imagination and association, and all other means of weighing and measuring, trying and testing, fail to reveal the advantage of one set of desires over the opposing set, resort must be had to the Touchstone of Positivity so often referred to in this instruction. The Touchstone by which the Positivity of any mental state, thought, feeling, desire or action is determined is as follows: *"Will this tend to make me stronger, better and more efficient?"* In the degree that any mental state meets the requirements of this test, so is its degree of Positivity and consequent desirability.

In testing two sets of conflicting desires in this way, you ask yourself: *"Which of these two desires, if attained, will tend to make me stronger, better and more efficient?"* This is the Test Question. The answer should represent your final decision in the matter. The Touchstone is your Court of Last Resort, to be appealed to when all other tests have failed. Its report represents the best, highest and most valuable elements, mental, moral and spiritual, within your nature; all that is worst in you is absent therefrom. It represents your Summum Bonum—your Chief Good.

The Survival of the Fittest. By this time, your list of desires has resolved itself into a schedule or inventory of a few strong, dominant, prime desires, and of a larger number of lesser ones. The strongest desires should be finally tested in order to discover whether they are merely "different" from each other, or whether they are essentially mutually antagonistic and contradictory.

If they come under the latter category, then they must be pitted against each other until one of the pair wins the victory, and one goes down in defeat; for two sets of this kind must not be permitted to dwell permanently in your region of Desire: "a house divided against itself shall not stand." There must be fought a fight to the finish. One of the opposing sets must be rolled in the dust, while the other stands proudly erect as the victor. The defeated one, thereafter, must be compelled to say, "After you, monsieur," as our French cousins politely express it.

If two sets of desires are merely "different,'" and are not essentially and necessarily conflicting and antagonistic, then they may be permitted to remain dwelling in mutual peace and harmony, at least for the time being. This permission, however, is conditioned by the fact that there must not be too many of such sets occupying the front seats of Desire at the same time. The tendency should always be in the direction of concentration and focused energy; you should beware of scattered power and energy arising from a great diversity of desires and aims.

If you discover that there are too many strong "different" desires left after you have reached this stage of selection and elimination, you should carefully weigh each remaining set, subjecting it to the tests of memory, imagination, association and rational judgment, discarding all that are not found profitable and sufficiently advantageous. If you find that any of your desires cost you more than you get out of them; get rid of all those which do not pay for their keep."

Continue until you have left only a comparatively few sets of desires, all of proved value and superlative emotional strength and depth. These should be recognized as well worth the price which you are prepared to pay for their maintenance and support. Treat in the same way any new desires which arise within you. Test them just as you have tested their predecessors, and insist that they prove that they are "worth while" before you decide to keep them. If they cost you more than you get out of them, discard them. Insist that they shall "pay their keep" and yield you some emotional profit beside. Run your emotional and desire establishment on business principles.

You have now finally reached the stage in which you have on your list nothing but your Dominant Desires—the survivors in the Struggle for Existence—the Survival of the Fittest. These Dominant Desires must thereafter rule your emotional realm. Any new comer must prove its worth by a test of strength with these Dominant Desires—if it shows its strength, and is able to hold its place, very well; it may be added to the list. Those going down in defeat must be eliminated. This will require strength and determination on your part—but you are a strong and determined individual, or at least are becoming one.

The process of Self-Analysis and Selection which you just considered will furnish you with two classes of reports, viz., (1) it will demonstrate to you your strongest classes of desires—your Dominant Desires; and (2) it will cause you clearly and definitely to picture and form a strong idea of each of such Dominant Desires. In both reports it will cause you to "know exactly what you want," which is the first requisite of the Master Formula of Attainment.

PUTTING POWER INTO YOUR DESIRE

According to the Master Formula you must not only "know exactly what you want," but must also "want it hard enough," and be "willing to pay the price of its attainment." Having considered the first of the above stated three requisites for obtaining that which you want, we ask you now to consider the second requisite, i.e., that of "wanting it hard enough."

You may think that you "want it hard enough" when you have a rather keen desire or longing for anything, but when you compare your feeling with that of persons manifesting really strong, insistent desire, you will find that you are but merely manifesting a "wish" for that for which you have an inclination or an attachment. Compared to the insistent "want" or "want to" of thoroughly aroused Desire, your "wish" is but as a shadow. The chances are that you have been a mere amateur—a dilettante—in the art and science of "wanting" and "wanting to." Very few persons really know how to "want" or "want to" in such manner as to arouse fully the elemental forces of Desire Power.

An old Oriental fable illustrates the nature of Desire aroused to its fullest extent. The fable relates that a teacher took his pupil out on a deep lake, in a boat, and then suddenly pushed him overboard. The youth sank beneath the surface of the water, but rose in a few seconds, gasping for breath. Without giving him time to fill his lungs with air, the teacher forcibly pushed him under once more. The youth rose to the surface the second time, and was again pushed under. He rose for the third time, almost entirely exhausted; this time the teacher pulled him up over the side of the boat, and employed the usual methods to restore him to normal breathing.

When the youth had fully recovered from his severe ordeal, the teacher said to him: "Tell me what was the one thing that you desired above all other things before I pulled you in—the one desire to which all other desires seem like tiny candles compared with the sun?" The youth replied, "Oh, sir; above all else I desired air to breathe—for me at that time there existed no other desires!" Then said the teacher, "Let this, then, be the measure of your desire for those things to the attainment of which your life is devoted!"

You will not fully realize the measure of Desire pointed out in this fable, unless you employ your imagination in the direction of feeling yourself in the drowning condition of the youth—until you do this, the fable is a mere matter of words. When you can realize in feeling, as well as recognize in thought, the strength of the desire for air present in that youth, then, and then only, will you be able to manifest in expression a similar degree of Desire for the objects of your prime "wants" and "want tos." Do not rest satisfied with the intellectual recognition of the condition—induce the corresponding emotional feeling in yourself to as great a degree as possible.

Varying the illustration, you will do well to induce in yourself (in imagination) the realization of the insistent, paramount desire for food experienced by the starving man lost in the dense forest in mid-winter. The chances are that you never have been actually "hungry" in the true sense of the term; all that you have mistaken for hunger is merely the call of appetite or taste—the result of habit. When you are so hungry that an old, stale, dry crust of bread will be delicious to your taste, then you are beginning to know what real hunger is. Those men who, lost in the forest or shipwrecked, have tried to satisfy intense hunger by gnawing the bark of trees, or chewing bits of leather cut from their boots—these men could give you some interesting information concerning hunger. If you can imagine the feelings of men in this condition, then you may begin to understand what "insistent desire" really means.

Again, the shipwrecked sailors adrift at sea with their supply of water exhausted; or the desert-lost man wandering over the hot sands with a thirst almost inconceivable to the ordinary person; those men know what "insistent desire" means. Man can live many days without food; but only a few days without water; and only a few minutes without air. When these fundamental essentials of life are withdrawn temporarily, the living creature finds his strongest and most elemental feelings and desires aroused— they become transmuted into passions insistently demanding satisfaction and content. When these elemental emotions and desires are thoroughly aroused, all the derivative emotional states are forgotten. Imagine the emotional state of the starving man in sight of food, or the thirst-cursed man within reach of water, if some other person or thing intervenes and attempts to frustrate the suffering man's attainment of that which he wants above all else at that time.

Other examples of insistent desire may be found in the cases of wild animals in the mating season, in which they will risk life and defy their powerful rivals in order to secure the chosen mate. If you ever have come across a bull-moose in the mating season, you will have a vivid picture and idea of this phase of elemental desire raised to the point of "insistent demand."

Again, consider the intense emotional feeling, and the accompanying desires experienced by the mother creature in connection with the welfare and protection of her young when danger threatens them—this will show you the nature and character of elemental desire aroused to its fullest extent. Even tiny birds will fight against overwhelming odds in resisting the animal or man seeking to rob their nests. It is a poor spirited mother-animal which will not risk her life, and actually court death, in defense of her young. The female wild creature becomes doubly formidable when accompanied by her young. "The female of the species" is far "more deadly than the male" when the welfare of its young is involved. The Orientals have a proverb: "It is a very brave, or a very foolish, man who will try to steal a young tiger-cub while its mother is alive and free in the vicinity."

We have called your attention to the above several examples and illustrations of the force of strongly aroused elemental emotions and desires, not alone to point out to you how powerful such desires and feelings become under the appropriate circumstances and conditions, but also to bring you to a realization of the existence within all living things of a latent emotional strength and power which is capable of being aroused into a strenuous activity under the proper stimulus, and of being directed toward certain definite ends and purposes indicated by the stimulus. That this strength and power is aroused by, and flows out toward, the particular forms of stimulus above indicated is a matter of common knowledge. But that it may be aroused to equal strength, power, and intensity by other forms of stimulus (such stimulus having been deliberately placed before it by the individual) is not known to the many; only the few have learned this secret.

We ask you to use your imagination here, once more, for a moment. Imagine an individual who has "his mind set upon" the attainment of a certain end or purpose to such a degree that he has aroused the latent Desire Power within him to that extent where he "wants" or "wants to" that end or purpose in the degree of strength, power, insistency and fierceness, manifested by the drowning man who "wants" air; by the desert lost man who "wants" water; by the starving man who wants food; by the wild creature who "wants" its mate; by the mother animal who "wants" the welfare of its young. This is the individual in whom the elemental Desire Power has been aroused to such an extent, and directed toward the attainment or achievement of his Dominant Desire. How would you like to compete with such a man for the attainment of that object of his Desire Power? How would you like to be the opposing obstacle standing directly in his path of progress and attainment? How would you like to play with him the part analogous to that of one who would try to snatch away the bone from a starving wolf, or pull the tiger cub from the paws of its savage mother?

This is an extreme case or illustration, of course. Very few individuals actually reach the stage indicated—though it is not impossible by any means; but many travel a long way along that road. The strong, successful men who have "made good," who have "arrived," who have "done things," in any line of human endeavor, will be found to have travelled quite a distance in that direction, on the road of Desire. They have aroused within themselves the strong, elemental Desire Power which abides in latency in the depths of the mental and emotional being—the "soul," if you will—of every human creature; and have caused that elemental force to pour through the channels of the particular Dominant Desires which they have brought to the surface of their nature from the depths of the subconscious self.

Look in any direction you may, and you will find that the strong, masterful, dominant, successful men are those in whom Desire Power has been aroused and directed in this way. These men "know what they want"—just as the drowning man, the starving man, the thirst-cursed man, the wild mating creature, the mother creature, each knows what he or she wants—they have no doubts concerning their Dominant Desires. And these men also "want hard enough" that which represents their Dominant Desires—just as did the drowning man, the starving man, and the rest of our illustrative examples. And, like those examples, these men were also "willing to pay the price."

Run over the list of the successful men and women with whose careers you are acquainted. Place on that list the great discoverers, inventors, explorers, military men, business men, artists, literary men and women, all those who have "done things" successfully. Then check off name after name, as you discover the biographical report of the Desire Power manifested by these individuals. You will find that in each and every case there were present the "Definite Ideals, Insistent Desire, Confident Expectation, Persistent Determination, and Balanced Compensation," which constitute the Master Formula of Attainment of our instruction. And this second requisite—the "Insistent Desire"—is found to be this elemental Desire Power directed into the appropriate channels of manifestation and expression. These individuals "knew just what they wanted"; they "wanted it hard enough"; and they were "willing to pay the price."

It is this spirit of "wanting it hard enough" that distinguishes the men and women of strong purpose and determination from the common herd of persons who merely "wish for" things in a gentle, faint, conventional way—that distinguishes the true "wanters" from the dilettante "wishers." It was the recognition of this spirit in men that caused Disraeli to say that long meditation had brought him to the conviction that a human being with a settled purpose, and with a will which would stake even existence itself upon its fulfillment, must certainly accomplish that purpose.

"But," you may say, "admitting the truth of your premise, how am I to proceed in order to arouse the dormant latent Desire Power within me, and to cause it to flow forth in the direction of the attainment of my Dominant Desires?" Answering the question, we would say, "Begin at the very beginning, and proceed to arouse and draw forth the latent Desire Power, by presenting to it the stimulus of suggestive and inciting ideas and pictures." For, from beginning to end, there prevails the principle expressed in that axiom of psychology which says: *"Desire is aroused and flows forth toward things represented by ideas and mental pictures; the stronger and clearer the idea or mental picture, the stronger and more insistent is the aroused desire, all else being equal."*

You should proceed to apply this principle from the very beginning even at the stage of semi-awakened Desire Power. There abides within you a great store of latent, dormant Desire Power—a great reservoir of Desire Power which is almost dormant, but which contains within itself the latent and nascent powers of wonderfully diversified manifestation and expression. You will do well to begin by "stirring up" this great reservoir of Desire Power—arousing it into activity in a general way, to the end that you may afterward direct its power and cause it to flow forth into and along the channels of expression and manifestation which you have provided for it.

In the great crater of a mighty volcano of Hawaii, in plain sight of the daring visitor to the rim of the abyss, there abides a large lake of molten lava, seething and bubbling, boiling and effervescing in a state of hissing ebullience—a lake of liquid fire, as it were. This great fiery lake is comparatively calm on its surface, however, the ebullition proceeding from its depths. The whole body of fiery liquid manifests a rhythmic tide-like rise and fall, and a swaying from side to side of the crater. The observer is impressed with the recognition of a latent and nascent power of almost immeasurable possibilities of manifestation and expression. He feels borne upon him the conviction that this seething, rising and falling, swaying, tremendous body of liquid fire, if once fully aroused into activity, would boil and seethe up to the edge of the crater, and overflowing, would pour down into the valleys beneath carrying before it and destroying every obstacle in its path.

This great lake of molten lava—this great body of liquid fire—is a symbol of the great body of latent and nascent Desire Power abiding within every individual—within YOU. It rests there, comparatively inactive on the surface, but ever manifesting a peculiar churning ebullition proceeding from its great depths. It seethes and boils, effervesces and bubbles, rises and falls in tide-like rhythm, sways in rhythmic sequence from side to side. It seems ever to say to you, "I am here, restless and disturbed, ever longing, craving, hankering for, hungering and thirsting for, desiring for expression and manifestation in definite form and direction. Stir me up; arouse my inner force; set me into action; and I will rise and assert my power, and accomplish for you that which you direct!"

Of course, we realize that this stirring up or agitation of your latent Desire Power is apt to—in fact, certainly will— create additional Discontent on your part; but what of it? Some philosophers praise the Spirit of Contentment, and say that Happiness is to be found only therein. Be that as it may, it may be as positively asserted that all Progress proceeds from Discontent.

While admitting the value of Content, at the same time we believe in preaching the "Gospel of Discontent" to a sane degree and extent. We believe that Discontent is the first step on the Path of Attainment. We believe that it is just this very Divine Discontent that causes men and women to undertake the Divine Adventure of Life, and which is back of and under all human progress. Content may be carried quite too far. Absolute Content results in Apathy and Lethargy—it stops the wheels of Progress. Nature evidently is not Content, else it would cease to manifest the process of Evolution. Nature has evidently been ever filled with the Spirit of Discontent, judging from her invariable manifestation of the Law of Change. Without Discontent and the Desire to Change, there would be no Change in Nature. The Law of Change shows plainly Nature's opinion on the subject, and her prevailing feelings and desires in the matter.

You will do well to begin by "treating" your great body of elemental Desire Power for increased activity, and for the transmutation of its static power into dynamic power— bringing it from its state of semi-rest into the state of increased restlessness and tendency to flow forth into action. You may do this in the same way that you will later employ in the case of specific, particular and definite desires, i.e., *by presenting to it suggestive and inciting ideas and mental pictures!*

Begin by presenting to your elemental Desire Power the suggestive idea and mental picture of itself as akin to the great lake of molten lava, or liquid fire, filled with latent and nascent energy, power and force; filled with the elemental urge toward expression and manifestation in outward form and action; able and willing to accomplish anything it desires to do with sufficient strength, providing a definite channel is provided for its flow of power. Show it the picture of itself as ready and willing to transmute its static energy into dynamic force, and to pour forth along the channels which you will provide for it—and above all else, quite *able* to do this if it will but arouse itself into dynamic action. In short, present to its gaze your idealistic and ideative mental equipment in the form of the surface of a great mirror, reflecting the picture of the elemental Desire Power as it presents itself to that mirror—let Desire Power see itself as it is. Supply Desire with its complementary Idea.

You will do well to accompany this mental picture with a verbal statement or affirmation of the details of that picture. Treat your elemental Desire Power as if it were an entity— there is a valid psychological reason for this, by the way—and tell it in exact words just what it is, what are its powers, and what is its essential nature displaying the disposition to express and manifest itself in outward form and activity. Pound these suggestive statements into it, as firmly, earnestly and persistently as you can. Supply the Desire Power with the element of Idea and Mental Pictures. Give it the picture of what it is, and the pattern or diagram of what it can do if it will.

The result of this course of "treatment" applied to your elemental Desire Power will soon show itself in an increased feeling of more vigorous rhythmic tidal-movement and side-to-side movement, as previously described; and in an increased rate and vigor of its seething, boiling, effervescing ebullition. From its depths 'will arise mighty impulses and urges, upheavals and uprisings. The great molten-lake of Desire Power will begin to boil with increased vigor, and will show an inclination to produce the Steam of Will. You will experience new and strange evidences of the urge of Desire Power within you, seeking expression and manifestation along the channels which you have provided for it.

But before reaching this stage, you must have created the channels through and in which you wish the overflowing Desire Power to flow when it reaches the "boiling over" stage. These channels must be built along the lines of those desires which you have proved to be your Dominant Desires. Build these channels, deep, wide and strong. From them you can afterward build minor channels for your secondary and derivative desires arising from your Dominant Desires. At present, however, your main concern is with your main channels. Let each channel represent the clear, deep, strong idea and mental picture of "just what you want" as you clearly see and know it. You have found out exactly what you want, when you want it, and how you want it; let your channels represent as closely as may be just these ideas. Build the banks high, so as to obviate any waste; build the walls strong, so as to stand the strain; build the channel deep and wide, so as to carry the full force and quantity of the current.

By "creating the channels" of your Dominant Desires, we mean establishing the paths to be traversed by the overflowing current of Desire Power which you have aroused from its latent and nascent condition. These channels or paths are created mentally by the employment of Creative Imagination and Ideation. These mental forces proceed to manifest in the direction of creating and presenting to your consciousness the ideas and mental pictures of your Dominant Desires which you have discovered in your process of Self-Analysis. The work of creating these channels is really but a continuation of the mental work performed by you in the discovery of your Dominant Desires. In creating these channels you should observe three general rules, as follows:

(1) *Make the Channels Clear and Clean* by creating and maintaining a clear, clean, distinct, and definite idea of each of your Dominant Desires, in which idea the entire thought concerning the Dominant Desire is condensed, and in which there is no foreign or non-essential material.

(2) *Make the Channels Deep and Wide* by forming mental pictures or suggestive ideas appealing to the emotional feelings associated with the Dominant Desires, and thus tempting the appetites of those desires by the

representation of the objects of their longing, and by the presentation of imaginative pictures of the joys which will attend their final achievement and attainment.

(3) *Make the Banks Strong* by means of the employment of the Persistent Determination of the Will, so that the powerful swift current may be confined within the limits of the Dominant Desire and not be permitted to escape and waste itself by scattering its energy and force over the surrounding land.

When your current is flowing freely, you will find it necessary to build minor channels serving to bring about the attainment of objects and ends helpful to the accomplishment of the objects and ends of the major channels. In building these minor channels, follow the same general rules and principles which we have given you. From the great main channels down to the tiniest canal the same principle is involved. *Always build clear and clean, by means of definite ideas and aims; always build deep and wide, by means of suggestive ideas and mental pictures; always build strong banks, by means of the determined will.*

In concluding this consideration of the second requisite, i.e., the element of "wanting it hard enough," we wish to impress upon your mind the tremendous vitalizing, and inciting power exerted by Suggestive Ideas and Mental Pictures upon Desire Power. Suggestive Ideas and Mental Pictures act upon Desire Power with a tremendous degree of effect in the direction of inciting, arousing, stirring, stimulating, exciting, spurring, goading, provoking, moving, encouraging, animating and urging to expression and manifestation. There are no other incentives equal to these. All strong desires are aroused by such incentives, consciously or unconsciously applied.

For instance, you may have no desire to visit California. Then your interest in that part of the country is aroused by what you read or hear concerning it, and a vague desire to visit it is aroused in you. Later, information in the direction of giving you additional material for suggestive ideas and mental pictures serves to arouse your desire to "go to California." You begin to search eagerly for further ideas and pictures, and the more you obtain the stronger grows the flame of your desire. At last, you "want to hard enough," and brushing aside all obstacles you "pay the price" and take the trip across the plains. Had you not been furnished with the additional suggestive ideas and mental pictures, your original desire would soon have died out. You know by experience the truth of this principle; you also know how you would use it if you wished to induce a friend to visit California, do you not? Then start to work using it on your Desire Power when you wish to incite it into "wanting hard enough" something that you know to be advantageous to you!

It is customary to illustrate this principle by the figure of pouring the oil of Idea upon the flame of Desire, thereby keeping alive and strengthening the power of the latter. The figure of speech is a good one—the illustration serves well its purpose. But your memory and imagination, representing your experience, will furnish you with one a little nearer home. All that you need do is to imagine the effect which would be produced upon you if you were hungry and were able to form the mental picture or create the suggestive idea of a particularly appetizing meal. Even as it is, though you are not really hungry, the thought of such a meal will make your mouth water.

Again, you may readily imagine the effect produced upon you, when you are parched and intensely thirsty on a long ride, by the vivid mental picture or strong suggestive idea of a clear, cold spring of mountain water. Or, again, when in a stuffy, ill-ventilated office you think of the fresh air of the mountain-camp where you went fishing last Summer,—when you picture plainly the joys of the experience—can you deny that your Desire Power is intensely aroused and excited, and that you feel like dropping everything and "taking to the woods" at once.

Raising the principle to its extreme form of manifestation, try to imagine the effect upon the famishing man of a dream of plentiful food; the dream of the thirst-cursed man in which is pictured flowing fountains of water. Try to imagine the effect upon the mate-seeking wild bull-moose of the far-off bellow of the sought-for mate—would you like to impede his path on such an occasion. Finally, picture the emotional excitement and frenzy of desire on the part of the tigress when she comes in sight of food for her half-starved cubs; or her force of desire when she hears afar-off the cry of distress of her young ones.

In order to "want" and "want to" as hard as do these human beings and wild things which we have employed as illustrations, you must feed your Desire Power with suggestive ideas and mental pictures similar in exciting power to those which rouse into action their dominant and paramount "want" and "want to." Of course, these are extreme cases—but they serve to illustrate the principle involved.

In short, in order to "want it hard enough," you must create a gnawing hunger and a parching thirst for the objects of your Dominant Desires; this you must intensify and render continuous by repeatedly presenting with suggestive ideas and mental pictures of the Feast of Good Things, and the Flowing Fountain, which awaits the successful achievement or attainment of the desires.

Or, you must be like the half-drowned youth wanting "a breath of air" above all else—wanting it with all the fierce energy of his soul and being; and you must ever keep before you the suggestive idea and mental picture of "all the air there is" which is to be found just above the surface of the water of Need in which you are now immersed. When you can create these mental and emotional conditions within yourself, then, and then only, will you really know just what it is to "want hard enough."

Think well over this idea, until you grasp its full meaning!

HOW TO OVERCOME TEMPTATIONS THAT SIDETRACK YOUR AMBITIONS

According to the Master Formula, "In order to get what you want you must not only know exactly what you want," not only "want it hard enough," but also "be willing to pay the price of its attainment." We have considered the first and second of these elements of successful attainment; let us now consider the third one, and learn what it means to "be willing to pay the price of attainment."

This final element of successful attainment—this last hurdle in the race—often is the point at which many persons fail; riding gallantly over the first several hurdles, they stumble and fall when they attempt to surmount this final one. This, not so much because of the real difficulty in passing over this obstacle, but rather because they are apt to underestimate the task and, accordingly, to relax their energies. Thinking that the race is practically over, they fail to observe care and caution and thus meet failure. With the prize almost in hand, they relax their efforts and lose it.

The Law of Compensation is found in full operation in the realm of Desire, as well as in every other field and region of life and action. There is always present that insistence upon Balance which Nature invariably demands from those who seek her prizes. There is always something to be given up, in order that something else may be gained. One cannot have his pie and his dime at the same time—he must spend the dime if he would buy the pie. Neither can one keep his dime and yet spend it. Nature boldly and plainly displays her sign, "Pay the Price!" Once more let us quote the old adage: "Said the gods to man, 'Take what thou wilt; but pay the price.'"

When in actual experience you perform the process of selection of the Dominant Desires, with its attendant Struggle for Existence and Survival of the Fittest among the competing desires, even then you are beginning to "pay the price" of the attainment of your Dominant Desires; this because you are setting aside and relinquishing one or more sets of desires in favor of a preferred set. Every set of desires has its opposing set, and also others sets which would to some extent interfere with its full manifestation; you must "pay the price" of attainment of the one set of desires by relinquishing the other sets.

In order to attain the object of your desire for wealth, you must "pay the price" of relinquishing desires for certain things which would prevent you from accumulating money. In order to attain the object of your desire for all possible knowledge in some particular field of study and research, you must "pay the price" of relinquishing your desires for a similar degree of knowledge in some other field of thought and study. In order to attain the object of your desire for business success, you must "pay the price" of hard work and the passing by of the objects of your desires for play, amusement, and enjoyment which would necessitate the neglect of your business. And so on; to attain the object of any one set of desires, you must always "pay the price" of the relinquishing of the objects of other sets of desires.

In some cases, this process of the inhibition of opposing desires is akin to that of weeding your garden, or of pruning your trees—getting rid of the useless and harmful growths which interfere with the growth and development of the useful and advantageous thing. In other cases, however, the desires which you must inhibit and put away from you are not in themselves harmful or useless. On the contrary, they may be very advantageous and useful in themselves, and may be actually worthy of being adopted as Dominant Desires by others; but, at the same time, they are of such a nature as to prove an obstacle to your progress along the line of your own chosen Dominant Desires.

Things may oppose and antagonize each other without either of them being harmful or "bad" in themselves. You cannot travel at the same time both forks of the road; nor can you travel north and south on any road at the same time; though either of these courses of travel may be good in itself. You cannot very well be a successful clergyman and a successful lawyer at the same time; if you have strong desires for both of these careers, you must choose the one you desire more and set aside the other. The girl with the two attractive suitors—the man with the two delightful sweethearts—the child with the dime, gazing longingly at the two different tarts—each must choose one and pass by the other, and thus "pay the price."

Not only in the preliminary process of discovering and identifying your Dominant Desires are you called upon to "pay the price," but you are equally called upon to do so at almost every subsequent step and stage of your progress in actual experience. There is always something presenting itself to tempt you into "sidetracking" your Desire Power; some alluring desires which beckon you from the straight Path of Attainment. Here you will find that it is hard to "pay the price"; and often you will gravely question yourself, asking if the things represented by the Dominant Desires are, after all, worth the price you are being called on to pay for them. These temptations and struggles come to all— they constitute one of the tests whereby it is determined whether you are strong or whether you are weak in regard to your Desire Power. Here is the real test of whether or not you "want it hard enough" to make you willing to "pay the price."

Particularly difficult to overcome and conquer are those temptations which induce you to relinquish your desire for future attainment in favor of the gratification of present desires; or which tempt you to forego the attainment of permanent future benefits in favor of temporary, ephemeral benefits. The tempter whispers in your ear that you are foolish to content yourself with the skim-milk of the present in the hope of obtaining the full cream of tomorrow. The ever-present suggestion to "Eat, drink, and be merry, for tomorrow we die" must be boldly confronted and conquered if you wish to attain the object of that which your reason and judgment, as well as your self-analysis, has shown that you really want above everything else. The habit of saying: "Get thee behind me Satan!" must be cultivated; and when you have got him behind you, look out lest he give you a push from behind!

Here you determine whether or not you really "want it hard enough." The drowning man is in no doubt concerning the value of the breath of air. He is willing to "pay the price of it," no matter how high that price may be. The famishing man knows the value of food—the parched man knows the value of water: they are willing to "pay the price," and are not liable to be sidetracked from their Dominant Desire. The bull-moose seeking his mate is willing to "pay the price" of danger and possible death lying in his path— but you cannot sidetrack him. The mother tiger cannot be sidetracked from the pursuit of food for her hungry cubs— she is willing to "pay the price" of risk of life without hesitation. When you begin to "want it hard enough" along the same lines, and reaching toward the same degree of intensity and insistence manifested by these creatures, then you will not hesitate to "pay the price"—to pay it in full, and without hesitation; when you reach this stage the tempter will whisper into ears deaf to his voice.

In order to hold the current of Desire Power within the bounds of your channels of Dominant Desire, the banks must be erected and kept in a state of strength by Will Power. The "Will to Will" must be called into manifestation. While Desire is one of the fundamental elements of Will, it is not all of Will. Will is a subtle combination of Conative Desire and of

Purposeful Determination. It springs from Desire, but it evolves into something which is capable of mastering Desire by its power of "Willing to Will."

Here follow three general rules which you should note very carefully in connection with the subject of inhibiting and setting-aside the temptations of conflicting desires—of those desires which are constantly springing up and tempting you to forego "paying the price," or to become "sidetracked" from the Path of Attainment of your Dominant Desires. Two of these rules are along the lines of which we have spoken in connection with the influence of Representative Ideas upon Desire Power.

I. Under temptation by sidetracking desires, use every effort to feed the Flame of Desire of your Dominant Desires, by an increased supply of suggestive ideas and mental pictures tending to stimulate its heat and incite its energy.

II. At the same time, strenuously avoid feeding the flame of the tempting desires by suggestive ideas and mental pictures likely to arouse or incite them. On the contrary, carefully and positively refuse to admit such ideas and pictures to your mind so far as is possible; seek to starve the fires of such desires by withholding from them the fuel necessary for their continuance and support.

The third rule involves another psychological principle, and is as follows:

III. So far as is possible, transmute the sidetracking desires into forms more in accordance with general trend of the Dominant Desires, thereby converting them into helpful rather than harmful emotional energy.

In the case of the first rule above stated, you tend to inhibit the energy of the sidetracking desires by imparting additional energy to the Dominant Desires. When the attention is strongly attracted or held by the suggestive ideas and mental pictures of a strong set of desires, it is not easily diverted by those of a weaker set. The strong light of the former tend to cast the latter into a comparative shadow. The attention firmly concentrated and held upon one particular set of ideas and mental pictures refuses to accept the demand of another set. Keep the attention busy with the advantageous set, and it "will have no time" for the consideration of the opposing set. With these opposing suggestive ideas and mental pictures kept out of the field of conscious attention, the desires associated with them tend to die down and finally to disappear.

In the case of the second rule above stated you deliberately and determinedly refuse to feed the flame of the sidetracking desires with the fuel of suggestive ideas and mental pictures. Instead, you proceed deliberately and determinedly to starve that flame. No flame of desire can long continue to burn vigorously if its supply of suggestive fuel be cut off from it. Cut off the fuel supply of any desire, and it will begin to decrease in vigor and force. Refuse to allow your mind to dwell upon the ideas or mental pictures tending to suggest the sidetracking desires. When such ideas and pictures intrude themselves and seek to attract the attention, you must deliberately turn your attention to something else—preferably to the suggestive ideas and pictures of your Dominant Desires.

The Roman Catholic Church evidently recognizes the value of this rule, for its teachers instruct their pupils to form the habit of turning their attention to prayers and certain forms of devotional exercises when temptations assail them. The attention being directed to and held firmly upon the devotional exercise or ceremony, it is withheld from the suggestive ideas and mental pictures of the tempting desire; and, accordingly, the latter loses strength and in time dies away. Without detracting from the value of the religious element involved, we may say that it is certain that the purely psychological effect of such course is highly advantageous. You would do well to apply the principle in your own case.

In the case of the third rule above stated, you transmute the energy of the sidetracking desire into that of desires more in accordance with the general trend of your Dominant Desires. In this way you not only obviate the danger of the interference and distraction of the sidetracking desires, but also actually employ the basic energy of Desire Power to feed the flame of the advantageous desires. Here, the principle involved is not so well known as are those involved in the other rules; but that principle is sound, nevertheless, and is capable of being employed with remarkable results by the individual possessing sufficient will power and determination to apply it.

As an example of this principle of the transmutation of the form of Desire Force, let us point you to a fact well known to scientific observers, viz., that the energy of the sexual passions may be transmuted into the energy of any kind of mental or physical creative work. This fact is also known to priests and others who are called on for advice from those wishing to control passions of this kind. The explanation probably lies in the fact that sexual desire is essentially *creative* in its fundamental nature, and therefore is capable of being diverted to other forms of creative activity. But whatever may be the true explanation, it is a fact that the person experiencing strong intruding sexual desires may proceed to master and control them by means of engaging in some form of creative work in which the elemental creative energy is transmuted into other forms of creative force.

For instance, one may *create* by writing, musical composition, artistic work, or making and constructing things with the hands—in fact, by any kind of work in which things are made, put together, constructed or created in any way. In all of such work, provided that sufficient interest is thrown into the task, it will be found that the strong impulse of the intruding sexual passions will gradually lose its force, and that the person will then experience a sense of new energy in the creative work which he has undertaken in order to transmute the previous form of Desire Power.

The experienced physician knows that the best possible prescription for certain classes of cases of this kind coming to him for treatment and advice is that of "interesting work" for head or hands or both. There is much truth in the old saying that "An idle brain is the devil's workshop," and the similar one that "The devil finds plenty of work for idle hands to do." This principle may be set to work against "the devil," by simply reversing its action by giving head and hands plenty to do.

Another illustration of this principle is found in the case of the beneficial effect of certain games—in fact, of nearly all games played in moderation. Here the sidetracking and distracting desires which seek to take one away from his appointed tasks, and from the manifestation of his Dominant Desires, are transmuted into the interest, feeling, and desires of Play. Play is a safety-valve of emotional feeling. It serves to transmute many a distracting desire into the conative energy expressing itself in an interesting game. This is true of games involving purely mental skill, as well as those in which physical skill is also involved. Baseball has been a wonderful benefit to the American people in this way. Golf is playing an important part in the direction of affording a "transmutation channel" of energy for busy men who tire under the somewhat monotonous strain of the strenuous pursuit of the object of their Dominant Desires. In cases of this kind, not only are the distracting desires transmuted in this way, but the games themselves give recreation, exercise and a restful change of occupation to the individual.

"Paying the price" of your Dominant Desires does not necessarily imply that you must give up everything in life not actually concerned in furthering the interests of those particular desires—in such case, indeed, you would probably actually injure your own interests by too closely restricting your circle of interest and attention. The real meaning of the injunction is that you must "pay the price" of *giving up, inhibiting, or at least transmuting any and all desires which directly and certainly oppose and seriously interfere with the attainment of the objects of your Dominant Desires.* That price, indeed, you must be prepared to pay. In many cases, such desires may be transmuted into forms which will in a sense "run along with" the pursuit of the objects of your Dominant Desires, and thus be rendered helpful rather than harmful. Many emotional elements may be turned to account in this way by the process of transmutation. You should give some thought to this matter of transmutation when you are threatened by distracting and sidetracking desires.

Another form of "paying the price" is that of the labor and work to be performed by the individual in his task of attainment of the object of his Dominant Desires. This work and labor, however, is not alone performed by the exercise of the Persistent Determination of the Will, though this is the active element involved; there is needed also the inhibition and starving out of the conflicting or sidetracking desires which strive to draw the individual away from his appointed tasks and toward the actions requiring less work, and which for the time being seem to be richer in promise of pleasure and satisfaction.

The price paid by the men and women who have achieved marked success almost always is found to include self-denial, and sometimes even actual privation during the earlier days of the undertaking; work far in excess of that rightfully demanded of the wage earner, both in amount and in time is demanded of them; application and unwearied perseverance are required of them; indomitable resolution and persistent determination must be "paid" by them. There is here the constant giving up of the present pleasure in favor of that hoped for in the future. There is here the constant performance of tasks which might easily be avoided, and which are really avoided by the average person, but which are required to be performed by the individual who is inspired by the Dominant Desire and who is working for the accomplishment of "the one big thing."

Napoleon "paid the price" in his earlier days when he refused to indulge in the frivolous pursuits of his fellow-students at Brienne, and instead, deliberately devoted his spare time to the mastery of the elements of military science and history. Abraham Lincoln "paid the price" when he studied the few books he could find by the light of the fireplace, instead of indulging in the pleasures and dissipations of the other young men of his neighborhood. Read the history of any successful man and you will find this invariable "paying the price" of study, application, work, self-denial, economy, thrift, industry and the rest of the needful things.

Never delude yourself with the thought that you can escape "paying the price" of the attainment of the objects of your strong desires. The price must always be paid— the greater the object of attainment the greater is the price demanded. But you will find that if you have learned how to "want it hard enough" then the price will be comparatively easy to pay—the thing will be deemed well worth it.

If you feel that the price that you are being called upon to pay for the object of your Dominant Desires is more than the thing is worth, then there is something wrong about the whole matter. In such case, you should carefully "take stock" of your feelings, weighing and comparing them carefully as we have suggested in our consideration of Self-Analysis, and selection of Dominant Desires. You may find that what you had supposed to be a Dominant Desire is not really such at all. Or you may find that you have failed to include some necessary element or phase of the Dominant Desire. Or, that you have failed to make some possible transmutation of distracting desires; or have failed to inhibit or starve out sidetracking desires. Or, possibly, that you have failed to feed the flame of your Dominant Desire properly. At any rate, there is something wrong in such a case, and you should seek the remedy.

While the Law of Nature provides that you must "pay the price" of any and all desires, it also provides that the attainment must always be worth the price. If you find that the present and probable future value of any object of your desire is not worth the price you must be called upon to pay for it, then you should carefully consider the whole matter most critically, viewing it from all angles, and in the light of all possible relations and associations, with full deliberation concerning the probable consequences of an opposite course, and with thoughtful judgment concerning all alternative courses. The dissatisfaction may be merely temporary and passing, or on the other hand, it may be growing in strength and promise of permanency.

Any desire which upon careful consideration, deliberation, and judgment may seem not to "pay for its keep"—to be not worth its storage charges or floor space in your emotional nature—is a fit object for a final retrial upon its merits, a re-valuation of its points, in order to decide whether it shall be retained and treated for additional strength, energy and emotional value, or else discarded and rejected. The test should always be: "*Is this really worth while—worth the price I am called on to pay for it; would its rejection cost me more than its retention?*" The Touchstone of Merit should be: "*Does this render me stronger, better and more efficient—and, therefore, more truly and permanently happier?*"

SUMMARY

You have seen that Desire is that emotional state which is represented by the phrase, *"I want!"* You have seen that *"Desire has for its object something which will bring pleasure or get rid of pain, immediate or remote, for the individual or for some one in whom he is interested."* You have seen that *"You always act according to your greatest 'like' or 'dislike' of which you are cognizant at the time."* You have seen that *"The degree of force, energy, will, determination, persistence, and continuous application manifested by an individual in his aspirations, ambitions, aims, performances, actions and work is determined primarily by the degree of his desire for the attainment of the objects thereof—his degree of 'want' and 'want to' concerning that object."* You have seen that *"Desire is the Flame that produces the Steam of Will,"* and that, therefore, Desire is the source from which all human action springs.

You have seen that not only does Desire Power directly or indirectly cause all human action, but that it also sets into operation the Life Forces which develop the mental and physical faculties and powers of the individual along lines designed to further and more efficiently manifest and express the dominant desires of the individual. You have seen how Desire Power presses into service the powers of the subconscious mentality in the work of manifesting and expressing the strong desires. You have seen how the subconscious powers act so as to attract to the individual the things, person, conditions and circumstances serving to enable him to better manifest and express his sovereign desires; and how, in the same way, they tend to attract the individual to those things, persons, conditions and circumstances. You have seen how Desire Attraction works silently, even when one is asleep, toward the end impressed upon it by the character of the strong desires.

You have discovered the importance of "knowing exactly what you want," and have learned how to gain such important knowledge by Self-Analysis and Selection. You have discovered the importance of "wanting it hard enough," and have learned how to feed the Flame of Desire so as to cause it to burn fiercely. You have learned how to set into motion and activity the great body of Elemental Desire, and how to cause it to flow forth through the channels of manifestation and expression which you have carefully built for its flood. You have discovered the necessity of "paying the price of attainment" of the objects of your desire, and have learned the general rules concerning such payment.

You have been informed concerning the tremendous power of the Desire Power within your being, and have become acquainted with the laws governing its manifestation and expression, and the rules regulating its control and direction. If you have entered into the spirit of this instruction, and have allowed its influence to descend into the subconscious depths of your mentality, you have already become aware of the aroused energy of the Desire Power in those depths. You will have found yourself filled with a new and unfolding consciousness of Personal Power within you. You will have experienced that intuitive feeling that there have been set into operation in you certain subtle but dynamic forces which will tend to make you "stronger, better and more efficient."

As you proceed to arouse into further activity these great forces of your nature, and to direct their channel of manifestation and expression, you will from time to time receive actual evidence and proof that you are travelling along the right road, and are employing the proper methods. You will be astonished to receive proofs and actual results in the most unexpected manner, and from sources and directions never dreamt of before. You will realize more and more, as you proceed, that you have set into operation one of Nature's most potent forces, in fact, "the force of forces." Finally, you will begin to realize that the very actual presence within you of a Dominant Desire which has won its place in the "struggle for existence," and which has stood all the tests, is practically "the prophecy of its own fulfillment."

You have been asked to consider the facts which have been discovered concerning the nature, character and modes of activity of Desire Power, that great elemental psychic energy which is seen to pervade all existence and to be present universally. Analyze the actions of any or every living thing, and you will find Desire Power inspiring and motivating it. Nay, examine the motions of the so-called inanimate objects of Nature, and you will find even there the energizing forces of "something like Desire Power."

If Nature be regarded as a magnificent Cosmic Machine—then Desire Power is the motive-power that runs that universal machinery. If Nature be regarded as a Living Macrocosm—then Desire Power is the living motive-power inspiring and causing its activities. From whatever angle Nature may be viewed, under whatever hypothesis or theory it may be regarded, Desire Power is perceived to be the Something or Somewhat directly responsible for making "the wheels go 'round." The old Hermetic axiom, "As above, so below; as within, so without; as in great, so in small," is seen to apply here: the individual and the Cosmos both are seen to have as their essential motive-power that original, aboriginal, elemental, fundamental Something which we know as Desire Power.

In view of this fact, you scarcely need to be urged to study the methods of operation of this mighty force, so that you may harness it to your machinery of life and action. Like Gravitation or Electricity, its power is available to all who have the courage, intelligence and perseverance to master it and to press it into service. It is as free as the air or the sunshine; it costs nothing to run your living machinery with it—nothing but persistence and determination. You do not have to supply it with power, or to add energy to it: it has within itself far more power, energy or force than you will ever have occasion to make use of. All that you need do is to tap on to its free energy, and to set it to work for you in the direction of running the mental and physical machinery with which you have provided it.

Let us ask you to consider the following remarkable statement of Wr. Wilfrid Lay. Speaking of the Desire Power of the Subconscious, Dr. Lay says:

I call your attention to the enormous power of the Subconscious. It is the accumulated desire in each one of us, of aeons of evolution, the present form, in each individual, of that vital force which has kept itself immortal through thousands of generations of men behind us, and millions of generations of animals behind them. It need not be anything but a source of power to us, power that we can draw upon, if we rightly understand it, just as we can turn on power from a steam pipe or an electric wire. It need not be destructive, indeed it is not destructive, except in the most distracted souls, but on the contrary ought in each one of us, when we have learned to manage it rightly, to be as much and as completely at our command as is the power in the automobile. As in the automobile, there are a few simple things that we have to learn and the rest is furnished by the maker of the car, and we do ill to tamper with it. The experience of having a two-hundred-horsepower car placed at one's command (if it is to be driven by oneself) is a situation into which there are many persons, both men and women, who are very loath to enter. And similarly there are many persons who for various causes would not be willing to have developed the two-hundred-thousand-generation-power which resides in them. To all intents and purposes, and as far as human flesh is able to bear the strain, this power which is largely in the hands of the Subconscious in most men and women is illimitable.

Desire Power is a Cosmic Force designed for the controlled and directed use of the strong. It is at the disposal of all—but only few are courageous and determined enough to avail themselves of its services. The masses of men merely dally with it, play with it, handle it gingerly: the Masters of Men boldly grasp its controlling levers, and turn its power into their mental and physical machinery. It is a Master Force fitted only for the service of Masters. It is the rightful servant only of those whose slogan is: "I Can, I Will; I Dare, I Do!"

You can be a Master of Desire Power, and thus a Master of Men, a Master of Circumstances, a Master of Life, if you but will to be so. You are the Master of your Fate—the Captain of your Soul—if you will but recognize, realize and manifest the Power of the "I AM I" which is your Real Self, and of which Desire Power is the willing servant.

YOUR SILENT PARTNER WITHIN

While the mental planes lying outside of and beyond the field of ordinary consciousness have been until recent years comparatively unexplored by psychologists, and in fact have been almost entirely ignored by western psychology until modern times, the best thought of the present time is in practical agreement upon the fact that on those hidden planes of mentality are performed the major portion of our mental work, and that in their field are in operation some of the most important of our mental processes.

The exploration of these obscure regions of the mind has been one of the most fascinating tasks of modern psychology; and the mines have yielded rich material in abundance. Many mental phenomena formerly either denied as impossible by the orthodox psychologists, or else regarded by the average person as evidence of supernatural agencies and forces, are now seen to fit perfectly into the natural order of things, and to operate according to natural law and order. Not only have such investigations resulted in a greater increase of the scientific knowledge concerning the inner workings of the mind, but they have also served to place in the hands of the more advanced psychologists the material which they have turned to practical and efficient use by means of scientific methods of application.

The effect of these discoveries has been the presentation of an important truth to the thinking individual—the truth that his mental realm is a far greater and grander land that he has heretofore considered it to be. No longer is the Self held to be limited in its mental activities to the narrow field of ordinary consciousness. Your mental kingdom has suddenly expanded until it now constitutes a great empire, with borders flung wide and far beyond the boundaries of the little kingdom which you have been considering as the entire area of the field of the forces, powers and activities of the Self.

The Self has often been likened to the king of a great mental kingdom; but, in view of the discovery of the new facts concerning the wonderful field of the unconscious, subconscious and superconscious mental activities, the Self is now more properly to be represented as a mighty emperor of a vast empire of which only a comparatively small portion has as yet been explored. You are being called upon to appreciate more fully the ancient aphorism: "You are greater than you know." Your Self is like a new Columbus, gazing at the great new world which it has discovered around itself, and of which it is the owner and the ruler.

Employing the term, "The Subconscious," to indicate the entire field of activities of the mind which are performed below, above or in anyway "outside of" the field or plane of the ordinary consciousness of the individual, we soon discover that the activities of the Subconscious extend over a very wide range of manifestation, and embrace a great variety of forms of expression.

In the first place, the Subconscious presides over the activities of your physical organism; it is the animating spirit of your physical processes. It performs the manifold tasks of digestion, assimilation, nutrition, elimination, secretion, circulation, reproduction—in short, all of your vital processes. Your conscious mentality is thus relieved of these great tasks.

Again, the Subconscious supervises the performance of your instinctive actions. Every action that you perform automatically, instinctively, "by habit," "by heart" and without conscious employment of thought and will, is really performed by your subconscious mentality. Your conscious mentality, thus relieved of this work, is able to concentrate upon those other tasks which it alone can perform. When you learn to perform an action "by heart," or "by habit," the conscious mentality has turned over this particular work to your Subconscious.

Again, the Subconscious is largely concerned with the activities of your emotional nature. Your emotions which rise to the plane or level of consciousness are but the surface manifestations of the more elemental activities performed in the depths of the ocean of the Subconscious. Your elemental and instinctive emotions have their source and home in the Subconscious; they have accumulated there by reason of habit, heredity or racial memory. Practically all the material of your emotional activities is stored on the planes and levels of the Subconscious.

Again, the Subconscious presides over the processes of Memory. The subconscious planes or levels of the mind constitute the great storehouse of the recorded impressions of memory. Moreover, on those planes or levels is performed the work of indexing and cross-indexing the memory-records, by means of which subsequent recollection, recognition and remembrance are rendered possible. These regions of your subconscious mentality contain not only the recorded impressions of your own personal experience, but also those racial memories or inherited memories which manifest in you as "instinct," and which play a very important part in your life.

Again, the Subconscious is able to, and frequently does, perform for you important work along the lines of actual "thinking." By means of "mental rumination" it digests and assimilates the materials furnished by your conscious mentality, and then proceeds to classify these, to compare them, and to proceed to form judgments and decisions upon them and from them—all below the levels of your ordinary consciousness. Careful psychologists have decided that by far the greater part of our reasoning processes are really performed on mental levels and planes outside of the field of the ordinary consciousness. Much of your creative mental work, particularly that of the constructive imagination, is performed in this way, the result afterward being raised to the levels of conscious thought.

Finally, there are levels and planes "above" those of the ordinary consciousness, just as there are those "below" the latter. Just as the lower levels are largely concerned with working over the stored-up materials of the past, so these higher levels are concerned with reporting that which may be considered to represent the future conscious activities of the human race. These higher regions of the Subconscious may be said to contain the seed or embryo of the higher faculties and powers which will unfold fully in the future stages of the mental evolution of the race; many of these higher faculties and powers are even now beginning to manifest in occasional flashes in the minds of certain individuals, and, as a consequence, such individuals are frequently regarded as "inspired" or as possessing that indefinable quality or power known as "genius."

On these higher planes of the Subconscious abide certain marvelous powers of the Self, which powers manifest and express themselves in that which we call genius, inspiration, illumination—the exceptional mental achievements of certain intellects which stamp them as above the average. On these high planes abide and are manifested those wonderful mental activities which we attempt to explain under the term "Intuition." These activities, however, are not contrary to reason, though they may seem to transcend it at times; it is better to consider them as the manifestation of a Higher Reason. The investigation and exploration of these higher realms of the Subconscious form one of the most interesting and fascinating tasks of modern psychology. Even now, the reports of the investigators and explorers are of surpassing interest; those which confidently may be looked for in the future bid fair to constitute a marvelous contribution to the pages of the history of modern scientific research.

We shall ask you to accompany us in an exploration of the various regions of the Subconscious—those wonderful realms of your mind—from the highest to the lowest. In this new land there are valuable deposits of material useful to you and to all mankind. It is our purpose to point out these to you, and to instruct you in the most approved methods of mining and converting them to practical uses. You are interested in the matter of being led directly to the mines containing these rich deposits, and in being told just how to conduct the mining operations and the converting processes. In this spirit, then, our journey of exploration shall be conducted.

The Secret Forces of the Great Subconscious, like all other great natural forces, may be harnessed and pressed into service by you. Like electricity, they may be so managed and directed into the proper channels that they may be set to work by and for you. You have been employing these forces, to a greater or less extent, in very many of your mental activities; but, in all probability, you have been employing them instinctively and without a full knowledge of the laws and principles involved in them. When you understand just what these forces are, how they work, and the methods best calculated to produce efficient results and effects, then you may proceed to employ them intelligently, deliberately and with conscious purpose and intent, end and aim.

The average man employs but about 25 per cent of the Subconscious Power. The man who understands the principles and methods to which we have just referred will be able to employ 100 per cent of his available Subconscious Power. This means that he will be able to increase fourfold his Subconscious mental work and activity, with correspondingly increased results and effects. Inasmuch as at least 75 per cent of man's mental processes are performed on the plane or level of the Subconscious, it will be seen that the benefits arising from quadrupling his Subconscious mental activities and available power are almost beyond the power of adequate calculation. This increased power and efficiency, moreover, are not obtained at the cost of increased effort and mental wear and tear: on the contrary, the man effectively employing his Subconscious relieves himself of a great portion of the mental strain incident to the employment of the conscious mentality.

In addition to the offices and powers of the Super-conscious which we have mentioned, there is another and a most important function of that phase of the mentality which may be called "the protective power." Many persons, most persons in fact, have at times experienced this beneficent power. They have felt strongly that they were in close contact with a force, power or entity of some kind which was in some way higher than themselves, but which was concerned with their welfare. This beneficent presence has been interpreted in various ways in accordance with the trend of thought of those experiencing it. Some of the ancients called it "the kindly genius"; others termed it "the guardian angel"; still others have thought of it as "my spirit friend"; while many others, though quite vividly conscious of its presence and power, have failed to give it a special name.

But by whatever name it may have been thought of, or even when no name at all has been applied to it, the mysterious something has been recognized as a beneficent presence-power—a hovering and brooding Something or Somewhat animated by a warm, kindly interest in the individual, and seemingly devoted to his interests and disposed to render to him useful services.

This beneficent presence-power has often acted as a warning guardian in the lives of many persons. In other cases it has been felt to have acted subtly to bring about advantageous results and conditions for the persons whom it protected. It has led some into circumstances and conditions calculated to be of advantage to them; it has drawn others away from conditions and circumstances calculated to bring harm to them. In short, it has played the part of "the kindly genius" or "the guardian angel" to many an individual.

The touch of this Unseen Hand has been felt by countless individuals—very likely by you who are now reading these lines. It has cheered men when the tide of circumstances seemed to be running against them; it has animated them with a new lively spirit, has encouraged them to renewed endeavor, has filled them with new courage when they needed it most. It has seemingly led persons into the presence of other persons and things, into conditions and environments, which have proved advantageous to them. Men in all ages—some of the most practical and "hard headed" men of affairs, among others—have felt the touch of this Unseen Hand, and have gratefully acknowledged its help in times of need, even though they have been perplexed concerning its real character.

To many careful thinkers who have earnestly investigated this phenomenon, it has seemed that this beneficent presence-power—this Unseen Hand that has reached out in times of need—is not an external power, nor an entity outside of themselves, but is rather a manifestation of that part of man's mental nature which we have here considered under the term "The Superconscious." Instead of being an entity outside of us, it is believed to be a part of ourselves— a phase, part or aspect of our Self that manifests above the levels or planes of the ordinary consciousness. In short, this "kindly genius" or "guardian angel" is your own Superconscious Self, manifesting on some of its higher levels or planes of activity and power.

In this Higher Self you have a friend far truer, more constant and more loyal than can be any other friend—for it is Yourself, in its essence and substance. Your interests are its interests, for you are one with it in essential being and power. It will manifest a fidelity to you, and a watchfulness over your real interests which is amazing in its devotion and constancy. It will manifest toward you, in turns, the protecting care of a father; the brooding watchful, loving care of a mother; and the helpful, fraternal care of a brother. It will be all of these things to you—and more—if you will but give it the chance to unfold its presence and to manifest its power in your life.

This Higher Self—this phase of your Superconscious—needs but the encouragement of your recognition and realization in order to manifest its power in your behalf. It is seemingly discouraged, disheartened and abashed by your indifference, unbelief and the failure to recognize its presence and to realize its power. It does not need "training" or "developing"—all that it asks is to be recognized and realized by you, and to have from you a kindly, sympathetic reception. It has done much for you in the past—it will do more for you in the future, if you will but meet it half way.

This higher part of your Self is full of discernment, and of cold, keen-edged wisdom. It can see far ahead, and is able to discern and select the right road for you to travel, and then to lead you into that road and to keep your feet on its solid substance, in spite of your efforts to take a side path or to wander into the ditches which lie on either side of the road. You will do well to "get off by yourself" once in a while, then and there to commune with your Higher Self—to have a little "heart-to-heart" visit with it. You will find this Higher Self to be a wonderful companion—one closer to you than can be any human being—for it is Yourself, and nothing but Yourself, manifesting on the higher planes and levels of your being. You will emerge from these periods of self-communion with renewed strength and vigor, filled with new hope and faith, animated by new ambitions and purposive determination.

We have presented to you a view of your New Mental Empire—a view of its lowest and its highest planes and levels, of its highlands and its lowlands. It is your own empire—YOURS! Yours it is to rule and to govern, to explore and to cultivate. You are at home in it. The many wonderful phenomena manifested in its immense region are your phenomena—yours to control, direct, develop, cultivate; yours to restrict, restrain, inhibit; at your will, as you will, by your will.

Do not allow yourself to be tempted by the wonderful powers manifested by some of your subordinate mental machinery or instruments; do not allow yourself to fall under the spell of any of the phenomenal manifestations in your mental wonderland. View all; respect all; use all; demand and secure aid and work from all; but never lose sight of the fact that YOU, your Real Self—the "I am I"—is the Master of this land, the ruler of this Empire, and that you rightfully have power and dominion over it, all its inhabitants, and all contained in its realm.

Your "I am I," your Real Self—YOU—are a centre of consciousness and will, of Personal Power, in that Infinite and Eternal Power, that Ultimate POWER from which all things proceed, and in which we live, and move, and have our being. Your physical body and your physical energies; your mental mechanism and its energies, manifesting on any or all the planes or levels of consciousness, subconsciousness, or superconsciousness; all these are but instruments or channels of expression of your Real Self, the "I AM I," of YOU.

YOU, the "I AM I" are the centre of your personal world of experience and manifestation. Keep ever your rightful place at the center of that world; observe all the rest whirling and revolving around that center, as the planets revolve, whirling, around the sun. YOU are the Sun! Do not lose your balance, nor be induced to move away from your central position to accommodate any of your subordinate planets—not even the greatest of them.

Hail! Mighty Emperor! Enter into and possess, rule and govern, your New Mental Empire! It is YOURS!

Let us remind you of the truth of the ancient aphorism:

"You are greater than you know!"

The Secret of Power

INTRODUCTION

What is the strongest political trend in the world today?

After the last war, it was towards democracy. But somehow democracy failed the average man. When the depression came and he found himself unable to provide food and shelter for his loved ones, he demanded something more than equality of opportunity. He demanded SECURITY from want.

To answer that demand came "Strong Men," so-called, Mussolinis and Hitlers and Antonescus and Francos and the like, and Fascism was born. Men achieved security, of a kind, but they bartered their freedom for it. And soon they learned that power feeds on power, and the only end of dictatorship is war, which destroys all.

And the reason? The same reason that has impelled man since time began—the longing for security, security for the home, security against want, security for old age.

Since time began, the search for security has been one of the strongest urges in all of nature. You see it in the animal in the way it conceals its nest and tries to make it safe from predatory creatures—man or animal. You see it in the records of early man in the caves he dug into the sides of the mountains, in the tree huts, in the cliff dwellings. You follow it down through the ages to the walled cities, the turreted castles, the inaccessible mountains in which men made their homes.

Throughout history, you see this search for security as one of the dominant characteristics of all human kind. And now that the common man has realized his power, you find him all over the world banding together to take over all property, to the end that he and his may find that security from want that he has so long worked for.

What he does not seem to realize is that the mere redistribution of property never has and never will solve his problem. It will provide him with temporary supply, yes— but supply is a continuing problem, and when his small share of the general distribution is gone, he will be worse off than he was before, because production will have either ceased or been greatly curtailed.

Redistribution is not the answer. It has been tried repeatedly, and always failed. You must go farther back than that. You must start with the source of things. And that is what we shall try to do in the following pages.

> Know this, ye restless denizens of earth,
> Know this, ye seekers after joy and mirth,
> Three things there are, eternal in their worth—
> LOVE, that outreaches to the humblest things:
> WORK, that is glad in what it does and brings;
> And FAITH, that soars upon unwearied wings.
> Divine the powers that on this trio wait,
> Supreme their conquest, over time and fate.

LOVE, WORK and FAITH, these three alone are great.

THE CREATIVE FORCE

The Spirit of the Lord is upon me,
Because he anointed me to preach good tidings to the poor:
He has sent me to proclaim release to the captives,
And recovering of sight to the blind,
To set at liberty them that are bruised,
To proclaim the acceptable year of the Lord."
In the beginning was the Word. And the Word was with
God. And the Word was God.

                                        —ST. JOHN

What is a word? A mental concept or image, is it not? In originating language, words were coined to represent certain images or objects. The word horse, for instance, calls to mind the image left upon the retina and the brain by what one has seen of that quadruped.

But what if there were no horses? What if one were called upon to create a horse, with no previous knowledge of such an animal? You'd have to build up a clear mental image of him first, would you not? You'd have to work out a mental picture of every part of his anatomy, every physical outline. You'd need a perfect mental concept of everything that is comprised in the word horse.

And that was what happened when God created the world. In the beginning was the "Word," the mental concept, the image in God's mind of what He planned. "And the Word was made flesh." It took on shape and substance. It grew into an habitable world. It developed creatures like the fish in the sea, the birds in the air, the beasts of the field. And finally man.

Life then, as now, was a continually developing process. Those early forms of life were threatened by every kind of danger—from floods, from earthquakes, from droughts, from desert heat, from glacial cold, from volcanic eruptions—but each new danger was merely an incentive to finding some new resource, to putting forth their Creative Force in some new shape.

To meet one set of needs, the Creative Force formed the Dinosaur; to meet another, the Butterfly. Long before it worked up to man, we see its unlimited resourcefulness in a thousand ways. To escape danger in the water, some forms of Life sought land. Pursued on land, they took to the air. To breathe in the sea, the Creative Force developed gills. Stranded on land, it perfected lungs. To meet one kind of danger, it grew a shell. For another, it developed fleetness of foot, or wings that carried it into the air. To protect itself from glacial cold, it grew fur. In temperate climes, hair. Subject to alternate heat and cold, it produced feathers. But ever, from the beginning, it showed its power to meet every changing condition, *to answer every creature need.*

Had it been possible to stamp out this Creative Force, or halt its constant upward development, it would have perished ages ago, when fire and flood, drought and famine followed each other in quick succession. But obstacles, misfortunes, cataclysms, were to it merely new opportunities to assert its power. In fact, it required difficulties or obstacles to stir it up, to make it show its energy and resourcefulness.

The great reptiles, the monster beasts of antiquity, passed on as the conditions changed that had made them possible, but the Creative Force stayed, changing as each age changed, always developing, always improving.

When God put this Creative Force into His creatures, He gave to it unlimited energy, unlimited resource. No other power can equal it. No force can defeat it. No obstacle can hold it back. All through the history of life and mankind, you can see its directing intelligence rising to meet every need of life.

No one can follow it down through the ages without realizing that the purpose of existence is GROWTH, DEVELOPMENT. Life is dynamic, not static. It is ever moving forward—not standing still. The one unpardonable sin in all of nature is to stand still, to stagnate. The Gigantosaurus, that was over a hundred feet long and as big as a house; the Tyrannosaurus, that had the strength of a locomotive and was the last word in frightfulness; the Pterodactyl or Flying Dragon—all the giant monsters of pre-historic ages—are gone. They ceased to serve a useful purpose. They stood still while the life around them passed them by.

Egypt and Persia, Greece and Rome, all the great empires of antiquity, perished when they ceased to grow. China built a wall around herself and stood still for a thousand years. In all of Nature, to cease to grow is to perish.

It is for men and women who are not ready to stand still, who refuse to cease to grow, that this book is written. Its purpose is to give you a clearer understanding of your own potentialities, to show you how to work with and take advantage of the infinite energy and power of the Creative Force working through you.

The terror of the man at the crossways, not knowing which way to turn, should be no terror for you, for your future is of your own making. The only law of infinite energy is the law of supply. The Creative Principle is your principle. To survive, to win through, to triumphantly surmount all obstacles has been its everyday practice since the beginning of time. It is no less resourceful now than it ever was. You have but to supply the urge, to work in harmony with it, to get from it anything you need. For if this Creative Force is so strong in the lowest forms of animal life that it can develop a shell or a poison to meet a need; if it can teach the bird to circle and dart, to balance and fly; if it can grow a new limb on a spider or crab to replace a lost one; how much more can it do for YOU—a reasoning, rational being, with a mind able to work with this Creative Force, with energy and purpose and initiative to urge it on!

The evidence of this is all about you. Take up some violent form of exercise, and in the beginning your muscles are weak, easily tired. But keep on a few days, and what happens? The Creative Force in you promptly strengthens them, toughens them, to meet their need.

All through your daily life, you find this Force steadily at work. Embrace it, work with it, take it to your heart, and there is nothing you cannot do. The mere fact that you have obstacles to overcome is in your favor, for when there is nothing to be done, when things run along too smoothly, the Creative Force seems to sleep. It is when you need it, when you call upon it urgently, that it is most on the job.

It differs from Luck in this, that fortune is a fickle jade who smiles most on those who need her least. Stake your last penny on the turn of a card—have nothing between you and ruin but the spin of a wheel or the speed of a horse—and the chances are a hundred to one that luck will desert you.

It is just the opposite with the Creative Force in you. As long as things run smoothly, as long as life flows along like a song, this Creative Force seems to slumber, secure in the knowledge that your affairs can take care of themselves. But let things start going wrong, let ruin or death stare you in the face–then is the time this Creative Force will assert itself if you give it a chance.

There is a Napoleonic feeling of power that insures success in the knowledge that this invincible Creative Force is behind your every act. Knowing that you have with you a force which never yet has failed in anything it has undertaken, you can go ahead in the confident knowledge that it will not fail in your case. The ingenuity which overcame every obstacle in making you what you are, is not likely to fall short when you have immediate need for it. It is the reserve strength of the athlete, the second wind of the runner, the power that, in moments of great stress or excitement, you unconsciously call upon to do the deeds which you ever after look upon as superhuman.

But they are in no wise superhuman. They are merely beyond the capacity of your conscious self. Ally your conscious self with that sleeping giant within you, rouse him daily to the task and those superhuman deeds will become your ordinary, everyday accomplishments.

It matters not whether you are banker or lawyer, business man or clerk, whether you are the custodian of millions or have to struggle for your daily bread. The Creative Force makes no distinction between high and low, rich and poor. The greater your need, the more readily will it respond to your call. Wherever there is an unusual task, wherever there is poverty or hardship or sickness or despair, there this Servant of your mind waits, ready and willing to help, asking only that you call upon him. And not only is it ready and willing, but it is always ABLE to help. Its ingenuity and resource are without limit. It is mind. It is thought. It is the telepathy that carries messages without the spoken or written word. It is the sixth sense that warns you of unseen dangers. No matter how stupendous and complicated, or how simple your problem may be, the solution of it is somewhere in mind, in thought. And since the solution does exist, this mental giant can find it for you. It can know, and it can do, every right thing. Whatever it is necessary for you to know, whatever it is necessary for you to do, you can know and you can do if you will but seek the help of this Genie-of-your-mind and work with it in the right way.

To every living creature, God gave enough of this Creative Force to enable it to develop whatever it felt that it needed for survival. Behind and working through every living thing was this Creative Force, and to each was given the power to draw upon it at need. With the lower forms of life, that call had to be restricted to themselves, to their own bodies. They could not change their environment.

They could develop a house of shell in which to live, like the crustaceans or the snail or the turtle. They could use the Creative Force to develop strength or fleetness or teeth and claws—anything within or pertaining to themselves. But aside from building nests or caves or other more or less secure homes, they could not alter conditions around them. To man alone was given the power to make his own environment. To him alone was given dominion over things and conditions.

That he exercises this power, even today, only to a limited extent, does not alter the fact that he has it. Man was given dominion. "And God said—Let us make man in our image, after our likeness, and let them have dominion over the fish of the sea, and over the fowl of the air, and over the cattle, and over all the earth, and over every creeping thing that creepeth upon the earth."

Of course, few believe in that dominion. Fewer still exercise it for their own good or the good of all. But everyone uses the Creative Force in him to an extent. Everyone builds his own environment.

"Don't tell me," some will say indignantly, "that I built these slums around me, that I am responsible for the wretched conditions under which I work, that I had anything to do with the squalor and poverty in which my family have to live." Yet that is exactly what we do tell you. If you were born in poverty and misery, it was because your parents imaged these as something forced upon them, something they could not help, a condition that was necessary and to be expected. Thinking so, they used the Creative Force working through them to fasten those conditions upon themselves as something they were meant to suffer and could do nothing about.

Then you in your turn accepted those conditions as what you were born to, and fastened them upon yourself by your supine acceptance of them, by failing to claim better ones, by making no great or sustained efforts to get out of them.

All history shows that the determined soul who refuses to accept poverty or lack can change these to riches and power if he has the determination and the perseverance. The great men of the world have almost all come up from poverty and obscurity. The rich men of the world have mostly started with nothing.

"Always the real leaders of men, the real kings, have come up from the common people," wrote Dr. Frank Crane. "The finest flowers in the human flora grow in the woods pasture and not in the hothouse; no privileged class, no royal house, no carefully selected stock produced a Leonardo or a Michelangelo in art, a Shakespeare or Burns in letters, a Galli Curci or Paderewski in music, a Socrates or Kant in philosophy, an Edison or Pasteur in science, a Wesley or a Knox in religion."

It is the NEED that calls forth such geniuses, the urgent need for development or expression, and it is because these men drew powerfully upon the Creative Force within them that they became great. As the poet put it:

> There is Power within me which is Life itself;
> I can turn to it and rest on it;
> As I turn to it and rest on it,
> It helps me and heals me all the time.

> There is Wisdom itself within me which is Life itself;
> I can turn to it and rest on it;
> As I turn to it and rest on it,
> It helps me and heals me all the time.

There is Love itself within me which is Life itself;
It can turn to it and rest on it;
As I turn to it and rest on it,
It helps me and heals me all the time.

"Look within," said Marcus Aurelius. "Within is the fountain of all good. Such a fountain, where springing waters can never fail, do thou dig still deeper and deeper."

God gave to man, and to man alone, the power to make his own environment. He can determine for himself what he needs for survival, and if he holds to that thought with determination, he can draw whatever is necessary from the Creative Force working through him to make it manifest. First the Word, the mental image, then the creation or manifestation.

Professor Michael Pupin says—"Science finds that everything is a continually developing process." In other words, creation is still going on, all around you. Use your Creative Force to create the conditions you desire rather than those you fear. The life about you is constantly in a state of flux. All you have to do is create the mental mold in which you want the Creative Force to take form, and then hold to that mold with persistence and determination until the Creative Force in it becomes manifest.

Dr. Titus Bull, the famous neurologist, says—"Matter is spirit at a lower rate of vibration. When a patient is cured, it is spirit in the cell doing the healing according to its own inherent pattern. No doctor ever cured a patient. All he can do is to make it possible for the patient to heal himself."

And if that is true of the body, it is just as true of conditions around you. Matter—physical materials—is spirit or Creative Force at a lower rate of vibration. The spirit or Creative Force is all around you. You are constantly forming it into mental molds, but more often than not these are dictated by your fears rather than your desires. Why not determinedly form only good molds? Why not insist upon the things you want? It is just as easy, and it works just as surely. "There is no great and no small," writes Emerson,

To the soul that maketh all;
And where it cometh, all things are;
And it cometh everywhere.
I am the owner of the sphere,
Of the seven stars and the solar year,
Of Caesar's hand, and Plato's brain,
Of Lord Christ's heart, and Shakespeare's strain.

"Give me a base of support," said Archimedes, "and with a lever I will move the world."

And the base of support is that all started with *mind*. In the beginning was nothing—a fire mist. Before anything could come of it there had to be an idea, a mental model on which to build. *The God Mind* supplied that idea, that model. Therefore the primal cause is mind. Everything must start with an idea. Every event, every condition, every thing is first an idea in the mind of someone.

Before you start to build a house, you draw up a plan of it. You make an exact blue-print of that plan, and your house takes shape in accordance with your blue-print. Every material object takes form in the same way. Mind draws the plan. Thought forms the blue-print, well drawn or badly done as your thoughts are clear or vague. It all goes back to the one cause. The creative principle of the universe is mind, and thought forms the molds in which its eternal energy takes shape.

But just as the effect you get from electricity depends upon the mechanism to which the power is attached, so the effects you get from mind depend upon the way you use it. We are all of us dynamos. The power is there—unlimited power. But we've got to connect it with something—set it some task—give it work to do—else are we no better off than the animals.

The "Seven Wonders of the World" were built by men with few of the opportunities or facilities that are available to you. They conceived these gigantic projects first in their own minds, pictured them so vividly that the Creative Force working through them came to their aid and helped them to overcome obstacles that most of us would regard as insurmountable. Imagine building the Pyramid of Gizeh, enormous stone upon enormous stone, with nothing but bare hands. Imagine the labor, the sweat, the heartbreaking toil of erecting the Colossus of Rhodes, between whose legs a ship could pass! Yet men built these wonders, in a day when tools were of the crudest and machinery was undreamed of, by using the unlimited power of the Creative Force.

That Creative Force is in you, working through you, but it must have a model on which to work. It must have thoughts to supply the molds.

There are in Universal Mind ideas for millions of wonders greater far than the "Seven Wonders of the World." And those ideas are just as available to you as they were to the artisans of old, as they were to Michelangelo when he built St. Peter's in Rome, as they were to the architect who conceived the Empire State Building, or the engineer who planned the Hell Gate Bridge.

Every condition, every experience of life is the result of our mental attitude. We can *do* only what we think we can do. We can *be* only what we think we can be. We can *have* only what we think we can have. What we do, what we are, what we have, all depend upon what we think. There is only one limit upon the Creative Force, and that is the limit we impose upon it.

We can never express anything that we do not first believe in. The secret of all power, all success, all riches, is in first thinking powerful thoughts, successful thoughts, thoughts of wealth, of supply. We must build them in our own mind first. As Edgar A. Guest so well expressed it,

> *You can do as much as you think you can,*
> *But you'll never accomplish more;*
> *If you're afraid of yourself, young man,*
> *There's little for you in store.*
> *For failure comes from the inside first,*
> *It's there if we only knew it,*
> *And you can win, though you face the worst,*
> *If you feel that you're going to do it.*

William James, the famous psychologist, said that the greatest discovery in a hundred years was the discovery of the power of the subconscious mind. It is the greatest discovery of all time. It is the discovery that man has within himself the power to control his surroundings, that he is not at the mercy of chance or luck, that he is the arbiter of his own fortunes, that he can carve out his own destiny. He is the master of the Creative Force working through him. As James Allen puts it: Dream lofty dreams, and as you dream, so shall you become. Your vision is the promise of what you shall one day be; your Ideal is the prophecy of what you shall at last unveil.

For matter is in the ultimate but a product of thought, the result of the mold into which you have put the Creative Force working through you. Even the most material scientists admit that matter is not what it appears to be. According to physics, matter (be it the human body or a log of wood— it makes no difference which) is made up of an aggregation of distinct minute particles called atoms. Considered individually, these atoms are so small that they can be seen only with the aid of a powerful microscope, if at all.

Until comparatively recent years, these atoms were supposed to be the ultimate theory regarding matter. We ourselves—and all the material world around us—were supposed to consist of these infinitesimal particles of matter, so small that they could not be seen or weighed or smelled or touched individually—but still particles of matter *and indestructible.*

Now, however, these atoms have been further analyzed, and physicists tell us that they are not indestructible at all— that they are mere positive and negative buttons of force or energy called protons and electrons, without hardness, without density, without solidity, without even positive actuality. In short, they are vortices in the ether—whirling bits of energy—dynamic, never static, pulsating with life, but the life is *spiritual!* As one eminent British scientist put it— "Science now explains matter by *explaining it away!*"

And that, mind you, is what the solid table in front of you is made of, is what your house, your body, the whole world is made of—*whirling bits of energy!*

To quote the "New York Herald-Tribune": We used to believe that the universe was composed of an unknown number of different kinds of matter, one kind for each chemical element. The discovery of a new element had all the interest of the unexpected. It might turn out to be anything, to have any imaginable set of properties.

That romantic prospect no longer exists. We know now that instead of many ultimate kinds of matter there are only two kinds. Both of these are really kinds of electricity. One is negative electricity, being, in fact, the tiny particle called the electron, familiar to radio fans as one of the particles vast swarms of which operate radio vacuum tubes. The other kind of electricity is positive electricity. Its ultimate particles are called protons. From these protons and electrons all of the chemical elements are built up. Iron and lead and oxygen and gold and all the others differ from one another merely in the number and arrangement of the electrons and protons which they contain. That is the modern idea of the nature of matter. *Matter is really nothing but electricity.*

Can you wonder then that scientists believe the time will come when mankind *through mind* can control all this energy, can be absolute master of the winds and the waves, can literally follow the Master's precept—"If ye have faith as a grain of mustard seed, ye shall say unto this mountain, Remove hence to yonder place; and it shall remove; and nothing shall be impossible unto you."

For Modern Science is coming more and more to the belief that what we call *matter is a force subject wholly to the control of mind.*

So it would seem that, to a great degree at least, and perhaps altogether, this world round about us is one of our mind's own creating. And we can put into it, and get from it, pretty much what we wish. "Nothing is," said Shakespeare, "but thinking makes it so." And the psychologist of today says the same in a different way when he tells us that only those things are real to each individual that he takes into his consciousness. To one with no sense of smell, for instance, there is no such thing as fragrance. To one without a radio, there is no music on the air waves.

To quote from "Applied Psychology," by Warren Hilton: The same stimulus acting on different organs of sense will produce different sensations. A blow upon the eye will cause you to "see stars"; a similar blow upon the ear will cause you to hear an explosive sound. In other words, the vibratory effect of a touch on eye or ear is the same as that of light or sound vibrations.

The notion you may form of any object in the outer world depends solely upon what part of your brain happens to be connected with that particular nerve-end that received an impression from the object.

You see the sun without being able to hear it because the only nerve-ends tuned to vibrate in harmony with the ether-waves set in action by the sun are nerve-ends that are connected with the brain center devoted to sight. "If," says Professor James, "we could splice the outer extremities of our optic nerves to our ears, and those of our auditory nerves to our eyes, we should hear the lightning and see the thunder, see the symphony and hear the conductor's movements."

In other words, the kind of impressions we receive from the world about us, the sort of mental pictures we form concerning it—in fact, the character of the outer world, the nature of the environment in which our lives are cast—all these things depend for each one of us simply upon how he happens to be put together, upon his individual mental make-up.

In short, it all comes back to the old fable of the three blind men and the elephant. To the one who caught hold of his leg, the elephant was like a tree. To the one who felt of his side, the elephant was like a wall. To the one who seized his tail, the elephant was like a rope. The world is to each one of us the world of *his individual perceptions.*

You are like a radio receiving station. Every moment thousands of impressions are reaching you. You can tune in on whatever ones you like—on joy or sorrow, on success or failure, on optimism or fear. You can select the particular impressions that will best serve you, you can hear only what you want to hear, you can shut out all disagreeable thoughts and sounds and experiences, or you can tune in on discouragement and failure and despair if these are what you want.

Yours is the choice. You have within you a force against which the whole world is powerless. By using it, you can make what you will of life and of your surroundings.

"But," you will say, "objects themselves do not change. It is merely the difference in the way you look at them." Perhaps. But to a great extent, at least, we find what we look for, just as, when we turn the dial on the radio, we tune in on whatever kind of entertainment or instruction we may wish to hear. Who can say that it is not our thoughts that put it there? And why shouldn't it be? All will agree that evil is merely the lack of good, just as darkness is the lack of light. There is infinite good all about us. There is fluid cosmic energy from which to form infinitely more. Why should we not use our thoughts to find the good, or to mold it from the Creative Force all about us? Many scientists believe that we can, and that in proportion as we try to put into our surroundings the good things we desire, rather than the evil ones we fear, *we will find those good things*. Certain it is that we can do this with our own bodies. Just as certain that many people are doing it with the good things of life. They have risen above the conception of life in which matter is the master.

Just as the most powerful forces in nature are the invisible ones—heat, light, air, electricity—so the most powerful forces of man are his invisible forces, his thought forces. And just as electricity can fuse stone and iron, so can your thought forces control your body, so can they win you honor and fortune, so can they make or mar your destiny.

From childhood on we are assured on every hand—by scientists, by philosophers, by our religious teachers, that "ours is the earth and the fulness thereof." Beginning with the first chapter of Genesis, we are told that "God said, Let us make man in Our image, after Our likeness; and let them have dominion over the fish of the sea, and over the fowl of the air, and over the cattle, and over all the earth—and over every living thing that moveth upon the earth." All through the Old and the New Testament, we are repeatedly adjured to use these God-given powers. "He that believeth on Me," said Jesus, "the works that I do shall he do also; and greater-works than these shall he do." "If ye abide in Me, and My words abide in you, ye shall ask what ye will, and it shall be done unto you." "For verily I say unto you, that whosoever shall say unto this mountain, Be thou removed, and be thou cast into the sea; and shall not doubt in his heart, but shall believe that those things which he saith shall come to pass; he shall have whatsoever he saith." "The kingdom of God is within you."

We hear all this, perhaps we even think we believe, but always, when the time comes to use these God-given talents, there is the "doubt in our heart."

Baudouin expressed it clearly:

To be ambitious for wealth and yet always expecting to be poor; to be always doubting your ability to get what you long for, is like trying to reach east by traveling west. There is no philosophy which will help a man to succeed when he is always doubting his ability to do so, and thus attracting failure.

You will go in the direction in which you face. . . .

There is a saying that every time the sheep bleats, it loses a mouthful of hay. Every time you allow yourself to complain of your lot, to say, "I am poor; I can never do what others do; I shall never be rich; I have not the ability that others have; I am a failure; luck is against me"; you are laying up so much trouble for yourself.

No matter how hard you may work for success, if your thought is saturated with the fear of failure, it will kill your efforts, neutralize your endeavors and make success impossible.

What was it made Napoleon the greatest conqueror of his day? Primarily his magnificent faith in Napoleon. He had a sublime belief in his destiny an absolute confidence that the obstacle was not made which Napoleon could not find a way through, or over, or around. It was only when he lost that confidence, when he hesitated and vacillated for weeks between retreat and advance, that winter caught him in Moscow and ended his dreams of world empire. Fate gave him every chance first. The winter snows were a full month late in coming. But Napoleon hesitated—and was lost. It was not the snows that defeated him. It was not the Russians. It was his loss of faith in himself.

THE KINGDOM OF HEAVEN

"The Kingdom of Heaven is within you." Heaven is not some faraway state—the reward of years of tribulation here. Heaven is right here—here and now! In the original Greek text, the word used for "Heaven" is "Ouranos." Translated literally, Ouranos means EXPANSION, in other words, a state of being where you can expand, grow, multiply and increase. This interpretation is strengthened by Jesus' own description of what the Kingdom of Heaven is like. "The Kingdom of Heaven is like to a grain of mustard seed, which a man took, and sowed in his field; which indeed is the least of all seeds, but when it is grown, it is the greatest among herbs, and becometh a tree so that the birds of the air come and lodge in the branches thereof." "The Kingdom of Heaven is like unto leaven, which a woman took and hid in three measures of meal, until the whole was leavened."

What is the property of a mustard seed? *It spreads*—a single seed will grow into a tree, a single tree will produce enough seeds to plant a great field. And what is the property of leaven or yeast? *It expands*—in a single night it can expand a hundred times in size. So when Christ said that Heaven was within us, He meant just what He said—the power to multiply our happiness, to increase our good, to expand everything we need in life, is within each one of us.

That most of us fail to realize this Heaven—that many are sickly and suffering, that more are ground down by poverty and worry—is no fault of His. He gave us the power to overcome these evils; the Kingdom of Expansion is within us, the power to increase anything we have. If we fail to find the way to use it, the fault is ours. If we expand the evil instead of the good, that is our misfortune. To enjoy the Heaven that is within us, to begin here and now to live the life eternal, takes only the right understanding and use of the Creative Force working through us.

Even now with the limited knowledge at our command, many people control circumstances to the point of making the world without an expression of their own world within where the real thoughts, the real power, resides. Through this world within, they find the solution of every problem, the cause for every effect. Discover it—and all power, all possession is within your control.

For the world without is but a reflection of that world within. Your thought *creates* the condition your mind images. Keep before your mind's eye the image of all you want to be and you will see it reflected in the world without. Think abundance, feel abundance, BELIEVE abundance, and you will find that as you think and feel and believe, abundance will manifest itself in your daily life. But let fear and worry be your mental companions, thoughts of poverty and limitation dwell in your mind, and worry and fear, limitation and poverty will be your constant companions day and night.

Your mental concept is all that matters. Its relation to matter is that of idea and form. There has got to be an idea before it can take form.

The Creative Force working through you supplies you with limitless energy which will take whatever form your mind demands. Your thoughts are the mold which crystallizes this energy into good or ill according to the form you impress upon it. You are free to choose which. But whichever you choose, the result is sure. Thoughts of wealth, of power, of success, can bring only results commensurate with your idea of them. Thoughts of poverty and lack can bring only limitation and trouble.

"A radical doctrine," you'll say, and think me wildly optimistic. Because the world has been taught for so long to think that some must be rich and some poor, that trials and tribulations are our lot. That this is at best a vale of tears.

The history of the race shows that what is considered to be the learning of one age is ignorance to the next age.

Dr. Edwin E. Slosson, Editor of SCIENCE SERVICE, speaking of the popular tendency to fight against new ideas merely because they are *new*, said: "All through the history of science, we find that new ideas have to force their way into the common mind in disguise, as though they were burglars instead of benefactors of the race."

And Emerson wrote: "The virtue in most request is conformity. Self-reliance is its aversion. It loves not realities and creators, but names and customs."

In the ages to come, man will look back upon the poverty and wretchedness of so many millions today, and think how foolish we were not to take advantage of the abundant Creative Force all about us. Look at Nature; how profuse she is in everything. Do you suppose the Mind that imaged that profuseness ever intended you to be limited, to have to scrimp and save in order to eke out a bare existence?

There are hundreds of millions of stars in the heavens. Do you suppose the Creative Force which could bring into being worlds without number in such prodigality intended to stint you of the few things necessary to your happiness or well-being?

Nature is prodigal in all that she does. Many insects increase at such a marvelous rate that if it were not for their almost equal death rate, the world would be unable to support them. Rabbits increase so rapidly that a single pair could have 13,000,000 descendants in three years! Fish lay millions of eggs each year. Throughout Nature, everything is lavish. Why should the Creative Force working through you be less generous when it comes to your own supply?

Take as an example the science of numbers. Suppose all numbers were of metal—that it was against the law to write figures for ourselves. Every time you wanted to do a sum in arithmetic you'd have to provide yourself with a supply of numbers, arrange them in their proper order, work out your problems with them. If your problems were too abstruse you might run out of numbers, have to borrow some from your neighbor or from the bank.

"How ridiculous," you say. "Figures are not things; they are mere ideas, and we can add them or divide them or multiply them as often as we like. Anybody can have all the figures he wants."

To be sure he can. And when you learn to use the Creative Force, you will find that you can multiply your material ideas in the same way. You will EXPAND the good things in your life even as Jesus did the loaves and fishes.

Thought externalizes itself, through the Creative Force working through us. What we are depends entirely upon the images we hold before our mind's eye. Every time we think, we start a chain of causes which will create conditions similar to the thoughts which originated it. Every thought we hold in our consciousness for any length of time becomes impressed upon our subconscious mind and creates a pattern which the Creative Force weaves into our life or environment.

All power is from within and is therefore under our own control. When you can direct your thought processes, you can consciously apply them to any condition, for all that comes to us in the world without is what we've already imaged in the world within.

The source of all good, of everything you wish for, is Mind, and you can reach it best through your subconscious.

Mind will be to you whatever you believe it to be—the kind and loving Father whom Jesus pictured, always looking out for the well-being of his children—or the dread Judge that so many dogmatists would have us think.

When a man realizes that his mind is part of the God Mind, when he knows that he has only to take any right aspiration to this Universal Mind to see it realized, he loses all sense of worry and fear. He learns to dominate instead of to cringe. He rises to meet every situation, secure in the knowledge that everything necessary to the solution of any problem is in Mind, and that he has but to take his problem to Universal Mind to have it correctly answered.

For if you take a drop of water from the ocean, you know that it has the same properties as all the rest of the water in the ocean, the same percentage of sodium chloride. The only difference between it and the ocean is in volume. If you take a spark of electricity, you know that it has the same properties as the thunderbolt, the same power that moves trains or runs giant machines in factories. Again the only difference is in volume. It is the same with your mind and the God Mind. The only difference between them is in volume. Your mind has the same properties as the God Mind, the same creative genius, the same power over all the earth, the same access to all knowledge. Know this, believe it, use it, and "yours is the earth and the fulness thereof." In the exact proportion that you believe yourself to be part of the God Mind, sharing in Its all-power, in that proportion can you demonstrate the mastery over your own body and over the world about you.

All growth, all supply is from the Creative Force working through you. If you would have power, if you would have wealth, you must first form the mold in this world within, in your subconscious mind, through belief and understanding.

If you would remove discord, you must remove the wrong images—images of ill health, of worry and trouble from within. The trouble with most of us is that we live entirely in the world without. We have no knowledge of that inner world which is responsible for all the conditions we meet and all the experiences we have. We have no conception of "the Father that is within us."

The inner world promises us life and health, prosperity and happiness—dominion over all the earth. It promises peace and perfection for all its offspring. It gives you the right way and the adequate way to accomplish any normal purpose. Business, labor, professions, exist primarily in thought. And the outcome of your labors in them is regulated by thought. Consider the difference, then, in this outcome if you have at your command only the limited capacity of your conscious mind, compared with the boundless energy of the subconscious and of the Creative Force working through it. "Thought, not money, is the real business capital," says Harvey S. Firestone, "and if you know absolutely that what you are doing is right, then you are bound to accomplish it in due season."

Thought is a dynamic energy with the power to bring its object out from the Creative Force all about us. Matter is unintelligent. Thought can shape and control. Every form in which matter is today is but the expression of some thought, some desire, some idea.

You have a mind. You can originate thought. And thoughts are creative. Therefore you can create for yourself that which you desire. Once you realize this, you are taking a long step toward success in whatever undertaking you have in mind. You are the potter. You are continually forming images—good or bad. Why not consciously form only good images?

More than half the prophecies in the scriptures refer to the time when man shall possess the earth, when tears and sorrow shall be unknown, and peace and plenty shall be everywhere. That time will come. It is nearer than most people think possible. You are helping it along. Every man who is honestly trying to use the power of mind in the right way is doing his part in the great cause. For it is only through Mind that peace and plenty can be gained. The earth is laden with treasures as yet undiscovered. But they are every one of them known to the God Mind, for it was this Mind that first imaged them there. And as part of Universal Mind, they can be known to you.

"TO THE MANNER BORN"

Few of us have any idea of our mental powers. The old idea was that man must take this world as he found it. He'd been born into a certain position in life, and to try to rise above his fellows was not only the height of bad taste, but sacrilegious as well. An All-wise Providence had decreed by birth the position a child should occupy in the web of organized society. For him to be discontented with his lot, for him to attempt to raise himself to a higher level, was tantamount to tempting Providence. The gates of Hell yawned wide for such scatterbrains, who were lucky if in this life they incurred nothing worse than the ribald scorn of their associates.

That is the system that produced aristocracy and feudalism. That is the system that feudalism and aristocracy strove to perpetuate.

What was it that Jesus taught which aroused the wrath of the Priests and the Rulers? What was it that made them demand His blood? NOT the doctrine of the One God. NOT the teachings of love instead of hate. But the fact that He went up and down the length and breadth of the land teaching that all men were equally the Sons of God. That would never do. That would ruin their system, spread discontent, cause uprisings against their authority. It must be stopped at any cost.

Yet Jesus' teaching has lived to become the basis of all democracies—that man is not bound by any system, that he need not accept the world as he finds it. He can remake the world to his own ideas. It is merely the raw material. He can make what he will of it.

It is this idea that is responsible for all our inventions, all our progress. Man is satisfied with nothing. He is constantly remaking his world. And now more than ever will this be true, for psychology teaches us that each one has within himself the power to use the Creative Force to become what he wills.

LEARN TO CONTROL YOUR THOUGHT

Learn to image upon your mind only the things you want to see reflected there.

You will never improve yourself by dwelling upon the drawbacks of your neighbors. You will never attain perfect health and strength by thinking of weakness or disease. No man ever made a perfect score by watching his rival's target. You have to think strength, think health, think riches. To paraphrase Pascal—"Our achievements today are but the sum of our thoughts of yesterday."

For yesterday is the mold in which the Creative Force flowing through us took shape. And cosmic energy concentrated for any definite purpose becomes power. To those who perceive the nature and transcendency of this Force, all physical power sinks into insignificance.

What is imagination but a form of thought? Yet it is the instrument by which all the inventors and discoverers have opened the way to new worlds. Those who grasp this force, be their state ever so humble, their natural gifts ever so insignificant, become our leading men. They are our governors and supreme law-givers, the guides of the drifting host that follows them as by an irrevocable decree. To quote Glenn Clark in the ATLANTIC MONTHLY,

Whatever we have of civilization is their work, theirs alone. If progress was made, they made it. If spiritual facts were discerned, they discerned them. If justice and order were put in place of insolence and chaos, they wrought the change. Never is progress achieved by the masses. Creation ever remains the task of the individual.

Our railroads, our telephones, our automobiles, our libraries, our newspapers, our thousands of other conveniences, comforts and necessities are due to the creative genius of but two per cent of our population.

And the same two per cent own a great percentage of the wealth of the country.

The question arises, Who are they. What are they? The sons of the rich? College men? No—few of them had any early advantages. Many of them have never seen the inside of a college. It was grim necessity that drove them, and somehow, some way, they found a method of drawing upon their Creative Force, and through that Force they reached success.

You don't need to stumble and grope. You can call upon the Creative Force at will. There are three steps necessary:

First, to realize that you have the power.

Second, to know what you want.

Third, to center your thought upon it with singleness of purpose.

To accomplish these steps takes only a fuller understanding of the Power-that-is-within-you.

So let us make use of this dynamo, which is *you*. What is going to start it working? Your *Faith*, the faith that is begotten of understanding. Faith is the impulsion of this power within. Faith is the confidence, the assurance, the enforcing truth, the knowing that the right idea of life will bring you into the reality of existence and the manifestation of the All power.

All cause is in Mind—and Mind is everywhere. All the knowledge there is, all the power there is, is all about you— no matter where you may be. Your Mind is part of it. You have access to it. If you fail to avail yourself of it, you have no one to blame but yourself. For as the drop of water in the ocean shares in all the properties of the rest of the ocean water, so you share in that all-power, all wisdom of Mind. If you have been sick and ailing, if poverty and hardship have been your lot, don't blame it on "fate." Blame yourself. "Yours is the earth and everything that's in it." But you've got to *take* it. The Creative Force is there—but *you* must *use* it. It is round about you like the air you breathe. You don't expect others to do your breathing for you. Neither can you expect them to use the Creative Force for you. Universal Intelligence is not only the mind of the Creator of the universe, but it is also the mind of MAN, *Your* intelligence, *your* mind. "Let this mind be in you, which was also in Christ Jesus."

> *I am success, though hungry, cold, ill-clad,*
> *I wander for awhile, I smile and say,*
> *"It is but a time, I shall be glad*
> *Tomorrow, for good fortune comes my way.*
> *God is my Father, He has wealth untold,*
> *His wealth is mine, health, happiness and gold."*
> —ELLA WHEELER WILCOX

So start today by *knowing* that you can do anything you wish to do, have anything you wish to have, be anything you wish to be. The rest will follow.

"Ye shall ask what ye will and it shall be done unto you."

A FUNNY WORLD

> *There is a world, a funny world, that's not a world at all;*
> *A world that has no shape nor size, that's neither sphere*
> *nor ball;*
> *You think at first that it exists; you think it very true;*
> *Then, finally, you see the point: that it's just fooling you.*
> *Perhaps, you once lived in this world with all its hates*
> *and fears;*
> *You were a glum and saddened soul, believed in pains*
> *and tears;*
> *You thought you had to be diseased and thought there*
> *was a hell;*
> *When, all at once, you learned the truth. This world just*
> *went pell-mell.*
>
> *And, then, this world, this shadow world, just disappeared*
> *from sight;*
> *And in its place a world of joy, of health, of love*
> *and light*
> *Came into view right where you were; you came to*

understand
That you abide in Heaven now and God is right at hand.
                    —FRANK BLENLARRY WHITNEY

THE GOAL

If you think success—success has begun;
If you think you can win, your battle is won!
Whatever you need you can have, you'll find:
It's all in the way you set your mind.

If you feel that your part in the world is small,
You may never achieve your work at all;
But feel that your life, of God's life is a part—
Then you'll work in the way you have set your heart.
If you know you are great, you will do great things;
Your thoughts will soar on eagle's wings;
Your life will reach its destined goal,
If you know the way to set your soul.
                    —KATHERINE WILDER RUGGLES

THE URGE

What is the strongest force in life? What is the power that carries those who heed it from the bottom-most pits of poverty to the top of the world—from the slums and ghettos to governorships and presidencies and the rulership of kingdoms?

The URGE for SECURITY—for ASSURED SUBSISTENCE AND SAFETY!

When the first primitive water plants appeared, living in the saturated soil along the shores of the waters, you might think the Creative Force would have rested content for a while. It had created something that lived and grew and reproduced itself. It was the first form of life upon this earth— the thallophytes.

As with the water plants, there came next the multiple-celled creature, each dependent for life upon drawing its own nourishment from the waters about. Then a central system corresponding with the stem and roots of the fern, finally evolving into distinct organs to take care of each function of life. And so was laid the foundation for all forms of animal life that have developed from this simple beginning. The principle had been perfected—it remained now only to develop every possible ramification of it, until the highest form should be reached.

When means of protection were found necessary for survival, the Creative Force developed these too. For those subject to the abrasive effects of sand and rocks, it developed shells. To the weak, it gave means of escape. To the strong, teeth and claws with which to fight. It fitted each form to meet the conditions it had to cope with. When size was the paramount consideration, it made the Gigantosaurus, over a hundred feet long and as big as a house and all the other giant monsters of antiquity. When smallness was the objective, it developed the tiny insects and water creatures, so that it takes a powerful microscope to see them, yet so perfectly made as to form organisms as exact and well-regulated as the greatest.

Size, strength, fierceness, speed—all these it developed to the last degree. It tried every form of life, but each had its weaknesses, each was vulnerable in some way. The Creative Force might develop forms that would grow, but nothing physical could be made that would be invulnerable, that would ever attain SECURITY.

To man has been given the job of emulating his Maker— of becoming a creator, finding new and broader and better ways through which to express the Creative Force in him. His is the work of creating beauty, or bringing more of comfort, of joy and happiness into the world.

To every living thing on earth is given a measure of Creative Power. Of the lower forms of life all that is required is that they bring forth fruit according to their kind—"some thirty, some sixty, some an hundred fold."

Of you, however, much more is expected. To bring forth fruit according to your physical kind is good—but that is no more than the animals do. More is required of you. You must bring forth fruit, according to your *mental* kind as well! You are a son of God, a creator. Therefore creation is expected of you. You are to spread seeds not merely of human kind, but of the intellect as well. You are to leave the world a better place than you found it, with more of joy in it, more of beauty, of comfort, of understanding, of light.

The real purpose of Life is expression, the constant urge onward and upward. Even in the smallest child, you see evidence of this. It plays with blocks. Why? To express the urge in him to build something. The growing boy makes toys, builds a hut. The girl sews dresses, cares for dolls, cooks, plays house. Why? To give vent to the inner urge in each, struggling for expression.

They reach the period of adolescence. They dance, they motor, they seek all manner of thrill. Why? Again to satisfy that constant craving of the Creative Force in them for *expression!*

True—at the moment, it is mostly a physical urge. But in some way, that urge must be translated into a mental one—*and satisfied!* It must be given an outlet for expression. It must be brought into the light of day, given useful, uplifting work to do, and it will then bring forth abundant fruit of happiness and accomplishment. Because no matter how it is repressed, no matter how deep it is buried in dark cellars, the Creative Force will still bring forth fruit—only then it may be fungus growths of sin and misery.

Through every man there flows this Creative Force, with infinite power to draw to itself whatever is necessary to its expression. It doesn't matter who you are, what your environment or education or advantages, the Creative Force in you has the same power for good or evil. Mind you, that Force never brings forth evil. Its life is good. But just as you can graft onto the trunk of the finest fruit tree a branch of the upas tree, and thereupon bring forth deadly fruit, so can you engraft upon the pure energy of your Creative Force any manner of fruit you desire. But if the fruit be bad, it is *you* who are to blame, not the perfect Force that flows through you.

> To every man there openeth
> A high way and a low,
> And every man decideth
> The way his soul shall go.

What is it makes a poor immigrant boy like Edward Bok overcome every handicap of language and education, to become one of the greatest editors the country has ever known?

Isn't it that the more circumstances conspire to repress it, the stronger becomes the urge of the Creative Force in you for expression? The more it lacks channels through which to expand, the more inclined it is to burst its shell and flow forth in all directions.

It is the old case of the river that is dammed generating the most power. Most of us are so placed that some opportunity for expression is made easy for us. And that little opportunity serves like a safety valve to a boiler—it leaves us steam enough to do something worth while, yet keeps us from getting up enough power to burst the shell about us, and sweep away every barrier that holds us down.

Yet it is only such an irresistible head of steam as that which makes great successes. That is why the blow which knocks all the props from under us is often the turning point in our whole career.

As Walt Whitman put it—

Oh, while I live, to be the ruler of life, Not a slave.
To meet life as a powerful conqueror . . .
And nothing exterior shall ever take command of me.

You cannot stand still. You must go forward—or see the world slide past you. This was well illustrated by figures worked out by Russell Conwell years ago. Of all the thousands who are left fortunes through the deaths of relatives, *only one in seventeen dies wealthy!*

Why?—Because the fortunes left them take away the need for initiative on their part. Their money gives to them easy means of expressing the urge in them, without effort on their part. It gives them dozens of safety valves, through which their steam continually escapes.

The result is that they not only accomplish nothing worth while, but they soon dissipate the fortunes that were left them. They are like kettles, the urge of life keeping the water at boiling point, but the open spout of ease letting the steam escape as fast as it forms, until presently there is not even any water left.

Why do the sons of rich men so seldom accomplish anything worth while? Because they don't have to. Every opportunity is given them to turn the Creative Force in them through pleasant channels, and they dissipate through these the energies that might carry them to any height. The result? They never have a strong enough "head of steam" left to carry through any real job.

"What shall I do to be saved?" begged the rich young man of Jesus. "Sell all that thou hast, give it to the poor and follow Me," the Master told him. Churches have used that to prove that poverty is necessary to salvation. But is that the lesson the Biblical writer meant to convey? If so, why is there no record of Jesus having ever given similar advice to Nicodemus, or Joseph of Arimathea, or any others of the rich who sought counsel of Him and at whose houses He frequently stopped?

Isn't the difference that these latter had made their mark in the world—expressed the Creative Force in them to some worth-while purpose—and in the expressing of it, the Creative Force had increased and multiplied and brought back to them goodly harvests of riches?

The young man, on the other hand, had done nothing to earn all the good things that were his. His life had been cast in pleasant places. The Spirit in him urged its need of expression, but Jesus saw that only by getting away from his life of ease was any worth-while expression possible. And the young man had not courage enough for that. Truly it is harder for a camel to go through the eye of the needle than for such a rich man to enter into the Kingdom of Heaven— the Land of Accomplishment.

You will be what you will to be;
Let failure find its false content
In that poor word 'environment,'
But Spirit scorns it, and is free.

It masters time, it conquers space,
It cows that boastful trickster Chance,
And bids the tyrant Circumstance
Uncrown and fill a servant's place.

Be not impatient in delay,
But wait as one who understands;
When Spirit rises and commands
The gods are ready to obey.
                          —ELLA WHEELER WILCOX

You are a channel for power. There is no limit to the amount of Creative Force that will flow through you. The only limit to what you *get*, is the amount that you *use*. Like the widow's cruse, no matter how much you pour out, there is just as much still available, but unlike the cruse of oil, your channel and your power grow with use!

What are *you* doing to satisfy the urge in you? What are you doing to give expression—*and increase*—to the Creative Force working through you?

Many a man and woman has the urge to write—or paint—or sing—or do some other worth-while thing. But does he? No, indeed. He is not well enough known, or has not the right training, or lacks education or opportunity or influence. Or else he has tried once or twice and failed.

What does that matter? It is not your responsibility if others fail in their appreciation. Your job is to express the Creative Force surging through you, to give it the best you have. Each time you do that, *you* are the better for it, whether others care for it or not. And each time you will give more perfect, more understanding expression to the Creative Force working through you, until sooner or later ALL appreciate it.

You don't suppose the great writers, the successful artists, were born with the ability to write or paint, do you? You don't suppose they had all the latest books or finest courses on the art of expression? On the contrary, all that many of them had was the URGE! The rest they had to acquire just as you do.

The Creative Force flowing through you is as perfect as the rose in the bud. But just as the life in the rose bush evolved through millions of less beautiful forms before it perfected the rose, so must you be satisfied to model but crudely at first, in the sure knowledge that if you keep giving of your best, eventually the product of your hands or your brain will be as perfect as the rose.

Every desire, every urge of your being, is Creative Force straining at the bonds of repression you have put upon it, straining for expression. You can't stand still. You can't stop and smugly say—"Look what I did yesterday, or last week, or last year!" It is what you are doing *now* that counts.

The Creative Force is dynamic. It is ever seeking expression—and when you fail to provide new and greater outlets for it, it slips away to work through some more ambitious soul who will. Genius is nothing but the irresistible urge for one particular channel of expression—an urge so strong that it is like a mountain torrent in flood, sweeping trees and bridges and dams and everything else before it.

So don't worry about whether those around you recognize your talents. Don't mind if the world seems indifferent to them. The world is too busy with its own little ways of expressing life to pay much attention to yours. To get under its skin, you must do something to appeal to its emotions.

You see, the world in the mass is like a child. Prod it, and you make it angry. Preach to it, or try to teach or uplift it, and you lose its attention. You bore it. But appeal to its emotions—make it laugh or weep—and it will love you! Love you and lavish upon you all the gifts in its power to give. That is why it pays a Crosby millions, and a great educator only hundreds. Yet the name of the educator may live for ages, while the entertainer will be remembered only until a better one displaces him.

So forget the immediate rewards the world has to offer, and give your energies to finding ways of better expressing the Creative Force in you. You are expressing it every day and hour. Try to express it better, to find ever greater channels through which to work. If your urge is to write a story, put into it the best you have, no matter if you know you could get by with a third of the effort. Work always for perfection, knowing that thus only can you be sure of the greatest help of the Creative Force working through you. "I can do all things through Christ which strengtheneth me," said Paul. And you can do all things through the Creative Force working through you.

That Creative Force is striving for a perfect body, perfect surroundings, perfect work. It is not its fault when you manifest less than these. Depend upon it, it is not satisfied with anything less. So don't *you* be! If you have the courage to refuse anything short of your ideal, if you have the dogged perseverance to keep trying, there's no power in the heavens or the earth that can keep you from success!

It's the way every great success has been won. Do you suppose if Michelangelo or Da Vinci had an off day and painted some imperfect figures into a painting, he left them there? Do you think he explained to his friends that he was under the weather that day, and so, while he was sorry it spoiled the picture, he could not be held accountable for it?

Just imagine one of these great painters letting something less than his best go over his name! Why, he would cheerfully destroy a year's work rather than have that happen. The moment he noticed it, he would hasten to scratch out the offensive figure, lest others might see it and judge his work by it. Or even if no one was ever to see it, he would do it because it failed to express the genius that was his!

That is how you must feel about your work before ever it can attain greatness. The Creative Force working through you is perfect, all-powerful, without limit. So don't ever be satisfied with less than its best! Follow its urge. Use every atom of strength and skill and riches you have to express it, serene in the knowledge that, like Paul, you can do anything through the Christ working in you.

Andrew Carnegie said:

Here is the prime condition of success, the great secret: Concentrate your energy, thought, and capital exclusively upon the business in which you are engaged. Having begun on one line, resolve to fight it out on that line, to lead in it, adopt every improvement, have the best machinery, and know the most about it. Finally, do not be impatient, for, as Emerson says, "No one can cheat you out of ultimate success but yourself."

Have you ever climbed a high mountain? Did you notice, as you kept getting higher and higher, how your horizon rose with you? It is the same with life. The more you use the Creative Force, the more you have to use. Your skill and power and resources grow with your use of them.

From earliest infancy, the Creative Force is trying to express something through you. First it is purely physical—a perfect body, and through it the generation of other perfect bodies. But gradually it rises above the physical plane, and strives to express itself in some way that will leave the world a better place for your having been in it—a memory of noble thoughts, of splendid deeds, of obstacles conquered and ideals won.

Do your part by never falling short of your best, no matter in how small a thing you may express it. Perfection, you remember, is made up of trifles, but perfection is no trifle.

It doesn't matter how small or seemingly unimportant your job may be. You have the same chance to attain perfection in it as the greatest artist has in his work. It doesn't matter how little others may believe that any good or great thing can come from you. It was said in the Scriptures of a far greater than you—"Can there any good thing come out of Nazareth?"

Who knows what good things may come from you?

There's nothing to fear—you're as good as the best,
As strong as the mightiest, too.
You can win in every battle or test;
For there's no one just like you.
There's only one you in the world today;
So nobody else, you see,
Can do your work in as fine a way;
You're the only you there'll be!
So face the world, and all life is yours
To conquer and love and live;
And you'll find the happiness that endures
In just the measure you give:
There's nothing too good for you to possess,
Nor heights where you cannot go;
Your power is more than belief or guess—
It's something you have to know.
There's nothing to fear—you can and you will,
For you're the invincible you.
So set your foot on the highest hill—
There's nothing you cannot do.

—ANONYMOUS

THE MENTAL EQUIVALENT

All the world's a stage,
And all the men and women merely players.

What part are you acting in the theater of life? What place have you assigned to yourself on that stage? Are you one of the stars? Do you bear one of the important parts? Or are you merely one of the "mob" scene, just background for the action, or one of the "props" for moving the scenery around?

Whatever part is yours, it is you who have given it to you, for as Emerson says, and the whole Bible teaches from one end to the other, "Man surrounds himself with the true image of himself."

"Every spirit builds itself a house," writes Emerson, "and beyond its house a world, and beyond its world a heaven. Know then that the world exists for you. For you is the phenomenon perfect. What we are, that only can we see. All that Adam had, all that Caesar could, you have and can do. Adam called his house, heaven and earth. Caesar called his house, Rome; you perhaps call yours a cobbler's trade; a hundred acres of plowed land; or a scholar's garret. Yet line for line and point for point, your dominion is as great as theirs, though without fine names. Build therefore your own world. As fast as you conform your life to the pure idea in your mind, that will unfold its great proportions."

All men are created free and equal, in that all are given the only tool with which you can really build your life. That tool is your thought. All have the same material with which to build. That material is the Creative Force working through you. As your interior thought is, so will your exterior life be. The Creative Force takes shape in the mold your thoughts give it. "We think in secret and it comes to pass; environment is but our looking glass."

"In all my lectures," declared Emerson, "I have taught one doctrine—the infinitude of the private man, the ever-availability to every man of the divine presence within his own mind, from which presence he draws, at his need, inexhaustible power."

> Think big, and your deeds will grow;
> Think small, and you'll fall behind;
> Think that you can, and you will—
> It's all in the state of mind.

"What sort of mental image do you hold of yourself?" Emmett Fox asks in one of his helpful books.

Whatever your real conviction of yourself is, that is what you will demonstrate.

Whatever enters into your life is but the material expression of some belief of your own mind. The kind of body you have, the kind of home you have, the kind of job you have, the kind of people you meet with, are all conditioned by and correspond to the mental concept you are holding. The Bible teaches that from beginning to end.

About twenty years ago, I coined the phrase "mental equivalent." And I am going to say that anything that you want in your life, anything that you would like to have in your life—a healthy body, a satisfactory vocation, friends, opportunities, above all the understanding of God—if you want these things to come into your life, you must furnish a mental equivalent for them. Supply yourself with a mental equivalent and the thing must come to you. Without a mental equivalent, it cannot come to you.

And what is this "Mental Equivalent"? What but your mental image of what you hope to be, plan to be. "Think and forms spring into shape, will and worlds disintegrate."

God hid the whole world in your heart, as one great writer tells us, so when any object or purpose is clearly held in thought, its manifestation in tangible and visible form is merely a question of time. Cause and effect are as absolute and undeviating in the hidden realm of thought as in the world of visible and material things. Mind is the master weaver, both of the interior garment of character and the outer garment of circumstance. Thinking for a purpose brings that purpose into being just as surely as a hen's "setting" on an egg matures and brings the chicken into being.

"Amid all the mysteries by which we are surrounded," wrote Herbert Spencer, "nothing is more certain than that we are ever in the presence of an infinite and eternal energy from which all things proceed."

That infinite and eternal energy or Creative Force is molded by our thought. For thousands of years, men of wisdom have realized this and have molded their own lives accordingly. The Prophets of old did their best to impress this fact upon their people. "My word (my thought or mental image) shall not come back to me void, but shall accomplish that whereunto it was sent," says one. And in a hundred places, you will find the same thought expressed. You are molding your tomorrows, whether you realize it or not. Make them the good you desire—not the evil you fear.

Clarence Edwin Flynn expresses something of the power of thought in his little poem:

> *Whenever you cultivate a thought*
> *Remember it will trace*
> *With certain touch, its pictured form*
> *A story on your face.*

> *Whenever you dwell upon a thought,*
> *Remember it will roll*

Into your being and become
A fiber of your soul.

Whenever you send out a thought,
 Remember it will be
A force throughout the universe,
For all eternity.

Remember that this holds good in all of your affairs. In your own thoughts, you are continually dramatizing yourself, your environment, your circumstances. If you see yourself as prosperous, you will be. If you see yourself as continually hard up, that is exactly what you will be. If you are constantly looking for slights, if you seek trouble in your thoughts, you will not be long in finding them in your daily life. Whatever part you give yourself in the drama of life in your own thought, that part you will eventually act out on the stage of life.

So give yourself a good part. Make yourself the hero of the piece, rather than the downtrodden member of the mob or the overworked servant. Set your lines in pleasant places. It is just as easy as laying them in the slums. As long as you are bound to dramatize yourself and your surroundings and circumstances anyway, try this:

1. Dramatize yourself, in your mind's eye, with the people and surroundings and things you want most, doing the things you would like most to do, holding the sort of position you long for, doing the work you feel yourself best fitted to do. Some may call it day-dreaming, but make it day-dreaming with a purpose. Make the picture as clear in your mind's eye as though you saw it on the screen of a motion picture theater. And get all the enjoyment out of it that you can. Believe in it. Be thankful for it.

2. Prove your faith in your dream by making every logical preparation for the material manifestation of your desires. Just as the kings of old did when they prayed for water, dig your ditches to receive it.

3. Alter minor details of your drama as you like, but stick to the main goal. Make it your objective, and like Grant in his successful campaign, resolve to stick to it "though it takes all summer."

4. Be a finisher as well as a beginner. Remember that one job finished is worth a dozen half finished. The three-quarter horses never win a prize. It is only at the finish that the purse awaits you. So complete your drama mentally before you begin to act it out, and then stick to it actually until you've made it manifest for all to see.

5. Keep that mental drama to yourself. Don't tell it to others. Remember Samson. He could do anything as long as he kept his mouth shut. Most people's minds are like boilers with the safety valve wide open. They never get up enough of a head of steam to run their engines. Keep your plans to yourself. That way they'll generate such power that you won't need to *tell* others about them— they'll see the result for themselves.

"The imagination," says Glenn Clark in "The Soul's Sincere Desire," is of all qualities in man the most God-like—that which associates him most closely with God. The first mention we read of man in the Bible is where he is spoken of as an "image." "Let us make man in our image, after our likeness." The only place where an image can be conceived is in the imagination. Thus man, the highest creation of God, was a creation of God's imagination.

The source and center of all man's creative power— the power that above all others lifts him above the level of brute creation, and that gives him dominion, is his power of making images, or the power of the imagination. There are some who have always thought that the imagination was something which makes-believe that which is not. This is fancy—not imagination. Fancy would convert that which is real into pretense and sham; imagination enables one to see through the appearance of a thing to what it really *is*.

There is a very real law of cause and effect which makes the dream of the dreamer come true. It is the law of visualization—the law that calls into being in this outer material world everything that is real in the inner world by directing your Creative Force into it. Imagination pictures the thing you desire. VISION idealizes it. It reaches beyond the thing that is, into the conception of what can be. Imagination gives you the picture. Vision gives you the impulse to make the picture your own by directing your Creative Force into it.

Make your mental image clear enough, picture it vividly in every detail, then do everything you can to bring that image into being, and the Creative Force working through you will speedily provide whatever is necessary to make it an everyday reality.

The law holds true of everything in life. There is nothing you can rightfully desire that cannot be brought into being through visualization and faith.

The keynote of successful visualization is this: See things as you would have them be instead of as they are. Close your eyes and make clear mental pictures. Make them look and act just as they would in real life. In short, day-dream—but daydream purposefully. Concentrate on the one idea to the exclusion of all others, and continue to concentrate on that one idea until it has been accomplished.

Do you want an automobile? A home? A factory? They can all be won in the same way. They are in their essence all of them ideas of mind, and if you will but build them up in your own mind first, complete in every detail, you will find that the Creative Force working through you can build them up similarly in the material world.

"The building of a trans-continental railroad from a mental picture," says C. W Chamberlain in "The Uncommon Sense of Applied Psychology," gives the average individual an idea that it is a big job. The fact of the matter is, the achievement, as well as the perfect mental picture, is made up of millions of little jobs, each fitting in its proper place and helping to make up the whole.

A skyscraper is built from individual bricks, the laying of each brick being a single job which must be completed before the next brick can be laid.

It is the same with any work, any study. To quote Professor James: As we become permanent drunkards by so many separate drinks, so we become saints in the moral, and authorities and experts in the practical and scientific spheres, by so many separate acts and hours of working. Let no youth have any anxiety about the upshot of his education whatever the line of it may be. If he keep faithfully busy each hour of the working day he may safely leave the final result to itself. He can with perfect certainty count on waking some fine morning, to find himself one of the competent ones of his generation, in whatever pursuit he may have singled out. . . . Young people should know this truth in advance. The ignorance of it has probably engendered more discouragement and faintheartedness in youths embarking on arduous careers than all other causes taken together.

Remember that the only limit to your capabilities is the one you place upon them. There is no law of limitation. The only law is of supply. Through mind you can draw upon the Creative Force for anything you wish. Use it! There are no limitations upon it. Don't put any on yourself.

Aim high! If you miss the moon, you may hit a star. Everyone admits that this world and all the vast firmament must have been thought into shape from the formless void by some God-Mind. That same God-Mind rules today, and it has given to each form of life power to attract to itself as much of the Creative Force as it needs for its perfect growth. The tree, the plant, the animal—each one finds supply to meet its need.

You are an intelligent, reasoning creature. Your mind is part of the great God-Mind. And you have the power to *say* what you require for perfect growth. Don't be a niggard with yourself. Don't sell yourself for a penny. Whatever price you set upon yourself, life will give. So aim high. Demand much! Make a clear, distinct mental image of what it is you want. Hold it *in your thoughts.* Visualize it, see it, *believe it!* The ways and means of satisfying that desire will follow. For supply always comes on the heels of demand.

It is by doing this that you take your fate out of the hands of chance. It is in this way that you control the experiences you are to have in life. But be sure to visualize *only what you want.* The law works both ways. If you visualize your worries and your fears, you will make them real. Control your thought and you control circumstances. Conditions will be what you make them.

To paraphrase Thackeray— "The world is a looking glass, and gives back to every man the reflection of his own thought."

Philip of Macedon, Alexander's father, perfected the "phalanx"—a triangular formation which enabled him to center the whole weight of his attack on one point in the opposing line. It drove through everything opposed to it. In that day and age it was invincible. And the idea is just as invincible today.

Keep the one thought in mind, SEE it being carried out step by step, and you can knit any group of workers into one homogeneous whole, all centered on the one idea. You can accomplish any one thing. You can put across any definite idea. Keep that mental picture ever in mind and you will make it as invincible as was Alexander's phalanx of old.

> *It is not the guns or armament*
> *Or the money they can pay,*
> *It's the close cooperation*
> *That makes them win the day.*
> *It is not the individual*
> *Or the army as a whole*
> *But the everlasting team work of every bloomin' soul.*
> —J. MASON KNOX

The error of the ages is the tendency mankind has always shown to limit the power of Mind, or its willingness to help in time of need.

"Know ye not," said Paul, "That ye are the temples of the Living God?"

No—most of us do not know it. Or at least, if we do, we are like the Indian family out on the Cherokee reservation. Oil had been found on their land and money poured in upon them. More money than they had ever known was in the world. Someone persuaded them to build a great house, to have it beautifully furnished, richly decorated. But the Indians, while very proud of their showy house, continued to *live in their old sod shack!*

So it is with many of us. We may know that we are "temples of the Living God." We may even be proud of that fact. But we never take advantage of it to dwell in that temple, to proclaim dominion over things and conditions. We never avail ourselves of the power that is ours.

The great prophets of old had the forward look. Theirs was the era of hope and expectation. They looked for the time when the revelation should come that was to make men "sons of God." "They shall obtain joy and gladness, and sorrow and sighing shall flee away."

Jesus came to fulfill that revelation. "Ask and ye shall receive, that your joy may be full."

The world has turned in vain to materialistic philosophy for deliverance from its woes. In the future the only march of actual progress will be in the mental realm, and this progress will not be in the way of human speculation and theorizing, but in the *actual demonstration* of the power of Mind to mold the Creative Force into anything of good.

The world stands today within the vestibule of the vast realm of divine intelligence, wherein is found the transcendent, practical power of Mind over all things.

> *What eye never saw, nor ear ever heard,*
> *What never entered the mind of man—*
> *Even all that God has prepared for those who love him.*

I AM

Years ago, Emile Coué electrified the world with his cures of all manner of disease—solely through the power of SUGGESTION!

"Nobody ought to be sick!" he proclaimed, and proceeded to prove it by curing hundreds who came to him after doctors had failed to relieve them. Not only that, but he showed that the same methods could be used to cure one's affairs—to bring riches instead of debts, success instead of drudgery.

Originally, Coué was a hypnotist. In his little drug store, he found occasional patients whom he could hypnotize. He hypnotized them—put their conscious minds to sleep—and addressed himself directly to their subconscious.

To the subconscious, he declared that there was nothing wrong with whatever organ the patient had thought diseased, and the subconscious accepted the statement and molded the Creative Force within accordingly. When the patient came out from under the hypnotic influence, he was well! It remained then only to convince his conscious mind of this, so he would not send through new suggestions of disease to his subconscious, and the patient was cured!

How account for that? By the fact that the disease or imperfection is not so much in your body as in your mind. It is in your rate of motion, and this is entirely mind-controlled. Change the subconscious belief, and the physical manifestations change with it. You speed up your rate of motion, and in that way throw off the discordant elements of disease. Doctors recognize this when they give their patients harmless sugar pills, knowing that these will dispel fear, and that when the images conjured up by fear are gone, the supposed trouble will go with them.

But Coué found many patients whom he could not hypnotize. How treat them? By inducing a sort of self-hypnosis in themselves. It is a well-known fact that constant repetition carries conviction—especially to the subconscious mind. So Coué had his patients continually repeat to themselves the affirmation that their trouble was passing, that they were getting better and better. "Every day in every way I am getting better and better." And this unreasoning affirmation cured thousands of ills that had been troubling them for years.

What is back of that success? A law as old as the hills, a law that has been known to psychologists for years—the law that the subconscious mind accepts as true anything that is repeated to it *convincingly* and *often*. And once it has accepted such a statement as true, it proceeds to mold the Creative Force working through it in such wise as to MAKE IT TRUE!

You see, where the conscious mind reasons inductively, the subconscious uses only deductive reasoning. Where the reasoning mind weighs each fact that is presented to it, questions the truth or falsity of each, and then forms its conclusions accordingly, the subconscious acts quite differently. IT ACCEPTS AS FACT ANY STATEMENT THAT IS PRESENTED TO IT CONVINCINGLY. Then, having accepted this as the basis of its actions, it proceeds logically to do all in its power to bring it into being.

That is why the two most important words in the English language are the words—"I AM." That is why the Ancients regarded these two words as the secret name of God.

You ask a friend how he is, and he replies carelessly—"I am sick, I am poor, I am unlucky, I am subject to this, that or the other thing,"—never stopping to think that by those very words he is fastening misfortune upon himself, declaring to the subconscious mind within him that he IS sick or poor or weak or the servant of some desire.

"Let the weak say—'I am strong!'" the Prophet Joel exhorted his people thousands of years ago. And the advice is as good today as it was then.

You have seen men, under hypnotic suggestion, perform prodigies of strength. You have seen them with their bodies stretched between two chairs, their heads on one, their feet on another, supporting the weight of several people standing on them, when they could not ordinarily hold up even their own bodies in that position. How can they do it? Because the hypnotist has assured their subconscious that they CAN do it, that they have the strength and power necessary.

"Therefore I say unto you, what things soever ye desire when ye pray, BELIEVE THAT YE RECEIVE THEM, and ye shall HAVE them." That was the assurance given us by the Master Psychologist of all time, the Great Healer, the Worker of Miracles. Again and again He told those He healed that it was their FAITH that made them whole. And where such faith was lacking, as when He went back to Nazareth, the home of his childhood, it is written that "There He did no mighty works."

How can you work up the necessary faith to accomplish the things you desire? By taking the advice of the wise men of old, of the Prophet Joel, of Jesus—by *claiming* it as yours, and setting your subconscious mind to work making those claims come true.

It is a sort of self-hypnosis, but so is all of prayer. Away back in 1915, the head of the Warsaw Psychological Institute conducted a series of experiments from which he concluded that the energy manifested by anyone during life is in direct ratio with his power for plunging himself into a condition of auto-hypnosis. In simple language, that means convincing yourself of the possibility of doing the things you want to do.

The subconscious in each of us HAS the knowledge, HAS the power to do any right thing we may require of it. The only need is to implant in it the confidence—the "BELIEVE THAT YOU RECEIVE" which Jesus taught.

In a case cited by Baudouin, the famous psychologist, a woman after using autosuggestion as a means of helping herself, declared: "I can do twice as much work as before. During vacation, I have been able to go through two extensive tasks, such as a year ago I should never have attempted. This year I systematized my work and said, 'I can do it all; what I am undertaking is materially possible, and therefore must be morally possible; consequently I ought not to experience, and shall not experience, discouragement, hesitancy, annoyance, or slackness.'" As a result of these affirmations, the way to her inner powers was opened and she was able to say truly, "Nothing could stop me, nothing could prevent my doing what I had planned to do; you might almost have said that things were done by themselves, without the slightest effort on my part." Not only did she find herself working with a high degree of success heretofore unknown, but with a certainty and calmness of mind beyond her previous attainment.

Emerson, with his genius for condensing great truths into a few words, wrote—"Do the thing and you shall have the power."

The wise men of old learned thousands of years ago that life is like an echo. It always returns the call sent out. Like the echo, the response is always the same as the call, and the louder the call, the greater the response.

You say—"I am sick, I am poor," and your words are forerunners of your circumstance. "Every idle word that men shall speak, they shall give account of in the day of judgment." And that day of judgment comes sooner than most people think.

Be careful to speak only those words which you are willing to see take form in your life, for remember the words of wise old Job: "Thou shalt also decree a thing, and it shall be established unto thee." Never speak the word of lack or limitation, for—"By thy words shalt thou be justified, and by thy words shalt thou be condemned."

Affirm constantly—"I have faith in the power of my word. I speak only that which I desire to see made manifest." Remember, "Behind you is Infinite Power, before you is endless possibility, around you is endless opportunity. Why should you fear?"

C. G. Tanner expresses the idea beautifully—

> *If you have faith in what you want to do,*
> *If you behold yourself a king's own son,*
> *Then you have asked God's power to work through you,*
> *And pledged yourself to see that it is done.*
> *'With faith I place it in God's hands', you say?*
> *God's hands are yours! Your good must come*
> *through you!*
> *God has no other hands with which He may*
> *Give unto you your sonship's rightful due.*
>
> *Faith and persistence travel hand in hand,*
> *The one without the other incomplete.*
> *If you would reach success, then take the stand,*
> *This I will try once more,' and no defeat*
> *Can cloud that beacon gleaming bright and clear,*

Or conjure up dread failure's haunting wraith!
You rest secure with God. No thought of fear
Can dim the shining armor of your faith.

Most people seem to think that we work to live, but there is a deeper purpose in life than that. What we really work for is to call forth the talents that are within our own soul, to give expression to the Creative Force working through us. That is the one big purpose for which we were born—to express the Creative Force in us, to give God the chance to express Himself through us. And we CAN do it. As the famous English poet Shelley put it—"The Almighty has given men arms long enough to reach the stars, if they would but put them forth."

And the first step lies in using what you have. The key to power lies in using, not hoarding. Use releases still more power for ever greater works. Hoarding builds a hard shell around the thing hoarded and prevents more from coming in. You may have what you want, if you are willing to use what you have now. You can do what you want to do if you are willing to do what there is to do right now. "The one condition coupled with the gift of truth," says Emerson, "*is its use.*"

Professor William Bateson of the British Society for Scientific Research said: "We are finding now beyond doubt that the gifts and geniuses of mankind are due not so much to something added to the ordinary person, but instead are due to factors which in the normal person INHIBIT the development of these gifts. They are now without doubt to be looked upon as RELEASES of powers normally suppressed."

And why are they suppressed? Because of doubt, of fear of failure, of procrastination, of putting things off till the morrow. "Straight from a mighty bow this truth is driven: They fail, and they alone, who have not striven."

Tomorrow you will live, you always cry;
In what far country does this morrow lie,
That 'tis so mighty long ere it arrive?
Beyond the Indies does this morrow live?
'Tis so far fetched, this morrow, that I fear
'Twill be both very old and very dear.
Tomorrow I will live, the fool does say;
Today itself's too late; the wise lived yesterday.

                                        —ABRAHAM COWLEY

"To begin," said Ausonius, "is to be half done." "Greatly begin!" wrote another sage. "Though thou have time for but a line, be that sublime." And the Easterners have a proverb that the road of a thousand miles begins with one step.

So make your start, and don't allow any thought of failure to stop you. Have faith—if not in yourself—then in the Creative Force working through you. Many a splendid work has been lost to mankind because the faith of its originator was not strong enough to release the Creative Force that would have enabled him to make his dream come true.

Remember that you cannot talk failure, or think failure, and reap success. You'll never reach the top of the ladder if doubt and fear and procrastination make you hesitate to put your foot on the first rung.

There is a Power working through you that can accomplish any aim you may aspire to. But to energize that power, you must harness it up with Faith. You must have the will to believe, the courage to aspire, and the profound conviction that success is possible to anyone who works for it persistently and believingly.

Three hundred and forty years ago, there sailed from Spain the mightiest fleet the world had ever known, Spanish galleasses, Portuguese caracks, Florentine caravels, huge hulks from other countries—floating fortresses, mounting tier upon tier of mighty cannon—140 great ships in all, manned to the full with sailors and soldiers and gentlemen adventurers.

The treasure of the Incas, the Plunder of the Aztec, had gone into the building and outfitting of this vast Armada. No wonder Spain looked upon it as invincible. No wonder England feared it. For this was the Armada that was to invade England and carry fire and sword through town and countryside. This was the Armada that was to punish these impudent Britons for the "piratical" raids of Sir Francis Drake, Morgan and all those hardy seamen who had dared death and slavery to pull down treasure ships on the Spanish Main.

The iron hand of Philip II of Spain rested heavily upon the Netherlands. It dominated all of Europe. Now he confidently looked forward to the time when England, too, would groan beneath its weight.

But he reckoned without one thing—faith! He put in charge of this invincible Armada, the Duke of Medina Sidonia, a man who had no faith in himself, no faith in his ability, no faith in his men. And when he did that, he blunted the point of every pike; he dulled the cutting edge of every sword; he took the mightiest naval weapon ever forged, and deliberately drew its sting.

Is that putting it too strongly? Just listen. Here is the letter the Duke wrote to the King, upon being notified of his appointment to the command:

My health is bad and from my small experience of the water I know that I am always seasick.... The expedition is on such a scale and the object is of such high importance that the person at the head of it ought to understand navigation and sea fighting, and I know nothing of either. . . . The Adelantado of Castile would do better than I. The Lord would help him, he is a good Christian and has fought in naval battles. If you send me, depend upon it, I shall have a bad account to render of my trust.

He had everything to succeed with—everything but faith in himself. He expected failure—and disastrous failure met him at every turn.

One hundred and forty mighty ships—the greatest ever built. And England, to meet that splendid Armada, had only 30 small ships of war and a few merchantmen outfitted and manned by private gentlemen. Yet England, while alarmed, was yet courageous and hopeful. For had not England Sir Francis Drake? And Lord Charles Howard? And a dozen other mighty fighters who had met and bested the Spaniards a score of times on the Spanish Main? And could they not do the same again?

So said England, believing in her leaders. And her leaders echoed that sentiment. Are not English sailors the hardiest seamen and finest fighters afloat, they asked. And believed in their men.

The English had 30 or 40 little ships against the Spaniards' 140 mighty men-of-war. The English had scarce two days' powder aboard—so penurious was their Queen— while the Spanish were outfitted with everything a ship-of-war could ask.

But Howard and Drake were not depending upon any Queen to fight their battles. They were not worrying about the size of the enemy. They were thinking—"There are the Spaniards. Here are we. We have fought them and whipped them a dozen times before. We can do it now. So let's get at them!"

They went out expecting victory. And victory met them at every turn.

From the Lizard in Cornwall to Portland, where Don Pedro de Valdes and his mighty ship were left; from Portland to Calais, where Spain lost Hugo de Moncado with the galleys which he captured; from Calais, out of sight of England, around Scotland and Ireland, beaten and shuffled together, that mighty Armada was chased, until finally the broken remnants drifted back to Spain.

With all their vast squadron, they had not taken one ship or bark or pinnace of England. With all those thousands of soldiers, they had not landed one man but those killed or taken prisoner.

Three-fourths of their number lost or captured, their mighty fleet destroyed. And why? Because one man lacked faith. Spanish soldiers were proving on a dozen fields that no braver fighters lived anywhere. The "Spanish Square" had withstood infantry, cavalry, artillery—then carried all before it. Yet these same soldiers, afloat in their huge fortresses, were utterly defeated by less than a fourth their number.

And the reason? Because they were a spear without a head—an army without a leader—riches and power without faith. Was ever a better example of the power of belief?

Men go all through life like the Duke of Medina Sidonia—looking ever for the dark side of things, expecting trouble at every turn—and usually finding it. It is really lack of courage—courage to try for great things, courage to dare disappointment and ridicule to accomplish a worthy end. Have you ever sat in a train and watched another train passing you? You can look right on through its windows to the green fields and pleasant vistas beyond. Or you can gaze at the partitions between the windows and see nothing but their dingy drabness. So it is with everything in life. You can look for the good, the joyful and happy—and not merely see only these but manifest them in your daily life. Or you can look for trouble, for sickness and sorrow—and find them awaiting you around every corner.

Pessimists call this the "Pollyanna Age" and ridicule such ideas as this. But ridicule or not, it works—in one's personal life as well as in business—and thousands can testify to its efficacy.

Perhaps one of the best examples of the difference that outlook makes is in the lives of Emerson and Thoreau. Emerson's philosophy of living can best be expressed in his own words—"Nerve us with incessant affirmatives. Don't bark against the bad, but chant the beauties of the good." And his tranquil and serene life reflected that attitude throughout.

Thoreau, on the other hand, was constantly searching out and denouncing evil. With motives every whit as high as Emerson's, he believed in attacking the problem from the opposite angle, with the result that he was constantly in hot water, yet accomplished not a tenth of the good that Emerson did. Like the man in d'Annunzio's play, LA CITTA MORTA—"Fascinated by the tombs, he forgot the beauty of the sky."

It is necessary at times to clean up evil conditions in order to start afresh. It is necessary to hunt out the source of pollution in order to purify a stream. But it should be merely a means to an end. And the end should always be—not negative like the mere destruction of evil, but the positive replacing of evil with good.

If you have ever walked across a high trestle, you know that it doesn't pay to look down. That way dizziness and destruction lie. You have to look forward, picking out the ties you are going to step on ten or twenty feet ahead, if you are to progress.

Life is just such a trestle. And looking downward too much is likely to make one lose his balance, stumble and fall. You must gaze ever forward if you are to keep your perspective.

There's a little poem by Edgar Guest that exemplifies the idea:

> Somebody said that it couldn't be done,
> But he with a chuckle replied
> That 'maybe it couldn't,' but he would be one
> Who wouldn't say so till he'd tried.
> So he buckled right in with the trace of a grin
> On his face. If he worried he hid it.
> He started to sing as he tackled the thing
> That couldn't be done, AND HE DID IT.

Most of the world's progress has been made by just such men as that. Men like Watt, who didn't know that steam could not be made to accomplish any useful purpose, and so invented the steam engine. Men like Fulton, who didn't know that it was foolish to try to propel a boat with wheels—and so invented the steamboat.

Men like Bell, Edison, Wright, who didn't know how foolish it was to attempt the impossible—and so went ahead and did it.

"For God's sake, give me the young man who has brains enough to make a fool of himself!" cried Stevenson. And when they succeed, the whole world echoes that cry.

There is no limit upon you—except the limit you put upon yourself. You are like the birds—your thoughts can fly across all barriers, unless you tie them down or cage them or clip their wings by the limitations you put upon them.

There is nothing that can defeat you—except yourself. You are one with the Father. And the Father knows everything you will ever need to know on any subject.

Why then, try to repress any right desire, any high ambition? Why not put behind it every ounce of energy, every bit of enthusiasm, of which you are capable?

Mahomet established a larger empire than that of Rome on nothing but enthusiasm. And Mahomet was but a poor camel-driver. What then can *you* not do?

Men repress their power for good, their capacity for success, by accepting suggestions of inferiority; by their timidity or self-consciousness; by fear; by conservatism.

Never mind what others think of you. It is what *you* think that counts. Never let another's poor opinion of you influence your decisions. Rather, resolve to show him how unfounded is his opinion.

People thought so poorly of Oliver Cromwell that he could not win permission to emigrate to the Colonies. When he raised his regiment of cavalry, that later won the name of "Ironsides" because of its practical invincibility, the old soldiers and the dandies of the day laughed at it. Seldom had a lot of more awkward-looking countrymen been gathered together.

Any soldier might have trained them. But the thing that made them invincible, the thing that enabled them to ride over and through all the legions of King Charles, was not their training, but their fervent belief in the justice of their cause, in their leader and in their God.

"Hymn-singing hypocrites," their enemies called them. But here were no hypocrites. Here were men who were animated by a common faith that God was with them as with the Israelites of old—and that with God on their side, nothing could withstand them.

That was the faith of Cromwell. And he instilled that faith into every man in his regiment.

And while Cromwell lived to keep that faith alive, nothing *did* withstand them. They made the man who was not good enough to emigrate to America, Ruler of England!

Nothing worth while ever has been accomplished without faith. Nothing worth while ever will.

Why do so many great organizations go to pieces after their founder's death? Why do they fail to outlive him by more than a few years?

Because the ones who take up his work lack the forward look, the faith, to carry on. His idea was one of service— theirs is to continue paying dividends. His thought was to build ever greater and greater—theirs to hold what he won.

"The best defensive is a strong offensive." You can't just hold your own. You can't stand still. You've got to go forward—or backward!

Which is it with you? If forward, then avoid the pessimist as you would the plague. Enthusiasm, optimism, may make mistakes—but it will learn from them and progress. Pessimism, conservatism, caution, will die of dry rot, if it is not sooner lost in the forward march of things.

So be an optimist. Cultivate the forward look.

The Optimist and Pessimist,
The difference is droll,
The Optimist sees the doughnut,
The Pessimist—the hole!

The good is always there—if you look for it hard enough. But you must look for it. You can't be content to take merely what happens to come into your line of vision. You have got to refuse to accept anything short of good. Disclaim it! Say it is not yours. Say it—and believe it. Then keep a-seeking—and the first thing you know, the good you have been seeking will be found to have been right under your nose all the time.

What is the backbone of all business? Credit. And what is credit but faith—faith in your fellow-man—faith in his integrity—faith in his willingness and his ability to give you a square deal?

What do you base credit-faith upon? Upon hearsay— upon what your prospective customer has done for others, his promptness in paying them, his willingness to cooperate with them. In many cases you have never seen him—you can't be certain of your own personal knowledge that such a person exists—but you believe in him, you have FAITH. And having faith, your business grows and prospers.

If you can have such faith in a man you have never seen, as to trust large portions of your earthly goods in his hands, can you not put a little trust in the Father, too?

True, you have not seen Him—but you have far greater proof of His being than of that of your customer thousands of miles away. You have far greater proof of His reliability, of His regard for you, of His ability and His willingness at all times to come to your assistance in any right way you may ask. You don't need money with Him. You don't need high standing in your community. You don't need credit.

What is it makes a successful salesman? Faith in his house. Faith in the goods he is selling. Faith in the service they will render his customers. Faith in himself. Have you faith in your "house"—in your Father—in the manifold gifts He offers you so freely?

Men can sell for a little while solely on faith in their own ability, they can palm off anything that will show a profit to themselves. But they never make successful salesmen. The inevitable reaction comes. They grow cynical, lose all faith in others—and eventually lose faith in themselves as well. The successful salesman must have a fourfold faith—faith in his house, faith in his product, faith in the good it will do his customer, faith in himself. Given such a faith, he can sell anything. Given such a faith in the Father, *you* can do anything.

It wasn't superior courage or superior fighting ability that enabled Washington's half-trained army to beat the British. English soldiers were showing all over the world that they were second to none in fighting qualities. And the American soldiers were, for the most part, from the same sturdy stock. It was their faith in a greater Power outside themselves.

What is it differentiates the banker from the pawnbroker? Both make loans. Both require security. But where the pawn-broker must have tangible, material property that he can resell before he will lend a cent, the really great banker bases his loans on something bigger than any security that may be offered him—his faith in the borrower.

America was built on faith. Those great railroad builders who spanned the continent knew when they did it that there was not enough business immediately available to make their investment profitable for a long time to come. But they had faith—a faith that was the making of our country.

That same faith is evident on every hand today. Men erect vast factories—in the faith that the public will find need for and buy their products. They build offices, apartments, homes—in the faith that their cities will grow up to the need of them. They put up public utilities capable of serving twice the number of people in their territories—in the faith that the demand will not only grow with the population, but the availability of the supply will help to create new demands.

Faith builds cities and businesses and men. In fact, everything of good, everything constructive in this old world of ours is based on faith. So if you have it not, *grow it*—as the most important thing you can do. And if you have it, *tend it*, water it, cultivate it—for it is the most important thing in life.

> When nothing seems to help, I go and look at a stone-cutter hammering away at his rock, perhaps a hundred times without as much as a crack showing in it. Yet at the hundred and first blow, it will split in two, and I know it was not that blow that did it, but all that had gone before.
>
> —J. A. RIIS.

TALISMAN

Like the waves of the sea are the ways of fate
As we voyage along through life.

'Tis the set of the soul which decides its goal
And not the calm or the strife.
                    —ELLA WHEELER WILCOX

What is the eternal question which stands up and looks you and every sincere man squarely in the eye every morning? "How can I better my condition?" That is the real life question which confronts you, and will haunt you every day until you solve it.

The answer to that question lies first in remembering that the great business of life is thinking. Control your thoughts and you mold circumstance.

Just as the first law of gain is desire, so the first essential to success is FAITH. Believe that you *have*—see the thing you want as an existent fact—and anything you can rightly wish for is yours. Belief is "the substance of things hoped for, the evidence of things not seen."

You have seen men, inwardly no more capable than yourself, accomplish the seemingly impossible. You have seen others, after years of hopeless struggle, suddenly win their most cherished dreams. And you've often wondered, "What is the power that gives new life to their dying ambitions, that supplies new impetus to their jaded desires, that gives them a new start on the road to success?"

That power is belief-*faith*. Someone, something, gave them a new belief in themselves and a new faith in their power to win-and they leaped ahead and wrested success from seemingly certain defeat.

Do you remember the picture Harold Lloyd was in some years ago, showing a country boy who was afraid of his shadow? Every boy in the countryside bedeviled him. Until one day his grandmother gave him a talisman that she assured him his grandfather had carried through the Civil War and which, so she said, had the property of making its owner invincible. Nothing could hurt him, she told him, while he wore this talisman. Nothing could stand up against him. He believed her. And the next time the bully of the town started to cuff him around, he wiped up the earth with him. And that was only the start. Before the year was out he had made a reputation as the most daring soul in the community.

Then, when his grandmother felt he was thoroughly cured, she told him the truth-that the "talisman" was merely a piece of old junk she'd picked up by the roadside— that she knew all he needed was *faith in himself*, belief that he could do these things.

Stories like that are common. It is such a well-established truth that you can do only what you think you can, that the theme is a favorite one with authors.

I remember reading a story years ago of an artist—a mediocre sort of artist—who was visiting the field of Waterloo and happened upon a curious lump of metal half buried in the dirt, which so attracted him that he picked it up and put it in his pocket. Soon thereafter he noticed a sudden increase in confidence, an absolute faith in himself, not only as to his own chosen line of work, but in his ability to handle any situation that might present itself. He painted a great picture—just to show that he *could* do it. Not content with that, he visioned an empire with Mexico as its basis, actually led a revolt that carried all before it—until one day he lost his talisman. Then the bubble burst.

It is your own belief in yourself that counts. It is the consciousness of dominant power within you that makes all things attainable. *You can do anything you think you can.* This knowledge is literally the gift of the gods, for through it you can solve every human problem. It should make of you an incurable optimist. It is the open door to welfare. *Keep it open*—by expecting to gain everything that is right.

You are entitled to every good thing. Therefore expect nothing but good. Defeat does not *need* to follow victory. You don't have to "knock wood" every time you congratulate yourself that things have been going well with you. Victory should follow victory.

Don't limit your channels of supply. Don't think that riches or success must come through some particular job or some rich uncle. It is not for you to dictate to the Creative Force the means through which it shall send Its gifts to you. There are millions of channels through which It can reach you. Your part is to impress upon Mind your need, your earnest desire, your boundless belief in the resources and the willingness of the Creative Force to help you. Plant the seed of desire. Nourish it with a clear visualization of the ripened fruit. Water it with sincere faith. But leave the means to the Creative Force.

Open up your mind. Clear out the channels of thought. Keep yourself in a state of receptivity. Gain a mental attitude in which you are constantly *expecting good.* You have the fundamental right to all good, you know. "According to your faith, be it unto you."

The trouble with most of us is that we are mentally lazy. It is so much easier to go along with the crowd than to break trail for ourselves. But the great discoverers, the great inventors, the great geniuses in all lines have been men who dared to break with tradition, who defied precedent, who believed that there is no limit to what Mind can do—and who stuck to that belief until their goal was won, in spite of all the sneers and ridicule of the wiseacres and the "It-can't-be-doners."

Not only that, but they were never satisfied with achieving just one success. They knew that the first success is like the first olive out of the bottle. All the others come out the more easily for it. They realized that they were a part of the Creative Force and Intelligence of the Universe, and that the part shares all the properties of the whole. And that realization gave them the faith to strive for any right thing, the knowledge that the only limit upon their capabilities was the limit of their desires. Knowing that, they couldn't be satisfied with any ordinary success. They had to keep on and on and on.

Edison didn't sit down and fold his hands when he gave us the talking machine. Or the electric light. These great achievements merely opened the way to new fields of accomplishment.

Open up the channels between your mind and the Creative Force, and there is no limit to the riches that will come pouring in. Concentrate your thoughts on the particular thing you are most interested in, and ideas in abundance will come flooding down, opening up a dozen ways of winning the goal you are striving for.

But don't let one success—no matter how great—satisfy you. The Law of Life, you know, is the Law of Growth. You can't stand still. You must go forward—or be passed by. Complacency—self-satisfaction—is the greatest enemy of achievement. You must keep looking forward. Like Alexander, you must be constantly seeking new worlds to conquer. Depend upon it, the power will come to meet the need. There is no such thing as failing powers, if we look to the Creative Force for our source of supply. The only failure of mind comes from worry and fear—and disuse.

William James, the famous psychologist, taught that— "The more mind does, the more it can do." For ideas release energy. You can *do* more and better work than you have ever done. You can *know* more than you know now. You know from your own experience that under proper mental conditions of joy or enthusiasm, you can do three or four times the work without fatigue that you can ordinarily. Tiredness is more boredom than actual physical fatigue. You can work almost indefinitely when the work is a pleasure.

You've seen sickly persons, frail persons, who couldn't do an hour's light work without exhaustion, suddenly buckle down when heavy responsibilities were thrown upon them, and grow strong and rugged under the load. Crises not only draw upon the reserve power you have but they help to create new power.

IT COULDN'T BE DONE

It may be that you have been deluded by the thought of incompetence. It may be that you have been told so often that you cannot do certain things that you've come to believe you can't. Remember that success or failure is merely a state of mind. Believe you cannot do a thing—and you can't. Know that you can do it—and you *will*. You must *see yourself doing it*.

> *If you think you are beaten, you are;*
> *If you think you dare not, you don't;*
> *If you'd like to win, but you think*
> *you can't,*
> *It's almost a cinch you won't;*
> *If you think you'll lose, you've lost,*
> *For out in the world you'll find*
> *Success begins with a fellow's will—*
> *It's all in the state of mind.*
>
> *Full many a race is lost,*
> *Ere even a race is run,*
> *And many a coward fails*
> *Ere even his work's begun.*
> *Think big, and your deeds will grow,*
> *Think small and you fall behind,*
> *Think that you can, and you will;*
> *It's all in the state of mind.*
>
> *If you think you are outclassed, you are;*
> *You've got to think high to rise;*
> *You've got to be sure of yourself before*
> *You can ever win a prize.*
> *Life's battle doesn't always go*
> *To the stronger or faster man;*
> *But sooner or later, the man who wins*
> *Is the fellow who thinks he can.*

There's a vast difference between a proper understanding of one's own ability and a determination to make the best of it—and offensive egotism. It is absolutely necessary for every man to believe in himself, before he can make the most of himself. All of us have something to sell. It may be our goods, it may be our abilities, it may be our services. You've got to believe in yourself to make your buyer take stock in you at par and accrued interest. You've got to feel the same personal solicitude over a customer lost, as a revivalist over a backslider, and hold special services to bring him over into the fold. You've got to get up every morning with determination, if you're going to go to bed that night with satisfaction.

There's mighty sound sense in the saying that all the world loves a booster. The one and only thing you have to win success with is MIND. For your mind to function at its highest capacity, you've got to be charged with good cheer and optimism. No one ever did a good piece of work while in a negative frame of mind. Your best work is always done when you are feeling happy and optimistic.

And a happy disposition is the *result*—not the *cause*—of happy, cheery thinking. Health and prosperity are the *results* primarily of optimistic thoughts. *You* make the pattern. If the impress you have left on the world about you seems faint and weak, don't blame fate—blame your pattern! You will never cultivate a brave, courageous demeanor by thinking cowardly thoughts. You cannot gather figs from thistles. You will never make your dreams come true by choking them with doubts and fears. You've got to put foundations under your air castles, foundations of UNDERSTANDING AND BELIEF. Your chances of success in any undertaking can always be measured by your BELIEF in yourself.

Are your surroundings discouraging? Do you feel that if you were in another's place success would be easier? Just bear in mind that your real environment is within you. All the factors of success or failure are in your inner world. *You* make that inner world—and through it your outer world. You can choose the material from which to build it. If you've not chosen wisely in the past, you can choose again now the material you want to rebuild it. The richness of life is within you. No one has failed so long as he can begin again.

> For yesterday is but a dream,
> And tomorrow is only a vision.
> And today well-lived makes
> Every yesterday a dream of happiness,
> And every tomorrow a vision of hope.

Start right in and *do* all the things you feel you have it in you to do. Ask permission of no man. Concentrating your thought upon any proper undertaking will make its achievement possible. Your belief that you *can* do the thing gives your thought forces their power. Fortune waits upon you. Seize her boldly, hold her—and she is yours. She belongs rightfully to you. But if you cringe to her, if you go up to her doubtfully, timidly, she will pass you by in scorn. For she is a fickle jade who must be mastered, who loves boldness, who admires confidence. Remember, you can have what you want if you will use what you have now. You can do what you want if you will do what there is to do right now. Take the first step, and your mind will mobilize all its forces to your aid. But the first essential is that you *begin*. Once the battle is started, all that is within and without you will come to your assistance, if you attack in earnest and meet each obstacle with resolution. But *you* have to start things. As the poet so well expresses it:

> *Then take this honey from the bitterest cup,*
> *There is no failure save in giving up—*
> *No real fall so long as one still tries—*
> *For seeming set-backs make the strong man wise.*
> *There's no defeat, in truth, save from within:*
> *Unless you're beaten there, you're sure to win.*

The men who have made their mark in this world all had one trait in common—*they believed in themselves!* "But," you may say, "how can I believe in myself when I have never yet done anything worth while, when everything I put my hand to seems to fail?" You can't, of course. That is, you couldn't if you had to depend upon your conscious mind alone. But just remember what One far greater than you said—"I can of mine own self do nothing. The Father that is within me—He doeth the works."

That same "FATHER" is within you, and back of Him and of you is all the Creative Force in the universe. It is by knowing that He is in you, and that through Him you can do anything that is right, that you can acquire the belief in yourself which is so necessary. Certainly the Mind that imaged the heavens and the earth and all that they contain has all wisdom, all power, all abundance. With this Mind to call upon, you know there is no problem too difficult to undertake. The *knowing* of this is the first step. *Faith.* But St. James tells us— "Faith without works is dead." And Emerson expressed it in the modern manner when he said: "He who learns and learns, and yet does not what he knows, is like the man who plows and plows, yet never sows." So go on to the next step. Decide on the one thing you want most from life, no matter what it may be. There is no limit, you know, to Mind. Visualize this thing that you want. See it, feel it, BELIEVE in it. Make your mental blue-print, and *begin to build!* And not merely a mental blue-print, but make an actual picture of it, if you can. Cut out pictures from magazines that symbolize what you want. Paste them on a large sheet of paper and pin them up where you can see them often. You'll be surprised how such pictures help you to form the mental mold, and how quickly the Creative Force will take shape in that mold.

Suppose some people DO laugh at your idea. Suppose Reason does say—"It can't be done!" People laughed at Galileo. They laughed at Henry Ford. Reason contended for countless ages that the earth was flat. Reason said—or so numerous automotive engineers argued—that the Ford motor wouldn't run. But the earth *is* round—and some millions of Fords did run—and are running.

Let us start right now putting into practice some of these truths that you have learned. What do you want most of life right now? Take that one desire, concentrate on it, impress it upon your subconscious mind in every way you can, particularly with pictures. Visualizing what you want is essential, and pictures make this visualizing easier.

Psychologists have discovered that the best time to make suggestions to your subconscious mind is just before going to sleep, when the senses are quiet and the attention is lax. So let us take your desire and suggest it to your subconscious mind tonight. The two prerequisites are the earnest DESIRE, and an intelligent, understanding, BELIEF. Someone has said, you know, that education is three-fourths encouragement, and the encouragement is the suggestion that the thing can be done.

You know that you can have what you want, if you want it badly enough and can believe in it earnestly enough. So tonight, just before you drop off to sleep, concentrate your thought on this thing that you most desire from life. BE-LIEVE that you have it. SEE it in your mind's eye, and see YOURSELF possessing it. FEEL yourself using it.

Do that every night until you ACTUALLY DO BELIEVE that you have the thing you want. When you reach that point, YOU WILL HAVE IT!

> *Do you accept the Power within,*
> *Or do you say— 'Tomorrow,*
> *Or after that, I will begin,'*
> *And try from time to time to borrow*
> *Sweet, precious moments, quickly sped,*
> *On futile paths by error led?*

> *Our God has willed a legacy*

To all of those believing.
So why not change your "it might be"
To just "I am receiving
A guiding hand in every task,
And full returns for all I ask."

Do you desire success to win?
Humbly accept the Power within."
                                        —JOHN GRAHAM

THE PERFECT PATTERN

In Chapter 4, we quoted Baudouin to show how a person can hypnotize himself into health, happiness, success.

This is not as foolish as it sounds, for self-hypnosis is nothing more nor less than deep concentration, and it is a well-known fact that we go in the direction of our thoughts. What we long for, or dread, or fear—that we are headed towards.

You see, man is inseparable from the Creative Force. God has incarnated Himself in man, and God is dynamic—not static. He cannot be shut up. He must be expressed in one way or another. We put His power into all that we do— whether towards failure or success.

How then can we use this Creative Power for good? How can we put it into our efforts toward success?

First, by convincing ourselves that we ARE successful, that we are on the road to riches or health or power. We must "believe that we receive." And the quickest, easiest, surest way to do this is through repetition. It is now generally known and accepted that one comes to believe whatever one repeats to oneself sufficiently often, whether the statement be true or false. It comes to be the dominating thought in one's mind.

Such thoughts, when mixed with a strong feeling of desire or emotion, become a magnet which attracts from all about similar or related thoughts. They attract a host of their relatives, which they add to their own magnetic power until they become the dominating, motivating master of the individual.

Then the second law begins to work. All impulses of thought have a tendency to clothe themselves in their physical equivalent. In other words, if the dominating thought in your mind is riches, that thought will tend to draw to you opportunities for riches that you never dreamed of. Just as the magnet attracts iron, so will you attract money and ways of making more money. Or if health be your dominating thought, ways and means of winning new health and strength will come to you. The same is true of love, of happiness, of anything you may greatly desire of life.

On the other hand, if you fill your mind with fear, doubt and unbelief in your ability to use the forces of Infinite Intelligence, these in turn will become your dominating thought and form the pattern for your life.

You will be lifted up, or pulled down, according to the pattern of your thought. There are no limitations upon the Creative Force working through you. The limitations are all in you, and they are all self-imposed. Riches and poverty are equally the offspring of your thought.

So if you desire anything of good, the first and most important thing you must do is to develop your faith that *you can have that good.* Faith, like any other state of mind, can be induced by suggestion, by repetition. Tell yourself often enough that you HAVE faith, and you will have it, for any thought that is passed on to the subconscious often enough and convincingly enough is finally accepted, and then translated into its physical equivalent by the most practical method available.

You remember the story of the king who felt that his child, if brought up in the court, would be spoiled by overmuch attention. So he put him in the family of an honest peasant, and had him raised as the peasant's own child. The boy had all the power, all the riches of the kingdom at his disposal—yet he knew it not. He was a great prince, yet because he knew nothing of it, he worked and lived as a lowly peasant.

Most of us are like that young prince, in that we are ignorant of our Divine parentage. We know nothing of the power that is ours, so we get no good from it. God is working through us, and there is nothing He cannot do, yet because we know nothing of Him, we are powerless.

There is no such thing as a human nobody. All have the Divine spark in them, all can kindle it into a glowing flame through faith. People let themselves be hypnotized by fear and anxiety, fear of poverty, of failure, of disease. They continually visualize these, and thus make them their dominant thought, using it as a magnet to draw these things to them.

Whatever form your thoughts and beliefs take, the Creative Force working through you uses as a mold in which to form your life and your surroundings. If you want to be strong, think of yourself as perfect. If you want to be prosperous, think not of debts and lacks, but of riches and opportunity. We go in the direction of our dominating thought. It strikes the keynote of our life song.

"The chief characteristic of the religion of the future," wrote Dr. Eliot, "will be man's inseparableness from the great Creative Force." We are in partnership with the Fountain Head of all good.

Emerson said that Christ alone estimated the greatness and the divinity of man. Christ constantly emphasized man's unlimited possibilities. He saw that God incarnated Himself in man.

Emerson goes on to say that man is weak when he looks for help outside himself. It is only as he throws himself unhesitatingly upon the Creative Force within himself that he finds the springs of success, the power that can accomplish all things. It is only when he realizes that all outside help amounts to nothing compared with the tremendous forces working through him that he stands erect and begins to work miracles.

Nearly every man has a habit of looking back and saying—"If I had that period of my life to live over again, if I could go back and take advantage of the chance at fortune I had then, I'd be rich and successful today."

Yet a year from now, or five or ten years from now, most of you who read this will be saying the same thing of today.

Why? Because your future depends upon the foundations you are digging NOW Yesterday is gone. There is no recalling it. And tomorrow has not come. The only time you have to work with is right now, and whether you will go up or down tomorrow, whether you will be rich or a failure, depends upon your thoughts today.

It took mankind thousands of years to learn how to control matter, how to provide comfort and safety and some degree of financial security. It has taken less than a generation to learn how to control one's own future. The knowledge is so new that most people are not yet aware of it. As David Seabury put it in his book—"They know that science and mechanics have made over the face of the earth. They do not know that psychology and its kindred sciences are making a like change in man's handling of his own nature."

Do you know why so few people succeed in life? Because it is so EASY that most people cannot believe in the methods that really make men successful. They prefer to look upon success as something arduous, something practically impossible for them to attain—and by looking upon it that way, make it so for themselves.

YOU CAN HAVE WHAT YOU WANT—if you know how to plant the seeds of it in your thought. To know that is the most important thing that anyone can learn. It is not fate that bars your path. It is not lack of money or opportunity. It is yourself—your attitude towards life. Change it—and you change all.

Ask yourself this important question: Are you a victim of self-pity? Are you embittered at life and at those more successful than yourself? Do you think fortune has played you a scurvy trick? Or are you cheerfully, steadfastly, confidently working out ways of meeting and bettering the situations that life presents to you?

Most people will dodge that question. They are more concerned in defending their ego and putting the blame for their failures on something outside themselves than they are in getting ahead. Failure comes from the inside first. It cannot be forced upon a resolute, dauntless soul.

How about YOU? Will you give yourself an honest answer to this important question—"Are you a victim of self-pity?"

Think of the times when you have yearned for a future— when you have grown impatient with the barriers that seemed to hold you down—when you have heard of the success of some acquaintance whom you knew to be inwardly no more capable than yourself. Are you willing to keep on *wishing* and *envying* and looking to the future for your success? Or will you start that success in the only time that will ever be yours to work with—the everlasting NOW?

Remember what Emerson told us: "There is one Mind common to all individual men. Every man is an inlet to the same and to ALL of the same. He that is once admitted to the right of reason is a freeman of the whole estate. What Plato has thought, he may think; what a Saint has felt, he may feel; what has at any time befallen any man, he can understand. Who hath access to this Universal Mind is a party to all that is or can be done; for this is the only and sovereign agent—of this Universal Mind each individual is one more incarnation."

The Creative Force of the Universe is working through you. You can be as great an outlet for IT as anyone who has ever lived. You have only to provide the mold in which it is to take shape, and that mold is formed by your thoughts. What is your dominant desire? What do you want most? *Believe in it*—and you can have it. Make it your dominating thought, magnetize your mind with it, and you will draw to you everything you need for its accomplishment.

"There is not a dream that may not come true," wrote Arthur Symons, "if we have the energy which makes or chooses our own fate. We can always in this world get what we want, if we *will* it intensely and persistently enough. So few people succeed because so few can conceive a great end and work towards it without deviating and without tiring. But we all know that the man who works for money day and night gets rich; and the man who works day and night for no matter what kind of material power, gets the power. It is only the dreams of those light sleepers who dream faintly that do not come true."

Knowing these things, can you ever again limit yourself, when you have such unlimited possibilities? Sure, there are times when you feel inferior. Everyone does. Just remember that, and realize that *you* are superior, one of the efficient few who take advantage of the Infinite Power inside them to carry you on to the heights of success.

Plato held, you remember, that in the Divine Mind are pure forms or Archetypes according to which all visible beings are made. And most of the great Mystery Schools of the older world held similar opinions. They taught growth by intent rather than by accident, a development from birth all through life towards the perfect image or Archetype of each of us that is held in Divine Mind. They visioned each of us growing into a destiny that had been imaged for him long before he was born.

Progress was movement in the direction of the perfect Archetype. Man became nobler as the interval between him and his perfect pattern grew less. To the Greeks, happiness meant peace between a man and his pattern, whereas if you lived in a manner inconsistent with your Archetype, you suffered from inharmonies of various kinds. They believed that it was not so much what you do that causes you to suffer, as it is the inharmony between what you do and what you SHOULD DO to match your perfect pattern.

There is a perfect pattern for YOU in the Divine Mind, a perfect Archetype that you CAN match. It has perfect form, perfect intelligence, all power necessary to make your surroundings perfect. Why not make yourself like it?

You CAN! Just let your Archetype be your model. Fill your mind with thoughts of its perfection, make it your dominant thought, and you can draw to yourself whatever elements you need to manifest that perfect image. And not merely the perfect image of yourself, but all that goes to make your surroundings and circumstances just as perfect. Remember, the only limit upon the Power working through you is the limit you impose. Bear these facts in mind:

1. Your subconscious mind is constantly amenable to control by the power of suggestion.

2. Its power to reason deductively from given premises to correct conclusions is practically perfect.

3. It is endowed with a perfect memory.

4. It is the seat of your emotions.

5. It has the power to communicate and receive intelligence through other than the recognized channels of the senses.

"Man contains all that is needful within himself," wrote Emerson. "He is made a law unto himself. All real good or evil that can befall him must be from himself. The purpose of life seems to be to acquaint a man with himself. The highest revelation is that God is in every man."

TO HIM THAT HATH

Jesus gave us the Fundamental Law of Increase when He told us that—"Unto everyone that hath shall be given, and he shall have abundance, but from him that hath not shall be taken away even that which he hath."

Sounds simple, doesn't it, yet it is the basic law of all success, all riches, all power. It is the way the whole universe is run. You live by it, whether you like it or not, or you die by it.

To many, this law seems unfair, but in this, as in all things, Nature is logical, and when you understand exactly how the law works, you will agree that it is eminently just and right.

You see, everything consists primarily of electricity—of tiny protons and electrons revolving about each other. It is of these that your body is made, it is of these that all plant life is made, it is of these that all so-called inanimate life is made. Wherein, then, is the difference between all these forms of life? Largely in their RATE OF MOTION!

Remember this: Starting with the individual cell in your mother's womb, you attract to yourself only those elements that are identical in quality and character with yourself, and that are revolving at the same rate of speed. Your selective ability is such that you are able to pick such material as will preserve your quality and identity.

This is true of your body, of your circumstances, of your environment. Like attracts like. If you are not satisfied with yourself as you are, if you want a healthier body, more attractive friends, greater riches and success, you must start at the core—within YOURSELF!

And the first essential to putting yourself in harmony with the Infinite Good all about you is to relax, to take off the brakes. For what is worry or fear or discouragement but a brake on your thinking and on the proper functioning of your organs, a slowing down of your entire rate of activity.

"Get rid of your tensions!" says the modern psychologist. By which he means—think more about the agreeable things and less about the disagreeable ones. You know how martial music stirs your pulses, wakes even the tiredest man into action. Why? Because it tends to increase the rate of motion in every cell in your body. You know how good news has often cured sick people, how sudden excitement has enabled paralyzed people to leap from their beds. Why? Because good news makes you happy, speeds up your rate of motion, even as sudden excitement stirs up the whole organism. You know how fear, hatred, and discouragement slow you down. Why? Because those feelings put a definite clamp upon your rate of motion.

Remember this: Hatred, anger, fear, worry, discouragement—all the negative emotions—not only slow down your rate of motion, and thus bring on sickness and make you old before your time, but they definitely keep the good from you. Like attracts like, and the good things you desire have a different rate of motion from these negative ones.

Love, on the other hand, attracts and binds to you the things you love. As Drummond tells us—"To love abundantly is to live abundantly, and to love forever is to live forever." And Emerson expresses the same idea—"Love and you shall be loved. All love is mathematically just, as much as the two sides of an algebraic equation."

> Whate'er thou lovest, man,
> That, too, become thou must;
> God, if thou lovest God,
> Dust, if thou lovest dust.

And that, again, is strictly logical, strictly in accord with Nature's law that like attracts like. Whatever your rate of motion, the elements of like quality with that rate of emotion will be attracted to you.

Which brings us back to the law enunciated by Jesus— "Unto everyone that hath shall be given, and he shall have abundance, but from him that hath not shall be taken away that which he hath."

Read the parable of the Talents, which brought forth this pronouncement of Jesus, and you will see that it is not mere money or possessions that attracts more money—it is the USE to which these are put. You can't bury your talent and expect increase. You must put it to good use. It is the rate of motion that attracts increase, what the modern merchant would call the "turn-over." The oftener he turns over his stock of goods, the more money he makes on his invested capital. But if he fails to turn it over, if his goods lie dormant on his shelves, they will gather dust or mold and presently be worthless.

The servant in the parable who had five talents put them to work and attracted five more; the servant with two talents did likewise and increased his by two more. But the servant with only one talent buried his in a field and let it lie idle. He got nothing, and the talent he had was taken away from him.

We see the same thing happening every day. Statistics show that of all those who inherit money, only one in seventeen dies with money; of all those possessed of fortunes at the age of 35, only 17 per cent have them when they reach 65.

The old adage used to be—"Three generations from shirtsleeves to shirtsleeves," but the modern tempo has speeded this up until now most fortunes hardly last out a single generation. Why is this? Because of the old law of the Rate of Motion. The man who makes the money has set in motion some idea of service that has attracted riches to him. More often than not, it is the idea or the service that is important in his mind. The money is incidental, and is attracted to him with other things of good because he has set in motion an idea that is bringing good to others.

But when he dies, what happens? Too often the business is carried on solely with the thought of how much money can be made out of it. Or the business is sold, and the money put out at interest, with the sole idea of hanging on to the money in hand. Naturally its rate of movement slows down. Naturally it begins to disintegrate and its parts are gradually drawn away by the stronger forces around it, until of that fortune there is nothing left.

You see exactly the same thing in Nature. Take any seed of plant life; take an acorn, for instance. You put it in the ground—plant it. What happens? It first gives of all the elements it has within itself to put forth a shoot, which in turn shall draw from the sun and the air the elements that they have to give; and at the same time, it puts out roots to draw from the earth the moisture and other elements it needs for growth. Its top reaches upward to the sun and air, its roots burrow deeply into the ground for moisture and nourishment. Always it is reaching out. Always it is creating a vacuum, using up all the materials it has on hand, drawing to itself from all about every element it needs for growth.

Time passes. The oaktree stops growing. What happens? In that moment, its attractive power ceases. Can it then live on the elements it has drawn to itself and made a part of itself through all those years? No, indeed! The moment growth stops, disintegration starts. Its component elements begin to feel the pull of the growing plants around them. First the moisture drains out of the tree. Then the leaves fall, the bark peels off—finally the great trunk crashes down, to decay and form soil to nourish the growing plants around. Soon of that noble oak, nothing is left but the enriched soil and the well-nourished plants that have sprung from it.

The Fundamental Law of the Universe is that you must integrate or disintegrate. You must grow—or feed others who are growing. There is no standing still. You are either attracting to yourself all the unused forces about you, or you are giving your own to help build some other man's success.

"To him that hath, shall be given." To him that is using his attractive powers, shall be given everything he needs for growth and fruition. "From him that hath not, shall be taken away even that which he hath." The penalty for not using your attractive powers is the loss of them. You are demagnetized. And like a dead magnet surrounded by live ones, you must be content to see everything you have drawn to yourself taken by them, until eventually even you are absorbed by their resistless force.

That is the first and fundamental Law of the Universe. But how are you to become an Attracter? How are you to make your start? In the same way that it has been done from the beginning of time.

Go back to the first law of life. Go back to the beginning of things. You will find Nature logical in all that she does. If you want to understand how she works, study her in her simplest, most elementary forms. The principles established there hold good throughout the universe. The methods there used are used by all created things, from the simplest to the most complicated.

How, for instance, did the earliest forms of cell life, either plant or animal, get their food? By absorbing it from the waters around them. How does every cell in your body, every cell in plant or tree or animal, get its food today? In exactly the same way—by absorbing it from the lymph or water surrounding it! Nature's methods do not change. She is logical in everything. She may build more complicated organisms, she may go in for immense size or strange combinations, but she uses the same principles throughout all of life.

Now, what is Nature's principle of Increase? From the beginning of Time, it has been—

DIVIDE—AND GROW!

That principle, like every other fundamental Law of Nature, is the same in all of life. It has remained unchanged since the first single-celled organism floated on the surface of the primordial sea. It is the fundamental Law of Increase.

Take the lowest form of cell life. How does it grow? It DIVIDES—each part grows back to its original size—then they in turn divide and grow again.

Take the highest form of cell life—MAN. The same principle works in him in exactly the same way—in fact, it is the only principle of growth that Nature knows!

How does this apply to your circumstances, to the acquisition of riches, to the winning of success?

Look up any miracle of increase in the Bible, and what do you find? First division—then increase.

When Russell Conwell was building the famous Baptist Temple in Philadelphia, his congregation was poor and greatly in need of money. Through prayer and every other means known to him, Conwell was constantly trying to help his flock.

One Sunday it occurred to him that the old Jewish custom had been, when praying to God, to first make an offering of the finest lamb of the flock, or of some other much-prized possession. Then, after freely giving to God, prayer was made for His good gifts.

So instead of first praying, and then taking up the collection, as was the custom, Conwell suggested that the collection be taken first and that all who had special favors to ask of the Creator should give freely as a "Thank Offering."

A few weeks afterwards, Conwell asked that those who had made offerings on this occasion should tell their experiences. The results sounded unbelievable. One woman who had an overdue mortgage on her home found it necessary to call in a plumber the following week to repair a leak. In tearing up the boards, he uncovered a hiding place where her late father had hidden all his money—enough to pay off the mortgage and leave plenty over!

One man got a much-needed job. A servant some dresses she badly needed. A student the chance to study for his chosen vocation. While literally dozens had their financial needs met.

They had complied with the law. They had sown their seed—freely—and they reaped the harvest.

"Except a kernel of wheat fall into the ground and die," said the Master, "it abideth alone. But if it die, it beareth much fruit." You can't put strings on your seeds. You can't sow them and say—"I'll give you a chance to sprout and bring forth increase, but if you fail, I'll take you back and use you to make bread." You must give that seed freely, fully. It must be dead to you, before you can hope to get back from it a harvest of increase.

Many people will tell you—"I don't see why God does not send me riches, I have prayed for them, and promised that if I get them, I will use them to do good." God enters into no bargains with man. He gives you certain gifts to start, and upon the way you use these depends whether you get more. You've got to start with what you have.

And the place to start is pointed out in a little poem by Nina Stiles:

The land of opportunity
Is anywhere we chance to be,
Just any place where people live
And need the help that we can give.

The basis of all work, all business, all manufacturing, is SERVICE. Every idea of success must start with that. Every nucleus that is to gather to itself elements of good must have as its basis service to your fellow man. Carlyle defined wealth clearly when he said that "the wealth of a man is the number of things he loves and blesses, which he is loved and blessed by."

And that is the only kind of wealth that endures. Love and blessings speed up your rate of motion, keep your nucleus active, keep it drawing to you every element of good that you need for its complete and perfect expression. They are, in effect, a constant prayer—the kind of prayer Coleridge had in mind when he wrote—

He prayeth well who loveth well
Both man and bird and beast.
He prayeth best who loveth best
All things both great and small;
For the dear God who loveth us,
He made and loveth all.

Remember that the only word often used in the Old Testament to signify "prayer" means, when literally translated—"To sing a song of joy and praise." In other words, to speed up your rate of motion with joy and thanksgiving. And you have only to read the Old Testament to know how often the great characters of the Bible had recourse to this method.

What do *you* want from life? Speed up your rate of motion and overtake it. Is it health you want? Then start by relaxing, by letting go of all your fears and worries. In a recent article, I read: "Dr. Loring Swaim, director of a famous clinic in Massachusetts, has under observation 270 cases of arthritis which were cured when they became free from worry, fear, and resentment. He has come to the conclusion after some years that no less than 60 per cent of his cases are caused by moral conflict."

In the Reader's Digest some months ago, it was stated that "Personal worry is one of the principal causes of physical ailments which send people to hospitals. It is literally possible to worry yourself sick; in fact, the chances are better than even that if you are ill, worry is causing the symptoms."

That is not a modern discovery, by any means. In Proverbs, you will find the statement—"A merry heart causeth good healing, but a broken spirit drieth up the bones." And Plato observed 19 centuries ago—"If the head and the body are to be well, you must begin by curing the soul."

So the first essential in curing yourself of any ailment would seem to be to let go of your resentments, your worries and fears. Make peace within yourself, within your thoughts. Laugh a little, sing a little. Dance a little, if you can. Exercise speeds up your rate of motion, but it should be joyous exercise. Do something you enjoy, something that speeds up your mind as well as your muscles. Dance, if you like dancing. Swim, ride horseback, play tennis—do something exhilarating to the spirit as well as the body. Mere routine exercises that soon become a chore do little good and often are harmful. Unless you can get mental as well as physical exhilaration out of your exercise, don't bother with it at all.

Do you want money, riches? Then use what you have, no matter how little it may be. Speed up your rate of turnover, as the merchant speeds the turnover of his stocks. Money is now your stock. Use it! Pay it out joyfully for any good purpose, and as you pay it, BLESS IT! Bless it in some such wise as this:

I bless you . . . and be thou a blessing; May you enrich all who touch you. I thank God for you, but I thank Him even more that there is unlimited supply where you came from. I bless that Infinite Supply. I thank God for it, and I expand my consciousness to take in as much of it as I can use ... As I release this money in my hand. I know that I am opening the gates of Infinite Supply to flow through my channels and through all that are open to receive it. The Spirit that multiplied the loaves and fishes for Jesus is making this money attract to itself everything it needs for growth and increase. All of God's channels are open and flowing freely for me. The best in myself for the world—the best in the world for me.

There is no quicker way of speeding up your rate of motion than by *giving*. Give of your time, of your money, of your services—whatever you have to give. Give of that you want to see increased, for your gift is your seed, and "everything increaseth AFTER ITS KIND!"

Solomon was the richest man of his day, and he gave us the key to his riches and success when he wrote:

There is that scattereth, and increaseth yet more. And there is that witholdeth more than is meet. The liberal soul shall be made fat, and he that watereth, shall be watered himself.

And one even wiser than Solomon told us: "Give, and it shall be given unto you, good measure, pressed down and shaken together and running over, shall men give into your bosom. For with the same measure that ye mete withal, it shall be measured to you again."

Do you want power, ability, greater skill in what you are doing? Then use what you have, use it to the greatest extent of which you are capable. The Sunshine Bulletin had an excellent little piece along these lines:

There is a task for today which can be done now better than at any other time. It is today's duty. And we are writing now a judgment upon our lives by our faithfulness or unfaithfulness at the present moment.

This moment has its own priceless value, and if wasted, it can no more be recovered than jewels that are cast into the depths of the ocean.

Each day has its share in the making of our tomorrow; and the future will be nobler or meaner by reason of what we now do or leave undone.

What is ambition but the inner urge that speeds up your rate of motion and makes you work harder and longer and more purposefully to the end that you may accomplish something worth while? What is perseverance but the will to carry on in spite of all difficulties and discouragements? Given that ambition and that perseverence, there is nothing you cannot accomplish, nothing with a rate of motion so high that you cannot overtake it.

It is in loving, not in being loved,
The heart is blessed.
It is in giving, not in seeking gifts,
We find our quest.

If thou art hungry, lacking heavenly bread,
Give hope and cheer.
If thou art sad and wouldst be comforted,
Stay sorrow's tear.

Whatever be thy longing or thy need,
That do thou give.
So shall thy soul be fed, and thou indeed
Shalt truly live.

—M. ELLA RUSSELL

EVERYTHING HAS ITS PRICE

Dear God, help me be wise enough to see
That as I give so it is meted out to me!

Help me to know that with my every thought
The good or ill that's mine myself I've wrought!
Help me to place all blame of lack on me,
Not on my fellow man, nor yet on Thee.
Give me the courage, God, truly to know
That as I'd reap in life thus must I sow!

–VERA M. CRIDER

In his essay on Compensation, Emerson says:

"What will you have?" quoth God
"Pay for it, and take it!"

How can we buy the things we want at the counter of God? What pay can we offer?

Perhaps the answer lies in the ancient Law of Karma. Karma is Sanskrit, you know, and means "Comeback." It is one of the oldest laws known to man. It is the law of the boomerang. Jesus quoted it when He said—"Whatsoever a man soweth, that shall he also reap."

In the parlance of today, it is—"Chickens come home to roost." Even in science we find it, as Newton's Third Law of Motion—"Action and reaction are equal to each other." Ella Wheeler Wilcox expressed the Law beautifully when she wrote—

There are loyal hearts, there are spirits brave,
There are souls that are pure and true;
Then give to the world the best you have,
And the best will come back to you.

Give love, and love to your heart will flow,
A strength in your utmost need;
Have faith, and a score of hearts will show
Their faith in your word and deed.

For life is the mirror of king and slave,
'Tis just what you are and do,
Then give to the world the best you have
And the best will come back to you.

One of the best illustrations of the working of the Law lies in the two seas of Palestine, the Sea of Galilee and the Dead Sea. The Sea of Galilee contains fresh water and is alive with fish. Green trees adorn its banks and farms and vineyards spread all around it. The River Jordan flows into it, and all the little rivulets from the hills around feed its sparkling waters.

The Dead Sea, on the other hand, knows no splash of fish, has no vegetation around it, no homes, no farms or vineyards. Travelers give it a wide berth, unless forced by urgent business to use its shores. The air hangs heavy, and neither man nor beast will drink of the waters.

What makes the difference? The River Jordan empties the same good waters into both seas. So it is not the river. And it is not the soil or the country round about.

The difference lies in the fact that the Sea of Galilee gives as it receives; for every drop of water that flows into it, another flows out. Whereas the Dead Sea holds on to all it receives. Water leaves it only through evaporation and seepage. It hoards all it gets, and the result is that the water stagnates, turns salt and is good for naught.

"Unless a kernel of wheat fall into the ground and die," Jesus told us, "it abideth alone. But if it die, it beareth much fruit." In other words, if you put your kernel of wheat safely away to keep, you will never have anything but a kernel of wheat, and in time it will mould and rot away, but if you sow it freely (let it die to you), it will bear much fruit. It is another way of saying—"Cast thy bread upon the waters and it will return to you after many days increased an hundredfold."

In all of Nature, the only known law of increase is that you must give to get. If you want to reap a harvest, you must first plant your seed. If you want to increase your strength, you must first break up the muscle cells, and stimulate them to divide and grow.

Division and growth is the way that all of life increases. Watch a single cell at work in your body, in a plant, or in any form of life. What happens? It first divides, then each half grows until it reaches its normal size, when it divides and starts growing again. Without division, there is no growth—only atrophy and decay. You must divide to grow, you must give to get.

John Bunyan knew nothing of the law of cell growth, but he expressed it just as well when he wrote—

> A man there was and they called him mad;
> The more he gave, the more he had.

And Moffatt had the same thought in his couplet:

> *One gives away, and still he grows the richer;*
> *Another keeps what he should give, and is the poorer.*

Even the thoughts we send forth return to us laden with a harvest of their kind. That which we put into our thought comes back into our own lives, because for every thought there is a response, a return of the pendulum we have started swinging. It is the Einstein doctrine of the extended line, which must return to its source.

There is no use saying you have not enough money or abilities to be worth starting with. Just remember the parable of the talents. The servant who was given five talents put them out at interest and made more, as did the one who was given two talents. But the servant who received only one talent felt that it was too little to do much with, so he buried it. And you know what happened to him when the Master came back.

Start with what you have and plant your seed, no matter how small and unimportant it may seem. You remember Jesus told us that the Kingdom of Heaven (or Expansion) is like a mustard seed—"Which indeed is the least of all seeds, but when it is grown, it is the greatest among herbs, and becometh a tree, so that the birds of the air come to lodge in the branches thereof."

What you have to start with can hardly be smaller than the tiny mustard seed. If it can grow into a tree, think what your seed may grow into.

"*Do the thing* and you shall have the power," says Emerson. "But they that do not the thing have not the power. Everything has its price, and if the price is not paid—not that thing but something else is obtained. And it is impossible to get anything without its price. For any benefit received, a tax is levied. In nature, nothing can be given—all things are sold. Power to him who power exerts."

> *You are not higher than your lowest thought,*
> *Or lower than the peak of your desire.*
> *And all existence has no wonder wrought*
> *To which ambition may not yet aspire.*
> *Oh man! There is no planet, sun or star*
> *Could hold you, if you but knew what you are.*

The key to power lies in using what you have, for use releases more power, just as using your muscles builds them into greater muscles, and failing to use them makes them weak and useless. "The one condition coupled with the gift of truth," Emerson tells us, "is its USE! That man shall be learned who reduces his learning to practice."

And Goethe expressed it even more strongly when he wrote—

> Lose this day loitering, it will be the same story
> Tomorrow, and the rest more dilatory;
> Thus indecision brings its own delays
> And days are lost tormenting over other days.
> Are you in earnest? Seize this very minute;
> What you can do, or dream you can, begin it;
> Boldness has genius, power, and magic in it;
> Only engage and then the mind grows heated;
> Begin, and then the work will be completed.

YESTERDAY ENDED LAST NIGHT

I said to the man who stood at the gate of the year: "Give me a light that I may tread safely into the unknown." And he replied: "Go out into the darkness and put your hand into the hand of God. That shall be to you better than a light and safer than a known way."

What do you want from life? Whatever it is, you can have it—and you have the word of no less an authority than Jesus for that.

"Seek ye first the Kingdom of God and His Righteousness," He told us, "and all these things (all the riches and power and other material things you have wanted) shall be added unto you."

Does that mean that you must become saintly in order to amass material possessions? Experience would seem to indicate that it seldom works out that way. The saintly are not often burdened with worldly goods. No, saintliness is not the answer. Then what is?

Let us examine the meaning of "righteousness" and see if the answer does not lie in it. The word used for "righteousness" in the ancient Greek text of the original Gospels is "dikaiosune," which, literally translated, means the absolute dictatorship of the spirit within you.

Translated thus the passage reads—"Seek ye first the Kingdom of God and His absolute dictatorship of the spirit within you, and all these things shall be added unto you." In other words, put the problem up to God in You, the part of Divinity that is the Creative Force in you, and leave it to Him to work out while you rest in serene faith that it IS done.

How would this work out in practice? There was an article in UNITY recently that exemplified the idea so well that I quote it here:

Let us say we are planning a business venture, or a social event, or a religious meeting, or the recovery of the sick. We are ready to pray over the situation. Now instead of futurizing our prayers and asking for something to take place tomorrow, let us imagine (imagination is an aid to the release of faith power) that everything has turned out just as we desired it. Let us write it all down as if it were all past history. Many of the Bible predictions are written in the past tense. Let us try listing our desires as if they had already been given us.

Of course we shall want to write down a note of thanksgiving to God for all that He has given us. He has had it for us all the time or else we should not have received it. More than this, God has it for us or we could not even desire it now or picture it in our imagination.

What happens? After we have written down our desires in the past tense, read them over carefully, praised God for them, let us then put away our paper and go on about our business. It will not be long before we actually see the desired events taking place in ways so natural that we may even forget that God is answering our prayers.

Imagination helps us to have faith, for it pictures the thing desired and helps make it real. After we have tried this experiment a few times we shall find that our imagination has increased our faith, and faith has turned to praise, and praise has opened our eyes to see what God has for us.

The habit of thanking God ahead of time for benefits about to be received has its firm basis in past experience. We can safely look upon it as a sure formula for successful prayer because Christ used it. David always praised and thanked God when he was in trouble. Daniel was saved from the lions through the praise of God. Paul sang songs of praise and liberated himself from prison. And don't you, and everyone else, find satisfaction in being praised for a task well done?

Wrote William Law: If anyone could tell you the shortest, surest way to all happiness and all perfection, he must tell you to make it a rule yourself to thank and praise God for everything that happens to you. For it is certain that whatever seeming calamity happens to you, if you thank and praise God for it, you turn it into a blessing. Could you therefore work miracles, you could not do more for yourself than by this thankful spirit; for it... turns all that it touches into happiness.

And Charles Fillmore adds: Praise is closely related to prayer; it is one of the avenues through which spirituality expresses itself. Through an inherent law of mind, we increase whatever we praise. The whole creation responds to praise, and is glad. Animal trainers pet and reward their charges with delicacies for acts of obedience; children glow with joy and gladness when they are praised. Even vegetation grows better for those who love it. We can praise our own ability, and the very brain cells will expand and increase in capacity and intelligence, when we speak words of encouragement and appreciation to them.

So don't let anything that has happened in your life discourage you. Don't let poverty or lack of education or past failures hold you back. There is only one power—the I AM in you—and it can do anything. If in the past you have not used that power, that is too bad as far as the past is concerned, but it is not too late. You can start NOW. "Be still, and know that I AM God." What more are you waiting for? God can do for you only what you allow Him to do through you, but if you will do your part, He can use you as a channel for unlimited power and good.

The difference between failure and success is measured only by your patience and faith—sometimes by inches, sometimes by minutes, sometimes by the merest flash of time.

Take Lincoln. He went into the Black Hawk War a Captain—and came out a private. His store failed—and his surveyor's instruments, on which he depended to eke out a livelihood, were sold for part of the debts. He was defeated in his first try for the Legislature. Defeated in his first attempt for Congress. Defeated in his application for Commissioner of the General Land Office. Defeated for the Senate. Defeated for the nomination for the Vice Presidency in 1856. But did he let that long succession of defeats discourage him? Not he. He held the faith—and made perhaps the greatest President we have ever had.

Then there was Grant: He failed of advancement in the army. Failed as a farmer. Failed as a business man. At 39, he was chopping and delivering cordwood to keep body and soul together. Nine years later he was President of the United States and had won a martial renown second in this country only to Washington's.

Search the pages of history. You will find them dotted with the names of men whom the world had given up as failures, but who held on to their faith, who kept themselves prepared—and when their chance came they were ready and seized it with both hands.

Napoleon, Cromwell, Patrick Henry, Paul Jones—these are only a few out of thousands.

When Caesar was sent to conquer Gaul, his friends found him one day in a fit of utter despondency. Asked what the matter was, he told them he had just been comparing his accomplishments with Alexander's. At his age, Alexander had conquered the entire known world—and what had Caesar done to compare with that? But he presently roused himself from his discouragement by resolving to make up as quickly as might be for his lost time. The result? He became the head of the Roman Empire.

The records of business are crowded with the names of middle-aged nobodies who lived to build great fortunes, vast institutions. No man has failed as long as he has faith in the Father, faith in the great scheme of things, faith in himself.

YESTERDAY ENDED LAST NIGHT

When Robert Bruce faced the English at the battle of Bannockburn, he had behind him years of failure, years of fruitless efforts to drive the English out of Scotland, years of heart-breaking toil in trying to unite the warring elements among the Scotch themselves. True, at the moment a large part of Scotland was in his hands, but so had it been several times before, only to be wrested from him as soon as the English brought together a large enough army.

And now in front of him stood the greatest army England had ever gathered to her banners—hardy veterans from the French provinces, all the great English nobles with their armored followers, wild Irish, Welsh bowmen—troops from all the dominions of Edward II, over 100,000 men.

To conquer whom Bruce had been able to muster but 30,000 men, brave and hardy, it is true, but lacking the training and discipline of the English.

Was Bruce discouraged? Not he. What though the English had the better archers. What though they were better armed, better trained, better disciplined. He was fighting for freedom—and he *believed* in himself, he believed in his men, he believed in the God of battles.

And, as always, weight, numbers, armament, proved of no avail when confronted with determination and faith. The vast English host was completely defeated and dispersed. Bruce was firmly seated upon the throne of Scotland, and never more did an invading English army cross its borders.

It matters not how many defeats you have suffered in the past, how great the odds may be against you. Bulow put it well when he said—"It's not the size of the dog in the fight that counts, so much as the size of the fight in the dog." And the size of fight in you depends upon your faith—your faith in yourself, in the Creative Force working through you and in your cause. Just remember that yesterday ended last night, and yesterday's defeats with it.

Time after time throughout the Bible we are told that the battle is not ours—but the Lord's. But like all children, we know better than our Father how our affairs should be handled, so we insist upon running them ourselves.

Is it any wonder they get so tangled as to leave us in the depths of discouragement?

When the Black Prince with his little army was penned in by Philip of France, most men would have felt discouraged. For the hosts of France seemed as numerous as the leaves on the trees. While the English were few, and mostly archers. And archers, in that day, were believed to stand no chance against such armored knights as rode behind the banners of Philip.

The French came forward in a great mass, thinking to ride right over that little band of English. But did the Black Prince give way? Not he. He showed the world that a new force had come into warfare, a force that would soon make the armored knight as extinct as the dodo. That force was the common soldier—the archer.

Just as the Scotch spearmen overthrew the chivalry of England on the field of Bannockburn, just as infantry have overthrown both cavalry and artillery in many a later battle, so did the "common men" of England—the archers— decide the fate of the French at Crecy. From being despised and looked down upon by every young upstart with armor upon his back, the "common men"—the spearmen and archers—became the backbone of every successful army. And from what looked like certain annihilation, the Black Prince by his faith in himself and his men became one of the greatest conquerors of his day.

Troubles flocked to him, but he didn't recognize them as troubles—he thought them opportunities. And used them to raise himself and his soldiers to the pinnacle of success.

There are just as many prizes in business as in war—just as many opportunities to turn seeming troubles into blessings. But those prizes go to men like the Black Prince who don't know a trouble when they meet it—who welcome it, take it to their bosoms, and get from it their greatest blessings.

What is the use of holding on to life—unless at the same time you hold on to your faith? What is the use of going through the daily grind, the wearisome drudgery—if you have given up hoping for the rewards, and unseeing, let them pass you by?

Suppose business and industry did that? How far would they get? It is simply by holding on hopefully, believingly, watchfully—as Kipling put it: "Forcing heart and nerve and sinew to serve your turn long after they are gone, and so hold on when there is nothing in you except the will which says to them: 'Hold on'!"—that many a business man has worked out his salvation.

It is not enough to work. The horse and the ox do that. And when we work without thought, without hope, we are no better than they. It is not enough to merely hold on. The poorest creatures often do that mechanically, for lack of the courage to let go.

If you are to gain the reward of your labors, if you are to find relief from your drudgery, you must hold on hopefully, believingly, confidently—knowing that the answer is in the great heart of God, knowing that the Creative Force working through you will give it to you, the moment you have prepared yourself to receive it.

It is never the gifts that are lacking. It is never the Creative Force that is backward in fulfilling our desires. It is we who are unable to see, who fail to recognize the good, because our thoughts are of discouragement and lack.

So never let yesterday's failure discourage you. As T. C. Howard wrote in "Forbes" magazine:

> Yesterday's gone—it was only a dream;
> Of the past there is naught but remembrance.
> Tomorrow's a vision thrown on Hope's screen,
> A will-o'-the-wisp, a mere semblance.
>
> Why mourn and grieve over yesterdays ills
> And paint memory's pictures with sorrow?
> Why worry and fret—for worrying kills—
> Over things that won't happen tomorrow?
>
> Yesterday's gone—it has never returned—
> Peace to its ashes, and calm;
> Tomorrow no human has ever discerned,
> Still hope, trust, and faith are its balm.
>
> This moment is all that I have as my own,
> To use well, or waste, as I may;
> But I know that my future depends alone
> On the way that I live today.
>
> This moment my past and my future I form;
> I may make them whatever I choose
> By the deeds and the acts that I now perform,
> By the words and thoughts that I use.

So I fear not the future nor mourn o'er the past
For I do all I'm able today,
Living each present moment as though 'twere
my last;
Perhaps it is! Who knows! Who shall say?

"Duty and today are ours," a great man once wrote. "Results and the future belong to God." And wise old Emerson echoed the same thought. "All that I have seen," he said, "teaches me to trust the Creator for all I have not seen." In short, a good daily prayer might be one I read in a magazine recently—"Lord, I will keep on rowing. YOU steer the boat!"

Easy enough to say, perhaps you are thinking, but you never knew such disaster as has befallen me. I am broken down with sickness, or crippled by accident, or ruined financially, or something else equally tragic. Shakespeare wrote the answer to your case when he told us—"When Fortune means to man most good, she looks upon him with a threatening eye."

In the town of Enterprise, Ala., there is a monument erected by its citizens for services done them. And you could never guess to whom it is dedicated. To the Boll Weevil!

In olden days, the planters living thereabouts raised only cotton. When cotton boomed, business boomed. When the cotton market was off—or the crop proved poor—business suffered correspondingly.

Then came the Boll Weevil. And instead of merely a poor crop, left no crop at all. The Boll Weevil ruined everything. Debt and discouragement were all it left in its wake.

But the men of that town must have been lineal descendants of those hardy fighters who stuck to the bitter end in that long-drawn-out struggle between North and South. They got together and decided that what their town and their section needed was to stop putting all their eggs into one basket.

Instead of standing or falling by the cotton crop, diversify their products! Plant a dozen different kinds of crops. Even though one did fail, even though the market for two or three products happened to be off, the average would always be good.

Correct in theory, certainly. But, as one of their number pointed out, how were the planters to start? They were over their heads in debt already. It would take money for seeds and equipment, to say nothing of the fact that they had to live until the new crops came in.

So the townsfolk raised the money—at the Lord only knows what personal sacrifices—and financed the planters.

The result? Such increased prosperity that they erected a monument to the Boll Weevil, and on it they put this inscription: In profound appreciation of the Boll Weevil, this monument is erected by the citizens of Enterprise, Coffee Co., Ala.

Many a man can look back and see where some Boll Weevil—some catastrophe that seemed tragic at the time— was the basis of his whole success in life. Certainly that has been the case with one man I know.

When he was a tot of five, he fell into a fountain and all but drowned. A passing workman pulled him out as he was going down for the last time. The water in his lungs brought on asthma, which, as the years went on, kept growing worse and worse, until the doctors announced that death was only a matter of months. Meantime, he couldn't run, he couldn't play like other children, he couldn't even climb the stairs!

A sufficiently tragic outlook, one would say. Yet out of it came the key to fortune and success.

Since he could not play with the other children, he early developed a taste for reading. And as it seemed so certain that he could never do anything worth while for himself, what more natural than that he should long to read the deeds of men who had done great things. Starting with the usual boy heroes, he came to have a particular fondness for true stories of such men as Lincoln, Edison, Carnegie, Hill and Ford—men who started out as poor boys, without any special qualifications or advantages, and built up great names solely by their own energy and grit and determination.

Eventually he cured himself completely of his asthma—but that is another story. The part that is pertinent to this tale is that from the time he could first read until he was seventeen, he was dependent for amusement almost entirely upon books. And from his reading of the stories of men who had made successes, he acquired not only the ambition to make a like success of himself, but the basic principles on which to build it.

Today, as a monument to his Boll Weevil, there stands a constantly growing, successful business, worth millions, with a vast list of customers that swear by—not at—its founder.

And he is still a comparatively young man, healthy, active, putting in eight or ten hours at work every day, an enthusiastic horseman, a lover of all sports.

"There is no handicap, either hereditary or environmental, which cannot be compensated, if you are not afraid to try." Thus wrote one of New York's greatest psychiatrists. "No situation in our heredity or in our environment can compel us to remain unhappy. No situation need discourage one or hold him back from finding a degree of happiness and success."

Age, poverty, ill-health—none of these things can hold back the really determined soul. To him they are merely stepping-stones to success—spurs that urge him on to greater things. There is no limit upon you—except the one you put upon yourself.

> Ships sail east, and ships sail west,
> By the very same breezes that blow;
> It's the set of the sails,
> And not the gales,
> That determine where they go.

Men thought they had silenced John Bunyan when they threw him into prison. But he produced "Pilgrim's Progress" on twisted paper used as a cork for the milk jug.

Men thought that blind Milton was done. But he dictated "Paradise Lost."

Like the revolutionist of whom Tolstoy wrote—"You can imprison my body, but you cannot so much as approach my ideas."

You cannot build walls around a thought. You cannot imprison an idea. You cannot cage the energy, the enthusiasm, the enterprise of an ambitious spirit.

This it is that distinguishes us from the animals. This it is that makes us in very truth Sons of God.

> Waste no tears
> Upon the blotted record of lost years,
> But turn the leaf
> And smile, oh, smile to see
> The fair, white pages that remain for thee.
>   —ELLA WHEELER WILCOX

THE UNDYING FIRE

> I want to do one kindly deed each day
> To help someone to find a better way.
> I want to lend a hand to one in need
> Or find some lonely stray that I may feed.
> I want to sing for someone a loved song
> To give them courage when the road is long.
> If just one smile of mine can lighten pain
> Then I shall feel I have not lived in vain.

—LENA STEARNS BOLTON

In an old newspaper clipping, I read of a fire on the hearth of a farmhouse in Missouri, that has not been out for a hundred years. When the builder of that old homestead left Kentucky with his young bride a hundred years ago, he took "with him some live coals from the home fireplace, swinging in an iron pot slung from the rear axle of his prairie schooner. Matches were unknown in those days, and the making of fire from flint and steel was too uncertain. So all through the long trek from Kentucky to Missouri, he kept that little fire alive, finally transferring it to his new log cabin home.

There his children grew and prospered. There he lived and there he died—by the light and warmth of that living fire. And so it must be with love—an undying fire.

The ancient Greeks had a legend that all things were created by love. In the beginning, all were happy. Love reigned supreme, and life was everywhere. Then one night while Love slept, Hate came—and everything became discordant, unhappy, dying.

Thereafter, when the sun of Love rose, life was renewed, happiness abounded. But when the night of Hate came, then came discord also, and sorrow and ashes. And truly without love, life would be dead ... a thing of wormwood and death.

I have seen tenderness and pity trace
A line of beauty on a homely face,
And dull and somewhat ordinary eyes
Made brilliant by a flash of glad surprise,
And lips relax and soften happily
At unexpected generosity.
But, oh, what strange, delightful mystery
Is there in love's breath-taking alchemy,
With power to take a drab, gray chrysalis
And form such radiant loveliness as this!

—OPAL WINSTEAD

The most fascinating women in history—Cleopatra, Helen of Troy, Catherine the Great, Queen Elizabeth, the Pompadour—none of them had beautiful features. Cleopatra's nose was much too big—but that didn't keep her from holding the ruler of the then-known world under her thumb for ten long years, and after his death, subjugating Anthony in his turn.

Of course, she had something else—as did all these famous women of history—something stronger, more subtle, more fascinating than beauty. She had charm—that enticing, bewildering thing called feminine charm. The same charm that is born in every daughter of Eve who has the brains to use it.

What is charm? Charm is something in the glance of the eyes, the turn of the head, the touch of the hand, that sends an electric thrill through every fiber of the one at whom it is directed, that speeds up his rate of motion. Charm is taking the gifts that God has given you and keeping them supernally young and fresh and alive. Charm is being so exquisitely buoyant and full of life, *keeping the magnet within you so surcharged with the joy of life*, that even poor features are lost sight of in the bewitching attraction of the whole.

Charm is keeping your loveliness all through life. It is holding on to your ability to stir the pulses and speed up the rate of motion of the one you love.

> *For those we love, we venture many things,*
> *The thought of them gives spirit flaming wings,*
> *For those we love, we labor hard and long,*
> *To dream of them stirs in the heart a song.*
> *For those we love, no task can be too great,*
> *We forge ahead, defying adverse fate.*
> *For those we love, we seek Life's highest goal,*
> *And find contentment deep within the soul.*

"Though we travel the world over to find the beautiful," wrote Emerson, "we must carry it with us or we find it not." Charm is not to be bought in jars or bottles. Nor is beauty. Both must come from within. Both spring from that magnet of life which is the Creative Force within us.

There are women who seem to have been born tired— never exactly sick, never entirely well. They don't go out because they don't get any fun out of play. They are sallow, listless, having neither charm nor personality, because they have allowed the magnet of life within them to run down. To them I would say—renew your health first, renew your energy and vigor, renew your interest in those around you, speed up your own rate of motion—*then* begin to look for love. "For love," says Browning, "is energy of life."

> *For life, with all it yields of joy or woe*
> *And hope and fear,*
> *Is just our chance of the prize of*
> *learning love—*

How love might be, hath been indeed, and is.

How to inspire love in another? By first cultivating it in yourself. Love begets love, you know. Charge your mental magnet with thoughts of unselfish love and devotion, give to the loved one in your thoughts the admiration, the appreciation, the idealized service you would like to give in reality—and as you give, love will come back to you.

Love is giving. It cannot be jealous, for it seeks only the good of the one loved.

"Blessed is he that truly loves and seeketh not love in return," said St. Francis of Assisi. "Blessed is he that serves and desires not to be served. Blessed is he that doeth good unto others and seeketh not that others do good unto him."

Love such as that is never lost or wasted. It comes back as surely as the morrow's sun—oftentimes not from the one to whom you sent it, but it comes back, nevertheless, blessed and amplified. As Barrie says—"Those who bring happiness into the lives of others, cannot keep it from themselves."

And Ella Wheeler Wilcox wrote—

> *Who giveth love to all*
> *Pays kindness for unkindness, smiles for frowns*
> *And lends new courage to each fainting heart,*
> *And strengthens hope and scatters joy abroad.*
> *He, too, is a Redeemer, Son of God.*

A woman once went to Krishna and asked him how to find the love of God. He inquired of her—"Whom do you love most?" "My brother's child," she answered. "Then go," he told her, "and love the child still more!" She did so, and behind the figure of the child, she presently saw the form of the Christ child.

> *True happiness doth lie in store*
> *For those who love their neighbor more;*
> *'Tis blessed more to give than get.*
> *Come, do your part, our cause abet.*

'Tis blessed more—and it does more to speed up your rate of motion. Though that statement would seem to be belied, at times, by young mothers who work so hard over their families.

Why is it that many married women grow old quickly, lose their youthful lines and rounded cheeks, get sallow and wan while their husbands are still in their prime?

Bearing children? There are thousands of women with three and four and five children who still look as youthful as when they married.

Work? A reasonable amount of work is good for every woman.

Then what is the reason?

STRAIN—unending, unceasing strain. There is not a servant in this country that you could hire to work every day and all day, without any period of freedom, any day of rest. Yet many men think nothing of making their wives do it.

When Taylor, the great efficiency engineer, was called in to re-organize the work of a certain foundry, he found a number of men with wheel-barrows engaged in carting pig iron from the pile in the yard to the cupola. They worked continuously, without rest except for lunch, and careful checking showed that each man carted from twelve to fifteen tons of pig iron a day. At the end of the day they were worn out.

Taylor took one of the men (an entirely average man), stood over him with a watch, and had him work exactly in accordance with his directions. He would have him load his barrow with pig iron, wheel it over to the cupola, dump it— then sit down and rest, utterly relaxing for a minute or more. When the minute was up, he would go through the same performance—and again rest.

It took two or three days to figure out the best periods of rest, but at the end of the week, Taylor's man was carting forty-five tons of pig iron every day, where before he had carted twelve to fifteen! And at the end of the day he was still fresh, where before he had been worn out.

If you have ever seen an army on the march, you know that no matter how great the hurry, the men are allowed to fall out for five minutes in every hour, and completely relax. Why? Because it has been found that this relaxation and rest enables them to march farther and faster.

There is not an organ in the body that does not require and take its period of rest, from the heart and lungs to the stomach and digestive tracts. Yet many a wife and mother goes all day and every day with never a moment of relaxation, never a minute when her nerves are not taut with strain. Is it any wonder they grow old years before their time? Is it any wonder they are nervous and irritable, unhappy themselves and making those around them depressed and unhappy?

To every such mother, I would say, first—relax! Sit down, lie down, every chance you get—and *just let go!* Don't listen for the baby—don't worry about dinner. Just blissfully relax—even if only for a minute or two at a time. If you can multiply those minutes by a dozen times a day, you will be surprised how much better you feel when night comes.

Give your inner magnet a chance to renew itself. Remember, the first essential toward speeding up your rate of motion is to relax, to get rid of your tensions, to LET the Creative Force work through you. Only then can you draw to you kindred elements of good.

> *I pray the prayer the Easterns do,*
> *May the peace of Allah abide with you.*
> *Wherever you stop—wherever you go—*
> *May the beautiful palms of Allah grow;*
> *Thru days of love and nights of rest*
> *May the love of sweet Allah make you blest.*
> *I touch my heart as the Easterns do*
> *May the love of Allah abide with you.*

PRAYER

> *But the stars throng out in their glory,*
> *And they sing of the God in man;*
> *They sing of the mighty Master,*
> *Of the loom His fingers span,*
> *Where a star or a soul is part of the whole,*
> *And weft in the wondrous plan.*
>   —ROBERT SERVICE

If you would know the surest way of speeding up your rate of motion, and overtaking the things you desire, try PRAYER! But when I say "prayer," I don't mean the begging kind. I don't mean a lot of vain repetitions, that seldom have the attention even of the one repeating them, much less of the Lord. Go to the Bible, and you will learn how to pray.

Out of 600,000 words in the Old Testament, only six, when literally translated, mean to "ask for" things in prayer, and each of these six is used but once.

Against that, the word "palal" is used hundreds of times to signify "to pray." And "palal" means—"To judge yourself to be a marvel of creation; to recognize amazing wonders deep within your soul."

Wouldn't that seem to indicate that prayer was meant to be a realization of the powers deep within you? Wouldn't you judge that all you need to do is to expand your consciousness to take in whatever it is that you desire?

"What things soever you ask for when you pray, believe that ye receive them, and ye shall have them." You are not to think of your lacks and needs. You are to visualize the things you want! You are not to worry about this debt or that note, but mentally see the Infinite Supply all about you. "All that you need is near ye, God is complete supply. Trust, have faith, then hear ye, dare to assert the 'I.'"

Remember this: If you pray to God, but keep your attention on your problem, you will still have your problem. You'll run into it and continue to run into it as long as you keep your attention focused upon it. What you must do is fix your attention upon God—upon His goodness, His love, His power to remedy any ill or adjust any untoward condition. Focus your attention upon these, and these are the conditions you will run into.

Prayer is expansion, and expansion of yourself into the Godself all around you. As Kahlil Gibran describes it in his great book "The Prophet"—

For what is prayer but the expansion of yourself into the living ether. When you pray, you rise to meet in the air those who are praying at that very hour, and whom save in prayer you may not meet. Therefore let your visit to the temple invisible be for naught save ecstasy and sweet communion. I cannot teach you to pray in words. God listens not to your words save when He Himself utters them through your lips.

Prayer is a realization of your Oneness with God, and of the infinite power this gives you. It is an acceptance of the fact that there is nothing on earth you cannot have—once you have mentally accepted the fact that you CAN have it. Nothing you cannot do—once your mind has grasped the fact that you CAN do it.

Prayer, in short, is thanksgiving for the infinite good God *has* given you. The word most often used for "prayer" in the Old Testament means—"To sing a song of joy and praise."

And how often you see that method used by every great character of the Bible. Running through all of Jesus Christ's acts, as well as His teachings, you find the glowing element of praise and thanksgiving. When He looked at five loaves and two small fishes and realized that He had a multitude to feed, His first thought was a thought of praise. "And looking up to Heaven, He blessed." When He raised Lazarus from the dead, He first praised and thanked God.

When Paul and Silas lay in jail, bound with chains, did they repine? Did they get down on their knees and beg for help? On the contrary, they sang hymns of praise, and the very walls were shaken down and they were set free. "The righteous doth sing and rejoice." "The sons of God shouted for joy."

Go back over the Old Testament and see how often you are adjured to "Praise the Lord and be thankful, that THEN shall the earth yield her increase." Probably no life chronicled in the Scriptures was more beset with trials and dangers than that of King David. And what was his remedy? What brought him through all tribulations to power and riches? Just read the Psalms of David and you will see.

> Jehovah reigneth; let the earth rejoice;
> Let the multitude of isles be glad.
> Bless Jehovah, O my soul;
> And all that is within me, bless His holy name . . .
> Who forgiveth all thine iniquities;
> Who healeth all thy diseases.

Throughout the Bible we are told—"In everything by prayer and supplication WITH THANKSGIVING let your requests be made known unto God." Again and again the root of inspiration and attainment is stressed: *Rejoice, be glad, praise, give thanks!* "Prove me now herewith, saith the Lord of Hosts, if I will not open you the window of Heaven and pour you out a blessing, that there shall not be room enough to receive it."

The most complete interpretation of prayer I have heard came from the man who wrote—"Once I used to say 'Please.' Now I say, 'Thank you.'" "Enter into His gates with thanksgiving," the Psalmist bade us, "and into His courts with praise. Be thankful unto Him and bless His name." And Christ's apostles tell us the same thing—"Let us offer up a sacrifice of praise to God continually. In everything by prayer and supplication *with thanksgiving* let your requests be made known unto God."

Someone has said that prayer is the spirit of God pronouncing His works good. "This is the day Jehovah hath made. We will rejoice and be glad in it." It is sound psychology as well, as Prof. Wm. James of Harvard testified. "If you miss the joy," he wrote, "you miss all."

Complete, wholehearted reliance upon God—that is the prayer of faith. Not an imploring of God for some specific thing, but a clear, unquestioning recognition that the power to be and do and have the things you want is inherent in you, that you have only to recognize this power and put your trust in it to get anything of good you wish.

But perhaps you have prayed long and fervently for some particular thing, and it has not come? What then? Has it ever occurred to you that the answer was there, but you didn't receive it because you were not ready or willing to accept it?

God always answers prayer. Over and over He tells us this. The answer to your prayer is as sure as tomorrow's sunrise. YOU are the one who is not sure. You are not sure, and so you do not accept the answer.

If you accepted it, you would act on it, wouldn't you? Did you ever act upon the answer to those long and fervent prayers of yours? Yet that is the way it must be, if you are to pray for an answer—and GET it. If you pray for health, you must accept health. You must act as though you already had it. If you pray for other things, you must accept them at once and start doing—even on the smallest scale—the things you would do when the answer to your prayer became evident.

Dr. Alexis Carrel, the brilliant scientist who for many years headed the Rockefeller Institute, stated that "prayer is the most powerful form of energy one can generate."

"The influence of prayer on the human mind and body," Dr. Carrel went on to say, is as demonstrable as that of secreting glands. Its results can be measured in terms of increased physical buoyancy, greater intellectual vigor, moral stamina, and a deeper understanding of the realities underlying human relationships. . . . Prayer is as real as terrestrial gravity. As a physician, I have seen men, after all other therapy had failed, lifted out of disease and melancholy by the serene effort of prayer. It is the only power in the world that seems to overcome the so-called "laws of nature," the occasions on which prayer has dramatically done this have been termed "miracles." But a constant, quieter miracle takes place hourly in the hearts of men and women who have discovered that prayer supplies them with a steady flow of sustaining power in their daily lives.

An old peasant was kneeling alone in a village church, long after the services had ended. "What are you waiting for?" the priest asked him. "I am looking at Him," the peasant replied, "and He is looking at me." That is prayer, of the kind that Emerson said—"No man ever prayed without learning something."

I never try to do my work by my own power alone.
When I begin I make my prayer before God's holy

throne.
I ask that His Almighty power may work its will through me
And so each task is done with ease; I'm charged with
power, you see.

–HANNAH ORTH

In the eighteenth chapter of St. Matthew, Jesus gives us a method of praying that He assures us will bring us anything we ask for: "Again I say unto you, that if two of you shall agree on earth as touching anything they shall ask, it shall be done for them of My Father which is in Heaven. For where two or three are gathered together in My name, there am I in the midst of them."

That would seem simple enough, for two or three to gather together and agree upon some one thing that all should ask for. It is simple, too, and when properly done, it works wonders. In "The Magic Word," we give a number of true experiences in which little groups of people got together and prayed for the particular needs of some one of their number, with seemingly miraculous results.

It is the most effective method of prayer known, and the only reason it is not used oftener is that people so seldom agree upon what they shall ask for. They will get together and agree to pray for the health of some of their number, but where one may be thinking of health and strength, another will be dwelling upon his suffering, or the hardships it has brought upon his family or any one of a dozen other negative images. To get results, all must think of the health and strength they are praying for—not the sickness. They must dwell upon the power of God to heal the sick one, not upon the misery his sickness has caused.

Two thousand years before Christ, it was said in the Vedas that if two people would unite their forces, they could conquer the world, though singly they might be powerless. And psychologists and metaphysicians everywhere agree that the power of two minds united in a single cause is not merely their individual powers added together, but multiplied manifold.

Perhaps this can best be explained in terms of electrical power. Take an ordinary magnet capable of lifting, let us say, 10 pounds of iron. Wrap this magnet with wire and charge it with the current from a small battery, it will lift—not merely ten pounds, but a hundred pounds or more!

That is what happens when one person prays and believes, and another adds his prayer and his faith. Why did Jesus send out his disciples, two and two? Why was it that on the one occasion He went alone among a crowd of scoffers, He was able to do no mighty works—on the occasion of His visit to His home town of Nazareth? You find the answer written in the Bible—"Because of their unbelief!"

Before a miracle could be wrought, there had to be faith—not only on Jesus' part, but on the part of someone around Him. Read how often He told those He cured— "Thy faith hath made thee whole."

If you were stuck in a muddy road with a heavily loaded two-horse wagon, and I were stuck with another right behind you, what would be the quickest way out? To unhitch my horses, would it not, couple them on to your wagon tongue and let the two teams pull you out. They could then take my wagon in its turn and pull it onto solid ground. What neither team could accomplish alone, the two pulling together could easily do.

Have you ever noticed a locomotive pulling a long train of cars? To START such a train takes 90 per cent of the locomotive's power. To keep it running on a smooth stretch takes less than 1 per cent. So a freight locomotive must have nearly a hundred times as much power as it needs for ordinary smooth running.

You are like a locomotive in that. To start you on the road to success requires every bit of energy you can muster. To keep you there, once you have reached the top, needs only a fraction of your abilities. The locomotive must carry its extra 99 per cent of power as a reserve, to start it again when it stops for orders or water or to pick up or unload freight, or to carry it over a heavy grade. It can do nothing with all that extra energy at other times, except blow off steam.

But what about you? You need your full 100 per cent to get started. Probably there are many times when you draw upon all of it to carry you through some grave difficulty, to push aside some obstacle that bars your way. But for the most part, you just carry that extra energy as reserve. What can you do with it? Find outlets for it!

All around you are men and women—earnest, hardworking men and women—who have put their hearts into their work, but lack some of the 100 per cent energy that would start them on the road to success. They are like freight locomotives that are perfect engines, but not quite up to the task of starting as heavy a train as has been given them. Give them a push, help them to get started or over the hump of some obstacle or difficulty, and they will go far. But getting started is too much for them alone.

Why should you do this? Because only thus can you profit from that excess energy you have to carry for emergencies, but which you so seldom use. How do you profit? Through the additional reserve power it brings you. A stalled train is a useless thing. Worse than that, it is an encumbrance, in the way of everything else that uses the line. It may be generating all but 10 per cent of the power required to move it, but without that 10 per cent, the 90 per cent is useless. So the 10 per cent you furnish to get it started is of as much value to it as the 90 per cent it furnishes, and is entitled to as great reward. When you help another in that way, you have in effect grub-staked him, and you share in the spiritual power that his success brings him. As Edwin Markham put it in his little poem—

> *There is a destiny that makes us brothers;*
> *No man goes his way alone;*
> *All that we send into the lives of others*
> *Comes back into our own.*

So whenever you have some earnest purpose, or want to help a friend or loved one to accomplish some greatly-cherished ambition, follow the advice Jesus gives us and unite in prayer for a few minutes each day until you have brought about the answer to that desire.

And when praying alone, remember:

First, center your thoughts on *the thing that you want*— not on your need.

Second, read the 91st and the 23rd Psalms, just as a reminder of God's power and His readiness to help you in all your needs.

Third, *be thankful,* not merely for past favors, *but for granting of this favor you are now asking.* To be able to thank God for it sincerely, in advance of its actual material manifestation, is the finest evidence of belief.

Fourth, BELIEVE! Picture the thing that you want so clearly, see it in your imagination so vividly, that you can actually BELIEVE THAT YOU HAVE IT!

It is this sincere conviction, registered upon your subconscious mind, that brings the answer to your prayers. Once convince your subconscious mind that you HAVE the thing that you want, and you can forget it and go on to your next problem. Mind will attend to the rest. So "sing and rejoice" that you HAVE the answer to your prayer. Literally shout for joy, as did the Sons of God in days of old.

Fifth, remember Emerson's advice—"Do the thing and you shall have the power." Start doing—even on a small scale—whatever it is that you will do when the answer to your prayer is materially evident. In other words, ACCEPT the thing you have asked for! Accept it—and start using it.

> *If you have faith in God, or man, or self,*
> *Say so; if not, push back upon the shelf*
> *Of silence all your thoughts till faith shall come.*

No one will grieve because your lips are dumb.
                    —ELLA WHEELER WILCOX

The Law of the Higher Potential

P-R-A-I-S-E

Did you ever notice that if you leave off the "P" from the word Praise, what you have left is *"Raise"*?

That is no mere accident, for wise men have realized for thousands of years that to praise is to raise the spirits and increase the power of the one praised. In the same way, praise of God and thankfulness for His gifts raises the spirits of the one who sings those praises to the heights of rare accomplishment.

Just as praise and thanksgiving freed Paul and Silas from the chains of the dungeon, so can they free you from worry and fear and the dungeons of dark despair. "I will sing unto Jehovah," sang the Psalmist of old, "because He hath dealt bountifully with me." And if we would have Him deal bountifully with us, it behooves us to praise and be thankful for the good we now have, no matter how small that good may seem to be.

"The righteous doth sing and rejoice," we are told in the Scriptures. And the Hebrew word used for "sing" means "to sing out loud, even to shout for joy." To sing with joy is one of the long-neglected truths of POWER. "The Sons of God shouted for joy."

The Kingdom of Heaven is the Kingdom of Expansion, and the way to expand what we have is through praise and joy and thanksgiving. Seldom indeed in the Bible do you find that God provides supply out of thin air. Almost always He requires the recipients of His bounty to start with what they have. The widow with the oil and meal, that other widow with a little oil, the feeding of the multitudes with the loaves and fishes, and scores of other cases, all started with the supply in hand. God expanded what they had. And God will expand what you have, if you rightly use the power of praise and thanksgiving.

But mere expansion is not enough. You might expand all the water in the world into steam, and get no good from it— if you had no engine in which to use the steam. You must have a purpose in mind if you are to get the utmost of good from your expansion. You must set a goal. You must plan the *form* in which that expanded energy is to make itself manifest. It can be in your body, in your circumstances, in your surroundings—in anything of good you may desire.

Some years ago the "Journal of Education" had a story that expressed this idea clearly. "There was once a prince," it read, who had a crooked back. He could never stand straight up like even the lowest of his subjects. Because he was a very proud prince, his crooked back caused him a great deal of mental suffering.

One day he called before him the most skilful sculptor in his kingdom and said to him: "Make me a noble statue of myself, true to my likeness in every detail, with this exception—make this statue with a straight back. I wish to see myself as I might have been."

For long months the sculptor worked, hewing the marble carefully into the likeness of the prince, and at last the work was done, and the sculptor went before the prince and said: "The statue is finished; where shall I set it up?" One of the courtiers called out: "Set it before the castle gate where all can see it," but the prince smiled sadly and shook his head. "Rather," said he, "place it in a secret nook in the palace garden where only I shall see it."

The statue was placed as the prince ordered, and promptly forgotten by the world, but every morning and every noon and every evening, the prince stole quietly away to where it stood and looked long upon it, noting the straight back and the uplifted head and the noble brow. And each time he gazed, something seemed to go out of the statue and into him, tingling in his blood and throbbing in his heart.

The days passed into months and the months into years; then strange rumors began to spread throughout the land. Said one: "The prince's back is no longer crooked or my eyes deceive me." Said another: "Our prince has the high look of a mighty man." And these rumors came to the prince, and he listened with a queer smile.

Then went he out into the garden to where the statue stood and behold, it was just as the people said, his back had become straight as the statue's, his head had the same noble bearing; he was, in fact, the noble man his statue proclaimed him to be.

2500 years ago, in the Golden Age of Athens, when its culture led the world, Grecian mothers surrounded themselves with beautiful statues that they might bring forth perfect children and that the children in turn might develop into perfect men and women.

Eleven months from now, YOU will have an entirely new body, inside and out. Not a single cell, not a single bit of tissue that is now in you will be there then. What changes do you want made in that new body? What improvements?

Then start right now getting that new model clearly in mind. Buy yourself a scrap book. Cut from the magazines a picture of the finest figure of a man or woman that you can find, and paste it on page one. Cut out other pictures, that show clearly different parts of your body that need developing or perfecting, and paste them on other pages. Then cut pictures of people doing the sort of things you would love to do—dancing, swimming, riding horseback, rowing, fishing, playing golf or tennis, anything you like—and paste them on different pages of your scrap book.

At the top and bottom of each page, or alongside the pictures, put such reminders and affirmations as these: Father God, I thank Thee for my glorious strength, my abiding health, my tireless energy.

Vitalize Thy perfect image in me in perfect form.

I am strong in the Lord and the power of His might.

God made me in His own image. He is my strength and power. He maketh my way perfect. The joy of the Lord is my strength.

Know ye not that ye are the temple of God and that the Spirit of God dwelleth in you?

Divine Love protects and sustains me. I am the open channel through which the healing currents of life are now flowing. God is my life. God is my health. In God is my trust.

Under a picture showing someone with a splendid chest, taking breathing exercises, put—

The Spirit of the Lord hath made me, and the breath of the almighty giveth me life.

Under one bathing—

Wash me and I shall be whiter than snow. Under a picture of the eyes—

Open thou mine eyes, that in Thy light I may see the light.

Or, if your eyes are weak or troublesome, put—

Jehovah openeth the eyes of the blind. Blessed are the pure in heart, for they shall see God. I see God in my eyes, in their perfect life and strength and wholeness. If thou can'st believe, all things are possible to him that believeth. According to thy faith be it done unto you.

Under picture at a well-filled table—

Thou shalt eat thy bread with joy.

Under sleep—

They that rest in the Lord shall renew their strength like the eagle. They shall walk and not faint, they shall run and not be weary. Thy Spirit strengthens both my soul and my body, and I rest in peace of wholeness and health.

Under vigorous, happy, healthy older people—

As my days, so shall my strength be. Behold, all things are becoming new. Thou shalt make me full of joy in Thy presence. Passing years have no effect upon my spiritual body. I am alive in Jesus Christ forever. I am a tower of strength and stability in the realization that God is my health. God's life is constant, unbroken, eternal. I am quickened in His consciousness of life. His constant power and strength sustain me and I am healed. I AM a perfect idea of God and all of life is with me now and always.

A long time ago, Epictetus said: "God has delivered YOU to YOUR care, and this is what He says to you— 'I have no fitter to trust than YOU. Preserve this body for me just as it is by nature; modest, beautiful, faithful, noble, tranquil.'

You will find many affirmations to paste in your scrap book. Use any and all that seem helpful. But that saying of Epictetus is a good one to paste on the last page—a good one to bear always in mind. "God has delivered you to your care." And God gave you dominion. So think of yourself as well and strong. Think of your body as spiritual substance that is not subject to the ills of the flesh. Think of it as constantly changing, continually GROWING into the perfect image that you are holding before it.

The Kingdom of Heaven is the Kingdom of Expansion. If you have but a single perfect cell in your whole body, you can expand that cell into a perfect body, provided only that you hold before it the image of health and strength—not of sickness; provided only that you BELIEVE! "God made man but little lower than the Angels."

"Give Us This Day Our Daily Bread"

For your Prosperity and Abundant Supply Scrap Book, you cannot do better than start with that line from the Lord's Prayer—"Give us this day our daily bread."

Get a picture of a horn of plenty—a cornucopia—with all manner of good things pouring out of it, and paste it on the first page of your Scrap Book. Line the page with pictures of sparrows and lilies of the field, to remind you of Jesus' promise, and then put at the bottom of the page something like this:

O God, beginning now I shall forever LET Thy Spirit Infinite become the sole dictator of my soul; and I shall never more take anxious thought of anything, but grow as the lilies grow, in peace and power, so that I shall have all I need, forever more.

The next page, I'd head with the line—"I can have what I want—*if I plant it.*" Under it, paste pictures of farmers or gardeners planting seed, only take a pen or pencil and change those seeds into $$$. Under these pictures, put— "The riches of the Spirit now fill my mind and affairs. I think prosperity, I talk prosperity and I know that prosperity and success are mine."

On other pages, show pictures of growing grain or other plants, with $$$ at the top instead of the usual grain or fruit. Use such affirmations as—"God is my inexhaustible and omnipotent source of abundant supply." "I accept the will of God, which is abundant prosperity for me." "If I continue to desire you, I shall have you, because I trust in God for all things I desire."

Then on succeeding pages, show pictures of great piles of money—bags of money, piles of paper money and currency all around the pages, and pictures of yourself pasted in the center, surrounded by riches. If you can find pictures of men digging up treasure hoards, put them in. Put in all kinds of pictures that imply riches and prosperity. Put in pictures of the sort of surroundings you will have, when you have manifested the riches you desire. Get pictures of a beautiful home—the home of your dreams. Show if possible, each room as you would have it furnished. Show the outside, with a wide driveway, bordered by a beautiful lawn, shrubbery around the house, trees in the background, the kind of car you would like to own drawn up before the house. Show even the wardrobes of fine clothes you would have, show horses or bicycles or whatnot for the children, show the flowers in your garden.

"When I got the Lessons of THE GOD IN YOU," wrote Mrs. Caroline Kroll of Indianapolis, in December, 1939, "I had only $12.00 a month. Now I have a nice home and everything is paid for. I am so happy." Mrs. Kroll had written us in the fall of '37 expressing her great desire for a home, and we suggested to her this Treasure Mapping method. She says in her last letter—"I never faltered in my home making, and tonight I am sitting in a good home of my own and never was any happier in my youth."

Remember, the first step in supplying a need is to know that it IS already supplied in the Mind of God. God has already given you all of good. It is yours for the taking, and the most perfect prayer is the deep realization that your need is already supplied. You don't have to waste energy wondering about the supply. All you have to do is to focus your energy upon *being* one with it.

Your desires are like acorns—visions of the mighty oaks they can grow to be. What you desire is and always has been yours. What man can conceive, man can achieve. It is the eye that makes the horizon. No man ever bettered his position by limiting himself in his own mind to the one he had. No man ever made a success of his business by thinking failure. Every success is achieved first in your own thoughts. You must work first on yourself, because all trouble, limitation and the like are states of consciousness. Change your thought and you change all. You get the conditions that belong to your consciousness. As Emerson put it—"No man was ever ridden down or talked down by anything but himself."

Look within yourself for the source of all power. I AM the great power of God expressing as ME. I AM the great abundance for all my needs and a surplus to spare. That to which I give my attention reveals itself. So give your attention to the things you want! Fill your Scrap Book with pictures of them. Put over and under and around them such affirmations as these:

God is able to do exceeding abundantly above all that we ask or think, according to the Power that worketh in us. I rejoice in the bounty of God, constantly manifesting to meet my every need.

If ye abide in Me and my words abide in you, ye shall ask what ye will and it shall be done unto you. For herein is the Father glorified, that ye bear much fruit. Your Father knoweth what things ye have need of before you ask Him. Fear not, for it is the Father's good pleasure to give you the Kingdom. All that the Father hath is yours, and you are in all ways prospered.

I will give thee hidden riches of secret places, that thou mayest know that I am the God of Israel. If thou return to the Almightly, then shalt thou lay up gold as dust, and the gold of Ophir as the stones of the brooks. I will sing unto Jehovah, because He hath dealt bountifully with me.

Remember that—"According to thy faith be it done unto you." So believe that you RECEIVE! If your beliefs are all for the future, you will get them in the distant future but never NOW You will never quite catch up with them. "Now is the accepted time. Now is the day of salvation." Realize that all these good things are NOW coming into manifestation in your life. Bless and thank God for them NOW.

> *Instead of pleading, "God bless me,"*
> *And making such a weary fuss,*
> *How much better off we'd be*
> *If we would smile awhile and say,*
> *"I thank you, God, for blessing us today."*

> *Instead of begging, "God, give me*
> *And mine the things which our hearts crave,"*

How much happier we'd be
If we would laugh with life, and say,
"We thank you, God, for what we have today."
                            –MARION B. SHOEN

"But what shall we do about pressing debts?" many will ask. First, make a list of all of them. Then, thank God for having sent such trustful people to your aid, thank Him for the confidence they have shown in you. Next, see yourself in your mind's eye going the rounds of all your creditors, paying them in full. See their thankful, smiling faces. Hear yourself expressing to them your appreciation of their courtesy and forbearance, hear them telling you that they were glad to be of help, will be glad to extend the same credit to you in the future. Get pictures of people paying money over to merchants, paste in your own features over those of the debtors, and under them put such affirmations as these: Divine Love prospers all of us together NOW. God is our supply, through each of us to all, and through all of us to each. I speak for all of us the word that multiplies money to all of us. And my word accomplishes that whereunto I send it. In God is my trust.

When I worry, I am not trusting God. When I trust God, I have nothing to worry about."

I put the payment of these debts lovingly in the hands of the Father with a child-like trust. That which is for my highest good will come to me.

Then do your part by using some of whatever money you receive to pay these just debts, and as you pay out the money, bless it in some such wise as this: "I bless thee . . . and be thou a blessing! As I pay out this money, I bless it. May it enrich everyone who touches it. The value of this substance I hold in my hand is this day magnified, for I perceive that it is truly a symbol of my heavenly Father's inexhaustible riches. Go forth, increase, multiply and bring forth fruit and hundredfold!"

Here is a prayer suggested by R. A. D., in a recent issue of NAUTILUS, to be used in connection with your list of debts: Father, I thank Thee that thou hast opened the way for me to pay every bill on this list, sending the money for each one before it is due. I place this expense sheet absolutely and unconditionally in Thy hands, and from the depths of a rich consciousness, I thank and praise Thee that the money for each separate item already is provided, awaiting only my claim to bring it into evidence. The glory of Thy radiance shining before me, Infinite Father, has opened the way for my unfailing prosperity and for a success greater than I ever before have experienced. I put from me every thought of limitations or lack and go free to have an abundance of all good.

The right job is the most pressing problem for many people. And you can help yourself or others to that right work through "Treasure Mapping" in the same way that you can bring riches or health or any other good thing.

The first essential, of course, is to know what you want. What kind of work would you most like to do? What are you best fitted for? What is your ultimate ambition? Get a Scrap Book and paste in it first a picture of yourself. After deciding on the line of work you want to devote yourself to, take inventory of yourself and think in what position you are now fitted to start. Then get a picture from the magazines of someone working in that position, paste it in your Scrap Book, and if you have a snap-shot of yourself that you can substitute for the face in the picture, do so.

Decide then what is the next position you will be fitted for in the line of work you have adopted, and paste a picture of someone in that position on the next page of your Scrap Book. Fill succeeding pages with logical steps in your progress, right on up to the very top. When you feel that your work will entitle you to a private office, paste in a picture of someone representing yourself seated at a desk in a sumptuously furnished office, with his title lettered on the door or on the side of his desk, and then letter in you name over the title.

And remember, no one ever got a good job by limiting himself mentally to a poor one. Admit to yourself that you are good. Then let others find it out by the service you give. This is the key to any door you wish to unlock. Yourself PLUS is your fortune. Your affairs PLUS is success.

Paste over and under and around your pictures such affirmations as these: "God is with me in all that I do." "If God be for you, who can be against you?" "Know ye not that ye are Gods, sons of the Most High?" What should your situation be like? What is it like in the Divine Mind, in the Eternal Plan? "Your Father knoweth what things ye have need of before you ask Him. Fear not, for it is the Father's good pleasure to give you the Kingdom. All that the Father has is yours, and you are in all ways prospered." "If ye abide in Me and My words abide unto you, ye shall ask what ye will and it shall be done unto you. For herein is the Father glorified, that ye bear much fruit." "With good will, doing service as to the Lord and not to man." "Whether therefore ye eat or drink, or whatever ye do, do all to the glory of God."

The same principles that help you to a better position will help you to make your business grow and prosper, when you have a business of your own. Many a man has started with practically nothing, and built a fortune, simply by taking God into partnership with him.

Start your Scrap Book with a picture of yourself and of your business as it is now. Then on each succeeding page, show it growing bigger and better. Picture the service you want to give your customers. Picture thousands of them taking advantage of that service. Picture yourself and your helpers serving even greater numbers, picture your product in the hands of more and more users, picture its manufacture in great volume, its shipping, its sale, everything you can connect with it. And let every picture show progress, growth, *expansion*. See yourself serving the world.

Under those pictures, put inspiring affirmations. "I am a partner and co-worker with God." It is the purpose of the Universal Mind to see men prosper, that they may express more of life, love, happiness and understanding, thus reflecting more of God. Our product is the connecting link between this demand and God's supply. The need is expanding continually and we have the will and the intelligence to see and meet it. Therefore, there is a continually growing demand for our product, that increases as I realize the spiritual significance of my work and make better products for my customers. It is in my power to make my customers better qualified, through the equipment that I provide, for prosperity and success. I delight in that power. I increase that power by using it for the honor, glory and pleasure of my customers and myself."

"Father, this business has to be good, so You handle it for me. I put it and all my affairs lovingly in Your hands, with a child-like faith. That which is for my highest good will come to me. One on God's side is a majority, and I am together with You, so all things are working together for my good and I am working with them in the wisdom and the power of the Spirit."

"God is in control. God is Spirit, good omnipotent. Apart from Him, there is no overcoming power. God is life, love and peace. God's will now fulfilled in me is abundant work for our business."

"The Spirit that multiplied the loaves and fishes for Jesus increases my substance, and I manifest prosperity."

But remember to give "good measure" to all, customers and co-workers alike, for "All who joy would win must share it—*Happiness was born a twin*."

Many who have no business to worry about have homes or pieces of property or whatnot that they wish to sell, and at times this is a problem. Yet it is a problem that lends itself to the same methods outlined above, as you can judge from the following letter dated May 15th, 1940, from one of the subscribers to THE GOD IN YOU: When I received Robert Collier's Course THE GOD IN YOU, we were in debt and sometimes wondered what the next meal was to be, even though we owned our cottage and three lots. It seemed we couldn't get a buyer, nor could we even borrow on the property, even though it was clear, as it was in a run-down neighborhood.

Since reading the Course, we have sold all St. Louis County property and purchased this 96-acre farm at Belle, paying cash for it and clearing ourselves of debt, as we sold most of the property for cash, a thing we could not have done without the help of THE GOD IN YOU. I believe we are about to see another manifestation of God's goodness as we have deposits under our ground which may indeed show God's goodness through riches to us.

The first essential is to BLESS the property you wish to sell. Know that it is a perfect image in the Divine Mind, made for the express purpose of manifesting good to someone, and declare that it is now sold to the right party at the right price.

Paste a picture of it in your Scrap Book. Think of every possibility for its development, and paste such pictures in your book, too. Show pictures of people looking at similar properties, of a sale being made, of the developments that will take place on it.

L. C. B. told in a recent issue of UNITY how she put her house "lovingly in the hands of the Father," then used this affirmation: "You, Christ, will find for us the perfect purchasers, who will love our home as we have loved it and recognize it for theirs and have sufficient cash to pay for it and have it NOW. Only through You are we fully aware of our omnipresent good." Within a short time, the article states, the house was sold for cash, and at their own price!

In "Nautilus" sometime ago, there was a similar story, the affirmation used in that case being the following: God's loving Presence in all of us brings the right buyer NOW, who will pay the right price for the property and who will make money on the deal, while at the same time I will make money, God's money, in the selling. Divine Love now multiplies God's money and His Good to both buyer and seller, so that all shall be satisfied. All things now work together for good to me and to the new buyer of this property. We are the open channels through which Divine Love is now flowing to this property and through it to all the world. All the barriers are now dissolved by Divine Love and my customer comes quickly and gloriously. God is our prosperity here and now. In God I trust and I know that all things work together to manifest the good we desire.

Whatever your problem, whatever your difficulty, you can get guidance if you will seek it. Give the facts to the God in You, ask Him for the solution, then leave the problem with Him and FORGET it in the serene confidence that He can and will find the answer. Never force the issue. Have faith in that

God in You, and wait for a leading. "And thine ear shall hear a voice behind thee saying, this is the path; walk ye in it."

Our physical senses are able to discern only such objects as are on the same or a lower material plane than ourselves. Our ears, for instance, are attuned to but a few octaves of sound. Those of higher or lower wave lengths are inaudible to us. Yet the radio has taught us that all about us are sounds of music, of laughter, of drama and instruction.

The same is true with our eyes. We see only those things that are on the median light waves. The air may be full of television pictures, yet with our unaided eyes, we get none of them. Is it therefore so hard to believe that when the servant of the Prophet Elisha was fearful, because of the enemies all around, Elisha prayed and said—"Lord, I pray thee, open his eyes, that he may see. And the Lord opened the eyes of the young man; and he saw; And behold, the mountain was full of horses and chariots of fire round about Elisha."

May not the air around you be just as full of God's angels? May not Elisha's advice be just as good today— "Fear not, for they that be with us are more than they that be with them."

The Psalmist of old testified, you remember—"I have been young, and now am old, yet have I not seen the righteous forsaken, nor his seed begging bread."

Paste in your Scrap Book some of those old Biblical pictures of Angels guiding the children of God, of Guardian Angels, and over and under them put such affirmations as these: "God goes before me and opens the way." "Infinite Wisdom tells me just what to do." "I thank you, God, that you are here with us, and no matter what happens, we are all right." "Thou shalt not be afraid for the terror by night, nor for the arrow that flieth by day. He will cover thee with his pinions, and under his wings shalt thou take refuge."

Grace Crowell had a beautiful little poem along these lines in Unity Weekly:

> So often through God's Holy Book there shines
> Some clear-cut word, some strong and simple phrase
> That gleams like diamonds gathered from deep mines,
> Set polished there to light our earthly days;
> "And God was with the lad." The words, how brief,
> And yet what vital meaning in their sound,
> As spoken of that ancient child of grief
> Once left to die upon the hot, parched ground.

"And God was with the lad," One need not look
For further information; all is told.
No gifted hand on earth could pen a book
Of strange biography that would unfold
With clearer words, nor could it tell as well
The God-companioned life of Ishmael.

Such affirmations cannot help but bring you peace and serenity. In "Esquire" magazine some time ago there was an article telling about the fear-scent the body gives off, which is exceedingly irritating to any animal that senses it. "It is this fear-scent," said the article, "which causes dogs to attack people who have not molested them. A dog will respond quickly both in friendship and in training when he is approached without fear, but no one can fool him for a minute with a fearless exterior concealing a quaking heart, for the fear-scent is there.

It is usually the fear that a canoe will tip over that causes the occupant to move suddenly in the wrong direction and thereby upset it. The fear of drowning, when suddenly thrown into the water, causes one to struggle frantically, and incidentally force himself under. It is an interesting scientific fact that a baby, until 24 hours old, can swim. Beyond that, it starts to realize fear and will sink. Fear is really the mental hazard of crossing your bridges before you come to them.

Is it not likely that the strong odor of our "fear-scent" registers on all we come in contact with, even though it be but subconsciously with human beings? Certain it is that when we approach people fearfully, we seem to repel them, for we seldom make a favorable impression, seldom get from them what we want.

The remedy? To BLESS the Divinity in all we come in contact with. You remember how often Jesus used the greeting—"Peace!" "Peace I leave with you; my peace I give unto you." And to the wind and waves, He bade—"Peace! Be still." And immediately the storm abated. "Acquaint now thyself with God and be at peace."

When trouble threatens in your home or your business, bless all concerned and mentally affirm—"Peace! The love of God is at work here. All of my forces are peaceful and harmonious. There is no resistance in me against the Spirit of God's peaceful life. Every anxious thought is stilled. Thy mighty confidence and Thy peace enfold me. The Spirit of God fills my mind, and abundance is everywhere manifest." Then go up to the thing you fear, confidently, serenely.

Or if it is something you must do, do it! Once you have lost the fear of it, you will find it easy.

Evil? There is really no such thing. It is merely the lack of Good. Summon the Good and the evil vanishes. The same is true of enemies. Summon love for them, salute the Divinity in them and bless them, and you will find hate turned to love. Say mentally to the Divinity in those who appear to be your enemies—"I recognize you. You can't disguise yourself. You are a radiant child of God. God's creations are all excellent. I bless you in the name of Jesus Christ. Because you are a child of God, you speak the truth and you are ever honest, just and harmonious. My world is filled with splendid people, and I love them all."

Be noble, and the nobleness that lies in other men, sleeping but never dead, will rise in majesty to meet thine own. Trust men, and they will be true to you. Treat them greatly, and they will show themselves great.

Love overcometh, for all motion is cyclic. It circulates to the limits of its possibilities and then returns to its starting point. Thus any unselfish expenditure of energy returns to you laden with gifts. Any unselfish act done for another's benefit is giving part of yourself. It is an outward flow of power that completes its cycle and returns laden with energy.

The thoughts that we send forth always return with a harvest of their kind. That which we put into the thought comes back into our life. For our every thought there is a response, a return of the pendulum that we have started swinging. It is Emerson's Law of Compensation.

So you can see the wisdom in the dictum—"Into whatsoever house ye enter, first say—'Peace be to this house!'"

But do more than bless those you come in contact with. Act the part. Think kindly of them as well.

> *Believe not each accusing tongue,*
> *As most weak people do;*
> *But still believe that story wrong*
> *Which ought not to be true.*

It is as easy to add, you know, as it is to subtract. Love adds. Fear and hatred subtract. You can reinforce your efforts with all the universe through love, as easily as you can separate yourself from everyone through hatred and fear.

Remember, evil is usually in the eye of the beholder. There is an old poem that depicts this graphically:

Mistress Polly Wittenhouse
Lived on Whetstone Alley,
And she was like an angel
To little orphan Sally,
And she was like a harlot
To the lass across the way,

A "good 'un" to the slavey
Who made her bed each day.
And she was like a siren
With the devil in her eye
To any roving sailor man
As he was passing by.

So Mistress Polly Wittenhouse
Was either good or bad,
According to the need or greed
Each of her judges had,
According as her living
Threw a shadow on their own.
The sailors flung her kisses
And the lass she cast a stone.
And Sally and the slavey
They prayed for her each night,
And all of them that judged her
Knew that they judged her right.

A Scrap Book on Love is probably the most valuable one you can make. Put in it pictures of all your friends, all those you would have for friends. Paste in it pictures of the home of your dreams, of each separate room in it, of the furnishings, of everything about it.

Put in it every motto of peace and love and happiness you can find. Put in it pictures of children and toys and fireside scenes, dinners and parties and all the intimate happy things you can think of. Love that house and everything about it. Live in it mentally. Believe in it, and before long you will find that you ARE in it in actuality.

God lights the way, no more we grope
Nor stumble on in troubled hope.

We sow no seeds of care or strife,
But those of love and joy and life.
No more we strive to plan our lot,
The Father fills our cup, unsought.

Sow the seeds in your Scrap Book and in your life of love and joy and happiness, then leave it to the Father to provide the means of making these seeds grow and bear fruit. "I have planted, Apollos watered, but God gaveth the increase."

Remember, the I AM in you is your part of Divinity. Some sage put it—"Whatever the Creator is, I AM." How often have you said—"I AM poor, I AM sick, I AM ignorant, I AM weak"—and thus fastened these evils upon yourself? You acknowledged a lack of something. What can you build with minus quantities? Only emptiness, void.

Reverse all that. Whenever you say "I AM," whenever you thus call upon the God in You, make it something you WANT. "I AM rich. I AM powerful. I AM well and whole and strong. I AM happy. I AM perfect in every way."

Make an I AM Scrap Book, with your picture on the first page, then pictures of supermen or genii or whatever your idea of power may be scattered throughout the pages of the book. Put in it pictures of all the things you would like to be and do. And fill it with such affirmations as these: The Spirit of Prosperity fills my mind and overflows into my affairs. God is my perfect will; through me it is done. There is only one Presence and one Power in my life—God, the Good Omnipotent. God is my inexhaustible source of abundant supply. The riches of the Spirit now fill my mind and affairs. I think prosperity. I talk prosperity, and I know that prosperity and success are mine.

If we but touch the garment's hem,
Comes power surging through.
Try—play the part—stretch out your hand,
Then quiet—wait what comes to you.

God gave man power and dominion over all that is below him. "I said—Ye are Gods, and all of you Sons of the Most High." "As many as received Him, to them gave He power to become the Sons of God, even to them that believe on His name."

Will YOU receive Him? Will you believe in and accept the power He offers you? "God is able to do abundantly above all that we ask or think, according to the Power that worketh in us." Will you accept His Divine Sonship? Will you BE the God-man you were intended to be? Then cast off all fear of debt and lack and sickness and evil. Live in the world of love and plenty that was intended for you. Use the God-given power that is yours to first visualize the things you want—"In the beginning was the Word," the mental image, you remember—and then bring those mental images into actuality through your faith and your work.

Treasure Maps help to re-educate your mind, help you to visualize and hold in thought the images you wish to create. But visualizing and asking God's guidance is only half the battle. The other half is to make your start, to dig in and DO the first thing necessary towards bringing your desires into actuality.

The Kingdom of Heaven is the Kingdom of Expansion, but there must be something to expand. You can start a house with a single brick. You can start a fortune with a single dollar. But there must be that brick or that dollar or that first step to put your leaven into before you can make it expand and grow into the perfect structure of your dreams.

So do the thing, whatever it may be, that is necessary to your start. Make your picture, draw your Treasure Map, then take the first step that may be necessary towards bringing it into actuality. To begin is to be half done. You will be amazed how quickly you will reach your goal.

> To every man God gives a gift tonight;
> To king and peasant and to you and me:
> A shining year, clean, white, as crystal clear
> As tropic pools or stars above the sea.
>
> Oh, let us promise all the coming days
> To keep them pure, to keep them ever white!
> As, heaven born, one comes to us each morn,
> God, help us use it wisely in Thy sight.
>
> Whatever task, whatever joy be ours
> Throughout the year that now has scarce begun,
> Let us steadfastly claim in His own name
> The promised presence of the Holy One.
> —BERTHA M. RUSSEL

THE KINGDOM OF EXPANSION

Here is a secret of riches and success that has been buried 1,990 years deep.

Since time began, mankind has been searching for this secret. It has been found—and lost again—a score of times. The Ancients of all races have had some inkling of it, as is proven by the folktales and legends that have come down to us, like the story of Aladdin and his wonderful lamp, or Ali Baba and his "Open Sesame" to the treasure trove.

Every nation has such legends. Every nation has had its Wise Men, its men of genius and vision who glimpsed the truth that is buried in these old folktales and who understood at least something of how it works.

But it remained for Jesus to re-discover this secret in its entirety and then to show us clearly, step by step, how we might use it to bring us anything of good we might desire.

Make no mistake about this: The miracles of Jesus were not something super-natural that could be performed only by Him, else how could He have picked seventy disciples—ordinary men, uneducated, untaught, fishermen, farmers, tax-gatherers and the like—and sent them out two by two to perform miracles and wonders second only to His own so that they returned to Him with joy, saying, "Lord, even the devils are subject to us through Thy name." How could He have assured us—"The things that I do shall ye do also, and greater things than these shall ye do." The miracles of Jesus were divinely NATURAL. Instead of being departures from natural law, they were demonstrations of what the law will do for you—if you understand how to use it!

God does not deal in exceptions. Every force in Nature works along definite, logical lines, in accord with certain principles. These forces will work for anyone who possesses the key to their use, just as Aladdin's fabled Genie would respond to the call of anyone who rubbed the magic lamp. They can be neglected and allowed to lie idle, they can be used for good or evil, but the laws themselves do not change. It is merely the methods of using them that change.

An airplane or an automobile would have seemed as great a miracle to the people of Jesus' day as the curing of a leper. Sending sound waves through the ether, to be picked up by a little box called a radio, would have been as wonderful to our fathers as is the sending of our voice over a beam of light to us today. Yet there is nothing super-natural about either of these. The forces of Nature have always been there, ready for our use. It is our understanding of them that has changed, our knowledge of how to USE them.

Man in ancient times looked upon the lightning as the wrath of God, just as many deeply religious people look upon poverty and sickness and calamities today in the same way, as visitations of God. Yet man has learned to harness the lightning and make it serve him.

The laws governing electricity were there all the time, waiting only for the understanding of someone wise enough to show us how to put them to good use. Just so the power to BE and HAVE what you want is right here, needing only for you to learn how it works.

Nineteen hundred years ago, there came to this earth a Son of Man who proclaimed that His mission was—"That ye might have LIFE, and have it more ABUNDANTLY."

NOT, mind you, that you might learn how to die, and thus reach Heaven and a life of comfort, but that you might have LIFE—here and now. Over and over again He told us—"What things soever ye desire ... ye shall have them," and lest you might think that this referred to some future state, He assured us—"If two of you shall agree ON EARTH as touching anything they shall ask, it shall be done for them."

Furthermore, He gave exact instructions as to how to go about getting the things you desire. When you want more of the good things of life, when happiness or success or riches seem to elude you, there is a definite formula for you to use. "Seek ye first the Kingdom of Heaven," Jesus directed, "and all these things shall be added unto you."

"Ah ha!" you say. "There it is. You do have to die and go to Heaven in order to get the good you want." But Jesus must have anticipated that you might think just that, for He pointed out specifically that the Kingdom of Heaven is not afar off, in the clouds or in the next world. "The Kingdom of Heaven cometh not with observation," He said. "Neither shall they say, Lo here, lo there! For behold, the Kingdom of Heaven is within you."

WHAT IS HEAVEN?

That word "Heaven" is perhaps the most misunderstood word in the Bible. In the original Greek text, the word used for "Heaven" is OURANOS, which, translated literally, means EXPANSION. And what is expansion? It is increasing, spreading out, multiplying, is it not? "Seek ye first the Kingdom of EXPANSION, and all these things shall be added unto you." Seek a place or a state of being where you can expand, grow, increase, multiply, bring forth fruit.

But we don't need to seek such a place, for Jesus assured us that the Kingdom of Heaven is already within us. We must therefore look within ourselves for this faculty of expansion.

Now what, within us, has unlimited power to expand? Our muscles are elastic, our lungs and many of our organs can be expanded to an extent, but none of them can expand greatly without harm to itself and to the body.

The only thing in this body of ours that can expand without limit is our MIND, our imaging faculties. So Jesus' advice might be paraphrased—"Seek ye first the Kingdom of Mind, of imagery, and all these things shall be added unto you."

That would seem to fit in with Jesus' own description of what the Kingdom of Heaven is like. "The Kingdom of Heaven is like to a grain of mustard seed, which a man took, and sowed in his field; which indeed is the least of all seeds, but when it is grown, it is the greatest among herbs, and becometh a tree, so that the birds of the air come and lodge in the branches thereof." "The Kingdom of Heaven is like unto leaven, which a woman took and hid in three measures of meal, until the whole was leavened."

What is the property of a mustard seed? *It spreads*—a single seed will grow into a tree, a single tree will produce enough seeds to plant a great field. And what is the property of leaven or yeast? *It expands*—in a single night it can expand a hundred times in size.

Go back over any of the miracles of increase in the Bible and see if they are not all miracles of EXPANSION. How did Elijah make the oil and meal last, so that one measure of oil and a little meal fed him and the widow and her son for an indefinite period? How did Elisha increase the pot of oil for that other widow who came to him to save her sons from bondage, so that she had enough to fill all the vessels she could borrow from her neighbors?

By EXPANDING them, did they not? And that is how you can increase your substance, your happiness, your every good thing.

When the disciples asked Jesus how to pray, what did He teach them? "Our Father 'which art in Heaven, hallowed be Thy name, Thy Kingdom come, *Thy will be done on earth as it is in Heaven.*" In other words, may the good that you have imaged for me in the Heaven of your consciousness be made manifest here on earth.

God is MIND, and He dwells in the Kingdom of Mind or Heaven. There—in the mind and thoughts of God— all is good. He images you as perfect, your surroundings pleasant and comfortable, all your ways cast in pleasant places. He does not think up sickness and troubles for you. He images you as His perfect child, happy and care-free, with everything of good that makes life desirable. He is your Father, and what father, even among us here on earth, would plan anything but good for his children? As Jesus reminded us—"What man is there of you, whom if his son ask bread, will he give him a stone? Or if he ask a fish, will he give him a serpent? If ye then, being evil, know how to give good gifts unto your children, how much more shall your Father which is in heaven give good things to them that ask Him?"

In short, when you pray . . . "Thy will be done . . ." you are asking that everything of good that the Father has imaged for you in His mind should be made manifest for you here on earth. For His will, like that of every father, is that His children should be contented and happy, that they should have everything that is for their good.

How can we help to bring this about? By putting our own lives and especially our thoughts on the plane of the Kingdom of Heaven—in other words, by starting here and now to *live* in that Kingdom of Heaven.

When you meet evil on its own level, you meet it at a disadvantage. You may overcome it, but only after a terrific struggle. The only sure way to overcome evil is to get above it—to use the Law of the Higher Potential not merely to defeat the evil that confronts you, but to replace it with the perfect condition you desire.

That is what Jesus bade us do when He told us to "Seek first the Kingdom of Heaven (of expansion, of mind, of the imaging faculties)."

Seek in your own mind the ideal condition you would have, expand your thoughts to image it in every detail, see it as part of the Kingdom of Heaven, so that you can be thankful for it and praise God for it. See it, believe in it, until you can be happy over it and no longer fearful or worrying about seeming conditions around you.

In the beginning all was void—space—nothingness. How did God construct the planets, the firmaments, the earth and all things on and in it from this formless void? By first making a mental image on which to build.

That is what you, too, must do. You control your destiny, your fortune, your happiness to the exact extent to which you can think them out, VISUALIZE them, SEE them, and allow no vagrant thought of fear or worry to mar their completion and beauty. The quality of your thought is the measure of your power. Clear, forceful thought has the power of attracting to itself everything it may need for the fruition of those thoughts. As W. D. Wattles puts it in his "Science of Getting Rich": There is a thinking stuff from which all things are made and which, in its original state, permeates, penetrates, and fills the interspaces of the universe. A thought in this substance produces the thing that is imagined by the thought. Man can form things in his thought, and by impressing his thought upon formless substance, can cause the thing he thinks about to be created.

The connecting link between your conscious mind and the Kingdom of Heaven is thought, and every thought that is in harmony with progress and good, every thought that is freighted with the right idea, can penetrate to the Heaven Mind. And penetrating to it, it comes back with the power of God to accomplish it. You don't need to originate the ways and means. God knows how to bring about any necessary results. There is but one right way to solve any given problem. When your human judgment is unable to decide what that one right way is, turn to the Lord for guidance. You need never fear the outcome, for if you heed His advice you cannot go wrong.

Always remember—your mind is but a conductor— good or poor as you make it—for the power of the Universal Mind or God. And thought is the connecting energy. Use that conductor, and you will improve its conductivity. Demand much, and you will receive the more. The Lord is not a niggard in any of His gifts. "Ask and ye shall receive, seek and ye shall find, knock and it shall be opened unto you."

That is the law of life. And the destiny of man lies not in poverty and hardship, but in living up to his high estate in unity with the Heaven Mind, with the Power that governs the universe.

To look upon poverty and sickness as sent by God and therefore inevitable, is the way of the weakling. God never sent us anything but good. What is more, He has never yet failed to give to those who would use them the means to overcome any condition not of His making. Sickness and poverty are not of His making. They are not evidences of virtue, but of weakness. God gave us everything in abundance, and he expects us to manifest that abundance. If you had a son you loved very much, and you surrounded him with good things which he had only to exert himself in order to reach, you wouldn't like it if he showed himself to the world half-starved, ill-kempt and clothed in rags, merely because he was unwilling to exert himself enough to reach for the good things you had provided. No more, in my humble opinion, does God.

Man's principal business in life, as I see it, is to establish a contact with the Heaven Mind. It is to acquire an understanding of this power that is in him. "With all thy getting, get understanding," said Solomon.

> *Happy is the man that findeth wisdom,*
> *And the man that getteth understanding.*
> *For the gaining of it is better than the gaining of silver.*
> *And the profit thereof than fine gold.*
> *She is more precious than rubies:*
> *And none of the things thou canst desire are to be*

compared unto her.
Length of days is in her right hand:
In her left hand are riches and honor.
Her ways are ways of pleasantness,
And all her paths are peace.
She is a tree of life to them that lay hold upon her.
And happy is every one that retaineth her.

—PROVERBS

When you become conscious, even to a limited degree, of your one-ness with this God Mind, your ability to call upon It at will for anything you may need, it makes a different man of you. Gone are the fears, gone are the worries. You know that your success, your health, your happiness will be measured only by the degree to which you can impress the fruition of your desires upon mind.

The toil and worry, the wearisome grind and the back-breaking work, will go in the future as in the past to those who will not use their minds. The less they use them, the more they will sweat. And the more they work only from the neck down, the less they will be paid and the more hopeless their lot will become. It is Mind that rules the world.

You see, from an ordinary earthly point of view, any savage or even many animals are to all intents as good as you or I. They are stronger, have greater vitality, live longer comparatively, and some are surer of their sustenance. The only faculty in which we are their superior is our mind.

And the only faculty that can make us superior to those around us, that can keep us from being the sport of circumstance and lift us above all danger of want or sickness, is that same mind.

Why is it that fervent prayer often works what seems to us to be a miracle? Why does Treasure Mapping bring such marvelous results? Because both put us upon the Heaven-plane, the plane where the Father works with us to bring about the object we desire.

When you pray earnestly, you see in your mind's eye the condition or result you desire. When you Treasure Map, you picture on paper the condition you want to see realized. And that is exactly how God worked when He created the world. "In the beginning was the word (the mental image)." In the beginning, He formed a picture in His own mind of what He wanted to create. "And the word (the mental image) was made flesh." It was made manifest, became reality for all to see.

Your word—your mental image—can be made flesh in the same way. All it needs is to get on the same plane that God is on when He creates—the plane of the Kingdom of Heaven—of imagery and faith. Remember the words of the Psalmist—"In Thy Book, all my members were written, *when as yet there was none of them.*" And elsewhere in the Scriptures, you find—"The Lord made the earth and the heavens, and every plant of the field *before it was in the earth,* and every herb of the field *before it grew.*"

That is the way you must create the conditions you desire. Create them in your own mind first.

"The imagination," says Glenn Clark in "The Soul's Sincere Desire," "is of all qualities in man the most Godlike— that which associates him most closely with God. The first mention we read of man in the Bible is where he is spoken of as an 'image.' 'Let us make man in our image, after our likeness.' The only place where an image can be conceived is in the imagination. Thus man, the highest creation of God, was a creation of God's imagination.

The source and center of all man's creative power— the power that above all others lifts him above the level of brute creation, and that gives him dominion, is his power of making images, or the power of the imagination. There are some who have always thought that the imagination was something which makes-believe that which is not. This is fancy—not imagination. Fancy would convert that which is real into pretense and sham; imagination enables one to see through the appearance of a thing to what it really is.

There is a very real law of cause and effect which makes the dream of the dreamer come true. It is the law of visualization—the law that calls into being in this outer material world everything that is real in the inner world. Imagination pictures the thing you desire. VISION idealizes it. It reaches beyond the thing that is, into the conception of what can be. Imagination gives you the picture. Vision gives you the impulse to make the picture your own.

AS A MAN THINKETH

We cannot change the past experience, but we can determine what the new ones shall be like. We can make the coming day just what we want it to be. We can be tomorrow what we think today. For the thoughts are causes and the conditions are the effects.

Thought is the only force. Just as polarity controls the electron, gravitation the planets, tropism the plants and lower animals—just so thought controls the action and the environment of man. And thought is subject wholly to the control of mind. Its direction rests with us.

Walt Whitman had the right of it when he said— "Nothing external to me has any power over me."

Each of us makes his own world—and he makes it through mind.

Thoughts are the causes. Conditions are merely effects. We can mold ourselves and our surroundings by resolutely directing our thoughts towards the goal we have in mind.

Ordinary animal life is very definitely controlled by temperature, by climate, by seasonal conditions. Man alone can adjust himself to any reasonable temperature or condition. Man alone has been able to free himself to a great extent from the control of natural forces through his understanding of the relation of cause and effect. And now man is beginning to get a glimpse of the final freedom that shall be his from all material causes when he shall acquire the complete understanding that mind is the only cause and that effects are what he sees.

"We moderns are unaccustomed," says one talented writer, to the mastery over our own inner thoughts and feelings. That a man should be a prey to any thought that chances to take possession of his mind, is commonly among us assumed as unavoidable. It may be a matter of regret that he should be kept awake all night from anxiety as to the issue of a lawsuit on the morrow, but that he should have the power of determining whether he be kept awake or not seems an extravagant demand. The image of an impending calamity is no doubt odious, but its very odiousness (we say) makes it haunt the mind all the more pertinaciously, and it is useless to expel it. Yet this is an absurd position for man, the heir of all the ages, to be in: Hag-ridden by the flimsy creatures of his own brain. If a pebble in our boot torments us, we expel it. We take off the boot and shake it out. And once the matter is fairly understood, it is just as easy to expel an intruding and obnoxious thought from the mind. About this there ought to be no mistake, no two opinions. The thing is obvious, clear and unmistakable. It should be as easy to expel an obnoxious thought from the mind as to shake a stone out of your shoe; and until a man can do that, it is just nonsense to talk about his ascendancy over nature, and all the rest of it. He is a mere slave, and a prey to the bat-winged phantoms that flit through the corridors of his own brain. Yet the weary and careworn faces that we meet by thousands, even among the affluent classes of civilization, testify only too clearly how seldom this mastery is obtained. How rare indeed to find a man! How common rather to discover a creature hounded on by tyrant thoughts (or cares, or desires), cowering, wincing under the lash.

It is one of the prominent doctrines of some of the oriental schools of practical psychology that the power of expelling thoughts, or if need be, killing them dead on the spot, must be attained. Naturally the art requires practice, but like other arts, when once acquired there is no mystery or difficulty about it. It is worth practice. It may be fairly said that life only begins when this art has been acquired. For obviously when, instead of being ruled by individual thoughts, the whole flock of them in their immense multitude and variety and capacity is ours to direct and despatch and employ where we list, life becomes a thing so vast and grand, compared to what it was before, that its former condition may well appear almost ante-natal. If you can kill a thought dead, for the time being, you can do anything else with it that you please. And therefore it is that this power is so valuable. And it not only frees a man from mental torment (which is nine-tenths at least of the torment of life), but it gives him a concentrated power of handling mental work absolutely unknown to him before. The two are co-relative to each other.

There is no intelligence in matter—whether that matter be electronic energy made up in the form of stone, or iron, or wood, or flesh. It all consists of Energy, the universal substance from which Mind forms all material things. Mind is the only intelligence. It alone is eternal. It alone is supreme in the universe.

When we reach that understanding, we will no longer have cause for fear, because we will realize that Universal Mind is the Creator of life only; that death is not an actuality—it is merely the absence of life—and life will be ever-present. Remember the old fairy story of how the Sun was listening to a lot of earthly creatures talking of a very dark place they had found? A place of Stygian blackness. Each told how terrifically dark it had seemed. The Sun went and looked for it. He went to the exact spot they had described. He searched everywhere. But he could find not even a tiny dark spot. And he came back and told the earth-creatures he did not believe there was any dark place.

When the sun of understanding shines on all the dark spots in our lives, we will realize that there is no cause, no creator, no power, except good; evil is not an entity—it is merely the absence of good. And there can be no ill effects without an evil cause. Since there is no evil cause, only good can have reality or power. There is no beginning or end to good. From it there can be nothing but blessing for the whole race. In it is found no trouble. If God (or Good—the two are synonymous) is the only cause, then the only effect must be like the cause. "All things were made by Him; and without Him was not anything made that was made."

THE MASTER OF YOUR FATE

Orison Swett Marden wrote—"A highly magnetized piece of steel will attract and lift a piece of unmagnetized steel ten times its own weight. De-magnetize that same piece of steel and it will be powerless to attract or lift even a feather's weight.

Now, my friends, there is the same difference between the man who is highly magnetized by a sublime faith in himself, and the man who is de-magnetized by his lack of faith, his doubts, his fears, that there is between the magnetized and the de-magnetized pieces of steel. If two men of equal ability, one magnetized by a divine self-confidence, the other de-magnetized by fear and doubt, are given similar tasks, one will succeed and the other will fail. The self-confidence of the one multiplies his powers a hundred-fold; the lack of it subtracts a hundredfold from the power of the other.

When Frank A. Vanderlip, former President of the National City Bank, was a struggling youngster, he asked a successful friend what one thing he would urge a young man to do who was anxious to make his way in the world. "Look as though you have already succeeded," his friend told him. Shakespeare expresses the same thought in another way—"Assume a virtue if you have it not." Look the part. Dress the part. Act the part. Be successful in your own thought first. It won't be long before you will be successful before the world as well.

David V. Bush, in his book "Applied Psychology and Scientific Living," says: "Man is like the wireless operator. Man is subject to miscellaneous wrong thought currents if his mind is not in tune with the Infinite, or *if he is not keyed up to higher vibrations* than those of negation.

A man who thinks courageous thoughts sends these courageous thought waves through the universal ether until they lodge in the consciousness of someone who is tuned to the same courageous key. Think a strong thought, a courageous thought, a prosperity thought, and these thoughts will be received by someone who is strong, courageous and prosperous.

It is just as easy to think in terms of abundance as to think in terms of poverty. If we think poverty thoughts we become the sending and receiving stations for poverty thoughts. We send out a "poverty" mental wireless and it reaches the consciousness of some poverty-stricken "receiver." We get what we think.

It is just as easy to think in terms of abundance, opulence and prosperity as it is to think in terms of lack, limitation and poverty.

If a man will *raise his rate of vibration* by faith currents or hope currents, these vibrations go through the Universal Mind and lodge in the consciousness of people who are keyed to the same tune. Whatever you think is sometime, somewhere, received by a person who is tuned to your thought key.

If a man is out of work and he thinks thoughts of success, prosperity, harmony, position and growth, just as surely as his thoughts are things—as Shakespeare says—someone will receive his vibrations of success, prosperity, harmony, position and growth.

If we are going to be timid, selfish, penurious and picayunish in our thinking, these thought waves which we have started in the universal ether will go forth until they come to a mental receiving station of the same caliber. "Birds of a feather flock together," and minds of like thinking are attracted one to the other.

If you need money, all you have to do is to send up your vibrations to a strong, courageous receiving station, and someone who can meet your needs will be attracted to you or you to him.

When you learn that you are entitled to win—in any right undertaking in which you may be engaged—you will win. When you learn that you have a right to a legitimate dominion over your own affairs, you will have dominion over them. The promise is that we can do all things through the Mind that was in Christ.

The Heaven Mind plays no favorites. No one human being has any more power than any other. It is simply that few of us *use* the power that is in our hands. The great men of the world are in no wise SUPER Beings. They are ordinary creatures like you and me, who have stumbled upon the way of drawing upon their subconscious mind—and through it upon the God Mind. Speaking of Henry Ford's phenomenal success, his friend Thomas A. Edison said of him—"He draws upon his subconscious mind."

The secret of being what you have it in you to be is simply this: Decide now what it is you want of life, exactly what you wish your future to be. Plan it out in detail. Vision it from start to finish. See yourself as you are now, doing those things you have always wanted to do Make them REAL in your mind's eye—feel them, live them, believe them, especially at the moment of going to sleep, when it is easiest to reach your subconscious mind—and you will soon be seeing them in real life.

It matters not whether you are young or old, rich or poor. The time to begin is NOW. It is never too late. Remember those lines of Appleton's:

I knew his face the moment that he passed

Triumphant in the thoughtless, cruel throng—
I gently touched his arm—he smiled at me—
He was the Man that Once I Meant to Be!

Where I had jailed, he'd won from life, Success;
Where I had stumbled, with sure feet he stood;
Alike—yet unalike—we faced the world,
And through the stress he found that life was good.
And I? The bitter wormwood in the glass,
The shadowed way along which failures pass!
Yet as I saw him thus, joy came to me—
He was the Man that Once I Meant to Be!

We did not speak. But in his sapient eyes
I saw the spirit that had urged him on,
The courage that had held him through the fight
Had once been mine. I thought, "Can it be gone?"
He felt that unmasked question—felt it so
His pale lips formed the one-word answer, "No!"

Too late to win? No! Not too late for me—
He is the Man that Still I Mean to Be!

The secret of power lies in understanding the infinite resources of your own mind. When you begin to realize that the power to do anything, to be anything, to have anything, is within yourself, then and then only will you take your proper place in the world.

As Bruce Barton put it—"Nothing splendid has ever been achieved except by those who dared believe that something inside them was superior to circumstance."

THE MASTER MIND

The connecting link between the human and the Divine, between the formed universe and formless energy, lies in your imagining faculty. It is, of all things human, the most God-like. It is our part of Divinity. Through it we share in the creative power of the Heaven Mind. Through it we can turn the most drab existence into a thing of life and beauty. It is the means by which we avail ourselves of all the good which God is constantly offering to us in such profusion. It is the means by which we can reach any goal, win any prize.

Do you want happiness? Do you want success? Do you want position, power, riches? *Image* them! How did God first make man? "In his image created He him." He "imaged" man in His Mind.

And that is the way everything has been made since time began. It was first imaged in Mind. That is the way everything you want must start—with a mental image.

So use your imagination! Picture in it your Heart's Desire. Imagine it—daydream it so vividly, so clearly, that you will actually BELIEVE you HAVE it. In the moment that you carry this conviction to your subconscious mind— in that moment your dream will become a reality. It may be a while before you realize it, but the important part is done. You have created the model. You can safely leave it to your subconscious mind to do the rest.

Every man wants to get out of the rut, to grow, to develop into something better. Here is the open road—open to you whether you have schooling, training, position, wealth or not. Remember this: Your subconscious mind knew more from the time you were a baby than is in all the books in all the colleges and libraries of the world.

So don't let lack of training, lack of education, hold you back. Your mind can meet every need—and will do so if you give it the chance. The Apostles were almost all poor men, uneducated men, yet they did a work that is unequalled in historical annals. Joan of Arc was a poor peasant girl, unable to read or write—yet she saved France! The pages of history are dotted with poor men, uneducated men, who thought great thoughts, who used their imaginations to master circumstances and became rulers of men. Most great dynasties started with some poor, obscure man. Napoleon came of a poor, humble family. He got his appointment to the Military Academy only through very hard "work and the pulling of many political strings. Even as a Captain of Artillery he was so poverty-stricken that he was unable to buy his equipment when offered an appointment to India. Business today is full of successful men who have scarcely the rudiments of ordinary education. It was only after he had made his millions that Andrew Carnegie hired a tutor to give him the essentials of an education.

So it isn't training and it isn't education that make you successful. These help, but the thing that really counts is that gift of the Gods—Creative Imagination!

You have that gift. Use it! Make every thought, every fact, that comes into your mind pay you a profit. Make it work and produce for you. Think of things—not as they are but as they MIGHT be. Make them real, live and interesting. Don't merely dream—but CREATE! Then use your imagination to make that CREATION of advantage to mankind—and, incidentally, yourself.

Get *above* your circumstances, your surroundings. Get above your troubles—no matter what they may be. Remember, the Law is that Power flows only from a higher to the lower potential. Use your imaging faculty to put yourself and keep yourself on a higher plane, *above* trouble and adversity. "Circumstances?" exclaimed Napoleon when at the height of his power. "I make circumstances!" And that is what you too must do.

> "As the rain cometh down and the snow from heaven, and returneth not thither, but watereth the earth, and maketh it bring forth and bud, and giveth seed to the sower and bread to the eater; so shall my word be that goeth forth out of my mouth: it shall not return unto me void, but it shall accomplish that which I please, and it shall prosper in the thing whereto I sent it."
>
> —Isaiah.

DO YOU HAVE MONEY WORRIES?

Say to yourself and believe—"There is no lack in the Kingdom of Heaven." Then make a Treasure Map as suggested in The Magic Word, showing all the riches and supply you may long for. All this must start, you know with an idea, a mental image.

"All that the Father hath is mine," said Jesus. And all that the Father hath is yours, too, for all He has to begin with is IDEAS, *mental images,* and you can create these as easily as He. Make your mental image of the thing you want, picture it on paper in so far as you can to make it more real and vivid to you, then have FAITH!

Faith starts you DOING the things you need to do to bring your ideas into realities. Faith brings to you the opportunities and people and things you need to make your images realities.

All that the Father hath is yours—all the ideas, all the mental images, all the power to make them manifest.

Do you want riches? They are yours for the making. The ancient Alchemists who spent their lives trying to turn base metals into gold were trying and working from the bottom up. Power does not flow that way. You must start ABOVE the thing you want, working from the higher potential to the lower.

Riches, health, happiness, power, all are yours if you work for them in the right way—if you make them yours in Heaven first and then use your faith and your abilities to make them manifest here on earth.

"Thy will be done on earth as it is in Heaven," God's will for you is for riches, for happiness, for health. If you haven't these now, deny the lack. Deny the wrong conditions. Say to yourself—"There is no lack in Heaven. There is no disease there, no weakness, no trouble or conflict, no worries of any kind. There is only love and plenty."

Then take your beliefs out of the images around you, which are merely the result of your previous belief objectified and put all your faith, all your hopes, all your strength and abilities into making your new Heaven images come true.

You CAN do it. But you must believe so firmly that you can actually ACT the part. As the Prophet Noel told us "Let the weak say—I am strong!" And the poor say, I am rich. And the sick say, I am well. And the miserable say, I am happy. Say it, repeat it until you believe it—then ACT the part!

In one of Edgar Rice Burroughs' Martian stories, he told of a great walled city that had outlived its usefulness and was now peopled by only a few old men. But every time an invading army appeared before this city, it was driven away by hordes of archers that manned every foot of the walls and even swarmed out through the gates to meet the enemy in the open. When the enemy fled, the archers disappeared!

Where did the archers come from? According to the story, they came entirely from the minds of the old men who still lived in that almost-deserted city. These old men remembered the huge armies that had garrisoned the town in its heyday. They remembered former invasions when their soldiers had repelled every assault and then dashed out through the gates and swept the invaders into the sea. And by gathering together and visualizing those mighty armies of theirs as once more existent, they brought them into being so that their enemies too could see them and be driven into flight by them.

Does that sound far-fetched? Then remember that you have only to go back to the Bible to find a parallel. Just turn to II Kings, Chapter 6, and you will read how the King of Syria sent his horses and chariots and a great host to capture the Prophet Elisha, and how in the night they compassed him around.

And when the servant of the man of God was risen early, and gone forth, behold, an host compassed the city both with horses and chariots. And his servant said unto him, Alas, my master, what shall we do?

And he answered, Fear not! For they that be with us are more than they that be with them.

And Elisha prayed, and said, Lord, I pray thee, open his eyes, that he may see. And the Lord opened the eyes of the young man; and he saw: and behold, the mountain was full of horses and chariots of fire around Elisha.

Again, when the High Priest sent his soldiers to seize Jesus, and Peter struck one of the soldiers with his sword, Jesus rebuked him, saying: "Thinkest thou that I cannot now pray to My Father, and He shall presently give Me more than twelve legions of angels?"

The mountains can be full of chariots of fire for you, too. The Father can send to your help as many legions of angels as you may need. All it requires is the power to visualize what you want, the faith to believe that you receive, the serenity to sit back and LET God work through you.

However meager be my worldly wealth,
Let me give something that shall aid my kind,
A word of courage, or a thought of health,
Dropped as I pass for troubled hearts to find.
Let me tonight look back across the span
'Twixt dawn and dark, and to my conscience say—
Because of some good act to beast or man—
The world is better that I lived today.
—ELLA WHEELER WILCOX

LaVergne, TN USA
11 April 2010
178864LV00002B/13/P